Real Estate Principles

Robert Rico, Carolee Rico, and Chase Milner

Published by US Realty School, LLC

Real Estate Principles

12130 Millenium Drive, Suite 300
Los Angeles, CA 90094

AUTHORS
Robert Rico
Carolee Rico
Chase Milner

CONTENTS

CHAPTER 1
REAL ESTATE/REAL PROPERTY

CHAPTER 2
OWNERSHIP OF REAL ESTATE

CHAPTER 3
COMMON INTEREST PROPERTY OWNERSHIP

CHAPTER 4
ENCUMBRANCES TO REAL PROPERTY

CHAPTER 5
GOVERNMENT RIGHTS IN LAND

CHAPTER 6
TRANSFERRING OWNERSHIP OF REAL ESTATE

CHAPTER 7
LAW OF AGENCY

CHAPTER 8
REAL ESTATE CONTRACTS

CHAPTER 9
PURCHASE AND LISTING TRANSACTIONS

CHAPTER 10
REAL ESTATE LEASES AND RENTAL CONTRACTS

CHAPTER 11
ESCROW AND TITLE

CHAPTER 12
REAL ESTATE FINANCING

CHAPTER 13
APPRAISAL OF REAL ESTATE

CHAPTER 14
REAL ESTATE AS A BUSINESS

CHAPTER 15
ANTI-DISCRIMINATION LAWS AND DISCLOSURES/ SUBDIVISION LAWS OF CALIFORNIA/RESIDENTIAL DESIGN AND CONSTRUCTION

ACKNOWLEDGEMENTS

US Realty School would like to express its profound gratitude to Deborah Carlisle for her unwavering support and the wealth of expertise she brought to this textbook. Her many years of experience in the real estate industry provided an essential foundation for the concepts and insights presented here. Deborah's notable success in establishing well-regarded real estate education and publishing companies is a testament to her vision and dedication. Above all, her dream of helping students gain their real estate licenses and transform their lives continues to inspire every page of this work, as well as all those who have benefited from her guidance.

We would also like to extend sincere thanks to the following individuals for their invaluable contributions to the development of these materials. Their diligence, creativity, and commitment were instrumental in ensuring the clarity and quality of this textbook:

Michelle C. North
Elias Magers

Together, their efforts have enriched this textbook and helped bring it to fruition. It is with deep appreciation that we acknowledge each of these remarkable contributors, whose efforts have truly made a meaningful difference.

CHAPTER 1

REAL ESTATE/REAL PROPERTY

US
Realty School

REAL ESTATE/REAL PROPERTY

California law has determined that all property is either ***real property*** or ***personal property***. The term ***real estate*** refers to an estate or interest in **real property** or land. The terms ***real estate*** **and** ***real property*** are synonymous. They both mean an interest in land and all that is permanently attached to it, which are improvements or attachments. Real estate is considered anything that is immoveable or that which **"runs with the land,"** or is **appurtenant** to the land. **California Civil Code** defines real property to include all the following elements:

1. Land
2. Airspace
3. Improvements
4. Appurtenance or incidental to the land
5. Anything immovable by law

1. **LAND** is the soil or earth and includes all substances on and below the surface of the earth. Land, for legal purposes, extends to the center of the earth to include water, oil, gas, and all minerals that are found in the earth. *See Figure 1: Real Estate and Land Ownership.*

2. **AIRSPACE** is above the earth's surface for an indefinite distance as allowed by government controls and is also included in the definition of real estate. Airspace laws and rights have changed throughout history to accommodate changes in society. Originally, airspace was described as an infinite distance. The ***Federal Air Commerce Act of 1926*** and the ***Aeronautics Act of 1938*** allow use of airspace by aircraft, which affects the definition and limits airspace. Local laws impose limits on building heights based on local building codes. Many urban areas have developed airspace as a profitable business by using airspace for advertising.

3. **IMPROVEMENTS** are any items permanently affixed to the property such as houses and other buildings, fences, and trees and all plants that are in the ground, not in pots. These are immovable items also *shown in Figure 1, Real Estate and Land Ownership.*

4. **APPURTENANCE OR INCIDENTAL** refers to items that have a use particular to that property. Stock in a private water company is an appurtenance. If the property owner were to sell a property, they would not take the stock in the water company with them because there is no longer a need for the stock of a new property. In other words, the appurtenant item has no use other than for the property that it came with or for which it works or has value.

5. **ANYTHING IMMOVABLE BY LAW** is considered real property. Pictures that are hanging by a nail are movable and are therefore considered personal property. A built- in bookcase is permanently attached to the wall and will not stand on its own; therefore, it is immovable and is real property. A freestanding bookcase, however, is personal property because it will stand on its own and not permanently attached to the wall or structure. When determining if something is real property or personal property, consider the item's ability to be moved or the method of attachment.

Figure 1: Real Estate and Land Ownership

Possession	Own and use at will
Quiet Enjoyment	Enjoy without harassment
Control	Use as one chooses
Exclusion	Allow or prohibit access
Disposal	Sell, lease, donate/dedicate

Figure 2: Bundle of Rights

BUNDLE OF RIGHTS is the right associated with ownership of real property. This bundle demonstrates the legal rights of ownership as seen in Figure 2, The bundle of rights or legal rights of ownership are as follows: *See Figure 2: Bundles of Rights:*

- **POSSESSION:** The property owner has the right to possess or use the property at will.
- **QUIET ENJOYMENT:** A property owner has the right to enjoy or to live on the property without disturbance or harassment from others.
- **CONTROL:** Subject to local zoning regulations, a property owner has the right to control the use of their property as they choose, such as building a house or using the property for agriculture.
- **EXCLUSION:** A property owner has the right to allow or prohibit access to the property as they choose.
- **DISPOSE:** A property owner has the right to dispose or encumber their property with a mortgage; they may sell, lease, donate or dedicate, or trade the property at will.

RIGHTS IN LAND

A. **MINERAL RIGHTS** are included as part of the ownership of land and are concerning those minerals found beneath the surface of the earth that have a fugitive or fluid nature. The most commonly found substances are oil, gas, gold, coal, iron, and gemstones, such as turquoise and tourmaline. Underground water, which would require a well to extract, is also included in mineral rights.

A property owner has the right to transfer all or part of the mineral rights without actually transferring the land. It has been common practice in California, especially from the late 1800s through the mid-1900s, to sell land but retain the mineral rights. During this time, oil, gas, and gold had been found in California, making the mineral rights a valuable commodity.

Accessing the minerals requires either access through the property that you own, or access rights being retained along with the mineral rights. One will usually purchase the access rights along with the mineral rights. Slant drilling, or drilling at an angle, to access minerals under adjoining property that belongs to someone else is not legal.

Example: *Bob Jones has purchased a property adjoining land that has operating oil pumps in the hopes that his land will also be productive. Bob drills under his own land and finds nothing. He decides to slant drill under his neighbor's property since he already knows there is oil on the property.*

This is not legal. *A property owner has the right to dig only under their own property. Fluid substances, such as oil or water, can be accessed only when found within one's own property boundaries.*

B. **WATER RIGHTS** are also a part of real property and are classified as either riparian or littoral.

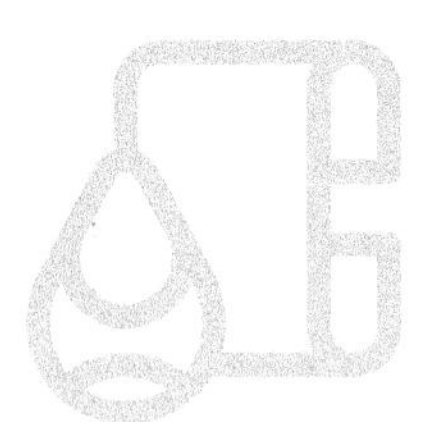

- **RIPARIAN RIGHTS** belong to owners of property bordering flowing water such as rivers or streams. The state owns the property beneath the waterway and the property owners have the right to reasonable usage in regard to their own property. If the body of water is navigable, the owner's property line stops at the high-water line. In the case of a waterway that is not navigable, such as a small stream, ownership is to the middle of the waterway.
- **LITTORAL RIGHTS** are the rights of property owners bordering a standing or still body of water such as lakes, oceans, or bays. Owners of littoral rights have the right of reasonable usage on their own property. Property lines for littoral rights are at the high-tide line with the exception of that waterway and land controlled by the Coastal Commission.
- **UNDERGROUND WATER RIGHTS** ***belong to landowners—the same as mineral rights. An owner of real property has a right to the use of the water beneath their own land. When underground water is not classified as a stream, it is referred to as percolating water. A property owner has the right to withdraw only for their own use on their own property.***
  - The ***water table,*** or ***groundwater,*** is the topmost limit of percolating water below the surface of the ground.
- **PERC TEST** - ***In preparation for the building of a septic drain field or infiltration basin, a "perc test" will be required to determine the water absorption rate of the soil, or its capacity for percolation. In its broadest terms, percolation testing is observing how quickly a known volume of water dissipates into the subsoil of a drilled hole of known surface area.***

A MUTUAL WATER COMPANY is formed when a development such as a subdivision is built that will be using a common source of water. The individual property owners each own an equal share of stock as they have an equal right to use of the water.

Stock in a mutual water company is an **appurtenance** as mentioned previously. To establish a mutual water company, it must be verified that there is a sufficient amount of potable water to support the community along with an adequate distribution system for both domestic use and fire protection. Additional requirements set forth by the ***California Corporations Code*** beginning with ***Section 14310*** must also be met by mutual water companies created on or after January 1, 1998, and reaffirmed by the Legislature in 2005. Mutual water companies are regulated by the Department of Financial Protection and Innovation (DFPI), ensuring compliance with relevant corporate and water use standards.

PERSONAL PROPERTY/CHATTEL

PERSONAL PROPERTY is also known as **chattel** and refers to anything that is not real property or real estate. Personal property is defined as anything that is moveable unlike real property, which is immovable.

It is possible to change an item from being personal property to real property by changing its nature. Once an item of chattel is permanently attached to the real property, it becomes an improvement and is then considered real property.

> ***Example:*** *A potted plant is personal property, and a seller of real estate would plan to take the plant with them when they move out of the property because it is movable. If the owner chooses to remove the plant from the pot and plant it in the ground, the plant becomes* ***realty, or real property*** *in the form of an* ***improvement.*** *It would no longer be acceptable for the plant to be taken with the seller once the property is sold because it is no longer movable and real property would actually be damaged by removing the plant from the ground.*

FIXTURES

FIXTURES are anything attached to real property. As simple as this explanation appears, it does not always provide a clear status of a fixture. Fixtures are items that were personal property before being permanently attached to real property. California has developed five tests to determine whether an item is in fact a fixture, which means that it is considered a permanent attachment to the property and is therefore **realty** rather than **personal property**.

The five tests for a fixture are:

1. **METHOD OF ATTACHMENT**: The more permanent the method of attachment, the more likely it is considered a fixture.

   Example: *A painting hanging by a nail on a wall is not a fixture, it is personal property. But a mural painted directly on the wall is a fixture, as the property owner would not remove the wall in order to take the mural with them when moving.*

2. **ADAPTABILITY:** The way in which the item works in conjunction with the property's use is referred to as adaptability. The better adapted the item is to the property, the greater the likelihood that it will be classified as a fixture. Custom fitted items, such as window blinds or drapes, are generally classified as fixtures. The brackets that hold the blinds and drapes are definitely fixtures.

3. **RELATIONSHIP OF THE PARTIES:** A tenant of a residential property may attach an item to their rented property. It is presumed to be the personal property of the tenant and will be taken with the tenant when the property is vacated. Courts will favor tenant over landlord; buyer over seller; and borrower over lender in such disputes.

   Example: *A tenant hangs a shelf on the wall by using screws and bolts. It appears to be a fixture for all intents and purposes; however, the tenant owns it and did not intend to leave the shelf when terminating the tenancy.*

4. **INTENT** when installing an item on land is the most important consideration. The intent may be for the purpose of health or safety instead of improving the property such as the installation of a wheelchair ramp, which will most likely be removed when there is no longer a need or when the occupant that uses the wheelchair no longer occupies the property.

5. **An AGREEMENT** of the parties involved, such as tenant and landlord, should put into writing items that will be installed and should have an agreement as to the disposition of the items. Such an agreement will help to avoid any ambiguity at a later date between fixture and personal possession.

When preparing a **listing agreement**, the agent should always identify and include in the listing agreement all items that the seller intends to remove from the property. One of the most disputed items is chandeliers. Sellers often plan to take down their chandelier to take with them and replace it with another; they are so proud of its beauty that they want to leave it hanging until the house sells. Potential buyers see the chandelier and naturally presume that it will stay with the property. Requesting in a purchase contract that items remain when writing an offer is equally important as inclusion in the listing. Disputes over fixtures cause a significant number of post-transaction lawsuits. Clarification of intention is of the utmost importance when property is being transferred.

Fixtures on leased property are common, especially in commercial property. There are several laws that apply to this practice; however, an agreement is always the best advice.

If a tenant has installed personal property to the premises, the property may be removed before the end of the term of the lease if:

- The property was installed for trade, business, manufacture, or domestic use, and the property can be removed without substantial damage to the premises.

A tenant may remove a fixture installed if they believed in good faith that the fixture could be installed and later removed. An item that has been attached for business use is commonly known as a **trade fixture** and may be removed prior to the end of the lease period. The tenant is responsible for all repairs necessary to correct any damage to the property caused by the removal of the items or fixtures.

When real estate is sold, fixtures are considered to be real property and ownership is expected to transfer to the buyer. Ownership and transfer of title to real property are subject to the laws of the state where the property is located. A court in another state cannot make decisions involving California real estate. The only exceptions are for federally owned property and federal proceedings, such as federal bankruptcy court. Ownership and transfer of personal property are subject to the laws of the state where the property owner resides even if the property is in another state.

CONTRACTS

CONTRACTS involving the transfer of real estate must be in writing, with the exception of a lease that is for twelve months or less.

The distinction between **real property** and **personal property** is also important in the formation of a contract.

A contract for **PERSONAL PROPERTY** is generally required only when the value exceeds a certain amount as established by the state in which the transaction is taking place. In California, a contract for the sale of personal property should be in writing for any amount of **$500** or more, or any amount if the sale is for a motor vehicle.

A written instrument may also be required for transactions involving personal property that fall within the rules of the **Uniform Commercial Code,** such as a bulk sale of goods, securities, and formation of security agreements. The sale of bulk goods in the real estate industry involves the sale of a business. Bulk goods are personal property that is included in the sale of a business, such as articles of clothing in the sale of a clothing store.

Ownership of real estate is transferred by an instrument called a **deed,** and transfer of personal property is transferred by an instrument called a **bill of sale.**

Deeds showing the transfer of real estate are generally recorded with the county recorder's office in the county where the property is located. A bill of sale or any instrument transferring personal property is generally not recorded, and recording may not be considered constructive notice of conveyance of personal property.

Real property and personal property are subject to different tax laws. Real property is subject to **property tax**, which is under the control of the county tax assessor and personal property is subject to **sales tax** under the control of the ***State of California Franchise Tax Board (FTB).***

EMBLEMENTS

EMBLEMENTS are cultivated crops. They are considered part of the land or realty until they are harvested. Once the crops are removed from the ground at harvest, they become personal property. When selling a producing farm, the emblements must be part of the negotiation to determine whether the buyer or seller owns the emblements. The seller usually retains the emblements and has the right to enter the property after transfer of ownership for the sole purpose of maintaining and harvesting the crop. Once the designated emblements have been removed, the seller no longer has any rights to that real property.

LAND DESCRIPTION

In order to have a definition of real estate, there must be a method of measurement or description in order to properly identify a particular parcel of real property. In urban areas, street names and numbers are commonly used as property identification. This describes the real estate and all improvements within the perimeter of an area of land or parcel. Use of street name and number only is not an infallible method of identifying property. Street names can change, addresses change with lot splits or combining lots, and property is often developed in a manner not conforming to the current identification method. Rural and undeveloped property cannot be identified by using street names and addresses. The nature of real estate makes this method impractical in many situations.

For this reason, legal descriptions are common practice in California and throughout the United States as a way of more accurately identifying a parcel of land. The **county tax assessor** in each county also establishes an identifying number known as the **assessor's parcel number** (APN). The best practice is to use the methods of identification in the following order:

- Legal description
- APN/assessor's parcel number
- Street address when available

Most deeds show the legal description and the street address, where available. In the United States, most properties are described using one of three methods of legal descriptions. More than one method may apply to the same property.

The three types of legal description used are:

1. Lot and block
2. Metes and bounds
3. Rectangular survey method

1. **LOT and BLOCK LEGAL DESCRIPTION,** or the lot and block method of property description, may also be called the lot, block, and tract system, or the subdivision system. When many urban areas are developed, subdivision maps are provided giving both a lot and block legal description and a street address. Both of these descriptions will be used on future legal documents such as deeds, which require adequate description. Lot and block is the most common method of legal description due to the high density of urban areas.

   The **SUBDIVISION MAP** gives a complete description of each parcel on the map including the measurement, usually in feet, of each border of the individual lots. The subdivision maps are filed by the developer at the county recorder's office. The map becomes the accurate record for all transfers in the future.

   For each property recorded on the **PLAT MAP** the description of each parcel of land refers to the tract, street, and lot as specified by the governing entity. A lot and block legal description generally describes the city, county, tract name and number, and block and lot numbers. The map book number and the page number are also included within the description along with the recording date of the map. *See Figure 3: Plat Map.*

   > ***Example:*** *Lot and block legal description: Lot 6 in Block 3of St. Francis Heights, in the city of Los Angeles, State of California as per map recorded in Book 22, Page 45 of maps in the office of the county recorder of said county.*

   The ***California Department of Finance*** has determined that the population of California was more than 38 million in January 2008 with constant and steady growth annually. Approximately 97 percent of the population of California lives in urban areas. The majority of development has been along coastal areas, primarily in and around San Francisco, Los Angeles, and San Diego. The large expanses of undeveloped land in the remaining areas of California necessitate methods of land description that will accommodate this land.

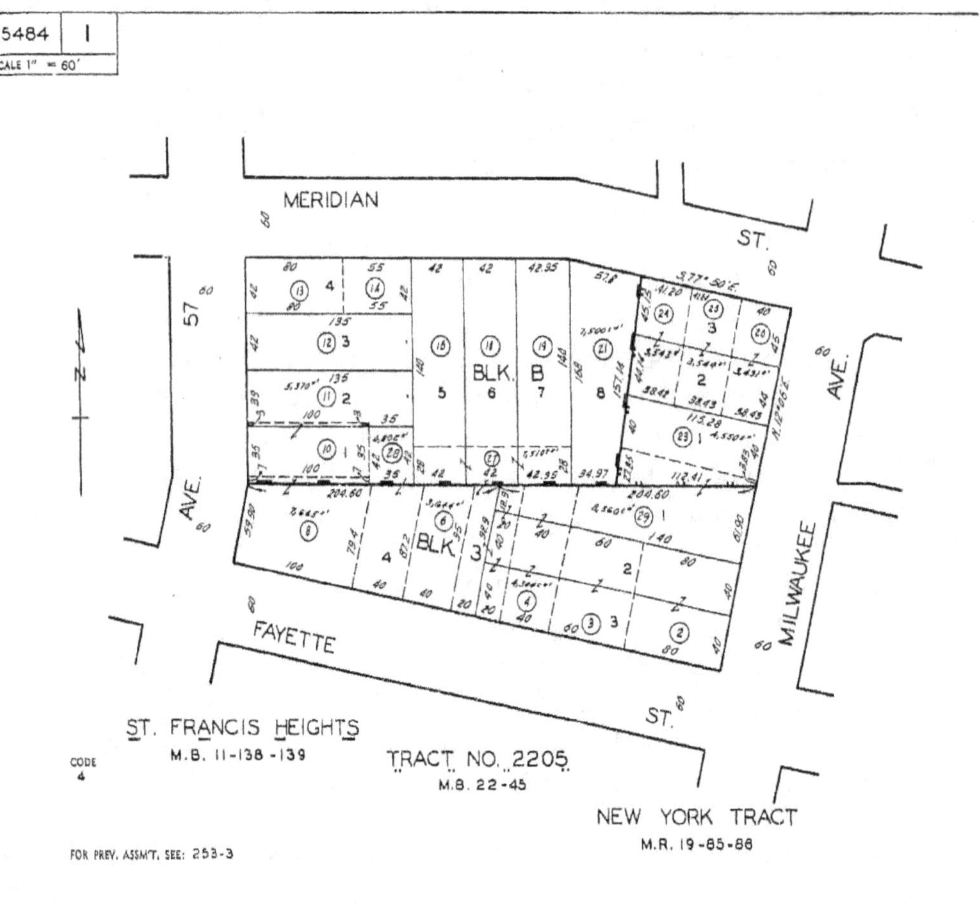

Figure 3: Plat Map

2. **METES AND BOUNDS** is used most often in rural areas and areas with uneven terrain, such as in the mountainous regions of California. This method works well for areas with irregular boundaries. It requires the use of markers, whether man- made or natural. Natural markers, such as a tree, rock, or river, can all move or be removed, causing a legal description to no longer be usable or at least not completely accurate. A legal description is created by following the borders of a property by using boundary markers.

   The term "metes" refers to distances, which may be measured in inches, feet, yards, or rods. Bounds are natural or artificial boundaries such as rivers, roads, property lines, or surveyor posts. Any boundary that is not directly following compass directions will be described by giving its angle, based on the degrees that it varies from the compass direction. *See Figure 4: Metes and Bounds.*

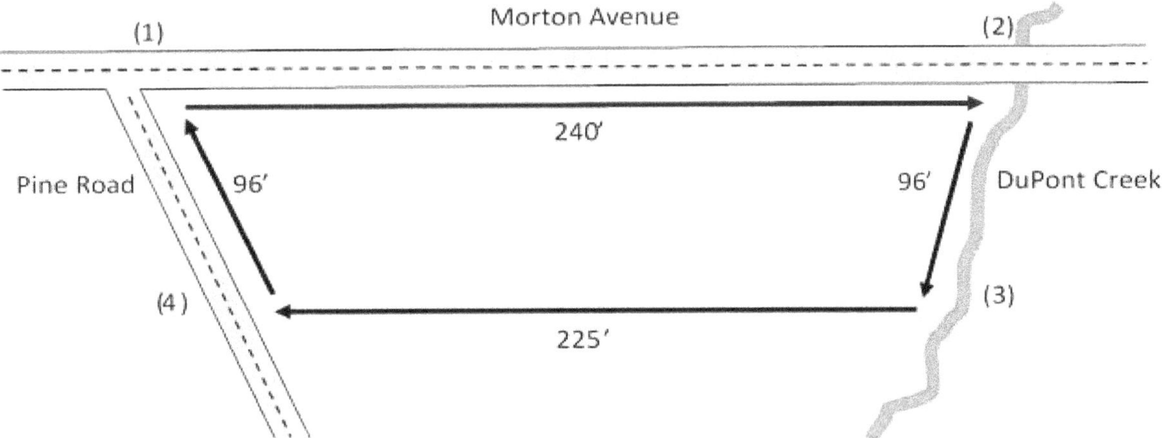

Figure 4: Metes and Bounds

A metes and bounds legal description starts at a beginning point and follows each boundary line for a given distance, in a given direction, and at a precise angle from point to point until the entire boundary has been enveloped.

> ***Example:*** *A tract of land in the Village of Fillmore described as follows: Starting at the beginning point (1) at the intersection of the east line of Pine Road along the south line of Morton Avenue traveling east 240 feet to the center of DuPont Creek (2); South 15° South West 96 feet, more or less, along the center of the creek; then (3) West 225 feet to the East line of Pine Road; then (4) North along the line of Pine Road to the point of beginning.*

3. **TOWNSHIP AND RANGE SURVEY SYSTEM,** also known as **rectangular survey** and the **U.S. Government Survey System** is used by the United States Surveyor general to measure and describe federal lands through survey. This system bases its descriptions of land on baselines which run east-west and meridians which run north-south from a specified reference point.

   There are three principle **BASELINES** and **MERIDIANS** used in California land descriptions:
   - The Mount Diablo Baseline and Meridian was established on Mt. Diablo in Contra Costa County in 1851.
   - The San Bernardino Baseline and Meridian was established on San Bernardino Mountain in San Bernardino County in 1852.
   - The Humboldt Baseline and Meridian was established on Mount Pierre in Humboldt County in 1853.

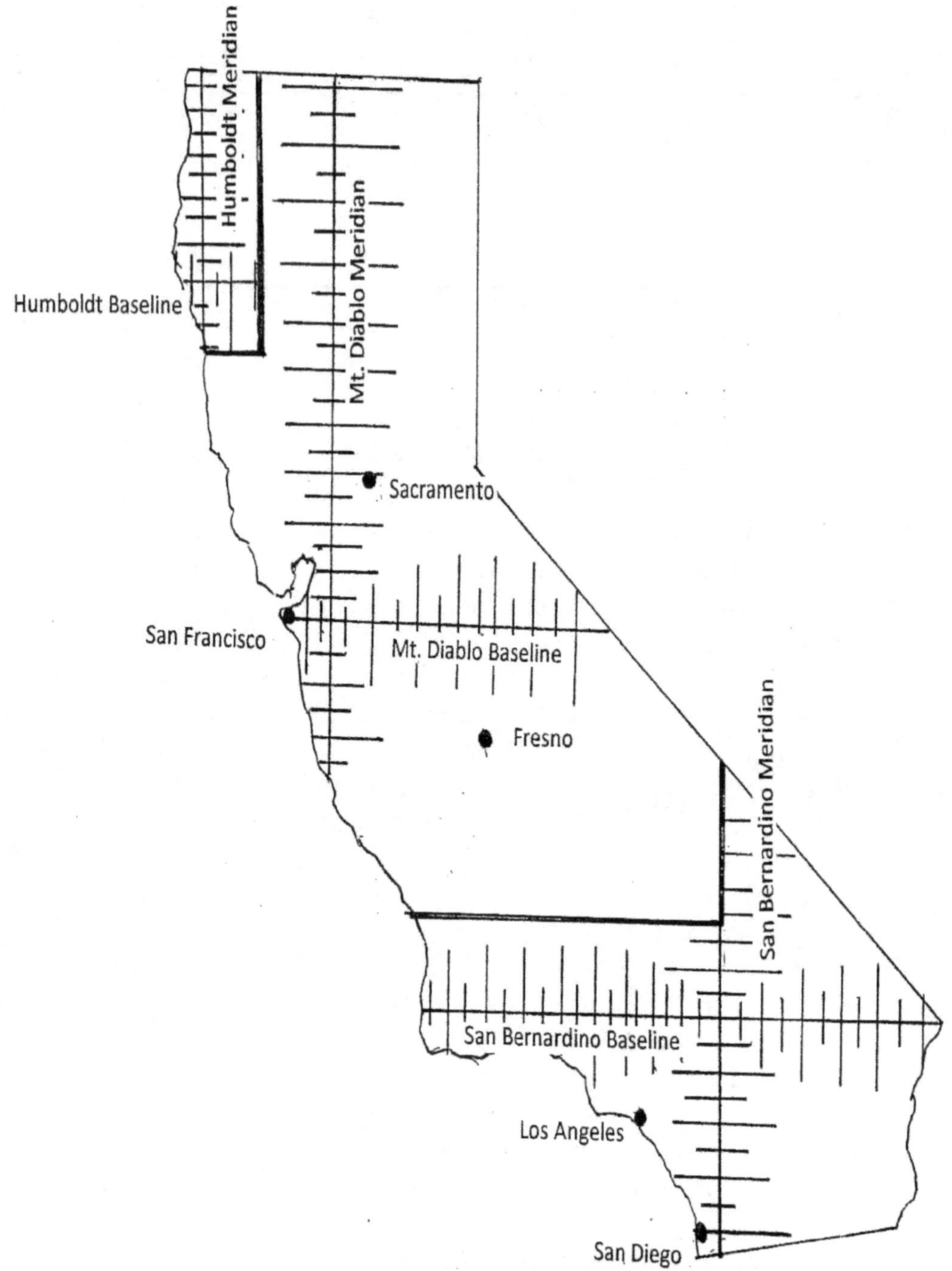

Figure 5: California Baselines and Meridians (Not to scale)

These baselines and meridians are used as a reference points from which a parcel can be located and described. Figure 5 shows the three main baselines and meridians used in California. *See Figure 5: California Baselines and Meridians.*

This method divides the land into **townships** that are numbered and measured in each direction from the point of intersection of the baseline and the meridian. The term "township" does not refer to an actual "town" or city; it is merely an expression used to define a square area which is six miles on each side or thirty-six square miles. Townships run east and west in **ranges** and north and south in **tiers.** As shown in Figure 6, T3N, R2E is the third tier north of the baseline and two ranges east of the meridian.

Each township has **36 Sections**, with each section being one square mile. One square mile contains **640 acres**. *See Figure 6: Township Identification Demonstration.*

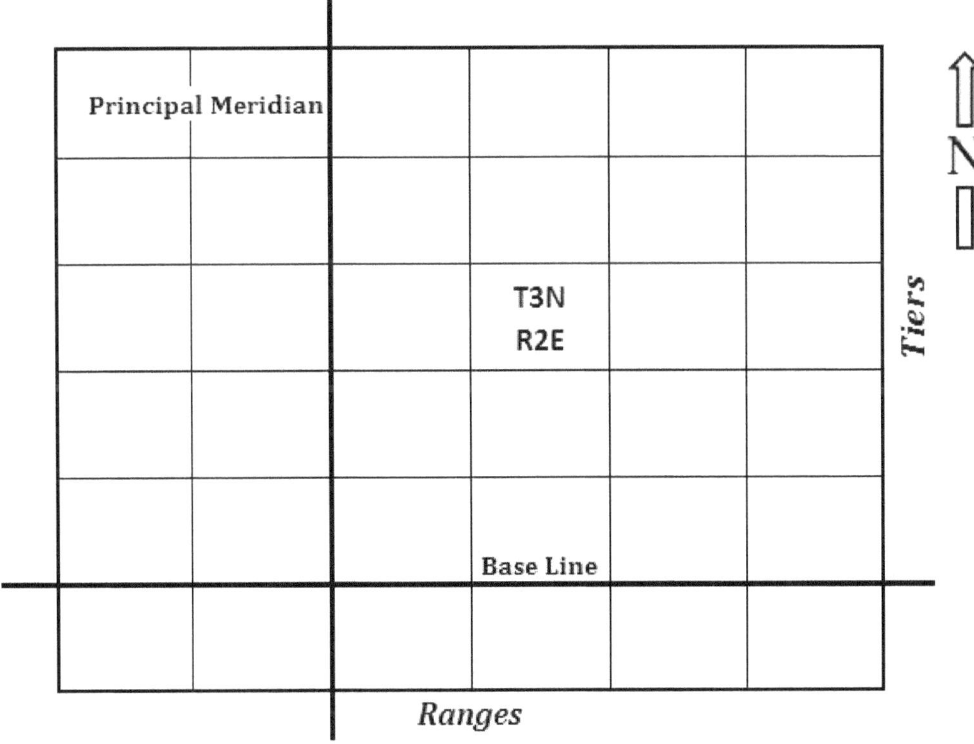

Figure 6: Township Identification Demonstration

A section can be broken down into smaller parcels. The sections within a township are numbered in a specific order starting with number 1 in the northeast corner of the section and running west to the end of the first row, then east in the second row, continuing in a serpentine pattern through Section 36. *See Figure 7: Township Grid.*

6	5	4	3	2	1
7	8	9	10	11	12
18	17	16	15	14	13
19	20	21	22	23	24
30	29	28	27	26	25
31	32	33	34	35	36

Figure 7: Township Grid

Due to the curvature of the earth and topography, the baselines and ranges, and the meridian and the tiers will not remain at an equal distance to form the intended measurements of 36 square miles in a township or one square mile in a section.

The method of measurement allows for a **correction line** in order to maintain the measurement system. When reading a legal description using this method, it will be read from the largest measurement to the smallest measurement, which means that the legal description will be read backward. Figure 8 demonstrates a common breakdown of a section done to provide a legal description. *See Figure 8: Section Breakdown and Measurements.*

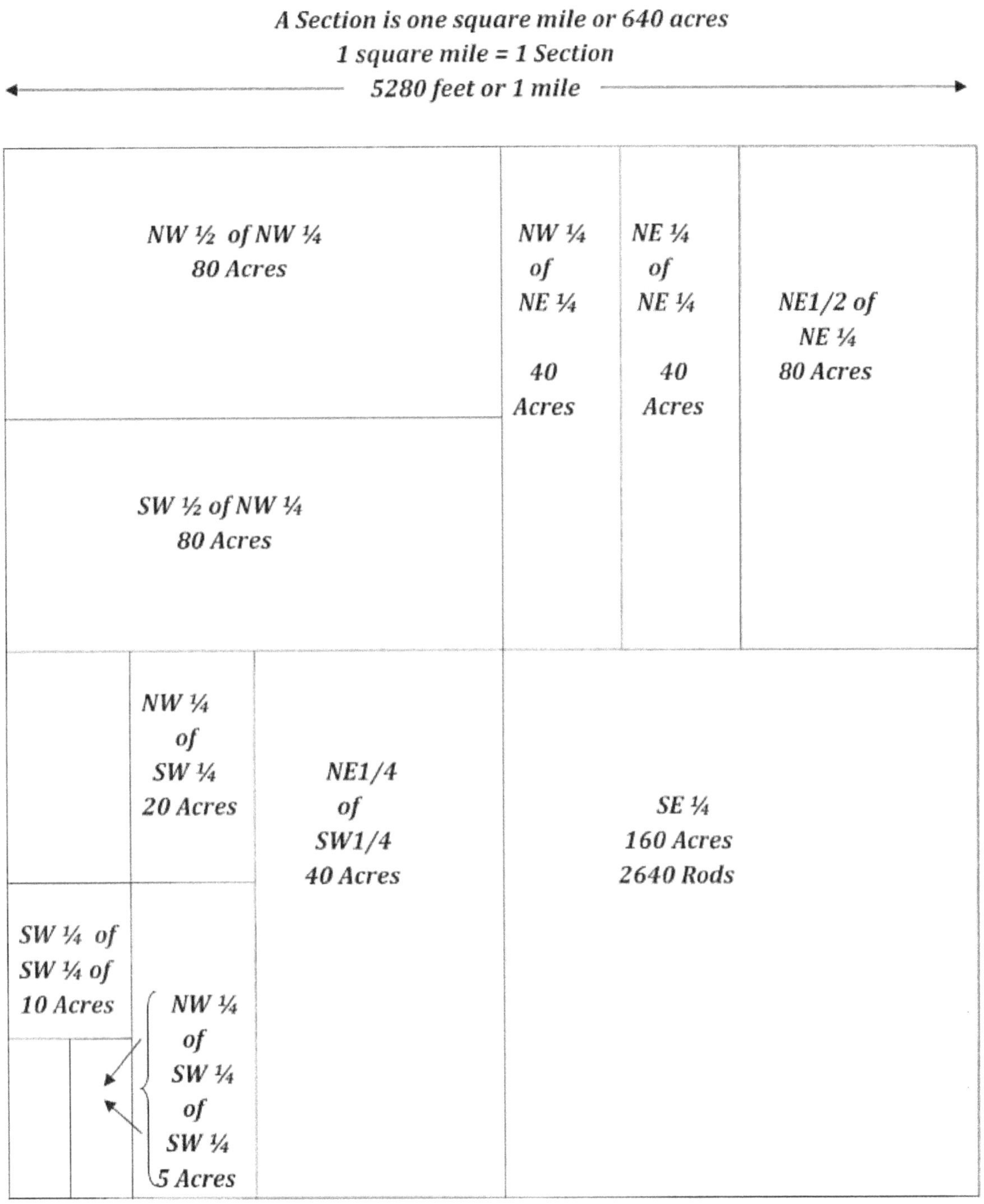

A Section is one square mile or 640 acres
1 square mile = 1 Section
5280 feet or 1 mile

NW ½ of NW ¼
80 Acres

NW ¼ of NE ¼
40 Acres

NE ¼ of NE ¼
40 Acres

NE1/2 of NE ¼
80 Acres

SW ½ of NW ¼
80 Acres

NW ¼ of SW ¼
20 Acres

NE1/4 of SW1/4
40 Acres

SE ¼
160 Acres
2640 Rods

SW ¼ of SW ¼ of
10 Acres

NW ¼ of SW ¼ of SW ¼
5 Acres

Figure 8: Section Breakdown and Measurements

All descriptions use the compass points north, south, east, and west.

> ***Example:*** *The east ½ of the northwest ¼ of the southeast ¼ of Section 21 of township T3N R2E of the San Bernardino Baseline.*

The area of a parcel can be computed using the rectangular survey system by multiplying the number of acres in a section by the fractional part of the section. We know that a section has 640 acres, so we can multiply 640 acres by the fractional parts of the sections involved. To calculate the size of the parcel in the previous example, always start from the end and work backward by starting at the largest measurement, or the total section, and work to the smallest measurement:

> ***Example:*** *Section 21 = 640 acres ÷ 4 (SE ¼) = 160 acres ÷ 4 (NW ¼) =40 acres ÷2 (E ½) = 20 acres total size of the parcel described*

There are several ways to calculate the size of a parcel of land. The one just demonstrated is merely a matter of dividing the total size down one piece at a time. There may be times when the total parcel of land will actually be spread over more than one section in which case, the total acreage is done with separate calculations then added together for the total.

Multiplying fractions is a faster way to calculate the measurements in sections once you fully understand the concept of this method of measurement:

(¼ x ¼ x ½) x 640 acres = total size of parcel
1/32 x 640 = total size of parcel
640/32 acres = 20 acres

Computing land area is done using the following units of measurement:

1 foot	12 inches
1 yard	3 feet or 36 inches
1 acre	43,560 square feet
1 rod	5 ½ yards or 16 ½ feet
1 furlong	40 rods
6.06 rods	100 feet
1 mile	5,280 linear feet, or 8 furlongs, or 320 rods, or 1,760 yards
1 league	3 miles

THE HISTORY OF CALIFORNIA REAL ESTATE

Many of the terms currently used in the practice of California real estate came from English common law during a time when the king of England owned everything, especially the land. As a reward for loyalty from his subjects, the king gave land grants to free men, or men who were not serfs. These land grants from the king were called **fees**. As property laws evolved, this became the commonly used term **fee,** or **fee simple ownership**. These rewards were usually granted for service during wartime.

When the Spanish, led by Vasco Nunez de Balboa, claimed California for the king of Spain, Spanish law was implemented in Mexico and the California Territory. Franciscan missionaries began to establish missions beginning in San Diego in 1769. The missions were established along El Camino Real, which is now essentially the path of Highway 101 and Route 1, or the Pacific Coast Highway. The king of Spain owned the land and gave rancho grants on a limited basis for farming and grazing. Pueblos, or cities, were also established by receiving four square leagues, with a league being equal to 4,400 acres of land. City officials granted housing and farming lots to residents of the pueblos.

The settlement of the California territory increased by both Mexican and American citizens when Mexico gained its independence from Spain in 1821. This eventually led to the Mexican-American War, which ended with the **Treaty of Guadalupe Hidalgo** in 1848. At that time, California became a possession of the United States.

Existing rights of Mexican citizens living in California were honored by the government of the United States and the government of the California territory.

OWNERSHIP OF PROPERTY BY WOMEN and COMMUNITY PROPERTY are both legal concepts that were part of the **Treaty of Guadalupe Hidalgo** and carried over to California law. Women were not allowed to own property in their own name under most laws of the time.

Community property laws apply to property acquired by either spouse during marriage as well as property owned separately obtained prior to or during marriage. *This will be discussed further in Chapter 5.*

Shortly after the end of the war, gold was discovered in California, giving new interest and value to the territory. With this came a large influx of new residents to the area. The added interest in the territory was influential in making California a state in 1850.

Spanish law and English Common law were combined with American law to create the laws that are used today. The transfer from Spanish and Mexican law to American laws meant a lot of change and adaptation of the various sets of laws and legal codes. The changing laws and combining of different laws caused misunderstandings and land disputes by the settlers of California. In 1851, Congress formed the **Board of Land Commissioners** for the purpose of settling claims to privately owned lands in California. The majority of the Mexican land grants were honored, taking land away from many new settlers to the territory, most of whom were squatters. Additional information regarding California history can be found on the California website: *www.ca.gov*.

When California became a state in 1850, the federal government retained certain rights in the state, as it has in all states. The State of California owns all lands that lie beneath navigable streams and lakes and up to the ordinary high-tide line. The federal government still owns approximately forty five percent of the more than one hundred million acres of land that make up the state. National parks make up a large portion of the state's territory.

Tidelands are held in a public trust for the use of fishing, recreation, and navigation. Under certain rights, public lands can be transferred to private ownership, allowing for income from oil and gas production, and other mineral mining. Other federal land grants were made to railroad companies for the development of transportation to help in the growth of the state.

CHAPTER 2

OWNERSHIP OF REAL ESTATE

US
Realty School

ESTATES IN PROPERTY

ESTATES IN PROPERTY are either **FREEHOLD** or **LESS-THAN-FREEHOLD,** depending on the degree of ownership and the duration of the interest held in the property. It is generally accepted that freehold estates are real property, while less- than-freehold estates are personal property that is giving rights to the use of the real property. The term **fee** or **fee simple ownership** came from the old English land grants from the king, which were called fees.

FREEHOLD ESTATE/ESTATE IN FEE

FREEHOLD ESTATE is also referred to as **fee simple absolute,** or the shortened term fee simple. Fee simple is the most complete form of ownership that one can have in property. Fee simple ownership provides the entire **bundle of rights** which includes possession, quiet enjoyment, control, exclusion, and disposal. There are no restraints on the ownership of a property held in fee simple other than those imposed by the government, such as zoning laws.

Fee simple ownership is for an undetermined amount of time, meaning that an owner of property in fee simple has no time restraints on their ownership. That person can own that property indefinitely within their lifetime, or until they choose to sell, lease, give, or otherwise deed the property to another person.

All transfers of real property are assumed to be fee simple (absolute) unless the granting portion of the deed states otherwise.

FEE SIMPLE DEFEASIBLE refers to ownership in property that has conditions or limitations attached to the ownership that could defeat a party's claim to the property.

> ***Example:*** *Mr. Smith wants to donate a parcel of land to the city for the purpose of creating a park for recreation. Mr. Smith declares in the deed that the property will belong to the city as long as the property is used for public recreation. The city cannot use the property for any other use and cannot sell the property to a private owner for personal use because of the* ***fee simple defeasible*** *condition. Once the property is no longer used for public recreation, the ownership of the property can revert to Mr. Smith or his heirs.*

The defeasible condition must be disclosed to the party receiving title to the property. The new property owner must meet the terms of the defeasible condition in order to retain their ownership. This condition is what makes the fee simple ownership defeasible.

> ***Example:*** *Mr. Smith donates his property to the city for a park for public use and recreation as long as the use of alcohol is not allowed on the property. The city sells the property to a private party. The new owner establishes facilities for the purpose of hosting private parties on the property. The parties are allowed to hire catering services which include the serving of alcohol. The defeasible condition, which was present prior to the sale of the property, is in effect even though the original receiver of the fee simple defeasible title no longer owns the property. The property can revert to Mr. Smith or his heirs if they choose to pursue the option.*

The wording creating any defeasible conditions would be on the **grant deed** creating a **fee simple defeasible**. A fee simple defeasible is a limitation to the deed or the ownership rights to a property.

LIFE ESTATE

LIFE ESTATE is interest in property for the duration of the life of a designated person or persons. The owner of a life estate, or the **life tenant**, has the right to use and possess the property for the duration of the life of the designated person. All interests held by the life tenant end when the designated person dies. The purpose of a life estate is generally to provide a lifelong home to the person receiving the life estate. The designated person, upon whose life the estate depends, does not have to be the life tenant.

The designated person can be anybody that the grantor chooses to name. They do not need to be related to the transaction in any other way.

When the **designated person** dies, the property ownership transfers to the party named as the receiver of the title to the property. This will be either the **remainderman,** who is the person designated to receive the property, or the **reversionary holder,** who is the original owner and the grantor of the life estate.

A **life tenant** of property has certain interests and obligations in conjunction with the ownership of the life estate. The life tenant's rights and obligations are as follows:

Rights of a life tenant:

- Physically possess the property as long as the life estate is in effect. They can live on the property or use it accordingly.
- Lease the property to another party and retain all rents.
- Sell or finance the property, but not beyond the term of the life estate.

The life tenant can sell the property, but on the demise of the designated person, the property will transfer to the specified remainderman. It is unlikely that financing would be available on a life estate to a life tenant as the loan would not be collectable in most circumstances after the death of the designated person or in case of a foreclosure.

Obligations of a life tenant:

- May not destroy any part of the property in a way that is detrimental to any subsequent owners.
- Must maintain the property in good repair but is generally not required to make major repairs.
- Is responsible for costs and expenses, such as and including property taxes and insurance.

A pre-existing mortgage or any other debt against the property that was in place prior to obtaining the property that is paid by the holder of a life estate, may require reimbursement by the **reversionary holder** or the **remainderman**. Payment of mortgage principal will benefit the ultimate property holder because they will ultimately own the property and may therefore require repayment to the life tenant. Mortgage interest that is due during their tenancy only, however, is considered the obligation of the life tenant.

ESTATE IN REVERSION is the term used to describe the situation that will return the property to the original grantor of the life estate upon the death of the designated person. The holder of the estate in reversion is called the **reversionary holder** because the property ownership reverts back to them when the designated person dies, and they will gain ownership to the property through reversion of the title.

Example: Sam gives his sister, Sally, a life estate on a piece of property that he owns. Sam names Sally as not only the life tenant, but also the designated person. Sam states in the grant deed that when Sally dies, the ownership of the property will revert to him. Sam has an estate in reversion.

If Sam dies before Sally, Sally is still the life tenant of the property for the term of her life. Sam's son Joe may claim ownership based on the inheritance from his father, Sam, but Sally does retain her right to the property as long as she lives because she is the designated person.

ESTATE IN REMAINDER is held by a person other than the original grantor and this person is called the **remainderman**.

Example: *Sam gives his sister Sally a life estate on his property, but upon the demise of Sally, the designated person, the property will transfer to his son, Joe. When Sally dies, ownership of the property transfers to Joe "in remainder" or as the "remainderman."*

The designated person is not always the life tenant. It can be any person that the grantor chooses. This can and has caused many problems and lawsuits. The life estate was used frequently in California in the late 1800s and the early 1900s. This is no longer a common practice in California, but it still exists and is legal.

Example: *Sam gave his sister Sally a life estate on his property, but upon the demise of the designated person, the property will transfer to his son, Joe.*

When Sam dies, ownership of the property transfers to Joe "in remainder," or as the "remainderman" or as the remaining person. Sally relinquishes her rights to the property if she is still living.

There are few of these circumstances remaining in California; however, they do exist, and they do provide a legal interest in the property for the holder of the life estate or the life tenant.

LESS-THAN-FREEHOLD ESTATE

In a recent transaction in the central coast area of California, the grantor passed away and the heirs wanted to sell the property, which included two houses. The tenant that was living in the smaller guest house had a life estate, which gave him the right to rent the house for $300 per month for the remainder of his lifetime. He was not related to the family but had been a handyman and later helped the couple as they aged. A strong friendship had developed, and the couple became dependent on his help. There were a number of offers, all of which conditioned for the life estate to be canceled, and the life tenant vacate the property.

The life tenant was offered as much as $50,000 by the heirs to release his interest in the estate and move. He declined based on advice from friends to wait for an offer of $100,000. An offer to purchase the property finally came in from a buyer that was willing to let the life estate remain in place, but for a purchase price $30,000 below the list price. The offer was accepted, and the transaction closed with the life estate in place. The sellers came out ahead of the previous offers by $20,000 because they did not have to pay the life tenant $50,000 or more to forfeit his interest in the property. The tenant was able to stay in the house he had lived in for many years, but without any additional cash.

LESS-THAN-FREEHOLD ESTATES provide the rights to the use of real property for a period of time. They are more commonly referred to as **leases** or **rental agreements**. The landlord or owner of the property is the **lessor,** or the person giving use of the property to another. The tenant or renter is the **lessee,** or the person receiving the right to use the property that belongs to another person.

CHATTEL REAL is another term used in reference to a less-than-freehold estate or lease. "Chattel" means personal property and "real" refers to real property; when combined, the phrase refers to a personal interest in real property.

A **LEASE** or **RENTAL AGREEMENT** gives a tenant various rights in the use of real property for a designated period of time. The lease or rental agreement is personal property because it is not true property ownership. It is only the right to use the property.

Only the lessor or landlord is required to sign a lease showing agreement to the terms. The lessee or tenant does not need to sign the lease. Taking possession of the property and paying the security deposit and rent shows agreement of the lease by the lessee.

NOTE

The State of California requires leases to be in writing if they are for a term of more than one year.

Four main types of less-than-freehold estates are in use as listed below.

1. **ESTATE FOR YEARS** is a lease for a fixed or specified period of time. This can be for a period of days, weeks, months, or years. The term can be deceiving because it does not necessarily designate that the term is for "years." It is a lease agreement whereby the landlord/owner/lessor and the tenant/lessee have agreed to a set date when the lease will expire.

Generally, an estate for years is in writing based on the fact that there is a pre- determined expiration date. **No termination notice is required with an estate for years because of the predetermined expiration date.**

> ***Example:*** *Mr. Jones owns a house that he rents to Mr. Smith for one year starting September 1st. The lease is in writing and the expiration date is August 31st of the following year. This is an estate for years because there is an expiration date.*
>
> *This example is for a period of one year and, therefore, does not need to be in writing. If the lease period had been from September 1st through September 1st of the following year, it would have been for a year and one day or more than one year and a written lease would be required.*

2. **ESTATE FROM PERIOD-TO-PERIOD** is a renewable agreement to rent or lease a property for a specified period of time such as month-to-month or year-to-year. This type of lease is generally used for shorter rental terms such as month-to- month but is not limited to that. There is no pre-determined expiration date in writing with this type of lease. When the term ends, it is understood that it will continue again for the period of time if the tenant/lessee pays the rent, and the landlord/lessor accepts the rental payment.

   The State of California requires a minimum of 30 days' notice from either party for termination of the agreement in most situations. The rule is that the Notice of Termination is to be for the length of time between rental payments. In other words, if rent is paid monthly, the Notice of Termination by either party should be given at least 30 days in advance.

   Up to a 60-day Notice of Termination is required in certain cases such as in the case of a disabled lessee or if there are minor children in the household. The minimum time for a Notice of Termination in California is seven days. The lease agreement and the terms can be whatever the lessor and lessee agree to within reason and within the law.

   > ***Example 1:*** *Prior to renting the house to Mr. Smith, Mr. Jones rented the same house on a monthly basis to Mr. Brown. The agreement was verbal, and Mr. Brown gave Mr. Jones 30 days' notice that he was vacating the premises on August 31st. This is an* ***estate from period-to-period.***

Example 2: *On September 1*st *at the end of the first year after Mr. Smith rented the house from Mr. Jones, Mr. Smith paid an additional month's rent to Mr. Jones. Mr. Jones accepted the rental payment, and the lease changed from an estate-for-years to an estate from period-to-period. They do not write a new lease. If they had written a new lease with a termination date, it would have remained as an* ***estate-for-years.***

3. **ESTATE-AT-WILL** can be terminated by either party at any time. This type of lease refers to a situation where a tenant's term of tenancy is indefinite. The State of California used to allow tenancy under an estate-at-will, which did not require a cancellation or notice of termination from either party. Now that a minimum notice is required, this type of lease is technically not in use under the law, an estate-at-will becomes an estate from period-to-period once the rent is paid and accepted.

   Example: *Mr. Smith continues to rent the property; however, he and Mr. Jones have agreed that he does not need to give a 30-day notice because he is purchasing a home and wants to move as soon as escrow closes.*

4. **ESTATE-AT-SUFFERANCE** occurs when the tenant remains after the agreed upon term either without paying rent or against the landlord's wishes—therefore the term "sufferance." Once the rent is paid by the tenant/lessee and is accepted by the landlord/lessor, the estate-at-sufferance becomes an estate-from period-to-period.

   Example: *Mr. Smith has continued to rent the property from Mr. Jones and the lease has expired. It is now September 5; but rental payment was due on the 1*st*. Mr. Smith did not pay the rent, yet he continues to occupy the property.*

   This is an estate-at-sufferance. Once Mr. Smith pays the rent and Mr. Jones accepts the rental payment, this becomes an estate-at-will.

TITLE IN REAL ESTATE

TITLE IN REAL ESTATE is obtained through a conveyance called a **grant deed**. The person who is conveying or granting the property is the **grantor**. The person receiving the property or the grant is the **grantee.**

The OR suffix is the party giving or the GIVOR and the party RECEIVING has the EE suffix. This rule applies throughout real estate terminology.

TITLE refers to and is used synonymously with ownership. If you own the property, it is said that your name is on title. Title can be held by an individual or by multiple parties. Title can also be held by a trust or a corporation. How parties choose to hold title or own property is a decision to be made carefully as it has tax and legal ramifications.

Giving advice to anyone regarding how they should hold title is a legal issue and should be referred to an attorney. Giving legal advice without a license to practice law is illegal.

The real estate professional may refer clients to the escrow company for help with the method of holding title. Escrow companies often have written information available that can provide definitions of the various forms of property ownership.

To begin with, it is important to establish the marital status of those taking title to a property. One of the following will apply to each person taking title and it is important to determine the appropriate status. **Legal ramifications apply if the marital status is misstated.** California is a community property state, which will be discussed later in this chapter. Consider the situation that may occur if a married person claims to be unmarried or single. The spouse may have a right to claim some ownership of the property upon discovery.

The common ways that a person may go on title are as follows:

- **Single:** Never been married.
- **Unmarried:** Currently not married but has been previously and is now divorced. A divorce decree may be required as verification if a loan is required to complete the real estate transaction.
- **Married:** Currently married, whether separated or living together.
- **Widow or widower:** Person whose spouse is deceased. A death certificate may be required as verification if a loan is required to complete the real estate transaction.
- **Trust:** Trust fund has been established for the management of personal and real properties for a person or persons.
- **Corporation:** Business entity that owns property.

OWNERSHIP IN SEVERALTY is when a person owns property solely or the owner is the sole person to enjoy the benefits of property ownership or the bundle of rights. The owner in severalty is also the only one responsible for the obligations of ownership, such as maintenance, taxes, debts, etc.

CONCURRENT OWNERSHIP is shared ownership, meaning that more than one person owns the property concurrently, or at the same time. As many individual owners can share the ownership as they choose; ownership can also be a combination of individuals, trusts, and corporations. There are four types of concurrent ownership. They are as follows:

1. **TENANTS IN COMMON** allows for any number of owners. The individual owners can be added onto title or removed from title at any time without affecting the other owners or the tenants-in-common designation.

   Each owner may own an equal or unequal share of the property as determined by the property owners. The owners do, however, have **unity of possession** which means that although they may own different shares, all owners have the right to use the entire property. No individual can claim a portion of the property for their personal use and no individual owner can be excluded by the co-owners.

   If the property is rented, the individual owners are entitled to a portion of the rent collected that is equal to their individual share of the ownership. In other words, if an individual owns one-fourth of the property, that individual is entitled to one-fourth of the rent collected. Property expenses are shared in the same way, based on the percentage of ownership.

   A **tenant-in-common** has the right to sell, give away, or leave their share to their heirs in a will, or devise their share or percentage of ownership in the property. The recipient of this transfer enjoys the same benefits of ownership as the donor had enjoyed. They will also share the same obligations and debts that the donor had.

   Upon the death of one of the tenants-in-common, the individuals share in the property passes to their heirs, not the other co-owners.

   A **CREDITOR'S SALE** can only affect the individual owners' share of the property. If a creditor successfully sues an owner of a concurrently owned property, that creditor can only attach the percentage of ownership held by that co-owner.

Example: *Tom owns property concurrently as tenants-in-common with Joe and Sam. They each own one-third of the property.*

Tom has defaulted on a debt and the creditor has sued him in court and won a judgment against him. The creditor has requested and been awarded a writ of execution in order to hold a creditor's sale. At the sale, the creditor is auctioning Tom's interest in real property, which includes the property that Tom owns with Joe and Sam.

The sale produces a successful bid for that property by George. George now owns one-third of the property concurrently with Joe and Sam with the same benefits and responsibilities that Tom had held prior to the sale.

PARTITION ACTION is a forced sale that can be accomplished by filing a lawsuit if the various owners cannot agree to a sale, and the settlement of the sale and proceeds of a concurrently owned property. If any of the individual owners of a tenancy-in-common wants to dissolve the shared ownership interest in property by sale of that property, all parties need to agree to the sale and settlement of any outstanding debts or obligations. The courts can settle a dispute between co-owners by requiring the sale of the property and division of the assets in an equitable manner after all debts and taxes have been paid in full.

Example: *Tom, John, Sally, and Jane buy a vacation property jointly for a purchase price of $100,000. They take the title as tenants-in-common. Tom puts $50,000 toward the purchase price to own 50%. John puts in $25,000 to own 25%, Sally and Jane each put in $12,500 to own 12.5%.*

They all have equal possession of the property. When they use the property for vacations, they can use any and all of the property without exclusion. In other words, Tom cannot mark off or lock certain areas denoted in his 50%.

They decide to rent the property for $1,000 a month. Tom will receive $500/month; John will receive $250/month; and Sally and Jane will each receive $125/month. Any expenses involved in renting the property will be shared accordingly. Taxes and mortgage payments will also be distributed according to percentage of ownership.

John unexpectedly dies. His share of the ownership does not pass to Tom, Sally, and Jane, but to his wife, Mary, who is his heir and is now a tenant-in-common with the other co-owners.

Mary decides that she does not want to own the property and offers her share to the other tenants in common. They do not wish to purchase her share from her at the requested price. She offers it to others, but no one chooses to purchase her share. Her option at that point is to file a partition action lawsuit against the other tenant-in-common owners. The courts sell the property and divide the profits according to percentage of ownership after the costs have been deducted.

2. **JOINT TENANCY** is a form of concurrent ownership allowing for co-ownership giving equal share or ownership. Joint tenants take title at the same time, on the same document, unlike tenants-in-common who may go on and off title without effect. There are four **unities of title that are an essential part of a joint tenancy**:
   a) **Unity of time:** Each owner takes title at the same time.
   b) **Unity of title:** Each owner receives title with the same deed.
   c) **Unity of interest:** Each owner has an equal share or interest.
   d) **Unity of possession:** Each owner has the right to use the entire property.

The joint tenant's **RIGHT OF SURVIVORSHIP** is provided for and is a distinguishing trait of joint tenancy. If the co-owner dies, the surviving co- owner inherits the property.

An individual joint tenant cannot bequeath, devise, or name an heir other than the co-owner.

There can be as many co-owners as the parties choose in a joint tenancy. A joint tenant can sell their interest to another party, but the new co-owner will be a tenant-in-common because of the unity of time, meaning that the title was not taken at the same time as the other owners. The joint tenancy will remain in place as long as there are two or more joint tenants remaining.

The right of survivorship applies only to the joint tenants, not to the tenant-in-common. If there are only two joint tenants, and one sells their interest in the property, there is no longer a joint tenancy, but a tenancy-in- common. Remember the unity of time and title. The definition of joint tenancy requires these unities.

Joint tenancy is most often used for married couples, mostly because of the right of survivorship. Joint tenancy is most often seen as "Husband and Wife as Joint Tenants." This form of ownership is, however, available for any who choose to own property in this manner.

3. **COMMUNITY PROPERTY** is a concept derived from Spanish law and instilled in California law as a result of the **Treaty of Guadalupe Hidalgo**. It is a form of ownership applying to both real and personal property pertaining to married couples. California, along with several other states, is a community property state, meaning that property acquired by a spouse during marriage usually belongs also to their spouse equally. Ownership may be acquired by taking measures to either include it as **community property** or exclude the property as **separate property**.

   Property may be acquired during marriage and owned as separate property. Real property that is owned as separate property is generally property that has been inherited or gifted but can also be property that is purchased as separate property while married. If a property is owned as separate property, the expenses and maintenance must be kept separate to retain the separate ownership status. Once the property has been shared with the spouse in any way to include shared funds used for expenses, the property may be considered community property. Separate bank accounts should be maintained for separate properties. Paying for anything as minor as a repair, such as replacing a switch plate, and paying from a joint checking account may qualify a property as community property.

   Property acquired prior to marriage may remain separately owned property after marriage. Separate property must be kept separate in order to qualify. This includes payment of debts and other obligations associated with the property. If property is acquired as separate property, but the taxes and maintenance expenses are paid from a joint bank account, it may be construed as community property.

   If one spouse owns property as **sole and separate** property, the non-owning spouse will need to sign a **quit claim deed** at the time of purchase or borrowing against the property. Signing a **quit claim deed** relinquishes their right and claim to the property.

A spouse has the ability to convey property held as community property by will or devise to someone other than the surviving spouse. The person that inherits the interest from the deceased spouse becomes a tenant-in- common with the surviving spouse. If either spouse dies without a will, the deceased spouse's surviving children will inherit the deceased spouse's interest, or 50% of the property.

4. COMMUNITY PROPERTY WITH RIGHT OF SURVIVORSHIP

Community property with right of survivorship (Civil Code 682.1) is a fairly new way for married couples to hold property title in California. It combines the best features of joint tenancy and community property and allows a property that was deeded after July 1, 2001, to pass to the surviving spouse without going through estate administration, known as ***probate.*** Furthermore, spouses *cannot bequeath* their shares of the community property to someone other than the spouse. **This new form of ownership combines the tax advantages of community property with the survivorship rights of joint tenancy.** The primary advantage to holding title as *community property with right of survivorship* is that upon the death of one spouse, the entire property receives a *step-up in basis* for tax purposes; that is, community property with right of survivorship will not be subject to capital gains tax when sold (*however,* this applies at a price not greater than the market value at the time of the decedent's death).

> **Title may be taken as "Husband and Wife, Community Property with Right of Survivorship."** This statement included on the deed and recorded with the county recorder's office will establish that, in the event of the death of either spouse, the surviving spouse will inherit the property solely and without probate.
>
> Not all states have **community property** laws. It is advisable to inform new residents of California of this unique set of laws. It is also important to inform clients of the effects that California laws may have on property owned by California residents in other states.

TRUSTS can hold title to real property for many different purposes, such as conveying property from the trustor to the trustee without probate and avoiding inheritance taxes following the death of the property owner. Trusts are also used by property owners as a way to transfer title to another and maintain controls to avoid mismanagement of assets by the grantee or beneficiary.

A trust may be established for the purpose of transferring property to a minor that would otherwise not be able to legally hold title to property. The trust may be used in this situation or anywhere the grantor has concern for the proper handling of assets by the beneficiary. The trust may name a trustee as a third party to manage the assets for the beneficiary, who is the actual owner of the property.

Trusts are used for a variety of reasons. They are often created to provide for a minor child until they reach maturity; to manage an estate with many heirs; or to avoid probate for heirs when the property owner meets their demise.

The terms and control of the property is stated in the trust agreement. A trust must conform to the laws of the state where it is drawn and the state where any property exists. A trust can be for a long or short period of time, depending on the purpose and the needs of the trustor, beneficiary, and trustee.

BUSINESS OWNERSHIP OF PROPERTY

Business Ownership of Property can take many forms. Businesses may purchase, sell, use, or lease property in the name of the business entity. The type of business structure will determine the extent of ownership and the capabilities allowed by law.

1. **SOLE PROPRIETORSHIP** is the ownership of a business by an individual. This type of business ownership allows for the fewest complications because the owner is the only person responsible for operating the business, and paying taxes and the debts associated with the business. Property is held in the name of the business owner as sole and separate property with inheritance as established by will or law.

2. **PARTNERSHIP** is a business that has two or more owners who share in the responsibility, expense, and liability of the business. A general partnership has established a partnership agreement as the guideline and terms of the business operation. The partnership may own business property, but the property will be purchased in the individuals' names.

   If the business of a partnership is ownership in a real estate business, all active partners must have a California real estate broker's license per the business and professions code and the California Department of Real Estate.

3. **TENANCY-IN-PARTNERSHIP** is a form of ownership allowing ownership by a business that is a legal partnership. Because the business is based on an agreement between individuals, the partners will hold title to any business property as **tenancy-in-partnership**. This is similar to tenancy-in-common unless the partners own the property as individuals on behalf of the business.

   The **partnership agreement** and the form of ownership of real property stated on the title establish the ownership of the property in the event of dissolution of the partnership or the death of one of the partners. The death of a partner dissolves the partnership unless the partnership agreement provides other provisions. When a partnership is dissolved, the assets are sold, and the profits are distributed among the partners after expenses are paid. If a partner dies and the business continues, the business property will generally go to the surviving partner. The heirs of the deceased partner have no right to the business property, but they do have a right to the deceased partner's share of business profit. This is common practice that can be done in any manner the partners choose and must be in writing in the partnership agreement. Partnership agreements do not need to be written by an attorney if the partners are able to prepare and agree on the terms; however, when real property is involved, preparation by an attorney is strongly recommended.

4. **LIMITED PARTNERSHIP** is a partnership with one or more general partner(s) who is responsible for the operations of the business and has the liability for the management decisions, debts, and obligations of the business.

   Limited partners are investors in the business who do not have any control of the management or operation of the business and therefore have only limited liability for the debts and obligations of the business, limited to the amount of their personal investment. But if a limited partner is involved in the operation of the business, they may lose their limited partnership status and become a general partner with all the responsibility and obligations that come with that status.

   A limited partnership business must file or register with the California Secretary of State. If a limited partnership business is operating as a real estate business, all general partners must have a California real estate broker's license. Any real property owned will usually be as individuals and in the name of the general partners.

5. **LIMITED LIABILITY COMPANY (LLC)** allows for many of the same benefits of a limited partnership with a few differences. An LLC provides for single taxation and limited liability. Unlike the limited partnership, an LLC allows the limited liability investors to take part in the operations of the business without losing their status or benefit of limited liability.

An LLC is an alternative to a limited partnership and an S-Corp *(see description below).* There is no restriction on the number of shareholders or investors. A written business agreement is not required. Taxes for an LLC are higher than taxes for a limited partnership or an S Corp.

The California Secretary of State requires that LLCs file or record the existence of the business with their offices. A California real estate broker's license is required to be held by the person or persons operating a real estate business.

6. **CORPORATION** is a legal form of business ownership established under the California Secretary of State. A corporation is managed by officers consisting of the president, vice president, secretary, and treasurer. The officers work closely with a board of directors when making business decisions. Investors in a corporation own a percentage of the business based on the amount of stock that they purchase or own. The sale of stock to the investors generates working capital for the operation of the business. The corporation must provide Articles of Incorporation to the California Secretary of State. The articles state the terms of ownership, the distribution of funds and assets, and the business purpose and structure.

   The individual shareholders are not personally responsible for business liability or the actions of the board of directors.

   A corporation is considered to be a legal entity and can hold title to property the same as an individual in perpetuity. The corporation can own, sell, lease, and give property as an individual entity. If a corporation is acting in the capacity of a real estate business, the president of the corporation must be a licensed real estate broker in California.

   A corporation has the disadvantage of double taxation. It is taxed first as a business, then the individuals receiving income from the corporation are taxed again on their personal returns.

7. **S-CORPORATION** is a legal entity which allows for the income to be distributed directly to the individual stockholders before taxation, eliminating double taxation. The S-Corp was created for small business entities and is limited to corporations with no more than thirty-five stockholders.

The stockholders of an S-Corp are acting as individuals and do not enjoy the legal protection offered by a corporation. They are also responsible for the liability of the business. Business property is owned as individuals and a real estate broker's license is required of the person in control of the operation of the business if the company's business is real estate.

8. **REAL ESTATE SYNDICATE** can be formed under various business types or legal entities but is most often created as a limited partnership. Real estate syndicates are a popular business for investors in California. They provide investors with the opportunity to make profitable investments in the real estate industry without the licensing requirements and without having to do the work or assume the responsibility.

   The real estate syndicate is a business that owns real property for rental or speculative purposes. The investors benefit from the income produced by the real estate owned. A real estate syndicate generally invests in large investment properties, such as commercial developments.

   If a syndicate has one hundred or more investors, it must have approval from the Department of Financial Protection and Innovation (DFPI) prior to offering properties for sale. Real estate syndicates are heavily regulated for the protection of not only the public but also the investors. Additionally, securities-related aspects of syndication may fall under the jurisdiction of the U.S. Securities and Exchange Commission (SEC) and relevant state securities laws.

   A real estate broker's license is required to be held by those in control. Business property is held in the names of the individuals in control of the real estate syndicate.

9. **REAL ESTATE INVESTMENT TRUSTS (REITs)** hold various forms of real property and mortgages for the income benefit of investors holding shares of the REIT. REITs are regulated at the federal level by the U.S. Securities and Exchange Commission (SEC) under the Securities Act of 1933 and the Securities Exchange Act of 1934. In California, REITs are subject to certain state securities regulations under the Department of Financial Protection and Innovation (DFPI). There is a requirement for at least one hundred investors in a REIT to qualify for tax advantages. Additionally, under the "5/50 Rule," no individual or a group of five or fewer investors is allowed to hold more than 50% of the REIT's shares during the last half of the taxable year to maintain its tax-exempt status.

   Like the real estate syndicate, the REIT creates income from investments in real estate. This type of business organization usually makes large investments, such as shopping centers, office buildings, and industrial properties.

   Seventy-five percent of the income must be derived from real estate with a minimum of 95% of the income generated from a variety of investments.

A real estate broker licensee must be in control of the management of the REIT and property may be held in the name of the business as an individual entity as a corporation.

The ***National Association of Real Estate Investment Trusts (NAREIT)*** serves REIT owners, managers, and investors. Information regarding REITs may be found on the website www.nareit.com.

Referring clients to dependable attorneys, tax preparers, and certified public accountants (CPAs) is advisable when they are interested in purchasing property in any type of business or trust.

Investigation of the professionals that specialize in this area of business may prove invaluable to your clients.

RESPA law requires that real estate licensees provide a minimum of five names when referring clients to any professional or service provider if a real estate professional chooses to specialize in this area researching the types of businesses further is essential. It is also important to have a good support system for the referral of clients.

The descriptions provided are abbreviated for the purposes discussed in this chapter. All laws discussed relate to California even where not stated. All states have laws regarding business ownership of land and the licensing of the various business types, which may vary from those of California.

Information and websites that may be helpful to both the real estate professional and their clients regarding the business forms of ownership are:

California Department of Real Estate - www.dre.ca.gov
Internal Revenue Service – www.irs.gov
National Association of REITs – www.nareit.com
Secretary of State – www.sos.ca.gov or www.sos.ca.gov/business

CONVEYANCE DEEDS

CONVEYANCE DEEDS, OR DEEDS, are used in California as a way of transferring ownership in real property. A deed is the document or instrument that is used to convey that transfer. There are several types of deeds that are commonly used for various types of property transfer.

VALID DEEDS must have several elements present to constitute the deed being valid. The elements of a valid deed are as follows:

- **WRITTEN DEED:** In California, transfer of ownership of real property must be in writing. Verbal transfer of real estate is not legally recognized in the California. The exception to this is a lease of 12 months or less.

- **DESCRIPTION OF THE PROPERTY:** Adequate or satisfactory identification must be included for a deed to be considered valid. A legal description is not necessary, but it is advisable. The property address is acceptable as long as it is a complete, legal address. Whatever description is used must positively identify the property.

  Example: *Mr. Green is transferring property he owns located at 508 W. College, LA, Ca. This is unacceptable as there may be a College Avenue, College Street, or College Way, etc. The proper address to use for a deed to be valid and to convey property is:*
  508 West College Avenue, Los Angeles, California

- **CAPACITY:** The grantor or the person conveying the property must be capable or able to execute a legal document. The grantor must be:
  - 18 years of age or older unless they are an emancipated minor by court order.
  - Married
  - In the military
  - Sane, or have the mental capacity to enter into legal transactions. A grantee or person receiving a property as a gift can be incompetent or can be a minor with a legal guardian to care for their interests.
  - Felons are not all capable of owning real property.

- **DESCRIPTION OF ALL PARTIES:** Must be present and sufficient to provide proper identification such as photo IDs. The full name of each person must be present, and their marital status should be included for legal purposes.

  Example: *Sam Smith should use his full name or sufficient enough to clarify which Sam Smith owns the property: Samuel A. Smith, A Married Man. The more common names should be as complete as possible such as: Samuel Anthony Smith, A Married Man.*

- **GRANTING CLAUSE:** Wording stating that the ownership is being transferred or conveyed to a new owner. Words of transference that must be included are "grant" or "convey." The habendum clause "To have and to hold" is not necessary for a deed to be valid.

  Example: *I, George Allan Green, do hereby grant the property at 508 West College Avenue, Los Angeles, California, to Samuel Anthony Smith.*

- **SIGNATURE OF THE GRANTOR:** Must be on the deed. The grantor must have the intention to convey the property. Signing the deed verifies the grantor's intention. The grantee does not need to sign the deed as acceptance of the deed verifies the intention of the grantee to obtain the property.

- **DELIVERY TO AND ACCEPTANCE BY THE GRANTEE**: If the deed is not delivered to the grantee, ownership has not been conveyed. If the grantee refuses or does not physically accept the deed, ownership has not been conveyed.

All of the abovementioned elements must be present or have taken place. If any are missing, the deed is not valid.

A deed also does not need to be recorded with the county recorder's office, although recording is strongly advisable. Not having a deed witnessed or recorded may lead to questions of fraud and validity in the future. The county recorder's office will refuse to record a deed that has not been notarized and a lender using the property as security for a debt will require that deeds be notarized.

A recording of the deed is a way of giving constructive notice that the ownership of the property has been conveyed to a new owner.

A deed is not a contract and, therefore, does not need consideration to transfer. A contract will require adequate consideration, but a deed can transfer based on love and affection.

CONVEYANCE of a deed with little or no consideration is legal; however, if this happens shortly before another event that would affect the property, there may be questions, and a court may choose to overturn the transfer.

This may happen in the event of an upcoming divorce settlement or just prior to an owner filing bankruptcy.

__Example:__ Mr. Jones is in a position of needing to declare bankruptcy. He owns an income property that he wants to retain because he has equity in it and the property is producing income. Prior to going to court for his bankruptcy case, he transfers the property ownership to his brother for $150,000 when the property is valued at $450,000. This appears to the courts as a straw sale to cheat the creditors from the collection of debt through the equity in the property.

The judge hearing the bankruptcy case demands that the property be transferred back to Mr. Jones and the property is to be sold to generate cash to pay his debts.

RECORDING is the act of filing a document with the county recorder's office in the county where the property is located. Property ownership and any other recorded documents are public information. Anyone can go to the county recorder's office and obtain information on any property within that county. Any information that may be recorded is available to the public, such as the lender on a loan secured by real property, divorce settlements, and lawsuits.

Recording a document gives constructive notice to the public of the information provided on the document being recorded.

The purposes of recording documents with the county recorder's office are numerous, but mainly an owner of real property wants to ensure that they actually own the property and no one else can claim that property. A general rule of recording is ***"first in time is first in right."*** This means that whoever files their document first has the priority position in the case of a claim against the property.

__Example:__ John deeds his property to his brother as a gift. His brother, Bob, does not record the deed. A month later, John discovers that his brother did not record the deed and has heard that the Doe family wants to purchase the property. John sells the property to the Doe family. Mr. Doe immediately records the deed. Bob sees that Mr. Doe has moved into the property and investigates. The fact that Mr. Doe recorded the deed established his claim to the property because he gave constructive notice by doing so.

Bob may be able to reclaim the property if he can provide sufficient proof of the previous gift transaction. The evidence of that proof is his responsibility; however, the burden of proof may be difficult. This example is an illegal act on the part of John because he no longer owned the property when he sold it to Mr. Doe.

Recording documents is also an advantage to any prospective buyers because it provides the opportunity to research the county records and verify that the actual property owner is the one that is being dealt with. All documents that are recorded are public records and are accessible to the public.

In the real estate industry, title companies work closely with escrow to aid in verification of ownership and any debts that may be due and payable prior to transferring title. Title companies provide a document called a preliminary title report, more commonly called a prelim to the real estate professional.

The title company researches the public records at the county recorder's office and compiles the information in the prelim. The information included is:

- Owner(s)
- Legal description
- Property tax records and any amount owed.
- Tax Assessor's Parcel Number (APN)
- Easements
- Mechanic's liens
- Judgments
- Liens and/or mortgages
- Address
- Plat map

Documents are recorded by the names of the parties to a transaction: both the previous owner and the new owner of a purchase transaction; property address, and date.

A CHAIN OF TITLE is available when researching real property and shows the activity that has transacted involving the property during the previous years. A chain of title are a series of documents maintained by the county recorder's office, which include deeds (transfer of ownership), mortgages and deeds of trust, liens and judgments, and easements and restrictions.

NOTARY AND ACKNOWLEDGEMENT is a way of verifying that the correct person has signed a document and that the transfer has been acknowledged. A notary public is a person who is licensed by the State of California to acknowledge signatures of individuals who want to have proof that they are in fact the party that signed a document. Any document can be notarized, and some documents require notarization. It is not required that all of the documents be recorded, and recording is not necessary to be valid, but if they are, they should be notarized or acknowledged. Most written instruments that effect transfer of title to real property are required by California law to be **acknowledged** or n**otarized** prior to being recorded. Some of these instruments include deeds, loan documents, option agreements, and affidavits concerning real property documents.

A **notary public** requires positive identification (ID) from the person signing a document. A photo ID, such as a driver's license or a passport, is the most commonly used form of ID used. If a party does not have ID, a person who will positively identify the person and provide their own photo ID is acceptable. *In January 2008, the practice of the notary acting as the third party was eliminated.*

Prior to that time, the notary was allowed to record in their journal that the individual signing was "Personally known to me." The notary will complete the

acknowledgment that is a part of the document being notarized, sign, and stamp the acknowledgement confirming that they have witnessed the signer's signature and verified the identity of that person. The notary also completes the information in their journal and requires the party to sign the journal.

A notary public in the United States is different from a notario publico licensed under Mexican law. A notario publico is an attorney and has the ability to perform many more acts under Mexican law than a notary public under U.S. laws. Many states that border Mexico will need to be careful when working with a notary public. A notario publico can only perform the duties as they apply to Mexican documentation.

TYPES OF DEEDS

DEEDS come in a variety of types and forms for the various uses of conveying ownership and interests in real property.

1. **GRANT DEED** is the deed that is used to convey or grant ownership of real property in California. The grant deed has a granting clause using the term "I hereby grant." There is a space to allow for the acknowledgement and for recording in the upper right corner. *See Figure 9, Grant Deed.*

There are **implied warranties** made by the grantor of the property when executing the deed. Implied warranties are legally enforceable even though they are not in writing. The implied warranties are:

- The grantor has not previously conveyed their interest in the property.
- There are no undisclosed debts against the property, such as liens, judgments, encumbrances, or unpaid taxes or tax liens.
- The grantor does not imply that they currently own the property. The grant deed is the only deed that will allow conveyance of **after-acquired title**. The after-acquired title transaction takes place when the grantor conveys title to property that they do not yet own. The grant deed will not be effective until the grantee receives the grant deed conveying ownership to them. Once they own the property, they become the grantor and the deed becomes effective. You cannot grant something you do not own so the after-acquired title cannot be a completed transaction until after the title has been acquired as the title indicates.

Recording Requested By:

When recorded mail document to:

NAME

ADDRESS

CITY
STATE & ZIP

APN:

Above Space for Recorder's Use Only

GRANT DEED

THE UNDERSIGNED GRANTOR(S) DECLARE(S)

DOCUMENTARY TRANSFER TAX is $_______________________CITY TAX $______________________________
☐ computed on full value of property conveyed, or
☐ computed on full value of items or encumbrances remaining at time of sale,
☐ Unincorporated area ☐ City of ____, and

FOR A FULL VALUABLE CONSIDERATION, receipt of which is hereby acknowledged,

____hereby

GRANT(s) to ____ the following

described real property in the City of _____________________County of _______________, State of California:

Dated: ________________________________ ________________________________

____

A notary public or other officer completing this certificate verifies only the identity of the individual who signed the document to which this certificate is attached, and not the truthfulness, accuracy, or validity of that document.

STATE OF CALIFORNIA}
COUNTY OF _________________} **SS**

On______________before me, ____________________________________a Notary Public, personally appeared ____who proved to me on the basis of satisfactory evidence to be the person(s) whose name(s) is/are subscribed to the within instrument and acknowledged to me that he/she/they executed the same in his/their/her authorized capacity (ies), and that by his/her/their signatures(s) on the instrument the person(s), or the entity upon behalf of which the person(s) acted, executed the instrument.

I certify under PENALTY OF PERJURY under the laws of the State of California that the foregoing paragraph is true and correct.

WITNESS my hand and official seal.

SIGNATURE_______________________ (SEAL)

MAIL TAX STATEMENT TO ADDRESS AS SHOWN ABOVE

Figure 9: Grant Deed

Example: ***Example:*** *Mary is in escrow to purchase a property. When she tells her friend, Sue, that she is purchasing the property, Sue tells her that she always wanted that house and is disappointed that she did not know that it was for sale. Mary says that she has had second thoughts about the property and will sell it to Sue. Mary gives Sue a grant deed before her escrow closes because Sue is giving Mary the money to complete the purchase. Once Mary's escrow closes, the grant deed that Mary gave Sue is now valid because at this point Mary owns the property. It is now legal to convey the ownership from Mary to Sue.*

2. **GIFT DEED** is a deed that is used when there is no monetary consideration. The real property is a gift. In the space for the "consideration paid," the words. **"Love and affection"** are used, making the transaction a gift.

3. **QUIT CLAIM DEED** is a deed used to waive or convey any interest in the real property. There are no express or implied warranties with a quit claim deed. A quit claim deed should not be used in place of a grant deed. Because California is a community property state, a quit claim deed is often used when one spouse is purchasing, financing, or conveying interest in real property as sole and separate ownership. The non-participating spouse will sign a quit claim deed in order to state that they have no rights or interest in the ownership of that property. See Figure 10, quit claim deed.

   Example: *Bill, a married man, is purchasing a property in California as sole and separate. His wife, Ellen, will not have ownership interest in the property. Ellen will sign a quit claim deed to state and clarify that she is quitting any claim to that property.*

   If Bill and Ellen already owned the property jointly or both names are on the title, and Ellen is now being removed from that title, a grant deed would be used. Ellen would be granting her interest to Bill in this situation.

   If a co-owner quit claims their interest in, they are still liable for any liens against the property that they had been responsible for or had signed for prior to being removed from the title such as a mortgage.

   A **quit claim deed** is also used as a way to **clear a cloud on title.** An example of this situation would occur when one has interest in a property, such as an easement or a right to use property that belongs to someone else.

Recording Requested By:

When recorded mail this deed and, unless otherwise shown below, mail tax statement to:

NAME

ADDRESS

CITY
STATE & ZIP

APN:

Above Space for Recorder's Use Only

QUITCLAIM DEED

THE UNDERSIGNED GRANTOR(S) DECLARE(S) DOCUMENTARY TRANSFER TAX is $_______________CITY TAX $_____________

☐ computed on full value of property conveyed, or

☐ computed on full value of items or encumbrances remaining at time of sale,

☐ Unincorporated area ☐ City of ______________________________________, and

FOR A FULL VALUABLE CONSIDERATION, receipt of which is hereby acknowledged,

____hereby

remise, release and forever quitclaim to

____ the

following described real property in the City of ____________________County of _______________, State of California:

Dated: ________________________________ ________________________________

____

> A notary public or other officer completing this certificate verifies only the identity of the individual who signed the document to which this certificate is attached, and not the truthfulness, accuracy, or validity of that document.

STATE OF CALIFORNIA}
COUNTY OF _________________} **SS**

On______________before me, ______________________________________a Notary Public, personally appeared
____who proved to me on the basis of satisfactory evidence to be the person(s) whose name(s) is/are subscribed to the within instrument and acknowledged to me that he/she/they executed the same in his/their/her authorized capacity (ies), and that by his/her/their signatures(s) on the instrument the person(s), or the entity upon behalf of which the person(s) acted, executed the instrument.

I certify under PENALTY OF PERJURY under the laws of the State of California that the foregoing paragraph is true and correct.

WITNESS my hand and official seal.

SIGNATURE______________________ (SEAL)

Mail Tax Statement to:

Figure10: Quit Claim Deed

Example: Joe has an easement for a driveway across Jim's property to access his landlocked property. Joe signs a quit claim deed in order to end that right to use Jim's property. He no longer needs the easement as his property is no longer landlocked. He is saying to the world that he no longer has a need to use the easement across Jim's property and he is, therefore, quitting his claim to Jim's property.

4. **WARRANTY DEED** expressly warrants or guarantees that the grantor has a good title. The liability for title flaws or errors is the responsibility of the grantor or seller of the property whether they knew of any problems, or not. The warranty deed is prepared by a title company or an abstract company after researching the public records. Most transactions in California are required to have title insurance provided as a means of relieving the grantor of the liability. The title insurance is an actual insurance policy that insures the title and condition of recorded and unrecorded information regarding real property. The title insurance company assumes the responsibility and expense of clearing any undisclosed property issues, such as unknown liens or claims to the title. Lenders will always require title insurance.

   Closing a real property transaction without using escrow and title can be risky for both the buyer and seller. This is especially an issue in "all cash" transactions or when there is no real estate professional involved providing the proper guidance, such as a "For Sale by Owner" transaction.

5. **TRUST DEED OR DEED OF TRUST** is used to give the property as security for a debt. The trust deed can be the loan that is procured for the purchase of the property or obtained any time during the ownership tenure. See Chapter 12 for information on real estate financing.
   - **A trustor is the borrower** or the person giving the trust interest in the property.
   - **A trustee** is the third party holding the title or interest in the trust. They remain the trustee until the debt is paid in full.
   - **A beneficiary, or the grantee,** is the lender or the party for whom the trust is created and held.

6. **RECONVEYANCE DEED** is used when a trust deed or a loan against the property is paid in full. The trustee will, on behalf of the beneficiary, provide a reconveyance deed to the trustor. The reconveyance deed reconveys the interest in the property and the deed back to the trustor. In this case, the lender and the trustee become the grantor and the borrower or property owner becomes the grantee.

7. **A TAX DEED** is used to convey ownership in real property when a property is sold at a tax sale as a result of non-payment of property taxes.

8. **SHERIFF'S DEED** is given to the purchaser of a court order to sell property to satisfy a judgment. There is no warranty with a sheriff's deed.

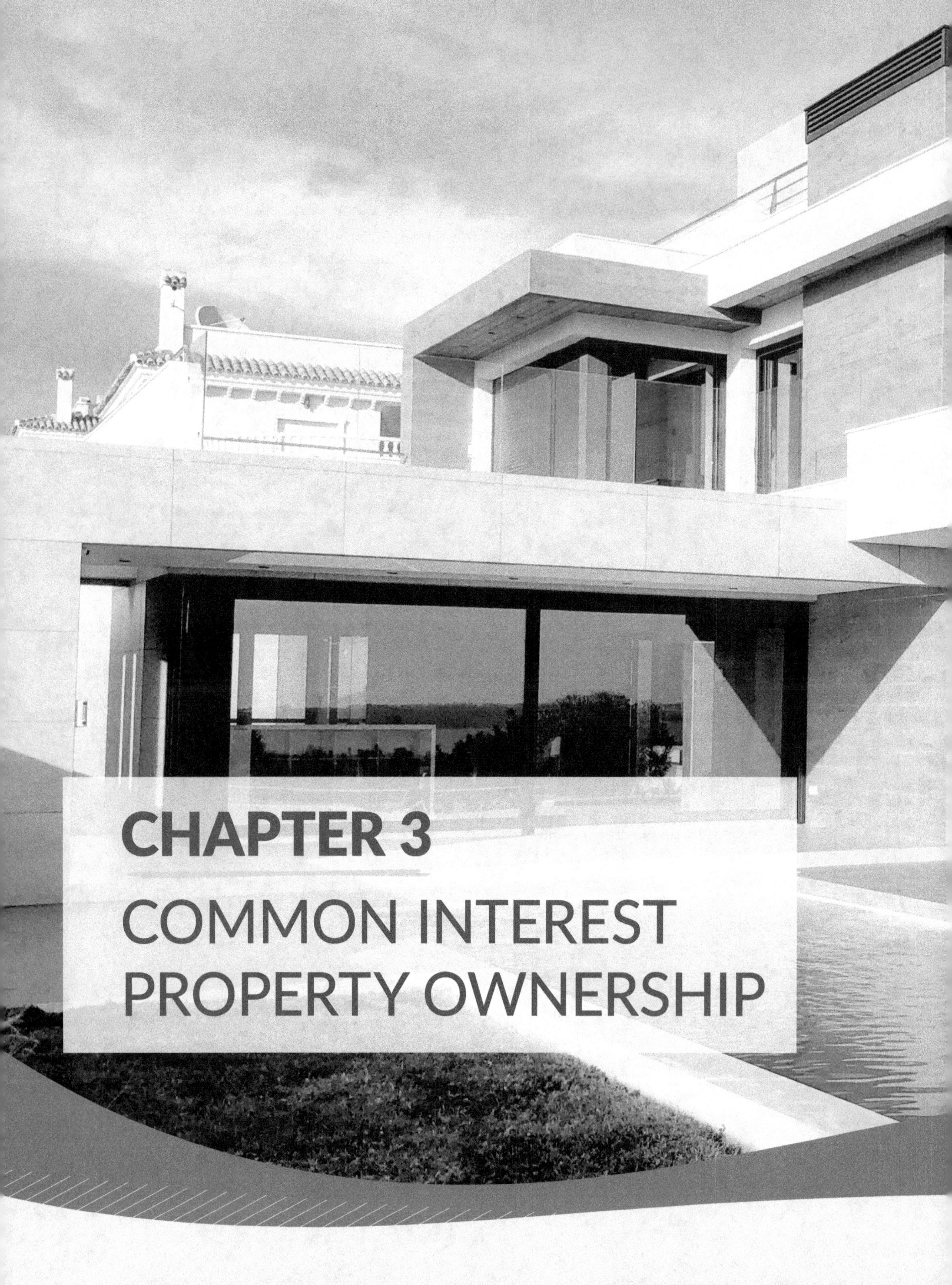

CHAPTER 3
COMMON INTEREST PROPERTY OWNERSHIP

US
Realty School

COMMON INTEREST PROPERTY

COMMON INTEREST PROPERTY OWNERSHIP is a form of ownership where a number of people share the ownership and rights of the same property. Multiple property owners have an interest or a share of ownership in a property as tenants-in-common in "common grounds" or a portion of the larger plot designated as shared property. At the same time, each owner has private ownership interests in a portion of the property that is designated as their private property, which is known as concurrent ownership.

This can be accomplished in a variety of ways, the most common of which is condominiums or "condos." These are legal forms of ownership that are held as tenants-in-common for the common areas and in whatever manner the individual homeowner chooses for their personal share or interest.

The common interest ownership complex or project is owned as tenants-in-common by all of the individual homeowners.

CONCURRENT OWNERSHIP means more than one person owns private interests in the same property at the same time or concurrently. This generally occurs within common interest ownership.

Each owner of a unit in a common interest property can choose to own their unit as sole & separate or in severalty, tenants-in-common, joint tenants, or community property, according to their own needs and circumstances.

CONDOMINIUM PROJECTS

CONDOMINIUM PROJECTS (CONDO) are currently a common type of common interest ownership in California. A condo is a legal form of ownership. A condo can be any architectural style or style of construction. The distinguishing element of a condo is the way in which the property owners hold title.

No individual homeowner owns any of the common areas separately from the other homeowners. Each homeowner owns an equal share of the common areas with all other homeowners in the project. A condo project is a property that has shared, or common, ownership of all of the common land including:

- Outer structural walls
- Roofs
- Lawn or green area
- Driveways and streets
- Fencing and boundary walls
- Garages
- Swimming pools
- Tennis courts

The individual homeowner owns their own unit within the complex separately from the other homeowners. The individual owner owns the unit exclusively from the other property owners. They do not, however, own the land that the unit is on. That is part of the common interest ownership and is owned by all of the unit owners. This is the most distinguishing feature of a condo as a legal form of ownership.

PLANNED UNIT DEVELOPMENT (PUD)

PLANNED UNIT DEVELOPMENTS (PUDs) share the elements of common interest ownership and are similar to condos.

The distinguishing difference of a PUD is that the individual unit owner owns the land beneath their own unit.

PUDs are most commonly used in common interest complexes that have less common ground. The commonly owned property may be no more than a shared swimming pool. PUDs are often used in common interest complexes that are gated communities. In this situation, the HOA owns the gate, surrounding wall, and private streets.

A **PUD** can be any of the architectural styles and can have any shared property interest desired. A property may be established as a PUD instead of a condo for a variety of reasons, but the developer will always consider the distinguishing feature of the ownership of the land beneath the individual's unit.

This type of ownership works best with properties that are townhouses, duplex to 4-plexes, or SFR-style homes because of the ownership of the land beneath the unit and the reduced common elements.

CO-OPERATIVE (CO-OP)

CO-OPERATIVE (CO-OP) complexes are corporations like a condo or a PUD and share the other features of common interest ownership.

The distinguishing difference of a co-op is that the individual unit owner owns stock in the corporation and a proprietary lease from the corporation for their individual unit.

The real estate professional will need to obtain a copy of the homeowner's stock certificates along with the usual common interest documentation, including CC&Rs, budget, insurance declaration (dec) page, and fidelity bond when handling a co-op transaction.

COMMUNITY APARTMENT

COMMUNITY APARTMENTS are owned by the individual owners who share a common interest in the land and structures as tenants-in-common and hold an exclusive right to occupy lease on their individual unit. This is similar to a co-op with the exception of not owning stock in the corporation. The property receives one tax bill, and any loans are against the entire property and are the responsibility of all of the owners. All other elements of common interest ownership apply.

TIMESHARE

TIMESHARES are most commonly used for vacation homes. Property is owned by a corporation or as a business entity. The individual unit owner receives the right to use a specified area or portion of the property annually for a specified period of time. This right is in perpetuity or as long as they own the time share interest, which may be for a predetermined number of years.

There is a three-day right of rescission when making an offer to purchase a timeshare. There must be a minimum of twelve separate interests for the project to be subject to DRE regulation. The twelve separate interests constitute twelve different ownership parties in the property.

TIMESHARE ESTATE is a timeshare which includes an **estate** interest which shows the individual owners on the title instead of the owners having an interest in property held under another form such as a business or a corporation.

Any property type can be designated a timeshare. In addition to the others named for all of the common interest ownerships, timeshares may also include properties such as campgrounds.

ARCHITECTURAL STYLE

ARCHITECTURAL STYLE does not determine the type of ownership. All of the following styles can be adapted to any form of common interest ownership. The following architectural styles are the ones most commonly used in today's real estate market.

1. **An APARTMENT STYLE** building is the most commonly known style when referring to condos, coops, or community apartments. The style is one that looks like an apartment building as far as the units sharing common walls within one building or a group of buildings and can be more than one story tall. Some condo and co-op projects are built in this style, while many apartment buildings were converted from apartments to condos or co-ops. If a complex is more than four stories high, it is considered a high-rise complex.

2. **A TOWNHOUSE** is an architectural style also known as row houses. Townhouses share one common wall on each side with the adjacent neighbor, while the front and back are usually open to the street and a yard. Each unit has a main entrance from the outside unlike an apartment style project that will generally have its main entrance, or front door, from an inside hallway of a large building.

NOTE

It is a common misconception that a townhouse is a legal form of ownership such as a condo. It is not. It is an architectural style and can be owned as a condo, PUD, coop, or as a single-family residence (SFR).

3. **A DUPLEX** is an architectural style with two residential units connected either with a common wall or an upstairs-downstairs design. A **triplex** is one with three units attached and a **fourplex** has four attached units.

4. **A SINGLE-FAMILY RESIDENCE (SFR)** style is a free-standing residential property that is designed as one unit or for one family's residence.

COVENANTS, CONDITIONS, AND RESTRICTIONS

COVENANTS, CONDITIONS, AND RESTRICTIONS (CC&Rs) are rules and regulations established by the developer to restrict land use and create an environment through restrictions for all of the common interest owners. The CC&Rs establish the rules and regulations that the homeowners agree to live by when sharing common property. CC&Rs run with the land or carry over to future owners as the ownership changes.

The CC&Rs address various issues that arise when groups of people gather to share living space. Some of the most common issues may include whether pets are allowed, and the use of a swimming pool or tennis court. Each property owner pays monthly dues to the homeowners' association. The homeowners' dues are used to maintain the commonly owned property and to pay the expenses of the complex, such as insurance and maintenance.

A. **COVENANTS** are promises by the owners to either do something or to not do something, such as the individual unit owner promising to maintain their property in a certain manner. Other homeowners or the HOA may seek an injunction from a court of law prohibiting the breaching party from further wrong-doing, or they may seek money damages for reparation or other losses.

   Example: *The CC&Rs of the Green Meadow Condos state that homeowners may not use their front entrance for storage and will maintain it in a presentable condition at all times.*

   Mr. Smith is short on storage space inside his unit and begins to stack boxes and other pieces of used furniture outside his front door on his entryway. The HOA confronts him with notice that he is in violation of the CC&R and must remove the debris within 30 days. The HOA also files an injunction against Mr. Smith to cease and desist from further misuse of the area.

This is a violation that is subject to a fine, and the HOA would have the right to hire a maintenance crew to remove the debris and then bill Mr. Smith for the work if he had not removed the debris within the 30-day time period.

B. **CONDITIONS** are more serious in nature and may result in loss or forfeiture of property.

Example: *The Freemont HOA conditions that pets larger than 50 pounds are not allowed in the complex. It also conditions that a business cannot be operated out of any of the individual units.*

Tom is raising and breeding greyhounds in his unit. The dogs are barking and disturbing the neighbors, and occasionally one or more of the dogs will get out and disturb other homeowners on their property. Tom also places a sign at his front door stating: "Freemont Dog Breeding and Training." His advertising creates additional traffic through the complex.

The HOA can take Tom to court for breach of two conditions. The courts may allow Tom a certain amount of time to remove all of the dogs from the complex or the property will be sold by the courts with the proceeds going to Tom minus any expenses due to the HOA for fees and damages.

Although an HOA cannot tell a person that they cannot work at home, they can restrict the operation of a business. The signage is not allowed and clearly indicates a clear violation of the condition. The intrusion on other property owners created by the presence of large dogs as well as the additional traffic on private streets is one of the reasons for establishing CC&Rs.

C. **RESTRICTIONS** are for the benefit of all property owners and to maintain the property.

Example: *Each property owner is restricted to the storage or parking of a maximum of two vehicles on the property and no campers or RVs are allowed other than the time required for loading and unloading of those vehicles. A notice, fine, or towing of additional vehicles should be sufficient to remedy any violation of a restriction.*

The homeowner has the bundle of rights in regard to their unit and the commonly owned grounds. The homeowner can live in their unit or use it as they choose and use the shared grounds within the guidelines of the CC&Rs.

NOTE

Nonpayment of HOA dues is a foreclosable violation of the CC&Rs.

PROPERTY TAXES are assessed and paid separately by each unit owner based on the price they paid for their unit. Property taxes in California are ***ad valorem,*** which means **"according to value;"** therefore, taxes are determined by the price the individual paid to purchase a property or the individual unit.

> ***Example:*** *The Smith family purchased Unit A for $200,000. The State of California has established a tax rate of 1.25%. The Smith's annual property taxes will be $2,500.*
> *$200,000 purchase price x 1.25% tax base = $2,500 annual taxes*
>
> *The Jones family purchased Unit B for $220,000. Their annual property taxes will be $2,750. $220,000 purchase price x 1.25% tax base = $2,750 annual taxes*
>
> *As demonstrated, each unit owner will pay their own property taxes on their individual unit and the amount will be determined individually based on the amount paid for their unit. The property taxes for the common grounds are calculated into the HOA dues and the Association will pay those taxes separately.*

HOMEOWNERS ASSOCIATION (HOA)

HOMEOWNERS ASSOCIATION (HOA) is made up of all of the individual homeowners for the purpose of ***management of the common areas*** and all matters concerning the common interest ownership. ***The HOA determines the annual budget, subject to approval of the homeowners.*** The HOA is required under the terms of ownership to have regular meetings open to all homeowners with annual elections for the purpose of electing the HOA officers to include president, vice-president, secretary, and treasurer. Many larger complexes hire management companies to handle the business of the HOA, such as maintenance, collection of dues, and bookkeeping.

The HOA maintains an insurance policy for the entire property. This policy will rebuild the structure if destroyed or damaged, but it does not cover the interiors of the individual units or the personal belongings of the owner. It is advisable for a unit owner to obtain an insurance policy separately from the HOA policy for the complex to protect their own property. The policy for a unit owner and their individual unit is similar to a renter's policy to replace or repair their personal interests.

The HOA insurance will replace the buildings and structures only; individual unit interiors and belongings are not covered.

THE COMMON INTEREST OWNERSHIP COMPLEX

THE COMMON INTEREST OWNERSHIP complex must be approved by the usual entities, such as the local *Department of Building and Planning*, whether it is a new complex or an apartment conversion. The State of California requires that common interest ownership projects be established as a corporation by filing Articles of Incorporation with the California Secretary of State, and that the Articles of Incorporation are included as a part of the CC&Rs.

SALE OR TRANSFER OF OWNERSHIP for a common interest property requires that the buyer must be provided with copies of the CC&Rs to include the Articles of Incorporation, current budget, insurance policy on the project, and the fidelity bond to protect the HOA from fraud or theft by employees or officers of the association. These items are all required to be maintained by the HOA.

The real estate professional needs to know that any potential lenders will require the HOA to maintain a budget balance equal to six months of the total HOA dues to be considered viable and stable.

Example: *Green Hills Condos charges each homeowner HOA dues in the amount of $350 per month. There are fifty units in the complex. When a unit sells, the lender of the buyer's new loan will require that the HOA carry a balance of $105,000.*
$350 HOA dues x 50 units = $17,500 x 6 months = $105,000

All of the previously stated laws, rules, and guidelines apply to all types of common interest ownership. Each type of common interest ownership varies from the others in some way.

CHAPTER 4
ENCUMBRANCES TO REAL PROPERTY

US
Realty School

ENCUMBRANCES TO REAL ESTATE

ENCUMBRANCES TO REAL ESTATE are the rights or interests in, or a claim on the real property held by someone other than the property owner. Something that encumbers property in some way hinders the use of that property. An encumbrance has an effect on the property owners' fee simple title, which is referred to as a **cloud on title**. The term "cloud on title" comes from the implication that the title is no longer clear, much like a "clear sky" versus a "cloudy sky." ***An encumbrance can restrict the property owner's ability to transfer title to the property.*** Depending on the type of encumbrance, it can also affect the use of the property. The two types of encumbrances that can be placed on real property are:

- ***Money encumbrances.*** These are liens placed on a property that affect a property's ownership. Liens such as mortgages and tax or mechanic's liens are common money encumbrances.
- ***Non-money encumbrances.*** These are interests that affect how a property can be used. Those physical encumbrances, such as a right-of-way across the property, could be in the form of an easement or encroachment.

DEED RESTRICTIONS AND **ZONING REGULATIONS** are encumbrances that may be considered a benefit to property owners.

DEED RESTRICTIONS are a means of establishing guidelines for homeowners within a community, such as a subdivision, for the purpose of maintaining the properties. They may also prevent changes that may affect the value of the other properties adversely, such as guidelines that restrict building height in order to have desirable views for the neighboring properties. Deed restrictions can be anything from dictating acceptable paint colors to the minimum size of a lot that a house can be built on.

In the past, there were deed restrictions that were discriminatory but are now illegal because of anti-discrimination laws. Any such deed restrictions must be considered illegal, even though they may still appear on the county records and will be reported on the preliminary title report.

ZONING REGULATIONS also are created and designed to give guidance to the usage of property to maintain the highest and best use for a community or neighborhood. This can also maintain property values by controlling growth and continuity of an area.

Encumbrances can affect the ***transferability of the property*** because they create a **cloud on title,** meaning that the title is less than perfect because something is hindering or blocking the owner's interest in the property. A less-than-perfect title may affect the marketability of the property because certain types of encumbrances affect the use of the land and therefore the value, while others do not. Some encumbrances may make the property non-transferable until corrected by release of the encumbrance or they may greatly reduce the value.

A buyer of real property may require that an encumbrance be removed from title prior to transfer of ownership. Loans, mechanics liens, life estates, judgments, and tax liens should always be removed prior to transfer. Escrow and title insurance should be used in a real estate transaction as a way of monitoring any potential

problems that may arise from liens. Part of the title company's job in a real estate transaction is to research the records of the county recorder's office. Any encumbrances in the form of a lien should be required to be paid in full prior to the closing of escrow. If liens are not paid in full through escrow, they will remain on the property and will become the responsibility of the new owner.

LIENS are a legal form of recording a notice that the property is security for payment of a debt. Liens can be voluntary in which case the property owner has chosen to place the lien against their property such as with a mortgage, or involuntary which means the property owner had no choice such as with tax liens.

- **VOLUNTARY LIENS** are generally in the form of a deed of trust or a mortgage. When a property owner chooses to finance or borrow money against their property, they voluntarily place the property as collateral or security as a part of the promise to repay the debt. The basis of a mortgage or trust deed is: *If you loan me money, I will pledge my property as a guarantee that I will pay my debt. If I don't pay you as agreed, you may take my house.*
- **INVOLUNTARY LIENS** are liens that have been placed against a property without the owner's consent or agreement such as with property taxes or income taxes. Involuntary liens are generally a government issue the basis of which is:

If you don't pay your property or income taxes, we will file a claim against your property. If you still do not pay your taxes, we will sell your property through a foreclosure sale.

LIENS are also either **GENERAL** or **SPECIFIC**.

GENERAL LIENS are placed against any and all property that a person owns in an attempt to collect a debt. A general lien is not related to or created as a result of one particular property. Because of the nature of a general lien, they are generally involuntary liens. Examples of general liens are judgments for a debt or child support.

SPECIFIC LIENS are placed only against specific, identified property usually relating to the debt, such as property taxes or a mechanic's lien. Because the debt is related to a specific property, a lien cannot be placed against other properties owned by the party involved unless those other properties were specifically named as collateral for the debt.

ATTACHMENTS are a lien or a legal hold against a party's title to property for a potential future judgment. When one party is in the process of suing another party and they are concerned that the party being sued, or the defendant, will try to hide their assets to avoid payment of the settlement, they may go to the courts and
request an attachment against the defendant's property. The party initiating the lawsuit or the plaintiff may request that the court seize the defendant's property prior to the settlement of the case to prevent this from happening. This seizure of the property is done by filing a lien against the property that is called an **attachment**.

A judgment is a lien that is issued by the court in a determination or settlement of a case giving an award to a creditor in the lawsuit when a party has a debt that has not been paid as agreed. The party that is owed the debt, or the creditor, will file a lawsuit requesting that the courts verify that the debt is owed to them and will instruct the debtor, or the party owing the debt, to pay.

The losing party in a case has a right to appeal the decision in a higher court. The judgment becomes final after due process or when any of the following has taken place:

- **No appeal filed** in the period allowed by law.
- **The higher court** upholds the lower court's decision.
- **Overturning or changing** the amount of judgment or other actions taken by the Court of Appeals.

ABSTRACT OF JUDGMENT is awarded to the creditor once they receive the final judgment. The abstract of judgment can be filed in any or all counties in California. The holder of the abstract of judgment will generally file the document in any and all counties where they believe the debtor owns property. The purpose of filing in multiple counties is to ensure that any properties owned by the creditor will have a lien placed against it.

A **judgment lien** or the ***abstract of judgment is effective for ten years*** against all non-exempt property and any property acquired during the judgment that term.

Homestead property is an example of exempt property and will be discussed further in this chapter.

If the award has not been collected in the first ten-year judgment period, the holder of the judgment can extend the collection term for an additional 10 years for a total of twenty years to collect on a judgment lien.

> ***Example:*** *Mr. Jones has a car accident and is taken to Community Hospital. His insurance pays all but $4,000. He finds it difficult to pay the debt and the hospital eventually sues him in court for nonpayment. The hospital wins the case and is awarded an abstract of judgment. Mr. Jones does not appeal the judgment and after the allotted time to file an appeal, the hospital files a judgment lien at the county recorder's office.*
>
> *When Mr. Jones sells his home, the title company finds the lien on the property and notifies the escrow officer. The escrow officer contacts Mr. Jones to ask if the lien is accurate, if it has been paid, or has it been disputed. Mr. Jones states that the debt is legitimate. The escrow officer will include that debt in the closing statement or HUD1 to be paid from the seller's proceeds at close of escrow.*
>
> *Escrow will forward the funds to the hospital and record a lien release to ensure that the lien is removed from the property title.*
>
> *If Mr. Jones had paid the bill, but it had not been released, he would either provide escrow with proof of payment or the creditor would be contacted to verify the payment had been made.*

A **WRIT OF EXECUTION** may be requested from the court by the lien holder providing the right to have any nonexempt properties sold to pay the judgment debt. If a judgment has not been satisfied and the creditor believes that it will not be paid prior to the expiration of the term, the creditor may present their case to force the sale of properties in order to satisfy the debt.

A DISCHARGE OF DEBT is provided when a judgment lien is paid in full or as agreed prior to the end of the judgment term and the debt is considered satisfied. Notice of the discharge should be filed with the county recorder's office in all counties where the judgment lien was filed. Partial payment of a debt may result in only partial release of an equivalent portion of the debtor's property.

> ***Example:*** *Sue made an investment in a business and later found out that it was a swindle. She sued the business owner, Mr. Green. Sue was awarded an abstract of judgment, which she immediately filed with the county recorder's office.*
>
> *After a few years of non-payment from Mr. Green, Sue went to the judge and requested a writ of execution against Mr. Green. The sheriff served Mr. Green with notice and a sale date was set for the auction of one of Mr. Green's properties. The sale did not produce the total amount that was owed to Sue. Sue released the judgment lien from that property only so that the sale could be finalized, and she could collect a portion of the debt owed to her.*
>
> *Mr. Green owned additional property, which provided Sue with the option to request the sale of Mr. Green's other properties to pay the balance of the debt.*

MECHANIC'S LIENS are used in securing payment for work that has been done for the purpose of maintaining or improving the real property on which the work is being done. The term "mechanic" refers to anyone that performs work directly or indirectly or provides supplies for the work. This includes architects, contractors, sub-contractors, laborers, lumber yards and other suppliers of materials and equipment.

A mechanic's lien can be used by any of the various parties to a job, many of whom the property owner may never deal with directly. A property owner may pay the general contractor as agreed, but if the general contractor fails to pay all of the others that provided services and supplies, the owner may be required to pay the debt again.

A **PAYMENT BOND** may be required of the contractor by the owner because of this potential for fraud. The bonding company will reimburse the property owner if the contractor defaults on payment to the subcontractors and suppliers. It may be advisable and can be arranged that the property owner pay the bills directly to the subcontractors and suppliers as each phase of the work is completed or as the supplies are delivered.

Notice and filing requirements are specified by law and must be strictly followed in order to obtain a mechanic's lien. This is a legal action and all actions taken in regard to mechanic's liens should be done with the advice and consultation of an attorney.

A **PRELIMINARY NOTICE** notifies all concerned that they have a right to file a ***mechanic's lien***. The preliminary notice is to be:

- **Filed within twenty days** of the time that the work begins, or the materials are delivered.
- **Hand delivered** to the property owner or sent by registered or certified mail.
- **Copy delivered** to the general contractor.
- **Copy delivered** to the lender if there is a construction loan for the project.
- **A written contract** will serve as notice.

The **START TIME** for the project is the date that the work begins or the date that the supplies are delivered to the project property, whichever is first. This date determines when the preliminary notice should be given, and the clock starts ticking for all subsequent filings and issues.

COMPLETION TIME is presumed to be when one or more of the following occurs:

- Project is completed.
- The building inspector has signed off on the building permits.
- Certificate of completion has been provided.
- Property owners begin to use the improvements.
- Work stops and the owner uses the improvement.
- The owner accepts the work.
- Work has stopped for sixty consecutive days.
- The owner files a notice of cessation after work stoppage of thirty consecutive days.

All recordings or filings are to be done with the county recorder's office in the county where the property is located as a means of providing constructive notice to the public.

- A certificate of completion should be filed by the property owner within 10 days of completion of the work.
- When a certificate of completion or a certificate of cessation is filed, a contractor for any of the project or the entire project has 60 days from that filing to file a mechanic's lien.
- When a certificate of completion or a certificate of cessation is filed, all others concerned with the project, such as suppliers, have 30 days from that filing date to file their mechanic's lien.
- If the notice or **certificate of completion or a notice of cessation is not filed** by the owner of the property, all claimants have **90 days** from the completion of the job **to file a mechanic's lien.**
- A mechanic's lien must be enforced within 90 days of the filing of the lien.
- **Notice of extension of credit** must be filed within 90 days of the lien filing and cannot be extended beyond one year from the completion date.

LIEN RELEASE is a notice to the public and all concerned that the claim of the mechanic's lien has been terminated. The claimant may file the lien release voluntarily with the county recorder's office. If the lien release is provided to the owner and not recorded, it is advisable that the property owner file the lien release with the county recorder's office to remove any cloud on the title. Even though the mechanic's lien is provided upon payment, it will not be removed from public records until the lien release is recorded.

Lien releases are often overlooked at the time that a debt is paid. This oversight will appear in future real estate transactions and the homeowner can provide proof of payment and the title company will obtain the necessary lien release from the creditor for filing with the county recorder's office.

NOTICE OF NON-RESPONSIBILITY is filed with the county recorder's office for the purpose of protecting a property owner from the responsibility and expense of unauthorized work and improvements. The owner of a property must post the notice of non-responsibility in a conspicuous place on the property, such as the front door, to notify any parties to the improvement that they will not be responsible for any of the work or supplies pertaining to that improvement project. Any persons with any interest in the property, such as a lessee, may and should post a notice of non-responsibility on the property. The notice of non-responsibility gives constructive notice to all concerned that the work has not been authorized by the person posting the notice.

The notice of non-responsibility must be posted and recorded within 10 days of learning of the work. The notice of non-responsibility must include:

- Name, address, and interest of the person giving notice whether ownership, lessee or other.
- The property description. This can be the address or some form of positively identifying the property in question.
- A statement that the person giving the notice is not responsible for any claims arising from the work being done.

Example 1: *The tenant of a commercial building has ordered remodeling work to suit his business, and he will be solely responsible for the costs. In this situation, the owner of the building will file a notice of non-responsibility and post it on the property in a conspicuous place because the work is the sole responsibility of the tenant.*

Example 2: *A homeowner arrives home from work to discover a load of shingles in their yard and a roofing truck in the drive. They are told that the homeowner ordered the work. If the contractor does not stop the work when told by the homeowner not to continue and that the work was not ordered by the homeowner, the homeowner should immediately file a notice of non-responsibility with the county recorder's office and post the notice in a conspicuous place on the property. In this case, it would be advisable for the homeowner to contact an attorney.*

Mechanic's liens are foreclosable liens. If a property owner believes that the mechanic's lien is incorrect, invalid, or in some way disputable, they are able to stop a **lien foreclosure** by filing a **lien release bond.** This bond must be:

- Issued by an authorized California surety company.
- For an amount equal to 150% of the claim or the portion allocated to a particular parcel in question if more than one parcel or property is involved. The amount required is to ensure sufficient funds to cover the claim and any expenses incurred.
- Filed with the county recorder's office.

A lien release bond can be filed by anyone involved with the property, such as a lender, contractor, sub-contractor, etc.

BANKRUPTCY

BANKRUPTCY is a process of eliminating one's debt. It falls under federal laws and is handled in federal bankruptcy court. There are several forms of bankruptcy identified by "Chapter." Chapter 7, Chapter 11, and Chapter 13 were created to provide different options for debtors.

- **CHAPTER 7** liquidates all debt through the court. This action is usually complete in about 3 months, depending on the back log of the court. This period will vary based on a number of factors affecting each separate court and the changing economy.

- **CHAPTER 11** reorganizes debt and allows the debtor time to pay the debts in full through the courts by making a monthly payment to the court, which is then disbursed to the creditors until the debts are paid in full. This method generally takes 3 to 5 years to complete.

- **CHAPTER 13** allows for reduction of debt. The courts establish the new debt balances based on the debtor's income and ability to pay. This type of bankruptcy is designed to benefit a debtor who has lost income, generally through disability, and will not be able to regain the previous income level.

The courts have the option and the right to sell the debtor's assets to pay off debt while they are in bankruptcy. Some assets are exempt from sale. A debtor is not allowed to assume any new debt during the bankruptcy period, or the bankruptcy can be dismissed.

While a debtor is in bankruptcy, ***a lender cannot foreclose on real property*** as the proceeding freezes all assets. Homeowners will often file bankruptcy as a means to stop a foreclosure while they find a way to bring their mortgage current.

Homeowners need to be aware that the foreclosure will proceed as soon as the bankruptcy is dismissed if not fully reinstated. At the time of the bankruptcy dismissal, the attorneys representing the lenders will be in court to verify their right to proceed with the foreclosure. A homeowner should be in the courtroom at that time to either pay to bring the mortgage current or to make a payment arrangement.

If a debtor's real estate is sold through the bankruptcy proceedings, a trustee to bankruptcy will hold the title to the property and be responsible for the sale of the assets. The buyer of the real property will receive a **trustee's deed** on conclusion of the sale.

EASEMENTS

EASEMENTS are used to give one person the right to use the property of another for a specific purpose. Most commonly, easements give a person the right to cross over another person's property to provide access to a particular place or their own property. This is called either **ingress**, entering into; or **egress,** exiting out of. An easement is limited to the use of property and does not allow for the right of possession unlike a lease that provides use and possession of the property.

Unlike other encumbrances, easements do not affect the title or ability to transfer title, it merely gives access or the right of one party to use the property of another party for a specific purpose.

> A **SERVIENT TENEMENT** is the holder of the property that the easement passes over. This property serves the needs of the party that needs the use or access.
>
> A **DOMINANT TENEMENT** is the owner of the land that has become accessible because of the easement provided by the servient tenement. The dominant tenement has a degree of **domination** over the servient tenement because they have the right to use the stated easement. The servient tenement cannot interfere with the easement by blocking or changing the grounds in any way. The dominant tenement likewise has no rights to anything beyond the use of the easement for the specified purpose and cannot change the servient tenement's property in any way other than agreed to by the easement. *See Figure 11, Easement with Servient and Dominant Tenement.*

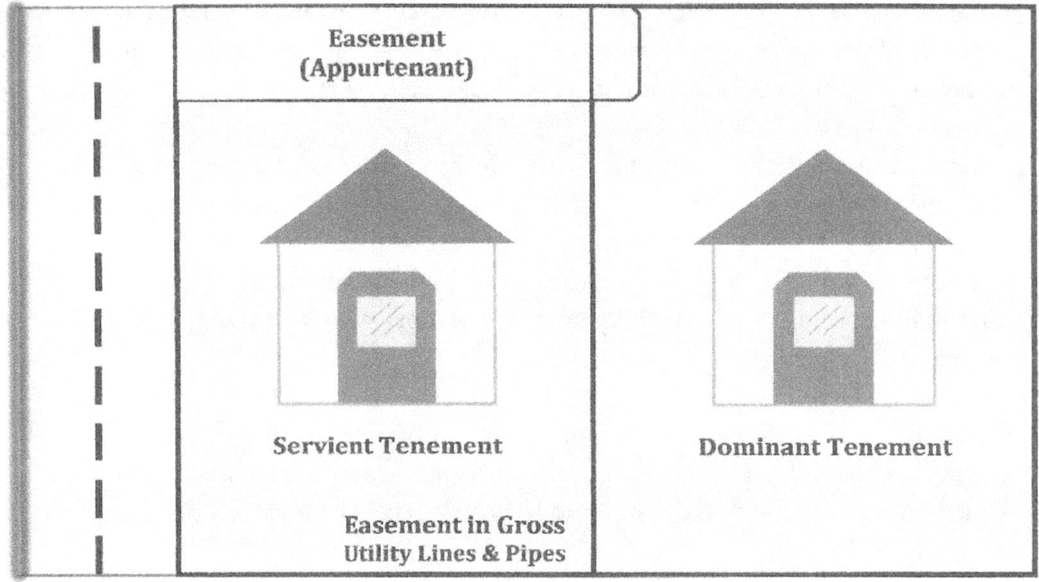

Figure 11: Easement with Servient and Dominant Tenement

EASEMENT APPURTENANT is an easement that **"runs with the land."** The expression "runs with the land" means that the easement appurtenant belongs with the land and will transfer to a new property owner and not go away with the change of ownership of the property. In other words, if the property of the servient tenement is sold, the easement still exists, and the new servient tenement cannot rescind the easement or the rights of the dominant tenement. Likewise, if the dominant tenement sells his property, the easement will be passed on to the new owner.

> ***Example 1:*** *John decides to do a lot split on his property and sell the lot that is to the back of the property. The lot does not have access to the street or is said to be* ***land locked****. In order to do this, John needs to provide a right-of-way across his lot, so he creates an easement across the ten feet of land running along the northern line of his property. John sells the property to George, who occupies the otherwise land locked property and uses the easement to access his property.*
>
> *John sells the servient property to Bob who wants to build a swimming pool along the northern line of the property which will eliminate the easement. This cannot be done as the easement is appurtenant and runs with the land. The easement cannot be terminated on this basis.*

EASEMENT IN GROSS is a right of a person to use the property of another yet it is not appurtenant to ownership in real property. An easement in gross does not run with the land, meaning that it usually cannot be passed on or granted to anyone other than the original holder of the easement because it is personal.

> ***Example1:*** *Joe has property adjacent to a river. His friend Dave enjoys fishing, and Joe has allowed Dave to park on and cross his property to fish at this favorite spot for a number of years. Dave has an easement in gross. Once Dave either stops using the easement or passes away, the easement terminates.*
>
> *Until that time, Dave has the right to use the land. Dave does not have the right to give, sell, or in any way transfer the easement to another person.*
>
> ***Example 2:*** *Pipelines and power lines give the utility companies the right to run pipelines and power lines across the servient tenement's property to the dominant tenement's property. It is not likely that the property owner would receive payment for this easement, and they may not benefit from the use.*
>
> *When the utility is no longer being used, the easement is terminated.*
>
> ***Example 3:*** *A railroad rarely owns the land that the tracks are on or any of the adjacent property. The railroad uses the property of others. Once the railroad abandons the tracks, the use reverts back to the servient tenement. The property owner in this situation is probably paid for the use and does not receive benefit.*

An easement in gross usually does not benefit the servient tenement.

CREATING AN EASEMENT can be accomplished in several different ways. Unless otherwise obtained through a court action, the owner of the servient property is the only person who can give an easement whether it is an easement appurtenant or a gross easement.

1.) **EXPRESS GRANT** is the most common way to provide an easement, and this is done by providing a **grant deed** *(Figure 9)*. An owner of real property provides to the dominant tenement a deed stating, "I hereby grant." The deed should be recorded to provide constructive notice of the right to use property that is owned by someone else. This will create a **cloud on the title** because it affects the servient tenement's use of the property, and it will **run with the land**. Most easements are removed by using a **quit claim deed** *(Figure 10)*.

2.) **RESERVING AN EASEMENT (BY DEDICATION)** is when selling property is done by the seller of the servient property when the seller chooses to retain an easement for their access. An example of this situation is when the seller is keeping the dominant tenement property and will need access to that property. This should be designated on a grant deed as part of the sales transaction.

3.) **CONTRACTS** may be used to create an easement. A written contract can be used much like a grant deed and must be signed by both the servient and dominant tenement to document that both parties agree to the arrangement. The contract should be recorded with the County Recorder's Office to provide constructive notice.

4.) **EASEMENT BY IMPLICATION OF LAW** can be found in a plat map for a subdivision showing streets, which imply an easement. This is also known as a public easement. Such easements are established at the time that the developer of a subdivision obtained the permits and approval from the governing agency. A plat map that is recorded with the county will disclose the easements.

Furthermore, an **IMPLICATION OF LAW** can be obtained by going to court to establish that there is a need, such as with land locked property. The State of California, along with most states, has determined that there cannot be a land locked property without allowing for an easement for the owner to access their property. In the earlier example in which John sold the back portion of his property, it was implied that he was providing an easement because the lot is land locked. This is also called an **easement by necessity**. When requesting an easement in this manner, the courts would give the shortest and most direct route to a public roadway within reason. Land locked property is property that is completely surrounded by property belonging to others to the extent that it does not provide public access for either ingress or egress to the property.

5. **EASEMENT BY PRESCRIPTION** occurs when a person uses another person's property over a period of years without the property owner's permission. The non-owner gains access through repeated and obvious use of the property. This circumstance is more likely to occur when the easement is the only access to the property of the dominant tenement. ***This does not need to be in writing to establish an easement or the need for an easement.***

Easement by prescription is obtained in much the same manner that real property is obtained using **adverse possession,** with the exception of paying the property taxes. An easement by prescription is gained by meeting the following requirements:

- ***Continuous use for five consecutive years.*** If the use ends for any period of time, the five-year requirement will need to start over from the day the property is re-occupied, or use of the easement begins again.
- ***Open and notorious use.*** The person using the easement must use it without hiding the action or use in any way.
- ***Exclusive use*** means that the easement is being used by individuals, even if more than one, for the exclusive purpose of access.
- ***Under claim of right or color of title*** which means that the person(s) using the easement believes that they are within their rights to use the easement because of having received permission of either the current owner or a previous owner.

Example: *Surfers in Malibu, California would park next to a fast-food restaurant and walk across the Pacific Coast Highway and a vacant lot to access the beach where they surfed regularly. This was a popular place partly because of the easy access and lack of obstruction to the beach and was used regularly for more than 20 years. The property was sold around the year 2000 and the new owner proceeded to build a house on the lot.*

As soon as construction started, the lot was fenced-off and the access to the beach was eliminated.

Several of the surfers sued the property owner on the premise that they had been using it for so many years openly and notoriously without hindrance. The surfers won the case and obtained a legal easement across the property. The owner provided a walkway at the outside edge of the property.

As a side note, it is interesting to know that the judge who heard the suit used to surf that beach and used that same access himself for a number of years.

6.) **EASEMENT BY CONDEMNATION** or **EMINENT DOMAIN** is obtained for the purpose of government use. Easement by condemnation condemns the use of the property based on the **highest and best use** principle. The principle is that the **highest and best use** for the designated property is no longer its current use but will be better used as the government needs easement by condemnation is often used by the government to obtain land for the purpose of providing new roads or to widen existing roads. This may require payment and may be of benefit to the servient tenement.

EMINENT DOMAIN was originally **created as a means to obtain property for public use as needed by the government**, most specifically for roads and other public access and uses. In recent years, this right has been abused by developers who used eminent domain as a way to obtain privately-owned property to build a variety of housing and commercial projects. They were not government projects, and they remained as privately-owned property. The local governments had been convinced that the planned projects were to better the community and would be of the highest and best use for the area. It has been determined that forcing the sale of property from private property owners to other private owners for the purpose of financial gain is not in the public's interest and this practice has been stopped. There were a number of lawsuits that ended in the Supreme Court, which ruled in favor of the public or the private owners that were being forced from their land. Many of these situations involved beach-front property and other equally valuable and desirable properties. Eminent domain has returned to its original purpose of truly accommodating the public and its best interest.

TERMINATION OF EASEMENT may be accomplished in a variety of ways:

1. **ESTOPPEL** is a legal term meaning terminating or preventing future actions, such as using an easement on someone else's property. Any easement may be terminated under the following circumstances:
    - No longer in use.
    - The owner of the dominant tenement no longer needs the easement.
    - The owner of the servient tenement uses the land where the easement is based on the indicated intent and there is no objection from the owner of the dominant tenement.

2. **EXPRESS AGREE MENT** is done by obtaining a quit claim deed from the dominant tenement declaring that they quit any claim to the use of the property. Quit claim deeds should be recorded with the county recorder's office as a way of giving **constructive notice** of the action or to release a cloud on the title.

3. **QUIET TITLE ACTION** is a lawsuit against anyone claiming a right to the use of the property owned by someone else. The term quiet title action comes from the type of lawsuit in which the servient tenement shows proof of the lack of need or continuous use by the dominant tenement. Basically, there is no noise or argument, therefore the action is quiet.

4. **ABANDONMENT** is lack of use by the dominant tenement. This usually occurs because there is no longer a need for the easement. Using the earlier example where John sold the back portion of his property, consider that now the city has put in a new street along the side of the property, so the back portion is no longer land locked. Abandonment is verified through either a **quit claim deed** or a **quiet title action**.

5. **A MERGER OF TITLE** is combining two or more lots into one lot. Using the same previous example, John sold his servient tenement lot to the owner of the dominant tenement, who then changed it back to one lot legally or began using it as one lot.

6. **An example of the DESTRUCTION** of the easement could be a fence owned by the dominant tenement that is on the servient tenement's property and is destroyed by any means. The easement is terminated, and the dominant tenement will need to get a survey verifying the property line prior to rebuilding the fence.

7. **ADVERSE POSSESSION** may be carried out by the servient tenement as confirmation of the abandonment or non-use by the dominant tenement. In the same manner that the dominant tenement obtained the easement by proving use through adverse possession, the servient tenement can prove their right to use by the same rules applying to adverse possession. On completion of the required five-year period to complete an adverse possession action, the easement can be terminated by going to court and requesting a **quiet title action**.

8. **EXCESSIVE USE** may be the cause for terminating an easement if the dominant tenement holder abuses the right and uses the easement for more than the intended use or uses more of the servient tenement property than allowed by the easement. This may happen if the dominant tenement starts to leave parked cars on the easement that was given for access only or if the dominant tenement uses the easement for storage instead of access.

LICENSE TO USE LAND

LICENSE TO USE LAND is the non-exclusive right or personal privilege to do something on the property of another. A license is for the use of personal property of another on a temporary basis, which can be terminated at any time by the owner of the property. The person receiving the license has no right or authority to exclude others from the property.

Example: *Mary wants to have a vegetable garden, but she lives in an apartment. Her friend, Sue, lets her use a space in her yard for her garden. Mary has the right to enter Sue's property as she needs to tend her garden, but Sue has the right to stop Mary at any time she chooses.*

RESTRICTIONS TO PROPERTY

RESTRICTION TO USE OF PROPERTY comes in a variety of forms other than easements.

COVENANTS, CONDITIONS, AND RESTRICTIONS (CC&Rs) are commonly used not only in common interest properties, but also in subdivisions. CC&Rs in subdivisions generally do not have an HOA or require dues, and there is rarely any common ground shared by the property owners. The purpose of CC&Rs in a subdivision is to restrict the property use and maintain the property condition and quality of the neighborhood.

CC&Rs are the same as discussed in Chapter 3 and carry the same enforcement and weight and they **run with the land** or will carry from owner to owner as property changes hands. It is often the situation that the purchaser of a real property in a subdivision may not be aware of the CC&Rs. It is important for the real estate professional to review the preliminary title report to be able to counsel the buyer of any restrictions on the title, including CC&Rs.

Example: *The Seaview Subdivision CC&Rs conditions that the properties will all be maintained and covenants that the architectural design must meet certain guidelines such as not allowing structures to be more than two stories high and must be Spanish style.*

CC&Rs can be changed by agreement of the property owners and the use of a quit claim deed for removal from the title.

DEED RESTRICTIONS are prohibitions against the property use imposed by a grant deed. HOAs will often use deed restrictions as a way to maintain neighborhood values through uniformity. Some deed restrictions may be unenforceable such as restricting the sale of property to persons of a certain race.

Examples of typical deed restrictions or CC&R conditions are as follows:

- Building exteriors will be maintained and painted as needed with a change in paint colors being pre-approved in writing by the HOA.
- Damage to the exterior of any structures or appurtenance to include windows, doors, deck, garage, and fencing will be repaired within 30 days.
- Lots must be landscaped, keeping lawns, trees, shrubs, and other plantings or ground cover trimmed and weeded to maintain a well-manicured appearance. Any trees or other plants overhanging streets, sidewalks, or neighboring lots must be kept trimmed so as to not become a nuisance.
- Accumulation of debris seen from the street or neighboring lots will not be allowed to remain beyond seven days or the next trash collection.
- Automobile repairs will not be allowed in the street or in driveways for more than 48 hours. Disabled vehicles will not be allowed to be parked on the street for more than 48 hours.
- The HOA reserves the right to take necessary actions affecting the appearance of the subdivision not previously mentioned.

**These are provided as examples of typical restrictions only.*

ZONING is an act of the government of the incorporated city or county. Zoning laws and ordinances determine the uses of a property within an area. Zoning was created in the 1900s as a way to promote public health and safety. It is also a way for the governing agency to maintain growth and public appeal for the community.

ENCROACHMENT

ENCROACHMENT is advancing beyond the designated or legal limits of a property. An encroachment is an encumbrance on another's property and occurs when one person builds or extends their property onto the property of someone else, usually a neighboring property. In real estate, the term is often used when referring to a fence that is built onto neighboring property, or a tree that is overhanging onto the neighboring property.

This occurs most frequently due to faulty surveys or measurements by the builder of a structure. Occasionally it is obstinacy on the part of the person encroaching onto their neighbor's property.

- The encroaching party may have the right to an easement either by **prescription or adverse possession** if certain conditions are met. The owner of the occupied property also has the right to bring a lawsuit against the encroaching property owner. The courts would decide based on several factors:
- Extent of the encroachment
- Difficulty of moving the obstruction
- Intent of the encroaching party

__Example:__ Sue was installing a privacy fence because she was having a swimming pool installed in her yard. The construction company filed the permits and performed the measurements for installation of the fence. An error in calculations put the fence twelve inches into the neighbor's yard. The mistake was not discovered until after completion of all the work.

The courts may determine that it is cost prohibitive for Sue to remove the fence and rebuild. They may determine that Sue should monetarily compensate the neighbors for the additional one foot that she has gained. There are a number of possibilities that the court may choose.

If the mistake is not discovered for several years, Sue may be able to claim an easement by prescription or through adverse possession because she has been using it openly and notoriously among the other qualifying elements.

HOMESTEAD

HOMESTEAD is a form encumbrance to the title of property which benefits the owner by providing protection from creditors provided for by state law. Some or all of the homeowner's equity in their **owner-occupied property** may be protected from creditors of an unsecured debt. The homestead applies to any type of property used as a residence including mobile homes and boats.

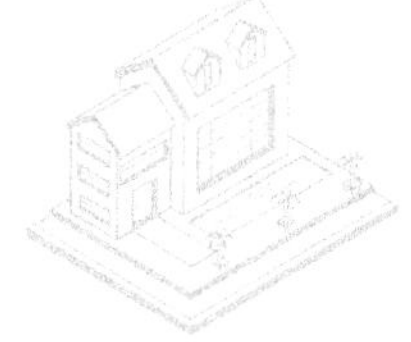

The form of ownership can be community property, separate property of a spouse, or separate property of an unmarried person or persons. If unmarried persons own a property, each can claim a separate homestead. The amount of the homestead depends on the marital status of the homeowner.

A homestead is not a lien or any kind of attachment to the property or the title. It is an encumbrance on the title for the protection of the homeowner's assets and equity.

After a party purchases a home and the deed has been recorded, the homeowner will receive a letter from the county recorder's office offering the right to file a homestead. *The real estate professional is often consulted by the new homeowner asking for an explanation of the letter and the process. It is advisable to be prepared with information for the homeowner that will be beneficial. An attorney is the best source for advice on this matter and the real estate professional should have a list of a minimum of five names to recommend to the client per RESPA law.*

The escrow officer is also a useful resource for the client. Escrow and/or the real estate professional may have printed information available for such situations. Valuable information for homebuyers can be obtained from the county, escrow, attorney, or a trustworthy website that provides legal information. **The real estate professional must never give legal advice unless also licensed as an attorney within the state where practicing.**

The equity in a property is the value of the property minus any loans secured by the property and any liens against the property, such as taxes and mechanic's liens. If the homeowner has more than sufficient equity to pay off all debts in question, after consideration of the homestead amount, the courts may require that the property be sold to satisfy the owner's debts. If there is not sufficient equity to pay mortgages and debts against the property after considering the homestead amount there would be no benefit to force a sale.

If the homeowner chooses to sell the property, the amount of the homestead exemption will be exempt from creditors as long as the funds are reinvested in a new owner-occupied property within six months of the sale. An indebted homeowner may use this law to be able to sell a more expensive home, pay debt, and obtain a home that is more easily maintained. There are tax benefits available for homeowners when downsizing from their primary residence.

AMOUNT OF HOMESTEAD EXEMPTIONS:

- Homeowner - $50,000
- Homeowner as a member of a family unit - $75,000
- Homeowner or spouse residing with homeowner 65 years or older -
- $150,000
- Homeowner or spouse residing with homeowner physically or mentally disabled and unable to be gainfully employed - $150,000.
- Homeowner 55 years or older with gross annual income of $15,000 or less, or married with total combined gross income of $20,000 or less and the homestead is subject to an involuntary sale - $150,000

FAMILY UNIT consists of two or more persons to qualify a homeowner for an exemption of $75,000. The forms of family units are as stated:

- Homeowner and spouse residing together.
- Homeowner and either their child or grandchild or that of their spouse whether living or deceased.
- Homeowner and their minor sibling or the child of a deceased sibling.
- Homeowner and their parent or grandparent or their spouse's.
- Homeowner and an unmarried adult relative who is unable to care for or support themselves.

- Homeowner's spouse and one of the other previously listed relatives who is unable to care for or support themselves.

The qualifying members and the homeowner must all reside in the subject property.

THE PRIORITY OF CLAIMS as established by law is the order in which creditors will be paid. Liens recorded against the subject property take priority over other debts and the recorded liens are paid in the order of recording. Liens are numbered according to this priority; for instance, property taxes are always #1 in the county recorder's records and on the prelim.

The proceeds of a forced sale will be paid in the following order:

- Tax lien
- Holders of any other lien or encumbrance
- Homeowner in the amount of the homestead
- Levying officer for reimbursement of costs of performing the sale if not paid in advance.
- Judgment creditors
- Any other claims against the property
- Homeowner for any remaining proceeds from the sale

CHAPTER 5
GOVERNMENT RIGHTS IN LAND

US
Realty School

LOCAL GOVERNMENT CONTROLS

LOCAL GOVERNMENT CONTROLS are created through the process of city planning. Fee simple ownership is the maximum rights that an owner has in real property; however, the local government has certain rights in all real property that cannot be avoided. These rights and the way they affect the property owner and the use of their land is an important part of the expertise of a real estate professional.

1. **CITY PLANNING** controls and directs the growth and land use of a community. How the land is to be used is originally established as it is needed by the persons settling an area; however, the residents of an area will need to establish a plan for future growth for the benefit of the public in the form of **city planning.**

2. **A GENERAL PLAN, OR THE MASTER PLAN,** sets the goals for the development of the community as part of the city planning. California law requires that all counties work through a **local planning commission** to adopt a long-term, comprehensive general plan for the purpose of development of the community within the local government's jurisdiction. The local government works with the planning commission through the Department of Building, the Zoning Department, the Building Inspector, and a variety of other committees, departments, and persons to maintain conformity with the master plan and the ultimate goals of the community.

   The plan should provide both current and desired demographics to include the history of the development and growth. Maps must be included to designate land use for residential and business use zones to include everything from small commercial through large manufacturing. Maps must also be provided to disclose plans and goals for the future. Government code requires that all general plans provide for the following:
   - **Land use** allows for population, commercial needs, and all other needs.
   - **Housing** for all population demographics.
   - **Circulation** allowing for transportation flow and utilities.
   - **Noise** issues both existing and potential.
   - **Safety** from fire, earthquake, or geographical.
   - Conservation of resources

- **Open space** for recreation and for public health and safety.
- Solid waste management
- **Airport land use** when a public airport is serviced by a certified air carrier.
- **Coastal development** when applicable.
- Mineral resources
- Forestry resources
- Historic preservation
- Seismic zones

GOVERNMENT CODES provide the procedures to be followed when either implementing a **general plan** or amending an existing plan. There must be a public hearing with the local **planning commission**. Once there is a majority vote, an additional vote by the local governing group will be required. The general plan must be adopted by resolution of the legislative body, which is either the city council or the county board of supervisors. When the general plan has been adopted, a **specific plan** can be formulated which will address and establish:

- Zoning
- Streets
- Utilities
- Projected population density
- Building codes and requirements
- Plan for population growth
- Topography and terrain

The ***White Paper on Smart Growth Policy in California*** states specific policy and planning reforms for the purpose of creating appropriate community growth. The system traditionally allowed for the various planning specialists to work separately from the other specialists while designing their particular area which left the separate components isolated without blending and creating urban sprawl.

California Assembly Bill 1268 was signed into law in July 2004 amending the ***white paper***, changing planning practices to support a new method called **form-based planning.** This allows the planning of all areas to be considered while planning each of the individual components. The reforms have helped reduce land consumption, improve accessibility, increase transportation, and achieve planning objectives.

POLICE POWER

POLICE POWERS in relation to real property is not as ominous as it sounds. Police powers have been created to provide the local governing agencies with the ability to control the use of land by the individual property owner. Various governing agencies regulate and pass laws that control the use of private land for the benefit of public safety, public health, and the general welfare of the public.

The property owner generally is not compensated for the use of the property when the use falls under the category of **police power**. The governing agency that is using or controlling a property will not pay the owner for any loss caused by the action taken under police power because there is no **"taking"** of land. In other words, the owner retains possession and ownership of the real property; the government does not take the land.

ZONING LAWS AND BUILDING CODES are examples of police power. Both of these may cause a gain or a loss in value when a property is re-zoned or when local building codes change. It is not accepted practice for a property owner to receive compensation for loss of value based on these situations; however, it can and has been overturned in the property owner's favor under various circumstances.

Although the homeowner is not usually compensated for actions taken under police powers, this example may be one instance when the homeowner may request compensation if damages occurred.

> ***Example:*** *During brush-fire events, firefighters will cross over private property in order to reach the fires. This is the use of police power. The use of the water in the property's pool is also a case of police powers. Any damage to the property may result in payment for repairs, but not for use.*

ZONING is the main method of controlling land use by the government provided under police power.

- The California Constitution provides a city the right to exercise zoning under police powers. Zoning is the act of dividing areas into specified sections or "zones" which are designated for specific uses. The most commonly used zones are categorized as residential, commercial, industrial/manufacturing, or agricultural. The creation of zones by the city planning agency can have the following effect on the community's growth:
- Maintain/retain the value of properties.

- Protect public health and safety by separating residential areas from the pollution of industrial areas.
- Create a desirable flow of the various areas.
- Attract and encourage growth.

CLASSIFICATION DESIGNATIONS vary somewhat throughout the state and each county is allowed to establish the designation that best suits local needs.

Classifications that are most commonly used to specify zoning use fall under the following classifications.

A. **RESIDENTIAL** property falls under zoning classifications allowing for single family homes or property providing accommodations from one-family dwellings up to dwellings for multiple families.
   - **R1** meaning residential property to accommodate one family. The acronym for **single family residence, SFR,** may also be used.
   - **R2** designates residential property that has **two** residences on one property or is one structure with two separate dwelling accommodations, which is called a **duplex**.
   - **R3** is residential property with **three** residences and is referred to as a
   - triplex.
   - **R4** usually refers to residential property with **four** units is a **fourplex**.
   - **R4** is also commonly used to designate any 1- to 4-unit residential dwelling. This is commonly used because the DRE licensing is concerned with 1-to-4-unit residential properties.
   - **R-multi** complexes of **five or more residential units** are generally considered **multi-family**. In some instances, these properties may be zoned as **commercial** with a designation such as **RC and** are usually handled as a commercial transaction by the real estate licensee.

The State of California recognizes all of these designations but will most commonly refer to any residential property **from two-to-four**-living units as **RM or R-multi** or **residential multi-family**. The real estate professional needs to be aware of the local zoning laws and designations.

Licensees of the California Department of Real Estate (DRE) are licensed for and concerned with transactions involving one-to-four-unit residential dwellings.

Although licensees often work with other properties, they are only required to be licensed for one-to-four-unit residential properties.

B. **COMMERCIAL** property will fall under several zoning designations as prescribed by the local planning board.
   - **C1** is often used for smaller businesses, such as small individual stores frequently found in older "downtown" areas.
   - **C2** may designate a commercial property such as a small strip center.
   - **C3** may designate a larger shopping center.

C. **MANUFACTURING AND INDUSTRIAL** properties will have similar zoning designations such as:
   - **M1** or **I1** is often used for small industrial areas.
   - **M2** or **I2** is often used for large industrial areas.

D. **AGRICULTURAL PROPERTY** will generally have one of the two designations:
   - **A1** may include small agricultural properties.
   - **AG** includes most agricultural properties.

E. **MIXED USE** can be a combination of any of the zoning designations. It is currently most commonly used for property that is a combination of residential and commercial.

   Example: *Downtown renovations of business districts are restoring shops and stores on the first floor with residential condos on the higher floors, creating mixed use zoning of commercial and residential.*

   This type of mixed-use property and zoning is an accepted and common practice in real estate sales and lending.

F. **PUBLIC PROPERTY** is that owned by any government agency, such as parks and recreation areas.

G. **BUFFER ZONES** are areas of land that separate properties of greatly varying types. These areas may often be owned by the local government and are used to promote public health and safety and also to promote the property values of the different use zones.

   Example: *Smith Development wants to build a subdivision of residential single-family homes. The adjoining property is a factory that manufactures electronics. They know that building homes next to the factory will be undesirable to any potential homeowners and that the homes directly adjoining the factory will decrease the value for the entire subdivision.*

They decided to donate an adequate piece of land dividing the subdivision from the factory to the county for the purpose of creating a park for public use.

Smith Development has increased the value of the houses for the remaining property by separating the residential area from the factory and by creating an area for recreation or a buffer zone.

ZONING LAWS AND REGULATIONS must be consistent with the general plan. The general plan will take precedence if there is a conflict. Zoning ordinances and specifications generally provide for:

- Permitted uses
- Minimum parcel size
- Building height limitations
- Lot coverage limitations
- Setbacks
- Density
- Changes and allowances

ZONING DEVIATIONS OR CHANGES are often required as a matter of course when dealing with the needs of a large group of people or the public. The general plan for a community addresses the possible ways to request and make the changes as presented by the public.

AMENDMENT is a zoning change for an entire area. Quite often an area that has been zoned residential will be rezoned as commercial to allow for additional business use. This often happens when an older area of residential properties gradually changes, such as the main street becoming a major thoroughfare. In order to accommodate the new businesses, the property owner(s) will approach the local zoning administrator and request that an amendment be made to the local zoning ordinances. There will be a hearing which is open to the public. Any member of the public has a right to request or dispute a zoning change.

NOTE

There is no uniform set of zoning classifications. Zoning designations can vary, and these are given as examples of common zoning designations. Knowing these sample designations will simplify recognition of local zoning for the real estate professional. Nearly all towns, cities, and counties in California have their own website. It is advisable that real estate professionals research their area and find the local zoning designations.

NON-CONFORMING USE occurs when such a zoning change is implemented, but a property owner chooses to continue to use their property according to the previously zoned use or designation. The existing use of the current properties does not always change immediately, and the property owners are not required to automatically change their property to accommodate the new zoning. Such a requirement would be considered cost prohibitive, and the government cannot place such a requirement on individual property owners. This is also called **grandfathered use** or **legal non-conforming**.

There are **restrictions** placed on the use of property that is **legal non-conforming or GRANDFATHERED IN**. Development plans and zoning ordinances place restrictions that will not allow improvements that will make the current structures larger than they are at the time of the re-zoning event, such as a room addition.

A structure can be rebuilt to the same size (square footage) and used if destroyed by natural causes such as fire or flood. Governing agencies will provide either a **rebuild letter** stating the policy in the event of destruction, or a **copy of the ordinance** providing for the rebuild. If the owner destroys the improvements intentionally, it cannot be rebuilt for its former use. It can only be rebuilt for the use designated by the current zoning.

> ***Example 1:*** *The neighborhood that Mr. Jones lives in has been rezoned from R1 to C1. He does not want to move from his house and does not want to change it into a business property. Mr. Jones continues to live on the property for several years following the zoning change before he decides that he wants to sell the property.*

He can sell the property as a residential property although it is zoned C1 for commercial use. The lender for the buyer of the property will require a **rebuild letter** from the governing agency. The letter will need to state that the property can be rebuilt "as is" if destroyed by natural causes such as fire, flood, etc.

> ***Example 2:*** *Mr. Jones' house is destroyed by fire. He can rebuild it as an 1800 square foot house because that is what it was at the time of the re-zoning event and at the time of the fire.*

The improvements cannot be expanded on. It can only be used as it was at the time of the re-zoning event. General remodeling and normal maintenance such as replacing a roof is acceptable.

__Example 3:__ Mr. Jones decides that he wants to add a room to his house and applies for the building permit. The permit is denied because the property is in a legal non-conforming zoning status.

If the property owner discontinues the original use, it cannot be changed back to the original use at a later date.

__Example 4:__ Mr. Jones decides to use the house as his office. He moves out of the property and converts it to operate his business from the former residence. After several years, he decides to sell it as a residential property. Now it can only be sold as a commercial property.

VARIANCE to a zoning ordinance allows an individual property owner to vary from the zoning in order to prevent a hardship, but it does not change the ordinance.

__Example:__ Mary lives in a residential neighborhood in the middle of her block. She needs to go back to work and would like to work from home because she has pre-school age children. If she can get a variance to the residential zoning, she will be able to operate a day care business from her home to alleviate the financial problems. The R1 zoning will not change. When she discontinues the business use, she will not be able to reuse it without getting a new variance.

CONDITIONAL USE PERMIT is a type of **variance** allowing a property to be used in a way that is not normally permitted under regular zoning. The terms may be used interchangeably or vary from county to county.

__Example 1:__ A congregation wants to build a new church in a residential neighborhood. They could be provided with a conditional use permit for the property so that they can build the new church.

__Example 2:__ The congregation may be given a conditional use permit for temporary use of a residence while the new church is being built nearby and when completed, the new church may be provided with either a __variance__ or __spot zoning__.

SPOT ZONING is used to rezone a small area within a larger, differently, and appropriately zoned area.

> ***Example:*** *A large new residential development is being built in an area that is zoned R1. The developer sees a need for a gas station and a small market because of the size of the development and for the convenience of the new residents. He requests a designated intersection to be spot zoned to accommodate the business needs of the neighborhood.*

DOWNZONING is rezoning of an area from a dense to a less-dense zoning designation. Industrial to commercial, and commercial to multi-residential, or multi-residential to R1 are examples of dense to less dense downzoning. The density or space used by industrial buildings is more than that of residential buildings. A high-rise apartment is denser than a four-unit apartment. The term dense is used to describe the building mass, not necessarily the number of people. Downzoning is used by city planners to control growth and sprawl.

> ***Example:*** *An area has been a commercial area, and the city has determined that the growth of the community requires additional housing. The current commercial community has moved away from the desired area and changing the zoning from C1 to R4 would provide for the housing needs and eliminate an area that is not currently being well used or is not at its highest and best use.*

PLANNED UNIT DEVELOPMENT OR PUD is a type of development, but it may also be a zoning classification because it has residential zoning, common grounds, and occasionally includes commercial areas. This is a newer use of development and zoning which is evolving on a regular basis. It may or may not be used as a zoning classification in any area of California. The real estate professional should be aware of the possibility of this zoning and how it affects real estate transactions and what it means to the area.

EMINENT DOMAIN

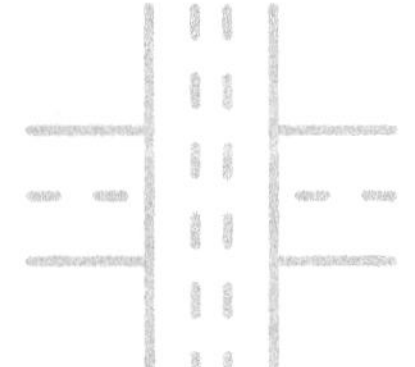

EMINENT DOMAIN is the right of the government to **"take"** private property when needed for the good of the public or for government needs. This is most often used for building public access, such as roads.

Because the government actually takes the land, the property owner receives **compensation or** is paid for the property. Compensation is based on the actual property values and involved expenses of the property owner as established by:

- Appraised value of the property
- Relocation or moving expense
- Tenant relocation expenses
- Mortgage penalty for pre-payment
- Business expenses incurred because of the action

Eminent domain is achieved through a process called **condemnation**. The government **condemns** the property usage or determines that the current use is not the highest and best use for the property in regard to the needs of the community.

> ***Example:*** *The freeway needs to be widened to create a sufficient number of lanes to accommodate the current road usage. The State of California determines that two properties on both sides of the existing freeway will be needed to accommodate the planned freeway project. All four property owners are notified that their property is being condemned and the state will purchase the property from them.*

Negotiations begin for the total purchase price based on the appraisal, the relocation costs, and any additional losses the property owner may incur through this transaction.

Relocation expenses and services are required to be paid under the Federal Uniform Relocation Assistance and Real Property Act of 1970 for any properties acquired by use of funds of the federal government. A significant amount of property obtained through eminent domain is for the purpose of road improvements, especially freeways. As these projects are generally funded by the federal government, this act applies. Recent reforms to the laws regarding eminent domain have been put in place to restrict the use for government purposes only rather than private enterprises. For more information see www.fighteminentdomain.com.

NOTE

Terms are open for negotiation; however, the property owner needs to remember that this is a right of the government and terms will be reasonable, and the appraiser is hired by the governing agency obtaining the property.

INVERSE CONDEMNATION is a process used by property owners that have been adversely affected by an act of the government. When the property value has decreased because of the actions of the government such as in the previous example, the injured party has a right to bring an inverse condemnation action against the government based on the **Tucker Act of 1887.** To continue with the previous example:

> ***Example:*** *The properties that were adjoining the four condemned properties that were obtained through eminent domain are now adjoining the freeway. They also now have the traffic signals for the on- and off-ramps at the corner of the properties. The value of all four properties has decreased because they no longer have the buffer of another property between them and the freeway, and they now have the annoyance of the on/off-ramps with the resulting traffic and noise. All four property owners have the right to file an inverse condemnation suit.*

TAXES

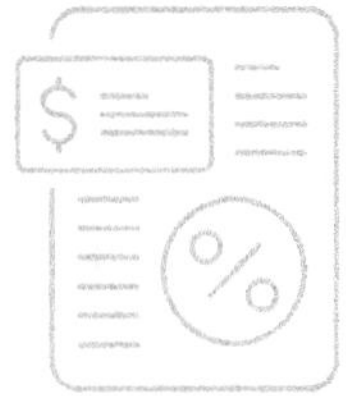

TAXES collected as **property taxes** are based on the value of the property. This is referred to as **ad valorem** which means **"according to value."** Most commonly, the value is determined by what a ready, willing, and able seller will accept, and a ready, willing, and able buyer will pay. The purchase price is the accepted determination of value plus an annual allowance of a 2% inflationary factor. This may vary if a tax event occurs to cause a reassessment by the county tax assessor. A transfer of ownership of real property must be reported to the county tax assessor's office within 48 hours of transfer.

PROPERTY TAX EVENTS that will cause a change in the amount of taxes owed by the property owner are improvements to the property that requires building permits or a drastic change in property values in the area. This applies to both an increase and a decrease in property values.

When a property owner applies for building permits to improve their property, the tax assessor's office is notified. Once the work is completed, the tax assessor will re-evaluate the property and adjust the taxes accordingly.

During times of economic inflation, property values increase. The tax assessor's office is aware of the values based on comparable sales in an area. The tax assessor has the right to look at all properties within an area to re-assess property values and adjust taxes accordingly. The tax assessor is responsible for the cost of an appraisal for an increase event.

A property owner can request in writing that the tax assessor reassess their property if values have decreased value drastically as in an economic recession. In this situation, the property owner is generally responsible for the appraisal cost.

PROPOSITION 13 amended the California Constitution to limit the state's ability to increase property tax assessments above the 1975 base values. Property taxes cannot be increased above that level unless there is a tax event which is most likely to be based on the sale of the individual property or the application for a building permit and the resultant notice of completion of the construction.

A property owner has the right to dispute the assessed tax amount. Any appeals must be made to the county tax assessor's office. There are time limits that must be met which will vary with each county. An appraisal of the property is the most valid form of proof concerning value.

Taxpayers' rights are spelled out in the ***Morgan Property Taxpayer's Bill of Rights***. The county tax assessor must provide for inspection and copying of documents including the auditor's notes and worksheets in regard to the subject property in the event of a dispute. Additional information regarding tax payers' rights is available from the local tax assessor's office and the State Board of Equalization: www.boe.ca.gov

State Board of Equalization
Taxpayers' Rights Advocate Office
P.O. Box 942879
Sacramento, Ca. 94279-0070
Phone (916)324-2798
Fax (916)323-3319

Information is available for each individual county on the appropriate website for each community such as Los Angeles:
https://lacounty.gov
https://assessor.lacounty.gov

BASE VALUE of a property for property tax purposes is the cash value established by the purchase price or any subsequent tax event that has occurred since February 28, 1978. The State of California uses 1.25% as the tax base for real property taxes. When the real estate professional is calculating costs and expenses for a potential buyer, multiplying the purchase price by 1.25% will provide the estimated annual tax payment. Divide that figure by 2 to obtain the bi-annual payment amount or divide by 12 to obtain the monthly tax expense for home expense budgeting purposes and for loan qualifying.

Example: *Based on a sales price of $450,000*
$450,000 (sales price) x 1.25% = $5,625 (annual property tax)
$5,625 (annual property tax) ÷ 2 = $2,812.50 (bi-annual tax payment)
$5,625 (annual property tax) ÷ 12 = $468.75 (monthly tax)

Every county in California has a **county tax assessor** who is responsible for **establishing the assessed value of real property**. Although there is a set tax rate or basis, which is usually 1.25% on real property, the tax assessor follows a set of determinations. This will generally vary somewhat from the amount obtained by the previous calculations because the tax assessor uses the tax base plus or minus assessments. The calculations shown will provide a usable calculation that will be close to the actual amount which can be used by the real estate professional for qualifying purposes.

THE COUNTY BOARD OF SUPERVISORS sets the tax rate for the county. There is an allowance for annual inflation which cannot exceed 2% above the current tax rate.

Counties can charge for debts that were approved by voters prior to Proposition 13 as well as bonded debts and special assessments approved by voters after July 1, 1978. These generally range from .20% to .25% and will appear on the property owner's tax bill as a special assessment.

SPECIAL ASSESSMENTS and BENEFIT ASSESSMENTS are created for the purpose of generating funds to pay for improvements for public use such as streets or sewers. The improvements and the resulting taxes are voted on by the public and the expense is usually paid for by property owners in the area that will benefit from the improvement. The property owners will receive the tax bill with the additional fee designated as "special assessment." It is to be paid at the same time as the regular property tax. Once the debt for the work has been paid in full, the special assessment will be eliminated from the property owners' tax bill. This is a temporary debt.

The benefit assessment is a term more often used for smaller areas or neighborhoods that will benefit directly from the assessment. Unlike other taxes and assessments, a benefit assessment is not a tax-deductible item for state or federal income taxes.

New legislation effective January 1, 2006, requires a seller of property or their agent to deliver to the prospective purchaser a disclosure notice regarding property taxes in at least 12-point type or a contrasting color that includes the following:

"Californian property tax law requires the Assessor to revalue real property at the time the ownership of the property changes. Because of this law, you may receive one or two supplemental tax bills, depending on when your loan closes. The supplemental tax bills are not mailed to your lender. If you have arranged for your property tax payments to be paid through an impound account, the supplemental tax bills will not be paid by your lender. It is your responsibility to pay these supplemental bills directly to the tax collector. If you have any questions concerning the matter, please call your local Tax Collector's Office."

A title must be included in at least 14-point type or a contrasting color that reads as follows:

"Notice of Your Supplemental Property Tax Bill"

The disclosure notice requirements of this section may be satisfied by including the required information in the **Mello-Roos Disclosure** (see *Part I, Section I, Subsection A, Item 5* – **Mello-Roos Bonds and Taxes**). Supplemental taxes may be assessed regardless of lending circumstances to include obtaining a new or existing loan, or to pay cash for the purchase of the property: *California Civil Code 1102.6c.*

Supplemental taxes are based on a voter approved improvement which has nothing to do with the sale of the property or the purchase price.

NOTE

The real estate professional should be aware of this to explain to clients. The preliminary title report will reflect any special assessment currently being paid on the subject property which will be transferred to the buyer of the property. If a property owner chooses to have their tax payments impounded with the mortgage payment, they need to know that special assessments will be billed separately and will not be included in the impound account.

MELLO-ROOS is a supplemental tax that was originally created in San Francisco as a way to increase funds for schools. Mello-Roos appears on the **Good Faith Estimate of Costs as "School Tax."** It has evolved into a supplemental tax that can be used for any needs that the local government may have and does not have to benefit the immediate area.

A **MELLO-ROOS DISTRICT** is most commonly attached to or created in new developments. Often, the developer will use it as a negotiating point to accommodate the needed facilities to be provided by the county or city where the property is being developed. The Mello-Roos tax appears much like HOA dues. The tax is generally for a twenty-year period, at which time it will no longer be an attachment to a Mello-Roos property.

The Mello-Roos Community Facilities authorize Mello-Roos bonds and taxes Act of 1982. "This act allows for the formation of community facilities districts, the issuance of bonds, and the levying of special taxes to finance designated public facilities and services. The seller of a property consisting of 1 to 4 dwelling units subject to the lien of a Mello-Roos community facilities district or subject to a fixed lien assessment collected in installments to secure bonds issued pursuant to the Improvement Bond Act of 1915 must make a good faith effort to obtain from the district a disclosure notice concerning the special tax and must give notice to a prospective buyer. If a district notice is not obtained, a notice obtained from a non- governmental source may be used, provided that it clearly and accurately describes the related tax liabilities." *California. Civil Code 1102.6b* as found on *https://www.dre.ca.gov*

NOTE

The real estate professional needs to be aware of the Mello-Roos attachment to any properties. This can be found on the preliminary title report under Item 1 Taxes. A notice must be given to any potential buyers of property designated Mello-Roos and the amount of the assessment must be disclosed prior to purchasing a property with a Mello-Roos lien.

COUNTY TAX COLLECTORS are elected officials that are responsible for **collecting property taxes.** If property taxes are not paid for five years, the county tax collector will be responsible for initiating foreclosure proceedings to include the foreclosure sale. When a tax foreclosure has concluded, the county tax collector's office will provide the purchaser with a **tax deed. If a property is sold through a tax foreclosure in California, the tax deed will be free and clear of any additional liens against the property.**

The property owner has five years from the date the property taxes becomes delinquent to redeem the property by paying the delinquent taxes plus the penalties and accrued interest. The five-year redemption period may be forestalled and re- started from the date of a disaster if the property is damaged or destroyed by a natural disaster, and the property is located in a declared a disaster zone.

A **CERTIFICATE OF REDEMPTION** will be provided to the property owner once all delinquent taxes are paid.

A "**TAX FEE**" will be charged by most mortgage lenders to the borrower at close of escrow. This fee pays for a service provided to lenders that notifies lenders when a property they have financed is tax default. Mortgage lenders will pay the delinquent property taxes prior to a foreclosure proceeding rather than lose their investment. The lender will increase the mortgage payment in an amount to repay the paid tax debt until the amount is repaid. The lender will then require that the taxes be impounded or included with the regular mortgage payment.

The **PROPERTY TAX YEAR** is from July 1 to June 30 based on the fiscal calendar. Annual property taxes are paid in two installments. Whenever the tax payment date falls on a weekend or holiday, the payment will be due by 5 p.m. on the following business day. A 10% penalty is charged for delinquent payments.

- **The first installment** ***is due November 1.***
- **Delinquent** ***if not paid by 5 p.m. on*** **December 10** ***of the same year.***
- **The second installment** ***is due February 1.***
- **Delinquent** ***if not paid by 5 p.m.*** **April 10** ***of the same year.***
- ***The tax lien takes effect January 1 of the calendar year.***

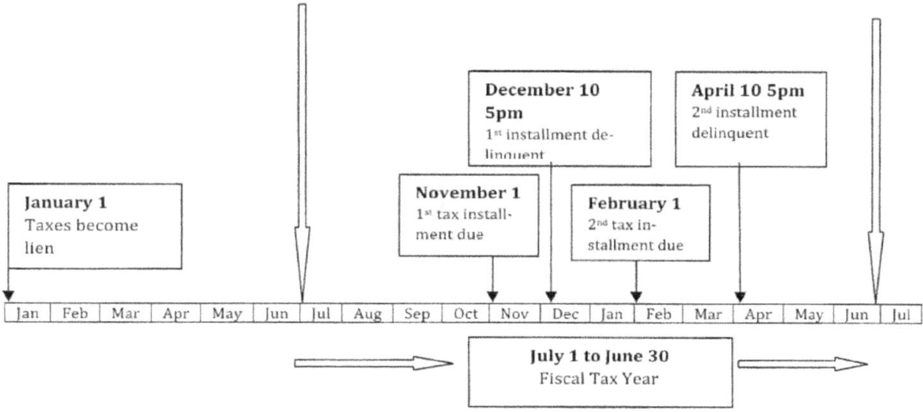

Figure 12: Tax Year and Installment Dates

Once the second installment is missed, a $10 fee is charged for the paperwork required to add the property to the Delinquent Property Tax Roll. The Delinquent Property Tax Roll is published in the local newspaper on June 8 of the same tax year. Past due tax amounts may be paid in five annual installments if a property owner starts to pay current property taxes along with the scheduled past due payments.

Property taxes go into effect on January 1 for the tax year beginning July 1 of that year. A lien in the amount of the assessed property taxes is placed against property on January 1. The first installment payment is not due until November 1 of that same year because the fiscal year does not begin until July 1.

PROPERTY OWNERS THAT ARE AGE 62 OR OLDER, DISABLED, OR BLIND can request in writing that their property taxes and interest be deferred under the **Property Tax Postponement Law.** The government allows senior citizens to set aside their tax payments until they vacate the property either by death or when they no longer occupy the property as their primary residence. The property taxes will be due and payable at that time including accrued fees and interest. The taxes can be paid from sale proceeds whether by the property owner or through the estate by the heirs. The property will not automatically be confiscated by the tax collector at the time of vacating the property. A reasonable amount of time will be allowed to settle the debt.

THE HOMEOWNER ASSISTANCE PROGRAM is also helpful by providing cash rebates to qualified property owners. Applications for property tax rebates are available from May 16 to August 31 of the current tax year.

ESCHEAT

ESCHEAT is the government's reversionary right in privately owned real property. When a property owner dies with no known heirs and with no will, the person is referred to as **intestate**. The State of California assumes that there are heirs and will bring a claim against the property and the estate of the decedent and hold it for a period of five (5) years. If no heirs have been located at the end of the five-year period, the state will take title to the property through the process called **escheat**.

GOVERNMENT LAND CONTROL

BUILDING CODES are established by the government by placing restrictions on building and construction on privately owned real estate. These building codes and standards are created for public safety in both private and public buildings by federal, state, and local governments.

NOTE

Whenever standards or restrictions conflict, the strictest will always prevail.

FEDERAL REGULATIONS are established by and for the Federal Housing Administration (FHA) and the Veterans Administration (VA). FHA insures loans and VA guarantees loans. Because the federal government has an interest in real property by virtue of the insuring and guaranteeing of loans, they have determined guidelines for construction of 1-to-4-unit residential dwellings. When a buyer is applying for a loan that will be insured by FHA or guaranteed by VA, the property will be required to comply with minimum property requirements (MPRs). These requirements were first established in 1934 when FHA was established. FHA has allowed local building codes to establish acceptable construction guidelines since 1986.

An **APPRAISER** approved by FHA and/or VA will prepare a **certificate of reasonable value,** which is an appraisal that will clarify and state any guidelines that are not met. If the subject property is inferior to MPRs, the loan may be subject to repairs and upgrades to be made prior to funding and, therefore, closing the purchase transaction.

MANUFACTURED HOMES are homes built in a factory per the federal definition. They are commonly called mobile homes; however, "manufactured" is the preferred term.
The Department of Housing and Urban Development (HUD) has established building codes for manufactured homes built since July 1976. The National Manufactured Home Construction and Safety Standards provide the rules and guidelines to include:

- Construction
- Design and floor plan
- Energy efficiency, insulation, and weatherproofing
- Fire resistance

Buyers of manufactured homes under the HUD code are to be given a homeowners' manual providing instruction for general maintenance, safety, and contact information for the state and federal agencies that enforce the standards.

STATE REGULATIONS are established through building codes and through the requirement of a contractor's license. The *state housing law* sets minimum construction and occupancy requirements for all residential dwellings, including apartments and hotels, under the administration of the *Codes and Standard Division of the* ***Department of Housing and Community Development.*** **Local building officials** and **building inspectors** are responsible for confirming the compliance of construction standards. The **local health officer** confirms compliance and enforces occupancy and sanitation standards.

The ***Commission of Housing and Community Development*** is required by the legislature to adopt regulations that comply with the Federal Uniform Building Codes that set the standards for the construction industry. Local building may be more stringent than the state building codes, but they must comply with the state regulations by not being more lenient.

Three major organizations in the United States merged in 2000 to create the International Code Council (ICC). The International Building Code and the International Residential Building Code were adopted by the ICC and are scheduled to be revised every 3 years thereafter. These standards are being adopted nationally. www.iccsafe.org

LOCAL BUILDING CODES are enforced by the appropriate municipal or county agency often called the **Department of Building and Safety**. The name will vary between counties. Applications for a **building permit** along with the plot plan, building plans, and specifications for the proposed structure or improvements is made to the local building official. A plans examiner will review the plans and address any problem areas and corrections that should or must be changed. The permit is issued when the application receives final approval from all departments involved.

The planning department of the local government regulates land use, fire safety, sanitation, density, building setbacks, and property line requirements.

A building permit must be obtained before construction is allowed to begin.

During the construction period, the building inspector will make inspections to ensure that code requirements are met. The building inspector will need to inspect and sign-off on each phase of the construction as it is completed, such as the electrical and plumbing before the drywall is hung.

On completion of a building, the local building inspector must approve the final work before the department issues a **certificate of occupancy**. A **temporary certificate of occupancy** may be issued to allow occupancy while minor work is still being done; however, all work must be successfully completed by the date stated in the temporary certificate.

The ***California Department of Health Services*** has the right to stop construction if there is contamination in the water supply, the drainage system, or the sewage disposal of the property. Local health officers are required in every county and city in California, providing a working relationship and direct contact with the Department of Health Services.

The local health officer must inspect and sign off on a project prior to the building inspector issuing the final inspection prior to the issuance of the **certificate of occupancy**.

The ***Commission of Housing and Community Development*** has required uniform codes to be made a part of local building codes since 1970. Local variations established to accommodate local conditions must be specifically approved by the state. Local codes may prohibit practices considered undesirable that are allowed by the uniform codes. For example, uniform building codes may only require a 2x4 in certain areas of framework, but the local building codes feel that a 4x4 is more substantial considering the earthquake potential in the area.

Local codes do not apply to the construction of HUD manufactured homes, which are governed by the Health and Safety Code, but local codes will apply to site improvements such as grading, foundation and anchoring, placement of the home on the site, and installation of utilities.

The ***Contractors State License Board*** under the **contractor's license law** licenses building contractors working in California. The license status of all California contractors can be checked at: www.cslb.ca.gov. Criminal charges can be brought against any unlicensed individual who works as a contractor who is not exempt from the licensing law.

No contractor's license is necessary for the following:

- Work including labor and material costing less than $500. (Worker must disclose that they do not have a contractor's license).
- Work done by the owner unless the owner is doing the work in preparation to offer the property for sale.

- Construction for certain agricultural purposes.
- Oil and gas operations.
- Work performed by public utilities for their purpose.

A person must meet both experience and knowledge qualifications to take the state exam to become a contractor. There are a variety of private schools throughout the state specializing in preparation for the contractors licensing exam. Once the requirements are met, the applicant for a contractor's license must post a bond or place a cash deposit with the state. The state fund is for the benefit of clients or anyone who is damaged or defrauded by a contractor in the conduct of business.

A contractor's license can be suspended or revoked for any of the following:

- Failing to follow plans and specifications.
- Abandoning a project.
- Diverting funds for a project to personal account or use.
- Violating building laws or safety regulations.
- Breaching a construction contract.

California's Mobile Home Accommodations Structures Law regulates buildings and other structures used with manufactured homes at grade level. The Mobile Home or Manufactured Homes Parks Act regulates construction and operation of parks for manufactured homes as well as parks for recreational vehicles. Both laws are part of the **Health and Safety Code.**

REDEVELOPMENT

REDEVELOPMENT of the deterioration of urban neighborhoods has served as the motivation for local redevelopment efforts. California's Community Redevelopment Law, which is found in the Health and Safety Code, provides for the creation of a **Community Redevelopment Agency (CRA).** The CRA either rehabilitates existing structures and neighborhoods or brings in new development to provide low- and moderate-income housing and to employ low-income persons.

The **GOVERNING BOARD OF CRA** is often composed of city council members. Redevelopment proposals must conform to the general plan, ***but do not need to conform to local zoning ordinances.*** The redevelopment plan must provide its own building use limitations to serve the needs and purpose of the redeveloped community or area.

The **CRA** can use the power of eminent domain to acquire property for the purpose of redevelopment. Funds can be borrowed from any source available to finance the purchase and construction required for redevelopment. The **CRA** can act as a developer.

Funding for CRA activities can come from a variety of bond programs, which may or may not require voter approval. Repayment can be through tax increment funding in order to be able to use the additional taxes produced by the redeveloped property.

Repayment also can be through the issuing of tax-exempt mortgage revenue bonds provided for purchaser of the redeveloped property. In 1979, the state legislature gave cities and counties the authority to levy special assessments on property within the redevelopment area in order to pay the indebtedness created by the redevelopment. This legislation is not limited by Proposition 13.

CHAPTER 6

TRANSFERRING OWNERSHIP OF REAL ESTATE

US
Realty School

TRANSFERRING OWNERSHIP RIGHTS IN REAL PROPERTY

Throughout history, property has changed hands in a number of ways, but this was basically done with only a proverbial handshake. There was often an item such as a bag of the soil or a branch of a bush or tree that was representative of the transfer of ownership of the property. Prior to California becoming a state, there were no formal written documents to verify transfer of property ownership. The new owner gave **constructive notice** by taking possession of the property. Once the state legislature was formed, written documents were created and authorized to either be held by the new owner or filed with the newly created public records in the county recorder's office.

TERMS were introduced and adapted from Spanish law and English common law, and from various other systems influencing the laws of the newly formed state of California. The following terms were adapted for use with the laws regarding the transfer of real estate.

1. **ACQUISITION** means to acquire or to obtain. Regarding the acquisition of real property, it can be accomplished in a number of ways that are currently accepted practice and within the guidelines of the laws. There are a variety of devices used to authenticate or verify the transaction. All of these will be discussed in this chapter.

2. **ALIENATION** is the act of removing oneself from the ownership or rights to a piece of real property. Alienation is derived from the root word "alien," or foreign to. If one alienates themselves, they remove or exclude themselves from the property and the property rights.

3. **TITLE** is a term that is commonly used synonymously with ownership. In the real estate industry, it is said that one **holds title** to property, meaning that they own it or that their name is on the **title** or **deed** to the property. **If one's name is on the deed, they own the property.**

NOTE

Terms that are used in the real estate industry vary from terms of other industries. Some commonly used terms are distinguished with the use of one of two suffixes. The "OR" suffix is always referring to the person that is giving, such as the grantor is giving land or a deed, or the landlord or lessor is giving a lease or the right to use property. The "EE" suffix refers to the person receiving property or the right to use property; for example, the grantee is the person receiving the grant deed or property, or the renter is the lessee or the person receiving the right to use the property.

4. **GRANT** is a term that means to give as with a grant deed. A **grant deed** is a written document that must contain the name of the grantor and the grantee. The following terms specify particular types of **grants** or **deeds** that are used for the transfer of real estate in California. Transfer of property may involve consideration or payment, or it may be a gift with no payment.

   - **PRIVATE GRANT** is the term used to describe the transfer of property from one individual or person to another individual with the use of a grant deed.

   - **PUBLIC GRANT** transfers real property from the government to an individual. When California became part of the United States, land that was not privately owned became the possession of the federal government and much of that land in turn became the property of California. When the government, whether state or federal, sells property, the transfer is done with a public grant, with the use of a grant deed used specifically for such transactions.

   - **DEDICATION** transfers real estate from an individual to the government. Most commonly used is when a subdivision is being built under the *Subdivision Map Act*, a developer will allow for a certain amount of the land to be dedicated to the government for public use such as for a park.

     This is a **statutory dedication** based on the requirements set forth under the *Subdivision Map Act* laws. It is held as **fee simple** ownership with the use of a deed.

NOTE

A corporation is considered to be a single entity the same as an individual person, therefore real property can be transferred to a corporation the same as to an individual.

- **PUBLIC DEDICATION** is the transfer of real property from the property owner or individual to the government for public use for a variety of reasons, which is commonly used for the creation of a roadway. This is also called a **common law dedication because it is not statutory or part of a law that requires certain dedications or contribution of land from the owner.**

ALIENATION BY OPERATION OF THE LAW

ALIENATION BY OPERATION OF THE LAW, OR COURT ACTION, is a way of clearing, establishing, or transferring title to real property to another person. This may even be in conflict with the person whose name is actually on title. **Transfer of ownership under this method may be an involuntary transaction on the part of the owner of the property.**

1. **QUIET TITLE ACTION** is a court action that is brought to force those persons who have claim to a property to prove their claims, or to have the courts rule the claims invalid. This clears any invalid claims against a property, thus the terms **clear title** or **clear clouds on title. Quiet title action** is often used for establishing title in an **adverse possession** claim (*to be discussed later in this chapter*). It is also used to remove abandoned easements from title which remove a person's right to use another person's property.

2. **PARTITION ACTION** is a court action brought by a co-owner of a property who wishes to divide or end the co-ownership of the property owned by more than one person. The co-owners may hold title as tenants-in-common or as joint tenants. The courts would try to find a settlement or order that the property be sold, and the proceeds divided according to the percentage of ownership of the individual parties. All proceeds will be given to the co-owners after any and all debts against the property are paid.

3. **POWER OF SALE** is a clause in the **note** that accompanies a **trust deed** which allows the trustee to sell the property to pay the balance of the debt if the property owner defaults on the loan agreement or fails to make payments as agreed. A mortgage agreement would have a similar clause allowing for the sale of the property to pay the debt. *See Chapter 12, Real Estate Financing.*

4. **A JUDICIAL FORECLOSURE ACTION** is requested by the trustee of the trust deed to request a court-supervised sale of the property to collect the debt that is owed under a default action.

5. **ACTION FOR DECLARATORY RELIEF** is brought by co-owners or those with rights in real property to request a clarification of their rights and obligations concerning a property. This is used to prevent future problems by the clarification when the deed is ambiguous or questionable.

6. **EXECUTION SALE** is a court action that allows for a party who has won a lawsuit and received a **judgment** against a person who owns real property to require the sale of the property to pay the debt. The party holding the judgment can request a court-supervised sale of any of the person's property within the state. The purpose of the sale is for the creditor or **judgment lien holder** to collect the money that is owed to them.

7. **A WRIT OF EXECUTION** is awarded to a **judgment lien holder** to allow and instruct the officials to perform the sale through public auction and use the proceeds to pay the **judgment lien holder** the amount owed plus expenses and court costs. The purchaser of property sold through an **execution sale** will receive a **sheriff's deed.**

8. **FORFEITURE** may be involuntary, which occurs when a condition of a deed is breached. This can happen with a **fee simple defeasible** ownership when a condition of the deed has been defeated or broken, or with a **trust deed** when the conditions have been violated as with payment default. The grantor of the deed has the right to reclaim the property.

   Forfeiture may also be on a voluntary basis, as when a property owner knows they are unable to meet the conditions of a deed and forfeits ownership. An example is **deed in lieu of foreclosure** situations. The owner /borrower realizes that they cannot make the payments for whatever reason and contacts the lender to offer them the deed and avoid the time of an expensive foreclosure process.

9. **MARRIAGE** in California provides for community property of all property acquired during marriage unless specifically designated otherwise. One spouse cannot defeat the other spouse's interest in jointly owned or community property.

10. **BANKRUPTCY** is under the auspices of the federal bankruptcy court. The bankruptcy court has the authority to sell a creditor's property to pay debts. If the court demands the sale of real estate through the court-appointed trustee, the successful bidder will receive a **trustee's deed.**

11. **ESCHEAT** is a process that takes place when a person dies **intestate** (without a will) and with no apparent heirs. The *California Attorney General* acts on behalf of the state to claim any property that is unclaimed by heirs within a five-year period following the real property owners' death.

12. **EMINENT DOMAIN** is the government's right to acquire property as needed for public use such as to build a roadway or expand a freeway. The real property in question will be **condemned** for its present use. This process involves declaring that the current use as a residential property; for example, is not the **highest and best use** for the property in question. The government will then declare that the property's **highest and best use** would be as a roadway to be used by the public. This declaration will clarify that the property is condemned for its current use.

    At this point, the government will obtain an appraisal to determine the **fair market value** for the purpose of establishing a purchase price to provide fair compensation to the owner of the property. *See Chapter 13, Appraisal*, for more information. The property owner will be compensated for the value of the property and expenses involved in vacating the property to include moving expenses and, in some situations, business expenses are included if the seller verifies the validity of the expense in association with the move.

    Neighboring or nearby properties are often affected by these improvements by virtue of the property value being reduced such as when expanding the freeway, the property that was condemned was creating a buffer between the neighboring property and the freeway. Now that the condemned property is part of the widened freeway, the neighboring property no longer has a buffer, and the value has been reduced because it is adjoining the freeway.

The property owner of such property has the right to file an **inverse condemnation** suit. This legal action allows the injured property owner to be compensated for the loss in value of their property.

13. **EQUITABLE ESTOPPEL** is a transfer referred to as **after acquired title**. This type of transaction occurs when a person conveys interest in real property prior to acquiring those rights. This is not necessarily considered fraud because the conveying party will acquire the property in the future. Once they actually acquire the real property interest, the previous conveyance will take place. **Originated as a common law theory, the equitable estoppel prevents the refusal to make the conveyance of real property.** Failure to convey the property once the rights are acquired will constitute fraud.

    Example: *Fred would like to purchase the property owned by Dave's aunt. Dave is her only heir and has been informed that he will inherit the property upon his ailing aunt's demise. Dave and Fred prepare a contract and a grant deed. Fred pays Dave a deposit with the balance of the purchase price to be paid once Dave legally owns the property. This is a legal and binding contract. Dave cannot renege on the agreement, and he cannot sell the property to anyone else.*

    Once Dave's aunt is deceased and the title is transferred to him, the transaction is completed, and the property ownership conveys to Fred with the balance of the purchase price being paid to Dave.

    If a party misrepresents themselves and their interest, which in turn causes the transfer of real property, the injured party has a claim of right.

    Example: *Using the above example, Dave and Fred are discussing the property owned by Dave's aunt and Fred expresses his desire to purchase the property.*

    Dave's brother, Ben, is with them and they both know that instead of Dave inheriting the property, Ben will inherit. Dave offers to sell the property to Fred as discussed in the previous example and Dave accepts the deposit money. Ben does not say a word in dispute and does not disclose the facts to Fred.

    When the aunt dies, Fred, as the injured party, may gain ownership of the property because Ben and Dave misrepresented the facts and Ben knowingly allowed Dave to make the agreement. This will probably require a decision in a court of law.

Equitable estoppel is occasionally used as a means to commit fraud by unsavory people. The real estate professional needs to be aware of the principles and the actual purpose of the option. The use of a straw buyer is not an acceptable use of equitable estoppel and is fraud.

CONVEYANCE OF PROPERTY AFTER DEATH

CONVEYANCE AFTER THE DEATH of a property owner may take place in more than one way. The most common is through **succession**, which is usually the result of a property owner dying **intestate**, which means without a will.

SUCCESSION most often occurs when the property is owned jointly, with the exception of tenants-in-common ownership, which does not have the right of Survivorship unless specified in the deed.

INTESTATE refers to property owners who have died without a will that would have stated who would inherit the property. California has made provisions for the legal succession or distribution of property, which is called **intestate succession**. The law applies to both real estate and personal property, or chattel. In California, the following intestate succession or right of succession applies:

1. **COMMUNITY PROPERTY WITH SURVIVING SPOUSE:** One-half is owned by each spouse. The deceased spouse's half is divided after the decedent's liabilities are paid:
   - One-third to the surviving spouse and two-thirds to any surviving children if there is more than one child.
   - One-half to the spouse and ½ to the child if there is only one child.
   - 100% to the surviving spouse if there are no surviving children.
   - 100% to the surviving spouse if title was taken as "community property *with the right of survivorship*".

2. **JOINT TENANCY:** is the same as with community property with the right of survivorship. The surviving spouse receives 100% property ownership.

3. **SEPARATE PROPERTY,** or property owned sole and separate or with no co-owner:
   - **Surviving spouse with no children:**
     - The surviving spouse receives half.
     - The surviving parent, brother, sister, or child of deceased sibling receives other half.
     - If none of these exist, the surviving spouse receives the remaining half.
   - **Surviving spouse with one child:**
     - The surviving spouse receives half.
     - Child receives half.
   - **Surviving spouse with more than one child:**
     - The surviving spouse receives one-third.
     - Children divide two-thirds equally.
   - **No surviving spouse or child:**
     - The property is distributed to next-of-kin according to California law in the following order: the surviving parent, brother, sister, or child of deceased sibling.
     - If no heirs exist, the property will go to the state through escheat.

TESTATE, or **with a will,** provides for the succession of an owner's property passing to the persons chosen by the deceased. A will is a document or a **devise** that is prepared by a **testator,** who is a legally competent person, to pass title to another after their demise. The testator dies **testate,** or with a will. A will cannot give something that the testator does not own, and it cannot override title.

> ***Example:*** *Joe dies testate. He has stated in the will that the ownership of all of his property is to pass to his son, Jim, after his death. Joe's residence is held as joint tenant with his wife Donna and his rental property is owned as tenants-in-common with 50% belonging to his brother Gerald.*
>
> *Jim cannot inherit the home his parents owned as joint tenants because the ownership passes to Donna based on the laws of joint tenancy. It was not Joe's to give. Jim will inherit only the percentage of ownership that his father owned in the rental property. The percentage of property owned by Gerald is not Joe's to give.*

DEVISE is the term given to the document or instrument that transfers real property, or the name given to a will that transfers real property.

A **DEVISOR** is the deceased person giving the property through a will or devise.

A **DEVISEE** is the party receiving the property through the will or devise.

BEQUEST of a LEGACY is the term used to describe the transfer of personal property or chattel though the use of a will. A legacy may include items such as money, jewelry, or furniture.

A **LEGATOR** is the person giving the **bequest or legacy** through the will.

A **LEGATEE** is the recipient of the **bequest or legacy** through the will.

NOTE

The OR suffix is used to indicate the giver (givOR) and the EE suffix is used to indicate the receiver (rEcEivEr).

Title of real property and ownership of personal property does not pass from the testator until after they have passed away. During the testator's lifetime, they have the right to change the contents of the will as they choose. The will can be completely rewritten by replacing the old will completely or the contents can be changed with a **codicil** or an amendment to the original will. A devisee has no
rights in the devisor's property until after the death of the advisor.

TYPES OF WILLS that are recognized in California are the witnessed will and the holographic will. *An oral will is not valid in California.*

1. **WITNESSED WILLS** are formal, written documents that have been signed in front of witnesses. The **witnessed will** is generally prepared by an attorney. An attorney prepares the will by listing the testator's property, both real and personal, along with the choices of heirs or devisees and legatees. Once the will is completed and accepted by the testator, that person signs the will. The signing is witnessed by the witnesses signing the will in the testator's presence. At least two people that are preferably not a party to the will are required by law to act as witnesses. The will may also be witnessed by a notary public.

2. **STATUTORY WILLS** are prepared forms that are completed by the testator by filling in the blanks and adding any amendments necessary. The statutory will is witnessed in the same way as the witnessed will. The statutory will may be purchased at various office supply stores, bookstores or online. Statutory wills may also be completely type written by the testator or any other party chosen as long as it meets the requirements established by law, which make it "statutory."

3. **HOLOGRAPHIC WILLS** are completely handwritten by the testator and cannot be typewritten. The holographic will must be signed and dated by the testator, but it does not need to be witnessed. If the will has typed sections included or is not entirely in the devisor's handwriting, it is no longer a **holographic will** and will be considered a witnessed will and will require witnesses.

PROBATE is a court process to distribute the property, both real and personal, of a person who is deceased. The probate court works with the person designated by the decedent (the person who is deceased) to oversee their property. This person is known as the **executor**. If the decedent has not named an executor, the probate court can name an **administrator**. The court will oversee payment of the decedent's debts, determination of the heirs, and transfer of title to any real property.

Probate will oversee the sale of real property through the executor or the administrator if the courts have determined that it is in the best interest of the estate to do so. The **executor** or the **administrator** can offer the real property for sale through a broker with an **exclusive right to sell agreement** for up to 90 days. *See Chapter 7 Real Estate Contracts.*

The court has the right to choose the broker/agent; however, the heirs have a right to provide their choice of a broker/agent for approval by the court. The probate court will determine the amount of commission to be paid by the estate. The administrator has the right to accept an offer from any prospective buyers with final approval and confirmation of the offer being given by the court.

ACCESSION

ACCESSION is the increase of property due to either man-made or natural causes. These additions add property to the owner's title by improvements, accretion, or reliction. Accession does not include property gained through fraud, misrepresentation, or even misinformation filed with the county records.

1. **IMPROVEMENTS** are any structures or fixtures that are added to the real property. Once added, the value of the property is increased. An improvement to the property may include anything from a fence to a house and more. A **fixture** refers to an item that is personal property until it becomes permanently attached such as an air conditioning system. Once a fixture is permanently attached, it becomes real property.

   Occasionally, an improvement will be added to the wrong property. This can occur through a variety of miscommunications and misinformation. When an improvement is placed on the wrong property innocently, the improvement can be removed from the property or the property beneath the improvement can be purchased. It is also possible for the owner of the property to purchase the improvement that has been placed on their property. The property owner must be compensated for any damage to the property.

   Example: *John is installing a new fence along the property line with his neighbor Betty. The fence was built where John believed the property line existed. Upon completion of the fence, Betty noticed that it was in the right place at the front of the lot; however, the fence angled onto her property as it approached the back of the lot. She approached John with this discovery and further investigation proved that the fence at the back of the property was in fact two feet onto Betty's property.*

   John and Betty had several options:
   John could move the fence to correct the error.
   John could give Betty monetary compensation for her loss of property.
   Betty could purchase the fence from John.
   The most practical option for John and Betty was for John to buy the land from Betty and compensate her for the lost property.

   Compensation would not be allowed or acceptable in a situation where an improvement was placed on the wrong property, or across property lines, and the property owner knew that it was being built on his property and said nothing. He viewed it as an opportunity to gain an improvement without the expense or to otherwise gain by the builder's error. This is tantamount to fraud and is unacceptable behavior. Likewise, if the property owner building the improvement intentionally built across property lines with the intention of gaining additional property through **adverse possession** or similar possessory rights would also be considered fraud and would be dealt with accordingly in the courts.

2. **ACCRETION** is the increase of land area through the forces of nature. Accretion may occur when a property is adjacent to or bordering a flowing waterway. The action is called accretion if the water adds soil to the property and increases the land area.
   - **ALLUVIUM OR ALLUVION** is the build-up of soil or land gradually over a long period of time. This process may be so gradual that it is not noticeable.

Accretion may also occur rapidly such as often occurs in the springtime when the snow melts on the mountains and the streams and rivers overflow. A fast-moving body of water may dislodge a large piece of soil in one area of the river and deposit it further downstream at another spot in the river, thus increasing the land mass or area at the newly attached property.

> ***Example:*** *John owns property adjacent to Mission Creek. During the winter storms, the creek flooded and carried large amounts of soil and debris from the mountains. As the creek flowed toward the ocean, soil was deposited along bends and flat areas. Several months after the storm, John conducted a survey and found that his property had increased by two feet.*

- **EROSION** is the gradual removal of land and can be caused by something as simple as rainfall or the constant flow of water. This is the opposite of accretion, as it erodes soil and land which decreases the land mass of real property.

- **AVULSION** is the sudden removal of land and, as stated in the above example, would be the situation of the land farther upstream that had suffered loss of property by the force of the water ripping away a large piece of land.

3. **RELICTION** occurs when waters permanently recede from a property, leaving newly exposed land which then becomes part of the existing property, increasing the land mass or the size of the owner's property. The receding of the water level on a permanent basis is an example of ***reliction***.

OCCUPANCY

OCCUPANCY OR POSSESSION of a property may establish ownership and be acquired in one of the following three ways:

1. **ADVERSE POSSESSION** is used to acquire title of property when the adverse possessor is acting under the belief that they actually have the right of ownership. More than one person believes they own a piece of real property, but only one occupies the property. The person occupying the property is known as the adverse possessor. This situation could actually happen in a number of ways; however, it was more common before the late 1900s. Prior to that time, communication and transportation were more difficult, creating greater periods of time when a property owner may be away from their property and ownership may have been more questionable. Property can be scrutinized more closely in today's world of technology.

   The primary purpose of adverse possession in the law is to cure defects in real estate titles by putting a statute of limitations on litigation when more than one party believes that they own a property. Without the adverse possession laws, a property owner would never know how secure their title is because there would be the potential for past owners and their heirs to claim the property.

   Adverse possession is based on the **legal doctrine of laches,** which states that "Neglect to assert a right of claim that together with lapse of time and other circumstances prejudices an adverse party. Neglecting to do what should or could be done to assert claim or right for an unreasonable and unjustified time causing disadvantages to another."

   If a person believes that they own a property but ignores the fact that there is a person living on the property, they create a moral issue. The person gives the impression that they are taking advantage of the person living there by letting the occupying person take care of the property through maintenance and paying taxes.

In order to obtain title, the adverse possessor must meet five conditions:

a) **Claim of title or right, color of title:** Claim of title or right of title refers to the right of ownership based on belief of that ownership. This belief may be due to the possession of a document that declares the adverse possessor is the owner whether valid or not. More than one document may exist declaring ownership to more than one party creating a **cloud on title** or **color of title**.

b) **Hostile to the true owner:** The adverse possessor must have taken possession of the property without the permission of the true owner or other party believing to own the property.

c) **Open and notorious use:** The adverse possessor must live in and use the property with no attempt to hide that fact.

d) **Continuous use:** The property must be occupied continuously for a period of five years. If the adverse possessor abandons the property for any reason during the five-year period and then reoccupies the property, the counting of the five-year period of time will begin from the day of their reoccupying.

e) **Pay all property taxes:** The adverse possessor must pay all of the property taxes for the five-year time period.

CLEAR TITLE to the property by the **adverse possessor** must be obtained through the courts. The adverse possessor would need to file a lawsuit to establish that they had met all requirements and request that the cloud on title be removed, and a clear title be provided. Once the courts recognize the ownership claim of the adverse possessor, the court decree can be recorded with the county recorder's office giving **constructive notice.**

Example: *Betty was living in a property owned by her grandfather. She had been told that since she had been living there so long and maintaining the property, she would inherit the property when her grandfather passed away. Betty's cousin George approached their grandfather and expressed his desire to purchase the property that Betty was living on. The grandfather agreed to sell the property to George, and they closed the transaction.*

He died before he could change his will to give Betty another property he owned and before he could tell her of the change. George did not file the grant deed that he received from his grandfather so that when the will was read, Betty received a grant deed from the probate court. George was not present at the reading because he had to be out of town on business and was unaware of the outcome. George also owned another property and was busy, so he did not worry about the property as he knew his cousin was taking care of it.

By the time George realized that there were two deeds to the property, Betty had been there with the belief that she owned the property for more than two years. George asked Betty to move out and she refused stating that she owned it. Betty continued to live on the property as she was secure in the belief that it belonged to her as she held a grant deed. The tax bills all came to the house and in Betty's name because she had recorded her deed. Betty made all of the tax payments and maintained the property. At the end of the five-year period, Betty filed an adverse possession action against George in order to gain a clear title.

Betty met all of the conditions of adverse possession law and was able to acquire a clear title through the courts. The lack of action on George's part may have indicated to the courts that he may have been taking advantage of his cousin to maintain the property and pay the taxes, leaving him with unfair gain. George's deed may or may not have been dated showing that he was first in time and, therefore, first in right; however, he did not act in a timely manner or within the statute of limitations, giving Betty the advantage and clear intentions in the eyes of the courts.

The **OCCUPANCY MUST BE FOR FIVE CONTINUOUS YEARS; however,** successive adverse possessors can pass their terms of occupancy to the next adverse possessor to compile the required five-year period. Each successive adverse possessor would need to gain possession through **color of title** by accepting a deed or document from the previous adverse possessor that appeared to give **good title**. Each adverse possessor must believe that they have the right to own and possess the property based on a deed or other document that would appear to be valid.

2. **PRESCRIPTIVE EASEMENT or EASEMENT by PRESCRIPTION** is a court ordered easement, allowing the right to use or to travel across the property that belongs to another person. Such an easement has been an unrecorded easement that has now been determined by the courts to be necessary and prescribes that there is a need for the easement. The prescriptive easement should be recorded for the purpose of giving constructive notice.

   A **prescriptive easement or easement by prescription** may be created by a person using the property of another for ingress or egress. After a period of time, if the use is undisputed by the property owner, it becomes accepted use. The prescriptive easement may also be created for a person who has obtained landlocked property and needs to be able to access that property.

   Prescriptive easement does not give the user ownership rights to the property, only the **right of usage**. In order to gain an **easement by prescription**, the following conditions must be met:
   - Open and notorious use
   - Continuous use for a minimum of five years
   - Hostile to the owner's interest
   - Claim of right

   These conditions are the same as for adverse possession with the exception of paying taxes.

   Example: *Surfers in Malibu had been parking at a fast-food restaurant and walking across the street through a vacant lot to their favorite surf spot on the beach. The vacant lot had been owned by the same family for many years and had never been used by them, just by the public for beach access. The property was sold and the new owner proceeded to build a new house on the lot. In doing so, he obstructed the beach access by building a fence around the property. The surfers that had been using the property as an easement to the beach took the property owner to court and requested an easement by prescription. The surfers won the case and were given easement across the new owner's property. The new owner relocated the fence by several feet, allowing an access path several feet wide from the street to the beach. This allowed for foot traffic only as was the extent of the use of the easement.*

3. **ABANDONMENT** occurs when a party vacates a property or forfeits their rights to a property of which they are in possession, such as a tenant or lessee that abandons property, which then reverts the right of possession of the property back to the landlord or lessor. This may occur in other situations regarding real property such as:
    - Adverse possessor vacates in less than five years.
    - An easement is not used for more than five years.
    - A life tenant abandons rights to the stated property.

DEEDS AND GRANTING

DEEDS are the documents that are used to transfer the ownership from one entity to another and verify the granting or giving of the real property. There are several types of deeds in California that are used to grant ownership.

***BILL OF SALE** is a document similar to a deed; however, it is used to transfer ownership of chattel or personal property such as a car.*

VALID DEEDS must have the following essential elements:

- **Written:** All real estate deeds and contracts must be in writing. Verbal contracts are not legal for real estate transactions in the State of California.
- **Granting clause:** "*I hereby grant*" must be in the document making a clear statement that the grantor fully intends to give or grant the deed in question.
- **Designated grantee**: The person receiving the deed must be named in the document. A deed can never be left blank concerning the recipient. A blank deed would be similar to a bearer bond, meaning that whoever held the document in their possession owned it.
- **Competent grantor**: The person giving or granting the property must be legally competent. A competent grantor must be:
    - **Sane.** ***A person who is not sane would either have been declared incompetent in a court of law or committed to a hospital for mental care.***
    - **18 years of age** ***or older*** **unless** ***the person is:***
        - Married
        - In the military
        - Emancipated by a court of law.
        - Free of certain **felony** convictions

- **Adequate description of the property:** A legal description is not necessary as long as the description is sufficiently adequate that it will not be confused with any other property. A complete address will usually suffice.
- **Executed by the grantor:** In real estate terminology, **"execute"** means **signed**. A **fully executed document** is one that has been signed by all involved persons. The grantor or the person giving the deed must sign the deed. The grantee or the person receiving the deed does not need to sign because acceptance of the physical document provides sufficient notice of the grantee's intent, and recording the deed by the grantee gives constructive notice.

Effective deeds must be **delivered by the grantor to the grantee** in order to transfer title. If the grantor does not deliver the deed to the grantee, it is not effective, and title or ownership will not be transferred. There must be a form of constructive notice by the grantor that clearly states the intent to transfer ownership. This intent is demonstrated by the physical delivery of the deed. If the grantee does not receive a deed, title does not transfer.

Once the grantor delivers the deed, that action has given notice of the intent to transfer ownership; however, the **grantee must accept the deed for the transfer to be complete**. If the grantee does not physically accept the deed, the transfer is incomplete and may be completed at a later date when the deed is accepted. If the grantee refuses the deed, title does not transfer.

Items that are not essential for a deed to be valid or effective:

- **Consideration:** Money or something of value, including love and affection. Consideration is essential for a contract to be valid, but not for a deed.
- **Signature of the grantee:** Acceptance by the grantee provides constructive notice of the transfer of the deed but is not necessary as taking possession of the property or the deed verifies transfer. Only the grantor must sign.
- **Date:** Not necessary, but advisable in case of any discrepancies in the future as to the rightful ownership.
- **Legal description:** An adequate description that adequately describes the property such as a full address is all that is required.
- **Recording:** Recording a deed with the county recorder's office in the county where the property is located is always advisable, but it is not necessary.

Recording gives constructive notice that the ownership or title has changed or that the rights to the real property have been altered in some way. Recording gives notice of the rights and the ownership of a given piece of real estate.

Unscrupulous sellers of property would actually be able to re-sell a property if there were no date and no recording. ***Constructive notice through recording is always advisable.***

TYPES OF DEEDS

TYPES OF DEEDS vary according to the purpose of transfer and the effect to be gained. deeds convey all interest that the grantor has in real property unless otherwise specified in the deed. If a property owner has a fee simple title, they will convey a fee simple title. A life estate holder can only convey the actual estate that they own, never more.

Either of these examples can convey a lesser interest such as the fee simple owner can convey with title with a condition or fee simple defeasible. The life estate owner can convey ownership interest, but when the designated person dies, the property ownership will pass to the **remainderman,** not the holder of the life estate.

1. **GRANT DEEDS** are documents that are used to transfer, grant, or give the ownership of real estate to another. The term grant deed refers to the document that is granting or giving the ownership of real property. A grant deed has a **granting clause** that states, *"I hereby grant." See Figure 9 in Chapter 2.* This is the most commonly used deed used in California today.

   Implied warranties as a part of a grant deed means that it warranties or guarantees that the **grantor has not previously conveyed title** to another. If a grantor has previously conveyed title, it is no longer theirs to transfer. A grant deed also warranties that **all encumbrances and other interests in the property having ownership have been disclosed.**

   Ownership does not transfer until **after the title is acquired**. The physical passing of the grant deed must take place before ownership transfers. This statement is as simple as the grant deed is passed from one person to the other, which constitutes acquiring title; ownership is transferred when this is complete. One does not own a piece of real property until the deed to that property is in their hands. As stated previously, **the grantor must deliver the deed, and the grantee must accept the deed in order for ownership to transfer.**

2. **GIFT DEED** is used to transfer ownership of real property when there is no monetary consideration involved or, as the name indicates, the property is being given as a gift from one owner to another. The chapter on contracts states that there must be consideration for a contract to be valid. Consideration is not required for a deed to be valid, but the consideration of "love and affection" usually does exist in the situation of a gift deed.

3. **QUIT CLAIM DEED** is a deed that quits any claim to the property that the grantor may have. *See Chapter2, Figure 10.* The grantor of a quit claim deed is giving constructive notice that they no longer have any claim on a piece of property, such as a person that had an easement across the property and is no longer using the easement, so they choose to give it up or to ***quit any claim*** or right they had to use property that belongs to another.

   Unlike the grant deed, the **quit claim deed** provides no warranties because the property probably never belonged to the grantor. If the property did belong to the grantor and they are now quitting their claim, it is most likely that the property is being given to their spouse, which is a transfer that does not require any warranty.

   The **quit claim deed** is often used to **clear a cloud on title** or to prevent any potential "clouds." Because of this, there is no need for a warranty whether implied or stated. A cloud on title refers to anything that is giving rights to another person other than the owner of the real property.

   Examples of this are easements, or the right to cross the property or use it in any way, or the right that another person may have as a claim to the ownership. Judgments and encumbrances would also be removed from title with the use of a **quit claim deed**.

   Example: *Mary bought her property from Mr. Jones. At the time, the property was land-locked meaning that there was no street access to her property, so Mr. Jones gave her an easement of ten feet to provide her with a driveway across his property. This provided a cloud on his title which gave Mary the right to use that portion of Mr. Jones' property. Since then, the city has put in a new street next to both lots and Mary now has access directly from the street, which means that Mary's property is no longer land locked. She no longer needs the easement across Mr. Jones' property, so she provides him with a quit claim deed. Mr. Jones records the quit claim deed with the county recorder's office and the easement is removed, clearing the cloud on title.*

California is a **COMMUNITY PROPERTY** state, which means that property that is gained in marriage is the possession of both spouses. This also applies to any property that has experienced a co-mingling of funds in regard to a property that has been acquired during or before marriage. Co-mingling of funds occurs when any income or expense from or for a property has been handled in a joint account for both spouses. Because California is a community property state, it is always required that a spouse not on title must sign a quit claim deed at any time that the owning spouse purchases, sells, or finances property that is held as "sole and separate." This will be required with every transaction for separately held property. The non-owning spouse signs the quit claim deed to state that they have no claim to that property.

4. **TRUST DEEDS** are the primary form of real estate financing in California. A **trust deed** is given from the **trustor,** who is also the **borrower** or property owner, to the **beneficiary,** who is the **lender**, as a means of placing their real property as security for a loan. The **beneficiary** hands the **trust deed** to a **trustee** who is a third party hired to maintain the trust that has been established. The **trustee** will oversee the loan payments and will notify the **beneficiary** of any defaults to the term of the **note** that accompanies the trust deed. The **note** spells out the terms of the loan, including the amount of payments and terms regarding any default of the payments.

   The **note** will also allow provisions for the **trustee** to take legal action against the **trustor** if there is non-compliance of certain terms. This will be discussed in more detail in *Chapter 12, Financing.*

5. **RECONVEYANCE DEED** is used by a lender to reconvey interest or give back the interest held by the lender to the property owner when the loan secured with a trust deed has been paid in full. Most states use mortgages when financing real estate. California uses trust deeds. A trust deed is similar to a mortgage and the term is used interchangeably; however, it is a separate document. Because of the nature of a **trust deed**, a **reconveyance deed** must legally be provided when the trust deed is paid in full. When a loan and a resulting trust deed have been obtained from a private individual, a reconveyance deed may often be overlooked at the time of payment in full. Private individuals are usually unaware of this document and do not know that it must be provided to the trustor/borrower when the loan is paid off. This will be discovered by the title company in the preliminary title report and can usually be completed without problems.

6. **TRUSTEE'S DEED** is used to transfer ownership to a successful bidder at a foreclosure sale or a bankruptcy sale when a trust deed was used as the security instrument for a loan against real property. The trustee of the property, or the party acting on behalf of the lender, is the grantor of a **trustee's deed**. The trustee is in charge of the disposal of the property and the foreclosure sale; therefore, they prepare and convey the deed, thus the term **"trustee's deed."** When a property owner has defaulted on the loan against the property securing the trust deed, the lender has the right to foreclose on the property or to claim ownership through the foreclosure process. Once the foreclosure process is complete, the trustee schedules a foreclosure sale to sell the property. Most foreclosure sales are public auctions. Once the sale is complete, the new owner is provided a trustee's deed in place of a grant deed. It serves the same purpose of transferring ownership.

7. **A SHERIFF'S DEED** is provided to the successful bidder of a property that has been sold through an execution sale to satisfy a judgment. A sheriff's deed is also similar to a trustee's deed except it is used when the financing instrument was a mortgage instead of a trust deed.

8. **A TAX DEED** is a deed that is used to transfer ownership to the successful bidder of a tax sale. If a property owner does not pay their property taxes to the county tax collector as required, the property can be sold through a foreclosure sale, much like the foreclosure sale by a lender. At the conclusion of the sale, which is in the form of an auction, the successful bidder is provided with a tax deed transferring ownership to the successful bidder.

9. **A WARRANTY DEED** as a way of giving a guarantee that the grantor/seller of the property owns a clear title and has the right to sell it to the grantee/buyer. The guarantee provided with the warranty deed covers not only the time the current owner has owned the property, but also back to the beginning of the recorded history of the real property. A warranty deed gives several traditional forms of covenants regarding the property, which fall under the two categories of present covenants and future covenants.
   - **PRESENT COVENANTS** - the seller guarantees:
     - **Right of ownership** – Has title and possession.
     - **Right to convey** – Can validly grant or convey.
     - **Against encumbrances** – There are no encumbrances other than those disclosed.

- FUTURE COVENANTS – the seller guarantees:
  - **Quiet enjoyment** – Protect buyer from others.
  - **Warranty** – No other can legally claim the title.
  - **Further assurances** – If anything is omitted that may cause the title to be invalid, the seller promises to do whatever is necessary to correct the problem.

TITLE COMPANIES are hired to perform a complete search of the title and the history of the title. Title insurance companies provide insurance to protect both the buyer and the seller from any errors or defects in the title that may result in a lack of validity and ownership of the property in question. California uses escrow companies and title insurance and, therefore, warranty deeds are not always used in the state. A warranty deed may be advised if the transaction is not being handled by an escrow officer and not using title insurance such as in an all-cash transaction. *Many states use abstract companies and attorneys to close real estate transactions, which require the use of a warranty deed.*

RECORDING

RECORDING is a way of providing **constructive notice** or announcing to the public that the transaction has taken place. Although **recording a deed** is not legally required, it helps ensure that the ownership of the property will not be questioned. After a **deed** is conveyed, the new **deed** is taken to the **county recorder's office** and the **recording** is requested. The **county recorder stamps the deed with the date and time that it was received**. The rule for recorded documents is ***first in time, first in right***. This means that the document that is delivered to the recorder's office first is considered to be the accurate one and will receive the claim of ownership or interest in the real property.

> ***Example:*** *Joe is selling his house to Tom. Escrow is closing and the title company has sent their representative to the county recorder's office to record the grant deed from Joe to Tom. The title company's person arrives at 8:45 a.m. and has the deed recorded. At 10:30 a.m. on the same day, Ace Roofing Company arrives at the county recorder's office to record a mechanic's lien against Joe's property. Joe no longer owns the property and has not owned the property since 8:45 a.m. Ace Roofing cannot record the mechanic's lien because the property is now owned by Tom and the lien was against Joe.*

PUBLIC RECORDING SYSTEMS are to the advantage of both buyers and sellers of real property. **Recording a deed** makes a statement and clarifies ownership.

Everything that is recorded is **"public information"** and because anyone is able to go into the **county recorder's office** and look up the recordings and records, it is less likely and more difficult for another person to claim a right to a piece of real property, which makes a recorded claim more secure to the owner. The **buyer** of real estate has the option and ability to **research** the **public records** to ensure that the seller has the right to sell and that there are no claims, encumbrances, liens, or easements recorded that may cause problems in the future.

TITLE COMPANIES are hired for the purpose of **researching the history** of the property ownership and rights, and to establish the accuracy of the recorded information and documents. Once the initial property search is completed, the **title company** prepares a document called the **preliminary title report**, commonly referred to as the **prelim**. The **prelim** is provided to the escrow officer who then forwards copies to the **seller, buyer, and real estate agents** for a sale transaction and to the **lender** for a financing transaction.

All parties to a transaction have the opportunity to review the prelim for accuracy and has the right to question or dispute any errors or recordings of concern. **In California, the title insurance company provides a title insurance policy to insure or guarantee the title**. *See Chapter 11, Escrow and Title.*

> *As stated previously, there are many states that do not use **title insurance** or **escrow companies**. In those states, an **abstract company** is used to research the recorded history of a property and provide a report to the parties involved in the transaction. The document is called an **abstract**. The **abstract** does not use the abbreviated format that a **prelim** uses. The **abstract** gives a history of ownership, claims, and any other recordings from the time that the property was first recorded with the public recording system. The history can go back centuries and reads much like a historical novel. A **prelim** is usually about eighteen pages long, but an **abstract** can be about one hundred pages. **Abstract companies** provide a copy to the **attorney** involved in a transaction who will use the information to form a **legal opinion** of the **state (condition) of the title**. Once the **opinion** is provided, a **warranty deed** can be prepared to **guarantee the title** by the seller.*

CHAIN OF TITLE is a statement made by the title company in the preliminary title report that declares any and all transfers or changes in ownership that have occurred on the subject property during the past twelve month- or twenty-four-month period as requested. This becomes an issue to lenders, in particular, during seller's markets when properties are changing hands rapidly because values are increasing. Lenders need to hold loans for approximately 18 months to start making back their investment. Rapidly changing ownership puts up red flags for potential problems.

DEEDS TO BE RECORDED must have the name of the property owner and the address of the **grantee** so the **tax bill** can be sent to the correct property owner.

Although recording a deed is not a legal requirement, the county tax assessor does have a requirement that the county recorder's office be notified of all transfers of ownership of real estate within three business days of the close of the transaction. The purpose is to provide accurate tax information to the owner of the property.

The **county recorder's office** has the right to add an additional charge to **real estate recordings** to be used for **real estate fraud** cases as needed by the **district attorney** for investigation and prosecution of such crimes.

ACKNOWLEDGEMENT is used as a way to verify the authenticity of documents. In the State of California, most **real estate documents** are required to be **acknowledged** prior to **being recorded with the county recorder's office. Acknowledgement** is most commonly referred to as **notarized.**

NOTARY PUBLICS are **certified** and **bonded** by the state in which they do business to perform **acknowledgements** and otherwise **witness signatures on documents** and **verify the identity** of those providing signatures. The purpose of requiring an **acknowledgement** is to prevent **fraud in real estate** transactions by verifying that the correct person is signing.

NOTE

A purchaser of real property should use their complete name as much as possible. The more complete the name, the easier it is to verify the correct owner, as many people have the same name. Including the first, middle, and last names is always a good practice. Use of initials and nicknames may only lead to confusion and the possibility of fraud. A real estate professional should always encourage parties to a real estate transaction to use given and complete names on legal documents.

A **notary** will require that the persons signing a document have at least one form of **photo identification** with them at the time of signing. The signers will also be required to **sign the notary journal** and provide a **thumbprint from their right hand** on all transactions involving conveyance of real property. California used to allow identification by the **notary** if the signing party was **"personally known"** to the **notary**. **This law changed on January 1, 2008, and the practice is no longer acceptable in California.** If a person signing a document does not have **photo identification,** such as a **driver's license**, they can bring a person with them that will testify that they are who they say they are. That third person will need to provide **photo identification** and also **sign the notary journal** along with their **right thumbprint**. Acceptable and frequently used forms of **photo identification** are:

- Driver's license
- Passport
- Employee ID from job

Laws and procedures have become more stringent over the years in an attempt to prevent fraud as much as possible. It is important to remember that any time there is a large amount of money involved, there is an increased potential for fraud and theft.

> ***Example:*** *In the 1980s in Los Angeles, a man sold his house and hired a woman with features similar to his wife's to sign the documents conveying title to the buyers. The wife was unaware of the sale until waking up one morning to find the buyers preparing to move into her house. The police were called to resolve the situation. The husband was found and arrested at LAX in the Bradley Terminal, which is the terminal for international flights. Funds were returned to the buyers and the wife retained the title to the property.*

NOTE

The real estate professional should be aware that these situations occur, and one should always be mindful of the possibility of such situations occurring. The real estate professional needs to take every precaution to avoid and prevent any and all fraud and NEVER PARTICIPATE or COMMIT FRAUD.

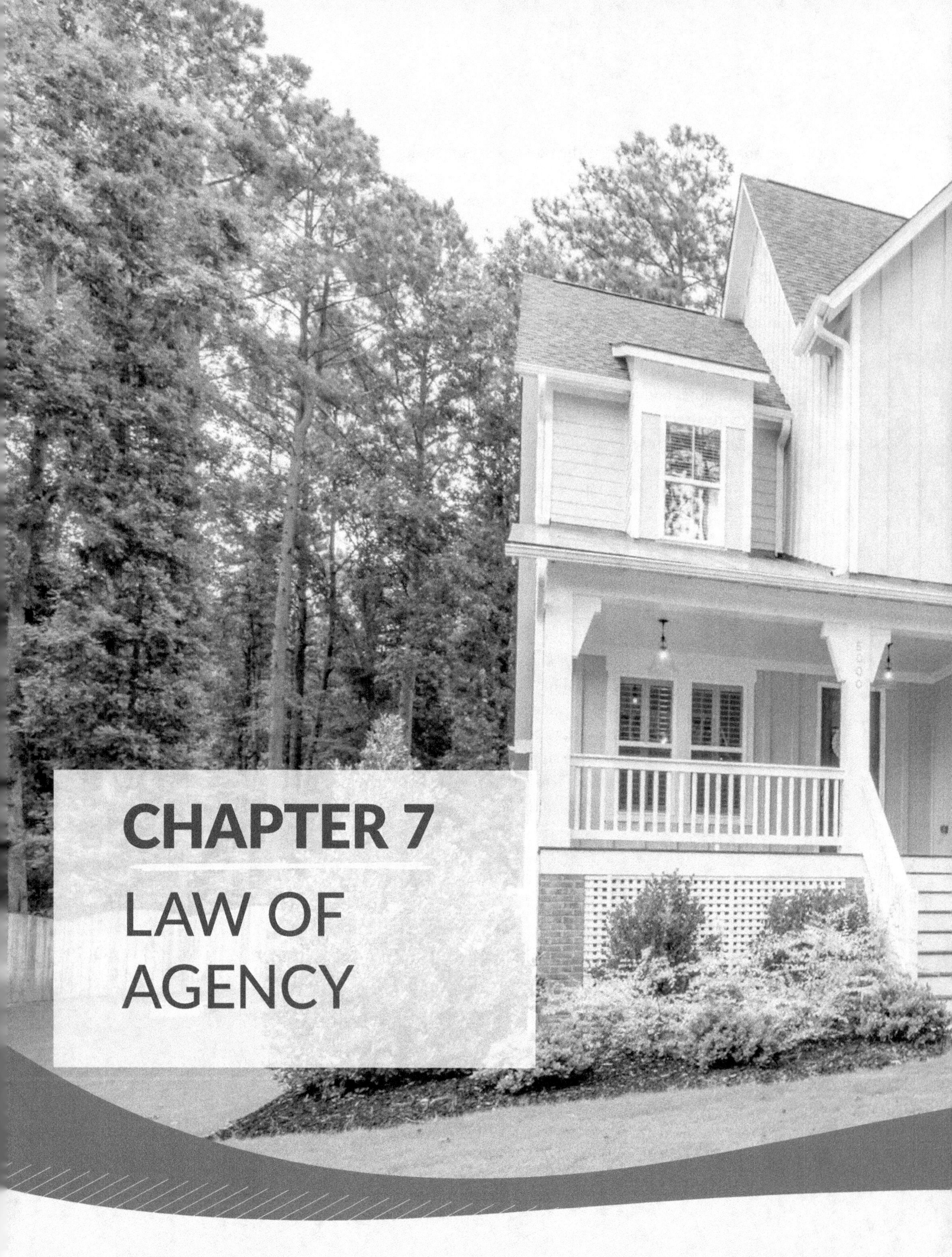

CHAPTER 7
LAW OF AGENCY

US
Realty School

CONCEPT OF AGENCY

AGENCY is a legal concept that refers to the relationship between the parties to a transaction. The concept of an agency establishes that once an agent/broker enters into a contract with a party, they are obligated to that party, or they owe that party fiduciary obligations whether or not money has changed hands.

Agency is created when a party either hires or enters into a contract with a real estate agent/broker. In a real estate transaction, the agency relationship is between the real estate broker and the client.

The terms agent and broker are used interchangeably in the real estate industry. The real estate licensee who is working for a broker is called an agent. The broker is the legal representative of the client and is also referred to as the agent.

The real estate laws used to view the creation of an agency as between the real estate agent and the party that was paying for the services. The seller was generally the party that paid the commission to the real estate agents; therefore, the seller was the party protected under the concept of agency. The buyer was not considered to be a part of the agency. It became apparent that the buyer was not being properly protected by the law as it was written. A buyer could spend months working with an agent that they believed was looking out for their best interest, when in reality, the agent owed their fiduciary relationship to the seller.

The law did change and now the real estate agent owes their fiduciary obligations to the party that has hired them. For further information, see www.leginfo.ca.gov. If an agent is working with the buyer, they owe the buyer their fiduciary obligations and if the agent is working with the seller, the fiduciary obligation is owed to the seller. The seller generally continues to be the party that pays the commissions to the agents/brokers involved in a transaction.

Real estate commissions are not paid until they are earned, and, in the eyes of the law, they are not earned until the transaction successfully closes. The real estate agent is not owed any commissions if the transaction does not close successfully. Expenses paid to others on behalf of the client can be charged in order to pay the outside provider, such as the cost to obtain an appraisal.

FIDUCIARY RELATIONSHIP

A FIDUCIARY RELATIONSHIP OR OBLIGATION is one of trust and loyalty to the party that has hired another to perform a service. All parties to real estate transactions have certain obligations to all other parties of the transaction. It is good to remember that the client is the "boss" during the time it takes to complete the transaction. The client cannot, however, obstruct the agent's activities within the laws, rules, and regulations of real estate. **A client has the right to cancel the contract or fire the agent if they are unhappy with the agent's work.** All parties must agree to the cancellation of a contract. Refusal to cancel by the agent/broker may cause bad feelings and inhibit future business and referrals.

OBLIGATION TO USE DUE DILIGENCE IS THE DUTY OF THE AGENTS to a real estate transaction and in all that they do in relation to the completion of the transaction. The real estate agent must do everything that they can and do it to the best of their ability to see that their client receives the best services the agent can provide.

The **fiduciary** or the person that has entered into a fiduciary relationship owes their client the following:

- **HONESTY AND GOOD FAITH OR FAIR DEALING** should always be the norm when working with clients. It is expected and should be provided. When working under a license from the DRE and working for a broker, the agent owes a fiduciary relationship to the client, either buyer or seller, and to their employing broker. **Being honest about the details of the transaction is necessary because a party to a transaction cannot make the proper decisions regarding the transaction if they do not know the facts.** Making wrong or bad decisions can only cause problems in the future and lead to potential lawsuits and even the loss of one's real estate license.

- **OBEDIENCE** to the client is one of the most important fiduciary obligations an agent owes. An agent must always consider the client's interests first. The client hires the agent and expects the agent to take care of their needs. Real estate agents are in control of what happens to their client's home and finances. **These are the largest, most important, and certainly the most emotional business transactions most people ever enter into.** Obeying the requests of a client may require such things as not placing a lock box on the property because they wish to control access to their home. The client's requests should be obeyed at all times.

  Example: *Agent Lopez meets with his client, Mr. Seller, to list the property. Mr. Seller informs Agent Lopez that he does not want any people of a certain race or religion to be shown his property. He also states that he will not accept any offers from such people. Agent Lopez informs Mr. Seller that he cannot fulfill that request because it is illegal. Mr. Seller insists that that is how it will be. Agent Lopez must refuse the listing under these circumstances.*
  - *Accepting such a listing is ethically and legally wrong.*
  - *Doing so may cause his license to be evoked.*
  - *Doing so may cause his broker to be fined, sued, and lose their license.*
  - *Doing so violates his fiduciary relationship by not being able to be obedient.*

NOTE

If a client makes a request that is illegal, the agent should let the client know that it is illegal and that they will not and cannot perform the duties with such requests in place. If the client refuses to remove the request or condition, the agent should refuse the client's business.

- **LOYALTY** is an **absolute** requirement on the part of the agent. The agent's loyalty must be held as a matter of respect for the person(s) being represented.

  An example of a situation that will constitute loyalty is when a client informs their agent that they will accept a certain amount if they must but prefer not to. This is a statement the agent should keep in the back of their mind, but not to tell the buyer's agent.

- **CONFIDENTIALITY** is expected in the real estate business as in any business transaction. The agent for a buyer or seller will be privy to many personal facts that are not meant for public knowledge, such as the client's personal finances or marital problems. An agent should never be involved in gossip in regard to a client transaction.

- **FULL DISCLOSURE** of **material facts (transfer disclosure statement)** in regard to a real estate transaction is a fundamental element of an open and honest transaction, and fair dealing. As stated earlier, a party to a transaction cannot make a good decision if they do not know all of the facts. It may feel uncomfortable giving bad news, but the sooner it is done the better. It is better to walk away from a bad transaction than to suffer the consequences.

  Example: *Agent Long saw the water stains on the ceiling of the subject property when he originally inspected the property and took the listing. He advised the seller to paint the ceiling and repair the roof as part of making the property look its best. When Agent Long sat down with the seller to complete the transfer disclosure statement (TDS) (to be discussed further), the seller did not mention the leaking roof. Agent Long asked the seller if the roof had been repaired and was told, "No, but if it doesn't rain, no one will know." Agent Long must disclose this fact to the potential buyer and their agent and require that the seller disclose these facts on the TDS.*

CREATION OF AGENCY

CREATION OF AGENCY occurs when a client or principal enters into a contract agreement or a verbal agreement with an agent or fiduciary to provide a service on the principal's behalf. *When a seller signs a listing agreement with an agent, (fiduciary relationship), an agency is created.*

PARTIES TO AN AGENCY RELATIONSHIP and, therefore, a fiduciary relationship include:

- **CLIENT OR PRINCIPAL:** Person or party who hires another to act on their behalf. *An example of a client or principal is a homeowner who wishes to sell their home, and they hire a real estate agent to act on their behalf.*

- **AGENT OR FIDUCIARY:** A party hired to perform a service for a fee. Under the *California Department Real Estate* (DRE), **only the broker is the agent.** ***A real estate salesperson licensee cannot enter into a contract independently.***
- **THIRD PARTY:** One with whom the agent conducts business on behalf of the principal, usually referring to potential buyers. This may also refer to others such as the escrow officer.
- **SUB-AGENT:** Is usually considered to be the buyer's agent. The party who has the listing is the seller's agent. Any other agents obtaining a purchase offer or working with the buyer is a sub-agent to the listing agent.

Following the change that made the buyer's agent truly an agent for the buyer and not the seller, the term "third party" lost its original meaning. The third party to a transaction was considered to be the buyer because all agents owed their fiduciary relationship to the seller because the seller was the party paying the commission. The term third party still means the buyer; however, it no longer carries the same connotation. Third parties may now be considered the "other parties," such as the escrow officer, appraiser, pest inspector, etc.

SUB-AGENT Agents representing buyers are sub-agents of the listing agent. The term originated based on the principle that the seller paid the commission; therefore, both the seller's agent and the buyer's agent worked for the seller, making the buyer's agent a sub-agent to the seller's agent and still applies. *A* ***sub-agent is not an associate licensee*** *who works for a broker who is the agent. It would be easy to construe the definition to fit that role, but the agent who works for a broker is an associate licensee.*

A SPECIAL AGENT is one who is hired to perform one particular service, and when that **job is completed, the agency agreement ends**. Real estate agents most often work as special agents.

> ***Example:*** *Agent Wong is hired to list and find a ready, willing, and able buyer for seller Joe's property. Agent Wong works diligently to market the property and finds a buyer for the property. The sale transaction is completed when escrow closes. The job that Seller Joe hired Agent Wong to perform is now completed and the agency agreement ends.*

A **special agency** would also end or cancel if a contract such as a listing agreement **expired** without finding a buyer. If the seller signed a new listing agreement with Agent Wong or with another agent, a new agency would be created.

NOTE

The special agency is created for the performance of one job or service only.

GENERAL AGENT This agency relationship is created when a broker is hired to perform ongoing jobs and duties. In the real estate industry, a property manager is an example of a general agent. A property owner hires a property manager to manage the property. The duties of a property manager will be ongoing, and the agency relationship will not terminate until the employment contract ends, which may be for months or years. A property manager will be responsible for any or all of the following duties:

- Show rentals units to potential tenants.
- Prepare leases.
- Collect rents.
- Maintain property.
- Manage or oversee maintenance work.

The work would be ongoing for an indeterminate period of time. A general agency is the result of such an employment contract because it is not for the purpose of performing one specific job or duty, but for multiple jobs for an extended period of time.

DUAL AGENCY situations occur when a broker is representing both the buyer and seller or both sides in a real estate transaction. A conflict of interest can arise easily in a real estate transaction, especially when working as a special agent. A conflict of interest between the parties involved can have a devastating effect on a real estate transaction if not handled properly. The most common incident of conflict of interest in the real estate industry takes place when the agent is a dual agent or in a dual agency situation.

> ***Example:*** *Agent Mary has a property listed for sale owned by Seller Smith. During an open house that Agent Mary holds at the property, she meets Buyer Jones and writes an offer to purchase the property from Seller Smith. The offer is accepted by Seller Smith and escrow is opened. Agent Mary provides both Seller Smith and Buyer Jones with an* ***agency disclosure*** *which reveals to them that Agent Mary is representing both parties.*

*Seller Smith is comfortable with Agent Mary representing both parties, which is known as **dual agency**. Buyer Jones is not comfortable. Buyer Jones now wonders if they might have been able to purchase the home for less money if they had been represented by an agent who did not also represent the seller.*

Agent Mary suggests another agent in her office but must disclose that this will also be a dual agency. Agent Mary also asks Buyer Jones if they know of an agent who they would prefer to work with. Buyer Jones considers the matter and decides that, even though another agent in Agent Mary's office will still constitute a dual agency, the situation will make it easier for the two agents to work together to complete the transaction. Buyer Jones agrees to the dual agency arrangement that will involve another agent in Agent Mary's office.

A **dual agency** must be clearly disclosed to all parties to the transaction. A dual agency also occurs when the buyer's agent and seller's agent both work for the same broker, whether in the same office or in separate branch offices under the same broker. The logic behind a dual agency being created is that when the agents work for the same broker, the associate licensees that work for the broker are not legally the agents; only the broker can be the agent. Because of this legality, the broker is a dual agent, not the individual sales associates.

A client may not want their agent to represent both parties in the transaction. Many people believe that it is impossible to represent both sides and be equitable to both. This is a valid argument and must be the decision of the clients.

If a client does not want their agent to represent both, they have the right to choose another agent or request that the other party choose another agent. Before an agent recommends a client to an agent who works in the same office or for the same broker, the parties to the transaction need to be given the facts. Again, it is the decision of the clients involved in the transaction to accept or reject an agent in the same office. Clients may still feel that this is too close and that they cannot be represented as a conflict of interest may occur.

An agent acting as a dual agent in a transaction must be careful not to disclose pertinent information. As in any real estate transaction, the price, terms, and motivation must never be disclosed to the other party without written permission from the party concerned.

SINGLE AGENCY occurs when the parties to a real estate transaction are represented by different agents who work under separate brokers. *This does not include agents who work for the same broker, but in a different branch office.*

An **AGENCY DISCLOSURE STATEMENT** OR **DISCLOSURE REGARDING REAL ESTATE AGENCY AGREEMENT** is a form that is required by the DRE to be completed and given to all parties to a real estate transaction involving one-to-four-unit residential dwellings by the real estate agents. The purpose of the form is to disclose the facts about agency and declare the type of agency in the current transaction.

The agency disclosure must be given to the seller of real property when the listing agreement is signed and to the buyer when the purchase offer is signed. If the seller's agent also becomes the buyer's agent, the agent must provide a new one to the seller disclosing the dual agency.

The **AGENCY DISCLOSURE STATEMENT** explains the fiduciary duties of the seller's agent and of the buyer's agent. The disclosure then explains what a dual agency is and what the ramifications are. There is a place for both the seller and buyer to sign the disclosure stating and verifying that they have been provided with the disclosure and the explanation. The agents for the transaction each sign the form and declare which party they represent and if they are a single agent or a dual agent. Each party to the transaction is given a copy of the disclosure for their records and a copy is provided to each broker to be maintained in the transaction file. One of the purposes of this disclosure is to allow the agent to:

- **Disclose** the nature of an agency.
- **Elect** the party or parties they are representing.
- **Confirm** their involvement to the clients.

The type of the real estate transaction the agent has been hired to perform is essentially an employment relationship. As stated earlier, the principal hires the real estate agent to perform a job or duty. This applies to both a special agency and a general agency.

When we refer to a **PRINCIPAL** in a real estate employment relationship, we are speaking of any of the following:

- **Seller** of real property.
- **Buyer** looking to purchase property.
- **Landlord** hiring a property manager.
- **Borrower** hiring a mortgage broker or loan officer to secure financing for real property.

An employment relationship or agency can be created in several different ways. In the real estate industry, the creation of a relationship is generally done by:

- EXPRESS AGREEMENT
- RATIFICATION
- ESTOPPEL, IMPLIED AGENCY, OSTENSIBLE AGENCY

1. **EXPRESS AGREEMENT** is created when the parties involved acknowledge that an agreement has been reached, such as when a seller of real property calls a real estate agent, and they mutually agree that the agent will be hired to sell the property on behalf of the seller. According to the ***Equal Dignities Rule***, the agreement does not need to be in writing unless it is required by law, or the agent is hired to perform an act that must be written.

   The ***Statute of Frauds*** designates that contracts must be in writing in order to be enforceable. The rules that apply to real estate contracts and transactions in California real estate law are required as follows:

   - **Employment agreements** between real estate broker and associate licensee must be in writing.
   - **Contracts for the sale of real property** that authorize an agent to find a purchaser for real property must be in writing.
   - **Lease of real property** for a term of longer than one year must be in writing. "Longer than one year" means twelve months and one day or longer; however, it is common practice to have any leases of twelve months also in writing.

NOTE

All contracts regarding real estate transactions in California must be in writing.

2. **RATIFICATION (AUTHORIZATION), or subsequent ratification,** creates an agreement through a contract that is subsequent to an action, or the contract is written after the action.

 Example: *Agent Smith is asked to keep an eye on his neighbor, Mr. Green's house while he is out of town for a week. Mr. Green asks him to go into the house to check on it and Mr. Green gives Agent Smith a key. Agent Smith meets Buyer Jones who describes the home that he is looking for and the description seems to fit that of Mr. Green's home. Agent Smith remembers having several conversations with Mr. Green about listing his home for sale. Mr. Green has told him that he is considering selling his home and when he is ready, he will list the property with Agent Smith.*

 Based on the conversations with Mr. Green that he may be interested in selling, Agent Smith shows Mr. Green's property to the Buyer Jones. Buyer Jones wants the home and Agent Smith prepares the written purchase offer. When Mr. Green returns from his trip, Agent Smith presents him with the offer. Mr. Green accepts the purchase offer from Buyer Jones. Agent Smith has also prepared a listing agreement to be signed by Mr. Green if in fact he is interested in entertaining the offer. Mr. Green signs the listing agreement after the purchase offer, making this an agreement by ratification or a subsequent ratification agreement.

 It is important for the real estate professional not to reveal the name of any potential buyers or clients to the seller or the opposite party to a transaction. If the opposite party knows the identity of the interested party, they may choose to bypass the real estate agent.

3. **ESTOPPEL AGREEMENT/ implied agency/ostensible agency** is created when a person declares that a particular agent is representing them in the performance of a job or duty. Once an individual states that the agent is representing them, they are committed to that agent and may owe them a commission if a resultant transaction closes.

 Example: *Mary is thinking about selling a property that she owns and has been renting to Tenant Dave. She has spoken to Agent Joe but has not made a final decision about selling. Mary is speaking with Tenant Dave about the house, and he expresses a desire to purchase the property.*

> *Mary is not sure about the price or other details, so she tells Tenant Dave that Agent Joe is representing her as the agent. Tenant Dave contacts Agent Joe and they write an offer to purchase. Mary accepts the offer, and they open escrow. Mary owes Agent Joe a commission because she told Tenant Dave that Joe was her agent and Agent Joe performed the duties of Mary's Agent based on Mary's declaration.*

This is also known as **IMPLIED AGENCY** because the property owner implied that there was already a relationship or agency. Another term for this type of agreement is **ostensible agency.**

AGENCY AGREEMENTS

AGENCY AGREEMENTS are the contracts that create an agency or are used as a part of the transaction that is a result of an agency. *Chapter 8: Real Estate Contracts* discusses the various contracts that are commonly used in real estate transactions.

VALID REAL ESTATE CONTRACTS must meet certain requirements to be considered valid:

- **The consent** of both parties to the terms of the contract must be verified by execution or signing of the contract.
- **Legal purpose** A contract cannot have an unlawful objective.
- **Consideration** must be included as a means of providing an obligation from both parties.

To demonstrate this: A **real estate listing agreement** requires the agent to find a **ready, willing, and able buyer** for the listed property. This is a **unilateral contract**, which is one that is one-sided, or requires the commitment of only one party. In a listing agreement, the seller is not committing to anything until a buyer is found. At that point, the listing agreement is replaced with a purchase offer which is a **bilateral contract,** meaning that it is a two-sided agreement, which is reciprocal by both parties or both parties are committing to perform an act.

When the agent agrees to the listing contract by signing, the agent makes a commitment to perform due diligence in finding a buyer. Likewise, the seller makes a commitment when they agree to the terms of the listing contract and sign.

Both parties have given consent by signing; the contract does not require an illegal act from either party, and they have both committed to performing a duty giving consideration to the other party.

The listing agreement is a **UNILATERAL AGREEMENT** because only the real estate agent is making a promise to perform. The duty of the seller is not required unless the agent performs successfully, at which time the purchase contract will replace the unilateral listing agreement. The **BILATERAL PURCHASE CONTRACT** requires a commitment to perform by both parties to the transaction.

***Bilateral** is based on the base "Bi" from the Latin for "two" which refers to a two-sided contract versus a **unilateral** contract from the base word "Uni" meaning one.*

Authority for a real estate transaction is declared in the contract to be used for a particular service. The authority derived by the real estate agent on behalf of the principal is limited in as much as the property owner is the "boss" of the real estate transaction because they hired the agent and they own the property, so the final decisions belong to the property owner. However, the real estate agent must be in charge because of the laws that control transactions involving one-to-four-unit residential properties. It is of the utmost importance for the real estate agent to remember that the property in question belongs to the principal. It is their home and the largest investment that most people make in their lifetime. The final decision as far as price and terms is that of the property owner, not the real estate agent, although the agent's expertise is important to the successful completion of a successful transaction.

- **The ACTUAL AUTHORITY** of the agent is specified in the agency disclosure with the specifics for the particular job in the real estate contract such as the listing agreement or the purchase offer. The duties include authority that is spelled out. For example, a listing agreement authorizes the agent to show and advertise the property.

NOTE

*Commissions paid for real estate services in the State of California are **always negotiable.** Any predetermination of a commission rate is considered a violation of the **Sherman Anti-Trust Act. Seller and broker may negotiate any rate that is agreeable to both.***

NOTE

The duties and obligations required by the agent to a real estate transaction are defined and declared in the agency agreement.

- **INHERENT AUTHORITY** is part of any real estate contract. Depending on the nature of the contract and the resultant duties, there are additional duties that the agent needs to perform even though they are not specified in the employment contract. Such duties are referred to as **due diligence,** or the work of the agent to perform the duties required by the contract based on laws and customs. Due diligence in performing the job which are considered to be inherent duties may include actions such as calling clients and other agents that may be interested in a new listing, placing Open House signs in conspicuous places to advertise, creating fliers and brochures to advertise a property. These are not duties that are necessarily specified in a listing agreement, yet they are inherent in the job of being a real estate professional who lists a property for sale.

- **APPARENT AUTHORITY** carries no obligation with the party that the agent is representing. When an agent acts in a way that is not specified in the contract and the **agent is not authorized**, however, the agent acts based on the fact that there is a contract, and the act must be performed. An example of this would be that the agent is not authorized to make any repairs or improvements to the property. There are, however, occasions when the agent would authorize repairs in case of an emergency, such as leaking water pipes when the property owner is unavailable or out of town. The agent would order the repair, and the authority would be apparent based on the fact the agent has a contract with the property owner. The agent may be liable for the buyer's expenses and the buyer may have the right to file a complaint with the ***Real Estate Commissioner*** for fraud and misrepresentation. Disciplinary action may adversely affect the agent's license and the ability to make a living.

DEPOSITS

HANDLING DEPOSITS by a real estate agent/broker is one of the most crucial duties of the agent/broker. When a buyer makes an offer to purchase, consideration is required for the contract to be valid. This means that the buyer must provide a deposit. The deposit funds or earnest money is generally in the form of a check that can be cashed immediately. The term "earnest money" is a somewhat antiquated real estate term that was derived from the word earnest, which means serious in intention.

NOTE

Real estate licensees must always exercise caution and care when assuming authorization on behalf of a property owner in regard to a transaction. Care and full disclosure are always recommended.

In other words, earnest money is to show that the potential buyer is earnest in their intention to purchase the subject property. Deposit money or deposit funds is the commonly used term; however, the term earnest money may still be used in the real estate industry.

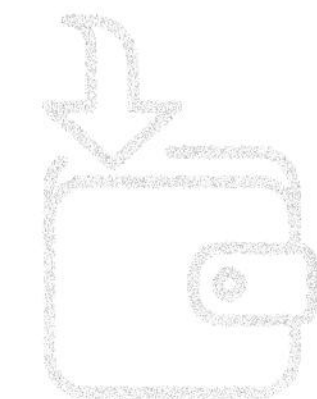

1. **DEPOSIT MONEY** in any form must be deposited within three business days of the offer being accepted into either the escrow company's trust account or into the broker's trust account. The deposit money should never be given directly to the seller except in rare circumstances of the purchase offer. The funds should always be held by a neutral third party for the protection of both parties involved in the transaction. If for any reason the transaction is canceled, a refund and distribution of the deposit money will be considerably easier if held by a neutral third party and not by the seller.

   The deposit funds may never be deposited into the broker's personal account or an account privately held by the associate licensee who wrote the purchase offer.

2. **TRUST FUND ACCOUNTS** are neutral checking accounts that are reserved for the client's funds only. The broker or escrow company cannot have any of their own funds in the trust account with the exception of $200, which is there to prevent any of the client's money from being charged bank fees and to guarantee that there are always sufficient funds to cover checks on behalf of the client. If a personal check for deposit funds was deposited into the trust account and the transaction is canceled, the broker or escrow should not refund the money to the client until the personal check has had time to clear their bank.

   The account must be balanced monthly. Individual accounting for each client must be maintained separately using columnar account methods. A signer for the account must always be available for immediate demand from the client for the funds. A signer can be the broker of record, a licensee in the broker's employment, a non- licensed employee that is bonded, or another broker with written authorization to sign for the broker of record.

3. **COMMINGLING** is the act of placing funds that belong to a client into a personal account or using the trust account for personal use. In other words, commingling is the act of mixing personal funds with client's funds. Commingling is illegal and is not only against DRE Rules & Regulations, but it is also a felony under the federal law ***Real Estate Settlement and Procedures Act (RESPA)***.

4. **CONVERSION** is the act of converting client's funds into personal funds. This act is also a felony. Occasionally, the funds will be in the form of cash, which must be handled quickly and properly to avoid any misconception or mishandling of funds or wrongdoing. The licensee who receives the deposit will show the form in which the funds were received on page one of the purchase offer.

The purchase offer acts as the deposit receipt for the funds; however, when the deposit is in the form of cash, it is recommended that the licensee accepting the deposit also provide the buyer an additional written receipt for the funds. It is recommended that the cash be deposited as soon as possible instead of waiting for three business days or the cash can be transferred into a cashier's check in the buyer's name and designated for that transaction only. The cashier's check can then be attached to the purchase offer for presentation to the seller and their agent.

NOTE

Never attach cash to an offer that is to be delivered to anyone other than the broker of record or the escrow officer.

Deposits can also be delivered in the form of a post-dated check or a promissory note. Both of these forms provide for payment of the deposit funds to be at a later date. This is legal in a real estate transaction, but not recommended. The real estate agent must disclose this form of deposit to the seller and their agent when the purchase offer is presented.

Sellers may base their decision to accept an offer to purchase on the form and amount of the deposit. Post-dated checks and promissory notes indicate that the potential buyer may not have money which ultimately means that they may not be able to complete the transaction.

When presented with this situation, the real estate agent should find out why the potential buyer needs to or wants to provide this type of earnest money deposit. The potential buyer may simply need to transfer funds into a different account. If it is because of lack of funds, the agent should quickly determine if the potential buyer can actually close the purchase transaction by qualifying the potential buyer.

Qualifying will be discussed further in *Chapter 12*. This is a delicate discussion, but one that the real estate agent needs to have with their client as soon as possible.

RIGHTS AND DUTIES

RIGHTS AND DUTIES OF THE REAL ESTATE AGENT will vary based on the duty being performed or the type of contract under which they are working.

BROKER AGENT AGREEMENTS are the first contracts that agents need to work with. Under the licensing laws of the DRE, one must have a real estate broker's license to own a real estate business, whether real estate sales, mortgage brokerage, or property management. Most licensees will obtain their real estate sales license first and work for a real estate broker. When working for a broker, DRE requires all licensees to have a broker agent agreement or contract, providing the terms of that employment arrangement.

CONTRACT EMPLOYEE is the way that most associate licensees will work. A contract employee is required under IRS laws to have an employment contract with their employing broker and report their income by filing an IRS Schedule C, Self-Employed Profit & Loss. A contract employee is basically a self-employed person who is working under the auspices of their broker. The broker will not withhold any taxes from the paychecks or provide any employee benefits such as insurance or unemployment insurance. A contractor will need to maintain records and be prepared to pay their self-employment withholdings and income taxes as a self-employed person.

The **BROKER AGENT EMPLOYMENT CONTRACT** will include the form and term of payment. The typical form of payment is commission and, as stated previously, the commission that the principal pays is first divided between the agents' offices in a purchase transaction and directly to the agent/broker in other real estate transactions such as mortgage brokering.

Example: *$400,000* *Sales Price*
X 6% *Commission Rate*
$24,000 *Commission Earned*
$24,000 ÷ 2 = $12,000 to sellers' agent
$12,000 to Buyers' agent
$12,000
x 55%
$6,600 *Associate Licensee's Commission*

A **CONTRACTOR** will also be in control of their time management. The broker cannot require that the associate licensee be in the office at specified hours.

According to IRS rules, a person is an employee if they have set office/business hours which will require that the agent be paid as a W2 or salaried employee. An associate licensee can work as a W2 employee if the broker chooses to pay that way; however, it is rare.

NOTE

A new associate licensee needs to remember that they are now self- employed and without a regular paycheck and should be prepared to have sufficient savings to cover approximately six months of living expenses. It generally takes that long for a new agent to start making an income.

LISTING AGREEMENTS/CONTRACTS are agreements between a seller of real estate and a real estate agent/broker to list the seller's property for sale to the public. The agent agrees to list, advertise, place a lockbox, and in general perform due diligence to provide the service requested. The ultimate outcome desired for the real estate broker is "to find a ready, willing, and able buyer."

The **seller** agrees to pay the agent a pre-negotiated amount which is usually in the form of a commission. The commission is most commonly a percentage of the sales price.

Example:	*$400,000*	*Sales Price*
	X 6%	*Commission Rate*
	$24,000	*Commission Earned*

The **agent** may be paid in a way other than a percentage of the sales price. The standard listing agreement used by the ***California Association of Realtors (CAR)*** has a space that allows for payment to be a predetermined, set dollar amount or even an hourly rate. Both of these methods of payment are options that are rarely used, but available if desired. They are legal forms of payment for a real estate transaction.

The **LISTING AGREEMENT** is between the seller/principal and the broker. The associate licensee cannot be the direct representative of the client. The *broker agent contract* defines the terms of the agreement between the agent and broker. **The agent or associate licensee represents the broker in a real estate transaction and the broker represents the principal, although the principal might never even meet the broker.** The agent represents the broker and must treat the principal and the transaction with the same ethics, principles, and laws as the broker. This is a legal determination.

REAL ESTATE LISTING AGREEMENTS

WRITTEN FORMS OF REAL ESTATE LISTING AGREEMENTS are summarized as follows:

1. **RESIDENTIAL LISTING AGREEMENT (Exclusive Authorization and Right to Sell Listing)** is currently the most commonly used **listing agreement** in California. This type of listing agreement allows the exclusive broker to be paid as the listing agent, no matter who procures the buyer. The total commission stated in the listing agreement is divided accordingly between the listing broker and the selling broker.
   - A **safety clause** in the listing agreement protects the listing broker from losing a client due to an expiring listing. The safety clause allows the listing broker to reserve any potential buyers they had been working with at the time the listing expires. **The seller will still owe the broker a commission after the expiration date if in fact any of the buyers on the broker's reservation list buys the property.**

   - The **Exclusive Authorization and Right to Sell** allows the broker to advertise the listed property for sale in the ***Multiple Listing Service (MLS)*** which provides an internet website to be shared with the public and also with other member brokers. The rules for advertising with MLS vary. MLS may require that all listings be placed on the service within a certain number of days while others may not require that all listings with a member broker be placed in MLS. The seller/principal has the right to decline listing with the MLS. The listing agreement provides the seller with a space to declare that option.

2. **EXCLUSIVE AGENCY LISTING** allows the broker to advertise and find a buyer or a cooperating broker to sell the property the same as the **Exclusive Authorization and Right to Sell Listing.**

NOTE

A definite termination date is required whenever a real estate broker is the exclusive agent for a seller. The Business and Professions Code calls for the revocation or suspension of a real estate license if the licensee receives any compensation under any Exclusive Listing Agreement if the agreement "does not contain a definite, specified date of final and complete termination."

The main difference between the two types of listings is that the exclusive agency listing allows the seller to find their own buyer without being required to pay commission to a broker.

3. **An OPEN LISTING** is also called a **non-exclusive listing**. The open listing derives its name from the fact that the listing is open to any broker who may procure a buyer, and the seller pays only the procuring broker. The open listing is rarely used in residential real estate because there is no assurance of being paid after doing the work. There is also the issue of verifying the procuring broker, creating disputes as to which broker actually earned the commission. While rarely used for residential property, the open listing.

4. **A NET LISTING** provides the broker's commission to be any amount in excess of the seller's sales price. The seller sets the price they want for the sale of their property and any amount beyond that figure is the broker's compensation for selling the property. The problem with this type of listing is that it lends itself to fraud on the part of the broker or the impression of fraud on the part of the seller. This type of listing is legal but is not advised. The broker is required by law to provide the seller with any anticipated profit as a result of the sale of the property.

   Example: *Seller Sam wants to list his property for sale with Agent Jane. He informs Agent Jane that he wants to clear for himself a dollar amount of $400,000. Anything above that will be her commission. Agent Jane knows that the property is worth $500,000. According to the terms of a net listing, Agent Jane could make $100,000. Agent Jane must disclose this anticipated income to Seller Smith.*

The possibility of fraud is great. If Agent Jane did not disclose the potential income to Seller Sam, Seller Sam could clearly construe her actions as misrepresentation and could file a complaint against her with DRE. It is likely that disclosing such a gain to a seller would most likely have them change their mind about the list price and their potential profit.

NOTE

The real estate professional should always advise their clients in accordance with what is best for the client.

5. **OPTION LISTING** is the exclusive listing of the broker that allows the broker to purchase the property. Like the net listing, full disclosure of anticipated profit is required. This type of listing is also legal, but not advised. Using the previous example:

    Example: *Agent Jane decides to purchase the property from Seller Sam for herself. She decides that she will then put it immediately back on the market for sale and make the $100,000 profit.*

    This does not generally refer to brokers who choose to purchase a home for their own use or to use as rental property; however, the **broker must never take unfair advantage**. When an agent is discussing the sale of a property with a potential client, they must always be honest and fair about the true value even when desiring the property for their own use.

DUTY TO THIRD PARTY

A THIRD PARTY to a transaction is generally the **buyer**. This term is from the time when all agents in a real estate transaction were agents of the seller. The laws regarding real estate most often refer to the seller of real property and many of the forms are directed toward the protection of the seller. The real estate professional must remember that they also owe fiduciary duties to the buyer of real property. If there is no seller, there is no transaction; but without a buyer to purchase a property, there is no transaction. The buyer's interest must also be considered throughout the transaction. **The agent who is representing the buyer owes a fiduciary relationship to their client**.

BUYER REPRESENTATION AGREEMENT is a relatively new contract for the real estate industry. This contract is not necessary to represent a buyer; however, it can help protect an agent from loss of income due to an undedicated buyer and it protects the buyer by defining the agent's duties to the buyer.

The b**uyer representation agreement** is an agreement committing the **buyer to the agent** by providing that the **agent** is paid even if another agent writes the purchase offer for the buyer. This may mean that the buyer is liable to the agent to pay out of their own pocket. This is a relatively new concept and should be approached with some education of the buyer by the agent.

The downside of the agreement is that a buyer may become committed to an agent that they later determine is not who they want to work with. On the other hand, the agent may not want to continue to work with the client.

The upside of the agreement is that the buyer has a committed agent, and one who feels comfortable investing their time and money taking care of a dedicated buyer.

> **NOTE**
> *The real estate professional should be willing to consider cancellation of any contract when warranted.*

Example: *Agent Sue spent many Fridays picking up her clients from LAX airport. She would take them to dinner, and then drop them at their hotel. On Saturdays, she would pick them up and take them to breakfast before spending the day driving the couple around Los Angeles showing properties. Sundays were spent taking the couple to breakfast then back to LAX to fly home.*

This routine continued once or twice a month for six months. Agent Sue had paid a considerable amount of her personal funds taking care of her clients. They called her unexpectedly on a Friday morning and said they would be at LAX that afternoon because the company that was transferring the husband wanted them to move within a month. They needed to find a home right away. Agent Sue picked them up and at dinner and showed them printouts of some of the properties she wanted to show them the next day. Agent Sue had a prior appointment and could not meet the couple until 11:00 a.m.

The next morning, Agent Sue received an excited call from the clients about 10:30 a.m. They had taken the printouts that Agent Sue had left with them and since one was having an open house, they decided to see the house. They loved the house and wrote an offer with the agent who was at the open house, not Agent Sue.

The couple could not understand why Agent Sue was not as happy as they were. Agent Sue did not receive any commission in spite of all her work.

If there had been a **buyer representation agreement** in this example, the buyers would have understood that Agent Sue was not being paid for all of her work and that her broker was not paying for all of the meals, gas, and money spent by Agent Sue. The couple would have known to wait until Agent Sue was available to write the purchase offer on their behalf.

The **buyer representation agreement** is an excellent tool to educate potential buyers regarding the way the real estate industry works, and the agents get paid. **It is often difficult for the average person to comprehend that agents do not earn a salary and are not on an expense account.**

Conversely, the agent owes the buyer due diligence and care in the work being done for the buyer. The real estate professional is considered to be the expert, and clients hire real estate agents because of that.

Easton v. Strassburger is a **real estate lawsuit** that demonstrates the care that an agent owes their client as a fiduciary. This case set precedence and has been the basis for a number new of laws, rules, regulations, and forms such as the transfer disclosure statement (TDS).

The decision derived in the *Easton vs. Strassburger* case determined that the real estate broker is responsible to the buyer to disclose all pertinent information regarding a property. It is the broker's duty to inspect the property to the best of their ability. This inspection does not include inaccessible areas or common areas of a condo or other commonly owned properties. The broker must disclose all information whether desirable or derogatory about the subject property that may affect the value or the habitability. The ***California legislature*** made the broker's duties a part of the ***California Civil Code*, beginning in *Section 2079*.** The laws apply to all one-to-four-unit residential dwellings.

The ***Easton v. Strassburger*** case involved a house that was built on a landfill. One of the agents noticed that the floor in one place was uneven, which usually indicates a cracked foundation. This fact should have sent up a red flag, encouraging further investigation. The seller of the property knew there had been land slippage and had reinforced a slope, and the swimming pool that had been damaged by the slippage was repaired. The seller knew that it would cost more than the property was worth to repair the problems caused by the settling of the landfill that was occurring. **None of this information was disclosed to the buyer.**

Property inspections were not used regularly at that time unless requested by the buyer. An inspection was not ordered because no one disclosed any of the information regarding the condition of the property.

The broker and the seller were both found to be responsible for the buyer's losses. The determination that resulted was that the broker needed to be cognizant of anything that may affect the value and habitability of the property, and the **broker is responsible to any buyer of real property to disclose all information that they did know and should have known. The broker is responsible for accessible areas only and is not responsible for any common areas of a condo or otherwise commonly owned property.**

> ***Example:*** *Buyer Tom was being transferred from Michigan to California. He contacted Agent Smith, and they worked online and by fax to get the transaction completed. Buyer Tom had not physically been to the property he was purchasing but had been assured by Agent Smith that everything was in order and "move-in ready."*
>
> *Buyer Tom arrived at the property with the moving van ready to move in. Tom used the restroom and discovered that the toilet did not have water to flush. He turned on the faucet in the sink and there was no water. Buyer Tom went through the house trying every faucet to find that none were working. When he went outside and looked under the house, he found that there was no plumbing in the house. The seller had been in the middle of replacing the plumbing when they received the offer to purchase from Buyer Tom. The seller decided to stop the work and save the money since the house was sold.*
>
> *The seller and Agent Smith were responsible for completing the plumbing job. They were also required to reimburse Buyer Tom for his added expenses incurred by staying in a hotel and storage of his belongings while the work was being done.*
>
> *Agent Smith* ***should have known that the plumbing job was being done and he should have known there was no water in the house****, making him equally responsible as the seller. The moral is to always turn on faucets when walking through a house with clients.*

Since the *Easton v. Strassburger* court action, inspections have become a regular part of a real estate transaction. The *Real Estate Transfer Disclosure Statement (TDS)* was also a result of this action.

NOTE

The real estate professional is responsible for knowing what needs to be known about a property. It has been determined that the agent/broker is responsible for what they do know and what they should know.

TRANSFER DISCLOSURE STATEMENT

Transfer Disclosure Statement (TDS) is a form that is required by law to be completed by the seller of one-to-four-unit residential dwellings. The disclosure provides for the seller to notify the buyer of real property of any defects or problems that they are aware of with the subject property such as a leaking roof or non-working dishwasher. The disclosure also informs the buyer of what is included in the sale such as the appliances, screens for windows and doors, and the type of furnace.

The **seller must complete their designated section**. The **agent cannot complete it for the seller.** The seller must disclose everything they know about the condition of the property. It is assumed that the property owner knows the property better than anyone. The exceptions to a seller providing a TDS are:

- Sale between co-owners
- Probate sale
- Foreclosure sale

All other **sales of one-to-four-unit residential dwellings** will require a **TDS** be provided to the buyer by the seller.

The **agent** must also complete a section of the TDS once the seller has completed their section. The **agent must disclose all that they know about the property.**

The purpose of this disclosure is to inform the buyer as much as possible about the actual condition and state of the property they are purchasing. This allows the buyer to make an educated decision. The disclosure of defects of a property does not require repairs, it only informs. The disclosure is to be delivered to the buyer as soon as practical after acceptance of the purchase offer.

The buyer has the right to cancel the transaction within three days of receipt of the TDS if it is hand delivered to them or within five days if the TDS is mailed to them. If the buyer does not receive a copy of the TDS, they may cancel the transaction at any time prior to the close of escrow.

NOTE

The real estate professional should provide the disclosure to the seller for completion within a day or two of the offer acceptance, then deliver to the buyer immediately.

TERMINATION OF AN AGENCY

TERMINATION OF AN AGENCY AGREEMENT can be accomplished in several ways.

- **CANCELLATION OF A CONTRACT** can be by either party. It does take the agreement of all parties to a contract to cancel it because it is a legally binding agreement.

- **PERFORMANCE** is the most desirable and obvious way to successfully complete the transaction and fulfill the contract. Once the contract is **COMPLETED**, it is terminated.

- **EXPIRATION** of a contract constitutes termination. Real estate contracts require expiration dates. If the date has passed and the terms of the contract have not been met, the contract expires with no further obligation by either party. As stated previously, a listing agreement contains a clause allowing the agent to earn the commission if one of their potential buyers purchases the property after the expiration of the listing as long as the agent had disclosed their list of potential buyers to the seller at expiration of the contract.

  Expiration of a contract that is in the process is usually continued such as a purchase transaction that is in escrow and within days of closing should be addressed by the buyer's agent by notifying the seller through their agent that they need an extension of the contract stating the number of days needed and the status of the transaction. The principals of any real estate contract have the right to cancel an expired contract even if it is within a day of closing. Communication is imperative to all parties to a contract, but this is especially true with one that is going to expire before it can be completed.

- **MUTUAL RESCISSION** occurs when both parties to the contract agree to cancel the transaction contract. This is a bilateral agreement and must be ratified by both parties to be canceled by mutual rescission.

  When a buyer or seller is committed to a purchase agreement and one of the parties chooses to cancel, there are issues to be addressed such as distribution of the deposit money. Distribution of the funds is handled by escrow and will not be completed until there is agreement by both parties about the distribution.

  Arbitration or lawsuits may arise as a result.

The purchase offer contains contingencies and if the contingencies cannot be met according to the terms of the contract, the buyer has a right to cancel the contract without reproach and the deposit money is refunded in full. This is a mutual rescission based on the terms of the purchase agreement because both parties accepted the offer with the contingencies included. A typical example of not meeting a contingency is when the appraised value is less than the agreed-on purchase price.

- **DESTRUCTION OF IMPROVEMENTS** automatically cancels a real estate transaction. The contract for a purchase transaction is canceled when the property is no longer in the condition that the offer is based on. The lender in a purchase transaction will not fund a loan on property that has been destroyed. This will apply also to a refinance transaction. In the case of a property manager, there is no longer property to manage; however, this statement is based on the presumption of total destruction and the lack of habitability. The property management contract may continue based on future business needs.

- DEATH OR BANKRUPTCY OF THE PRINCIPAL OR THE BROKER terminates a contract. If the seller or buyer of a property is deceased, the transaction cannot be completed, and the contract is terminated.

  The death of the broker of record to a transaction will also terminate a contract. If the broker of record dies, all of the files in the company are canceled because the broker owns all of the files. *The death of a salesperson who works for the broker will not affect the status of a real estate transaction.* The broker is the agent no matter who is working directly with the principal.

  A **principal** may have any number of reasons for canceling and their wishes should be respected. A principal may decide that they do not want to sell their home, or a buyer may have found a house they like better. A borrower may decide that a new loan is not going to work for them, or they have found a lender who will do the loan for less. The real estate professional should always ask questions to try to remedy the situation and also to protect themselves from unscrupulous clients. At times, a seller/principal will find a buyer and not want to pay the commission. Talking to the client and asking the right questions along with keeping an open mind can usually save a contract. There are times when the client is just not happy with the agent for any number of reasons. If the agent/client relationship is not good, it may be best to allow the cancellation of a contract. Refusing to cancel a real estate contract when requested by a client can only lead to hard feelings and lack of referral or repeat business.

CHAPTER 8

REAL ESTATE CONTRACTS

US
Realty School

DEFINITION OF A CONTRACT

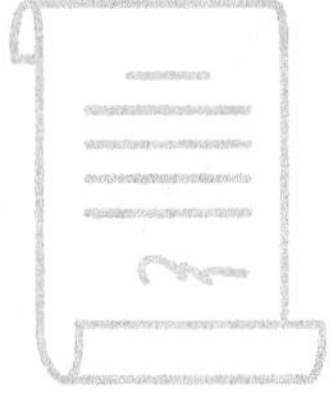

CONTRACT is an agreement between parties to perform an act or not to perform an act, or to fulfill a promise based on terms which can be upheld by law. The commitment that the parties to a contract make is a referred to as a **contractual obligation**. A valid contract requires that each party be contractually obligated to perform the duties or promise as specified in the contract. A contract must meet certain requirements to be considered valid or enforceable by law.

If any of the parties to a contract fails to fulfill their contractual obligations, they are considered to be in breach of contract. The breaching party or the party who does not fulfill their obligations may be liable to the non-breaching party of the contract because of their failure to perform. The liabilities may result in a lawsuit for monetary or financial losses and damages or for specific performance. (Specific performance is the requirement of the breaching party to complete the contract as originally agreed.)

BILATERAL CONTRACTS/AGREEMENTS are those that are committing both parties such as both the buyer and the seller. In an offer to purchase, the buyer is promising to pay a certain amount of money to purchase the property, and the seller is promising to deliver the property with equitable title to the seller.

UNILATERAL CONTRACTS/AGREEMENTS require a commitment from only one of the parties to a contract. An option to buy is a unilateral contract. The offeree, or the property owner, is promising to sell the property *if* the offeror ***decides*** to buy.
The offeree is committed to sell. The offeror is not committed to buy. If the offeror decides to buy, the option agreement then becomes a purchase offer, and at that time the contract becomes bilateral.

Example: *The Smiths have been renting a home from Mr. Jones. The Smiths approach Mr. Jones and tell him they would like to purchase the home but will not be in a position to do so for two years. Mr. Jones agrees to enter into an option to buy an agreement for a two-year period. The Smiths make a deposit of $5,000 as consideration and agree to continue to pay rent to Mr. Smith as agreed.*

Mr. Jones cannot sell the property to anyone else and is committed to the contract with a promise to sell the property if the Smiths decide to purchase the home in two years' time for the price agreed to today.

After twenty months, Mr. Jones is offered more for the property than the Smiths have agreed to pay. He wants to accept the new offer and gives the Smiths back the $5,000 deposit. If the Smiths accept the money, the contract is considered rescinded. Action must be taken within a reasonable amount of time or lack of action is considered acceptance. If the Smiths return the deposit money to Mr. Jones, the contract stands, and Mr. Jones is committed to selling to the Smiths as agreed. Mr. Jones is legally bound to perform per the terms of the contract.

ESSENTIAL ELEMENTS OF A CONTRACT

ESSENTIAL ELEMENTS OF A CONTRACT must be present in real estate contracts in California for a contract to be considered valid. The following are the essential elements required:

- **Consent**
- **Capacity**
- **Consideration**
- **Lawful objective**

A. **CONSENT OR MUTUAL AGREEMENT** is also called a meeting of the minds. The parties to the contract must agree to all of the terms as specified and the intent of the contract in order to have a "meeting of the minds." To reach a meeting of the minds, there must be **contractual intention** that occurs when both parties fully intend to meet the terms of the contract.

The **offer** of a contract is made by the offeror to the offeree. The offer may then be accepted or rejected. If accepted, the acceptance of the offer must then be communicated to the offeror before the contract is actually considered to be accepted. The offeror has the right to cancel the offer of a contract any time prior to being informed that the offer was accepted. Once the acceptance of the offer has been received by the offeror, there is a meeting of the minds, and the contract is legally binding.

If the offeree did not accept the contract, but did provide a counteroffer, the original contract is considered declined and the counteroffer becomes the offer, making the original offeror the party that is now receiving the offer or the offeree. The original offeree then becomes the offeror because the counteroffer is now the offer.

Revocation of the offer can occur at any time prior to the acceptance of a contract being communicated.

> ***Example:*** *Sam writes an offer to purchase the property owned by George. George has decided to accept the offer, but he has not returned the signed contract to Sam when Sam decides to rescind his offer. Sam contacts George and informs him that he is canceling the offer. George protests that he has already signed the offer.*
>
> *Sam does have the right to cancel the contract because he had not been told that the offer was accepted. It probably would have been advisable for Sam to have provided George with a written cancellation, but it does stand because George did not communicate to Sam that he accepted the offer prior to Sam communicating his rescission.*

FRAUD OR MISREPRESENTATION cannot be present or a part of a contract for there to be a meeting of the minds. The following issues fall under the categories of fraud and misrepresentation.

- **NEGLIGENCE** OR **MISREPRESENTATION** is the intent to deceive the other party. Criminal penalty will not apply for negligence or misrepresentation, but the contract may be considered voidable.
- **PUFFING** is a form of **misrepresentation**. The act of puffing is stating that something is **more than it is** such as the statement, "this is the best house on the block."
- **FRAUD,** or **actual fraud,** is the known **intent** by the party to **deceive** the other parties to a contract. **Fraud may constitute a felony.**
- **NO DURESS OR MENACE,** meaning **no force or threat,** is allowable or acceptable when working under contract or in the creation of a contract. **Duress** is putting pressure on a person to perform an act such as telling a person that if their yard is not maintained in a certain way, the property will be taken away from them. Threatening a property owner with harm is a menace. The elderly are often taken advantage of by use of either duress or menace.

- **UNDUE INFLUENCE OR UNFAIR ADVANTAGE** is not acceptable. If one party to a real estate transaction has knowledge of the property that the other party does not have, the party may have an unfair advantage.

  Example: *Agent Tom knows that a large lot is being purchased for the purpose of building luxury homes. He takes a listing on a home in the adjacent neighborhood of moderate homes. Agent Tom lists the home below market value then proceeds to make an offer on the home and purchases the home for considerably less than it should have sold for.*

  Agent Tom has used ***unfair advantage*** *and, therefore, there is not a meeting of the minds. Agent Tom knew that the property values for the adjacent neighborhoods would increase in value because of a new development of luxury homes to be built.*

- A **VOIDABLE CONTRACT** is one that has been created under fraudulent means and may be **voided** by the person injured by the fraudulent act. Action against the party committing fraud must be taken within a reasonable period of time from discovery of the action of fraud as set forth in the ***California Civil Code Statute of Limitations.*** *(To be discussed further under Status of Contracts later in this Chapter.)* The victim of fraud has the right to seek monetary and punitive damages. Criminal charges may also be brought against a perpetrator of fraud which could bring fines and/or imprisonment.
- **FRAUDULENT MISREPRESENTATION** is intentional fraud and carries felony penalties.
- **NEGLIGENT MISREPRESENTATION** is a result of carelessness or negligence and is not done with criminal intent if negligent misrepresentation does not result in criminal penalties; however, the contract is still voidable. Court discipline and civil damages can apply, depending on the degree of neglect and resulting damages.

To avoid negligent or careless acts, the real estate professional should always be fully aware of the subject matter of the contract and definite terms used and required within any contract. A contract should be prepared as completely and efficiently as possible.

NOTE

A real estate licensee who participates in a fraudulent action may lose their license to practice real estate and be fined and/or imprisoned.

The following items are points of particular concern when working with real estate contracts.

- **Adequate description** of the property concerned. The legal description is not necessary, but the description used must be adequate to positively identify the subject property, such as the complete address.
- **Terms** must be clear and concise. Any conditions to the terms or the contract must be understandable by all parties to the contract.
- **Identification of the parties** to the transaction must be as clear as possible. Each individual involved in the transaction should use as full a name as possible for proper identification. Generally, parties to a real estate transaction will use their full given name to avoid common names that others would also be identified by. It is common for persons to use their name as they are commonly known, such as by initials or a shortened form of their name such as "Betty" for "Elizabeth." It is the individual's choice of how they chose to have their name appears in the transaction paperwork, but proper identification is the goal.
- **Price** must always be included in the contract. Having clients sign an incomplete contract is a highly negligent act. Not including the price spelled out in numbers and words can be a disaster for all involved and would be highly negligent. The market value of a property is also an important part of a real estate contract and there should be a contingency to the contract providing for a determination or substantiation of that value by the use of an appraisal.
- **Time** allowed for the performance of the contingencies and conditions of the contract must be included. Real estate contracts carry the adage, "Time is of the essence." This means that the timeframes allowed for in the contract must be given consideration and adhered to as much as possible. There are times when the timeframes cannot be met. When this occurs, the real estate professional should notify the other party to the contract, giving the reason for the delay and requesting a new date or extension which is attainable.

Appraisals and loan approvals are the contingencies that most often require timeframes. There are times when an appraiser is unable to complete an appraisal, and a lender is unable to close a loan within the time allotted. These occurrences are common and should be given consideration. When the real estate industry is busy and properties are selling quickly, every aspect of the industry is busy, and it will take longer to get work completed.

NOTE

Having clients sign an incomplete contract is a highly negligent act.

B. **CAPACITY** is required for a person to enter into a valid contract. Capacity is the legal capacity or ability of a party to enter into a contract knowingly and with the capability to fulfill the terms. If a party to a contract does not have legal capacity, the contract is considered void, or it may be voided by the party lacking the capacity. To have capacity under the law, the parties to a contract must meet the following requirements:

- **Sane** as prescribed by the courts. A person who is confined to a hospital for mental incapacity cannot enter into a valid contract. A person who has been declared mentally incapacitated by a court of law cannot enter into a valid contract. A person cannot take control of another's property merely by stating that the party is mentally incapable of handling their affairs. **This is also a common problem with those taking advantage of the elderly.**

- **Eighteen years of age** or older is considered an adult. In the State of California, a minor or a person under the age of eighteen does not have legal capacity to enter into a contract with the ***exception of emancipated minors***, who are:
  - **Married** under the age of eighteen.
  - In the military service or armed forces.
  - **Emancipated** by the courts.

  If a minor inherits or is given property in some way, they will need a guardian to handle any actions involving the transfer of ownership or possession of that property such as leasing, listing, or selling until they reach the age of eighteen or become emancipated.

- **A drugged or intoxicated** person that enters into a contract can cancel or disavow the contract because they did not have capacity at the time that they entered into the contract. The contract is voidable, or they can choose to accept the terms of the contract.

- **Incarceration for certain felonies** may be considered to lack legal capacity to enter into a contract. The decision of capacity for felons is administered by the courts. Most incarcerated persons retain the legal capacity to enter into contracts and the individual status should always be confirmed prior to entering into a contract.

  FOREIGN LANGUAGE CONTRACTS are relatively common in California as the population is very international. The ability to understand the contract constitutes the capacity to enter into a contract.

Based on the history of California, Spanish is the second language for a large portion of the population and in many cases, Spanish is the only language. Because of the language needs, many contracts are negotiated completely or partially in Spanish (or other languages). ***Civil Code Section 1632*** provides for requirements for professionals such as real estate licensees engaging in and conducting business in a language other than English, whether written or oral.

The requirements apply to contracts for the following transaction:

- **Lease, sublease, or rental agreement** for longer than one month for a residential dwelling to include a house, apartment, or mobile home.
- **Loan** negotiated by a real estate broker and secured by real property on a one-to-four-unit residential property.
- **Broker disclosures** as required under the federal Truth-in-Lending Law and the State Financial Code.
- **Loan** secured by personal property for personal use, including the purchase or lease of a car or motor vehicle.
- **Contract or agreement** for legal services from one licensed to practice law.

The party to a contract that requires foreign language must be provided with an unexecuted version of the contract in the required language prior to signing the English version of the contract. This allows the party speaking a foreign language the opportunity to review the contract and understand the terms so when the contract is signed (executed), it is with an understanding by both parties constituting a meeting of the minds. The law does not apply if the party speaking a foreign language provides their own interpreter. A Spanish (or foreign) language notice must be provided and displayed in a conspicuous place at the main place of business or where contracts are being negotiated in any language other than, or in addition to, English.

C. **CONSIDERATION** is required for a contract to be valid and enforceable. Consideration can be in a variety of forms of something of value such as:

- Monetary
- Promise
- To do something
- Not to do something
- Personal goods
- Love and affection.

CONSIDERATION confirms the intent to be obligated by the parties to a contract by creating **mutuality of contract**. By providing consideration, a party to a contract is committing and mutually agreeing to the terms binding on the agreement.

- **VALUABLE CONSIDERATION** is used to describe items or services that have value. This usually refers to money or a service such as listing a property for sale. A party to a contract can give personal items as consideration if acceptable by the other party. Cars, boats, artwork, and household furnishings are examples of personal items of value that may be used as consideration.

- **GOOD CONSIDERATION** refers to love and affection. A parent will give their child a property out of love and affection for that child.

- **SUFFICIENT CONSIDERATION** is defined as enough consideration to make a contract binding. When making an offer to purchase a property, the buyer needs to give an amount sufficient to bind the contract based on several points. A buyer would not make a deposit of $500 on a purchase price of $1,000,000. Likewise, a buyer would not make a deposit of $15,000 on a purchase price of $50,000.

- **ADEQUATE CONSIDERATION** is defined as a sufficient amount of deposit to cover losses in the event of a contract cancellation or default. When making an offer to purchase a house that has tenants, it is common to require that the tenants vacate the property prior to the closing of escrow. If a buyer is making such a request, they should expect to make a large enough deposit to cover the seller's loss of rental income if the transaction does not close on time or if the transaction is canceled.

  Example: *Charles makes an offer to purchase a house that is currently rented. The offer is contingent on the tenants vacating the property prior to the close of escrow. The tenants had been paying $1,000 per month in rent so the seller agrees to have the tenants vacate, but the deposit is to be increased from $3,000 to $5,000.*

NOTE

There is no set amount or value that must be deposited to secure a real estate contract. The sufficient amount of deposit is whatever amount the offeror and the offeree feel is sufficient for that contract.

The tenants move out in time for the scheduled closing, but Charles asks for a thirty-day extension. The seller has now lost $1,000 in rental income because he has no rent to collect. After another 30 days, Charles still cannot close and asks for an additional 30-day extension and again for another 30 days.

The escrow is canceled, and the seller has lost a total of $3,000 in rental income. He puts the house back on the market and it takes four months longer to re-sell the property and close escrow. The seller has lost a total of $7,000 income from the time the tenants vacated the property until it is sold. The seller was able to retain the $5,000 deposit that Charles had made based on Charles' inability to close escrow and the requests that he had made which impacted the seller's income.

If Charles had been able to close escrow as scheduled, the $5,000 deposit would have been credited to Charles' price purchase and the seller would not have lost any income.

A buyer requesting an extended escrow period, especially when time is needed to sell their current home, should anticipate a larger deposit to entice the sellers' agreement. All of these are typical examples of circumstances affecting the amount of deposit and the real estate professional should consider the need and effect of providing sufficient consideration when preparing an offer to purchase.

A LISTING AGREEMENT is bound by or has the consideration of a **promise** by the real estate agent to give their due diligence in finding a ready, willing, and able buyer for the subject property at the price listed and the seller is doing nothing more than agreeing to pay the commission if the agent performs. The listing agreement is a unilateral agreement because the agent is the only party making an agreement to perform. If the agent performs, the seller will enter into a purchase contract, which will replace the listing agreement. The purchase offer is a bilateral agreement that will commit the buyer and the seller to perform acts in order to complete the contract.

A **PURCHASE AGREEMENT** is accompanied by a check or a **monetary deposit** as consideration by the buyer. The seller provides a promise to pay the agents, transfer the property, and deposits the deed with escrow as consideration.

An **OPTION** is accompanied by a monetary deposit as consideration from the optionor. The optionee gives a promise to sell the property to the optionor at a pre-determined price IF the optionor decides to exercise their option, making this a unilateral agreement.

FIRST RIGHT OF REFUSAL is a contract that gives the potential buyer the right to purchase or to choose not to purchase prior to the property being offered to another party. The contract does not contain a purchase price or any other terms. The only agreement is that the property owner will give the potential buyer the right to purchase the property if, at some time in the future, the owner decides to sell. There is no consideration.

D. **A LAWFUL OBJECTIVE** must be present for a contract to be valid. Lawful objective means that the purpose and terms of the contract are legal. An effective and valid contract cannot be for the purpose of performing an illegal act such as discriminatory requirements. If a contract has a legal and an illegal purpose, the contract is valid only for the legal purpose.

WRITTEN CONTRACTS

WRITTEN CONTRACTS are required for most real estate transactions in California. In short, it appears that the only real property contract that does not need to be in writing is a lease or rental agreement for a period of twelve months or less.

Although that agreement may not be required to be in writing, it is advisable to have it in writing. The ***California Civil Code Statute of Frauds*** lists the types of contracts that must be in writing to be valid and enforceable.

- Agreement that will not be completed within twelve months
- Agreement for the sale or the lease of real property
- Agreement authorizing an agent to make a sale or lease of real property on behalf of the owner.
- **Agreement employing an agent, broker**, or any other person to **perform** any of the following acts regarding **real property**:
    - Purchase or sale.
    - Lease for a period of more than twelve months/one year.
    - Locate a purchaser or seller of real property.
    - Locate a lessee or lessor of real property for a period of more than twelve months/one year.
    - Agreement by a purchaser of real property to secure a debt using real property as collateral.

PERFORMANCE OF CONTRACTS

EXECUTORY AND EXECUTED defines the current status of a contract as to whether it is still in process or completed.

1. **EXECUTORY CONTRACTS** have not yet been completed. There may be terms or conditions that still need to be met. When referring to a listing agreement, a buyer has not yet written an acceptable offer to purchase. A purchase contract may still have contingencies or conditions to be met, such as loan approval, appraisal, or termite work to be completed. The contingencies may have all been met and the parties are waiting for escrow to close, record, and transfer title.

2. **EXECUTED CONTRACT** is a contract that has been completed or "closed." All of the contingencies have been met or completed and the contract is complete. With a listing contract, a buyer has been found and an offer has been accepted, making the listing agreement completed or executed. When referring to a purchase transaction, escrow has closed, and title has transferred.

3. **ADDENDUM** to a contract is ***an addition to the existing contract becoming a part of the original contract***. The real estate form ***buyer's inspection advisory*** is an example of an addendum to the residential purchase agreement.

4. **AMENDMENT** to a contract is ***a change to a contract that is not a part of the original contract***. An amendment occurs after the fact. Common amendments to a real estate contract would include a price change based on a low appraised value or based on extensive termite damage. Amendments or changes to the terms of a real estate contract generally are done by amending the escrow instructions rather than changing the actual purchase offer.

   The escrow instructions are the more recent document involved in the transaction; therefore, they are considered to be the accurate document or the document to follow.

   The purpose of the escrow instructions is to define and instruct the parties on the terms of the contract and what they need to do to complete or execute the contract. Any amendment to the contract will be made with an amendment to escrow instructions.

NOTE

"Executed" is also used synonymously with "signed." When a contract has been fully executed, all parties to the contract have signed in all spaces required. Remember that the word "executed" has two meanings when referring to real estate contracts.

5. **ASSIGNMENT** of a contract transfers the rights and obligations of a contract to another party. The original party or assignor to the contract is still liable for the execution of the contract if the assignee defaults for any reason.

   Example: *Mary has entered into a contract to purchase a home. When she tells her friend Beth about the home she is buying, Beth tells her that she loves that house and has been waiting for it to go on the market. Mary agrees to assign the purchase offer to Beth. The assignment is made as an amendment to the escrow instructions and Beth as the assignee becomes the buyer.*

   Beth does not qualify for a loan under terms that she can afford, and she cannot meet the loan contingency. The contract reverts to Mary, who then completes the contingencies and purchases the home.

6. **NOVATION** is a way of substituting an existing contract with a new contract. Nova is the Greek word for "new."

   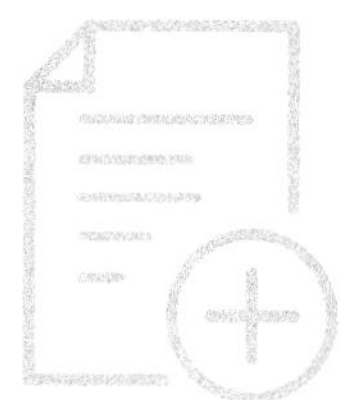

   Example: *Mary wants to transfer the purchase contract to Beth. She does not want to remain the secondary liability for the transaction because Mary has found another house that she wants to purchase. Instead of providing an assignment of the purchase offer, Beth provides a new purchase offer to replace the existing one that Mary had entered into.*

   The seller or the other party must agree to the novation, or replacement, of the original contract with the new contract. Once the novation is agreed to by the parties to the contract, the new contract is in place and the original contract is voided. This action releases Mary from her commitment and she is free to enter into another contract. If Beth for any reason cannot complete the contract, Mary has no obligation or responsibility to the seller.

7. **LEGAL IMPOSSIBILITY** refers to a contract, a portion of a contract, or a condition of a contract that cannot be met because it requires an illegal act. A party to a transaction cannot be required to perform or execute a contract that is illegal or requires illegal actions.

   Example: *Agent John meets with Mr. Z to lists his property for sale. As Agent John is preparing the listing agreement, Mr. Z informs Agent John that he does not want anyone of a particular ethnicity to be shown the home because the neighborhood is predominantly of the same ethnicity, and he does not want that to change. Agent John informs Mr. Z that this is an illegal request and that he cannot refuse to show the property to anyone who wishes to consider the home for purchase. Mr. Z insists on this condition.*

Agent John does not accept the listing because the listing would be an illegal contract if done the way that Mr. Z requires.

This is illegal under several discrimination laws and Agent John must not and cannot abide by this condition in the contract.

8. **DEATH** of the parties to a contract terminates the contract. If either party to a contract dies, the contract will be void. It is possible for the heirs to continue the contract if they choose to do so whether as the seller's heirs or the buyer's heirs. A purchase transaction is canceled if either buyer or seller dies. A mortgage loan would not continue.

   A lease agreement may not automatically terminate depending on the circumstances. **Death of a landlord** would not necessarily mean that the tenants had to vacate because the lease would not terminate; but if the tenant dies and was living alone, the lease will terminate. If a tenant dies, but the roommates choose to continue living in the property, they could do so as long as they are recognized as tenants by being named in the lease or having paid rent in their own name such as with a personalized check.

9. **MUTUAL RESCISSION** returns all parties in a contract to their position prior to the contract. Both parties mutually agree to cancel the contract with all deposits being returned without favor.

   Example: *Ron and George entered into a contract for Ron to purchase George's property for $350,000. Three weeks into the transaction, the appraisal is completed with a value $25,000 less than the purchase price agreed to in the contract. Ron offers to amend the purchase price to the appraised value of $325,000, but George refuses. George tells Ron that he is not willing to sell the property for that amount of money and would rather keep the property.*

   Ron and George agree to cancel the purchase contract by ***mutual rescission.*** *Ron's deposit is returned to him and George keeps his home. They are both exactly where they were prior to entering into the contract.*

NOTE

A contract is terminated if there is no one left to fulfil the terms of the contract. (This is an ambiguous statement which requires a degree of common sense and legal advice.)

CREATION OF A CONTRACT

Contracts are created in different ways, but they all are either created by an EXPRESS AGREEMENT or **an** IMPLIED AGREEMENT.

1. **EXPRESS CONTRACT** is created either in writing or orally. The term "express" means that the intention of entering into a contract was expressed or stated either by writing or speaking that intention.

   Example: *Bill and Tom were discussing the sale of Bill's property when Tom expressed an interest in purchasing the property and they verbally agreed on terms for the transfer of ownership to Tom. They orally created an express contract. Since oral contracts for such a real estate contract is not legal in California, Tom writes the offer to purchase according to the terms agreed on and Bill and Tom have entered into a legal, binding express real estate contract.*

2. **IMPLIED CONTRACTS** are those that have been created through actions, not writing. An implied contract occurs when one party acts in a manner that implies that there is a contract.

   Example: *Agent Sue is showing property to a potential buyer. The client's described dream home matches her neighbors' home. Agent Sue tells her neighbor that she would like to show their home to her client if they would be interested in entertaining an offer. The neighbor gives Agent Sue the house key. Agent Sue secures an offer to purchase on the neighbor's home.*

   The neighbor wants to accept the offer but insists that they did not list the home for sale with Agent Sue and should not owe a listing fee. The neighbor did in fact enter into an implied contract by virtue of handing a house key to Agent Sue to enter the home for the purpose of showing the property to potential buyers. This action implied the agreement to list the house for sale to that buyer.

   In the practice of real estate, a real estate professional should actually obtain a written listing agreement before showing a property even if it is for one client only. Another option that Agent Sue could have used would have been to inform the neighbor that she had secured a purchase offer and have the owner sign a listing agreement for that client only prior to presenting the purchase offer and revealing the client.

STATUS OF A CONTRACT

NOTE

Real estate contracts must be in writing with the exception of rental agreements for a period of twelve months or less.

1. **VALID CONTRACTS** are contracts that have all of the essential elements and meet the legal requirements of a contract. A valid contract has **mutual consent or meeting of the minds, legal capacity, consideration, and lawful objective.**

2. **VOID CONTRACTS** have no legal effect. A contract can be voided in several ways. The most common use of the term void contract is referring to a contract that is illegal such as the one in the example where the potential seller wanted to include discrimination as part of the contract. Such a contract is void by nature because it is illegal from the inception.

   A contract can also become void by a defaulting or breaching party. Once the contract is canceled because of a breach it is void. If a valid contract is canceled for any reason, even mutual rescission rather than executed, it becomes void.

3. **VOIDABLE CONTRACTS** are ones that have been violated by fraud or breach. A voidable contract is valid but may become void if the parties choose to cancel the contract. The disadvantaged, injured, or the non-breaching party has the right to void a contract. The breaching party cannot void the contract.

   Example: *Joe has entered into a contract to sell his home to Michael. Joe had received several offers to purchase at the same time. He chose to accept Michael's offer, even though it was for $15,000 less, because it could close escrow in 30 days based on it being an all-cash transaction.*

   *Michael does not have the cash to pay for the property and will need to get a mortgage loan. He wrote the offer as all cash to get a good deal and had no intention of paying all cash. He justified it by saying that once he got a loan, Joe would receive all cash. This is **intentional misrepresentation,** and Michael has breached the contract. Joe agreed to a shorter escrow on the property he was buying based on Michael's implied ability to close quickly. When Joe finds out that Michael lied and defrauded him, he has the right to:*
   - ***Continue** and close escrow.*
   - ***Void** the contract and sell the property to someone else.*
   - ***Sue for specific performance** which will require Michael to close within the terms of the contract.*

Joe is injured by Michael's actions because he is committed to the timeframe of another contract which could cost him money if he cannot perform because Michael cannot or does not perform. Joe also accepted $15,000 less than he could have gotten for his property based on Michael's lie. The decision of how to proceed is Joe's. Michael does not have a choice other than to abide by Joe's decision.

The real estate professional should be aware of their client's actions and must never be a party to misrepresentation and fraud.

4. **UNENFORCEABLE CONTRACT** is a contract that cannot be enforced because it is illegal. The unenforceable contract may have all of the essential elements of a contract, but will not be enforced by the courts based on any of the following ***Statutes of Frauds or limitations***:

   The Statutes of Frauds as found in the ***California Civil Code*** requires certain contracts to be in writing and signed to be enforceable.
   - **Transfer of interest in real property** with the exception of leases for twelve months or less.
   - **Debt agreements** secured by real property.
   - Listing agreements.
   - **Real property agreements** that will not be completed in twelve months or less such as long-term leases or property management agreements.

   The Statute of Limitations as found in ***the California Civil Code*** also establishes the time frames the non-breaching party has to take legal action against the breaching party.
   - **Breach of oral contract** – 2 years.
   - **Fraud** – 3 years from the date of discovery.
   - **Encroachment and trespass** – 3 years.
   - **Breach of written contract** – 4 years.
   - **Lawsuit to recover title** – 5 years.
   - **Court judgments** – 10 years and can be renewed for an additional 10 years for a total of 20 years to collect.

DISCHARGING A CONTRACT

DISCHARGING A CONTRACT is ***terminating a contract by completing or otherwise canceling a contract,*** which can be accomplished in several different ways. Some of the ways to discharge a contract have already been discussed as ways to change a contract.

1. IMPRACTICALITY OF CIRCUMSTANCES occurs when the circumstances change for one of the parties to a contract. Impracticality of circumstances may cause a contract to be discharged if there is an occurrence to either party such as:
   - **Loss of job** and can no longer qualify for the loan.
   - **Loss of value of cash assets** needed for the down payment to close escrow.
   - **Disability** occurring, creating impossibility to complete transaction based on loss of income.

   This is also called impracticality of performance or commercial frustration, and the party would be excused from the transaction.

2. IMPOSSIBLE TO COMPLETE the transaction may occur such as when the property is destroyed prior to close of escrow. If a property is destroyed prior to the closing of escrow, the seller is responsible for the replacement of the property if the buyer has taken possession of the subject property prior to the closing of escrow. The appropriate homeowner's insurance must be in place. This falls under the ***Uniform Vendor and Purchaser Risk Act*** which is found in the ***Civil Code.***

3. PERFORMANCE of the terms and conditions of the contract to a successful completion constitutes a discharge of the contract. A contract is for a specific purpose and when the purpose has been met, the contract is no longer an active document because it has been discharged by **completion** or through performance.

4. RESCISSION OR MUTUAL RESCISSION occurs when the parties to a contract agree to cancel the contract. This must be done by all parties to the contract.

5. RELEASE occurs with obligations such as debts, for example a mortgage loan, have been met or the debt has been paid by the party who owes the debt or obligation. The receiving party of the obligation or debt releases the contract which discharges the terms of the contract.

6. **NOVATION,** as discussed previously, is a way of substituting an existing contract with a new contract. As mentioned before, nova is the Greek word for "new." Once an existing contract is replaced by a new contract, the old contract is discharged as it is no longer needed.

7. **ASSIGNMENT** of the original contract does not constitute discharge because the original contract is still in place, only the parties to the contract have changed. It would only become a discharged contract if it were replaced with a new contract, in which case it would be a novation instead of an assignment.

8. **REFORMATION** is a way of making changes to an existing contract. A real estate contract is generally changed by writing a new contract to make the needed corrections or by amendment. Reformation is accomplished by rewriting the contract, therefore replacing the original contract with a new contract. The new contract makes the original one obsolete and discharges the original contract.

9. **BREACH OF CONTRACT** occurs when one of the parties to a contract fails to perform one or all of their duties as specified in the contract. The non-breaching party has the right to cancel or **discharge the contract.** As discussed previously, the injured party does have options:
   - **Void** the contract (discharge).
   - **Complete** the contract.
   - Sue for specific performance.

   SUING FOR SPECIFIC PERFORMANCE or any type of litigation concerning a real estate contract is expensive and time consuming. As long as there is sufficient money on deposit, litigation is generally avoided in real estate. The issue then becomes the distribution of the money which can usually be agreed to through arbitration rather than litigation.

CONTRACTS FOR BUSINESS ENTITIES

CONTRACTS FOR BUSINESS ENTITIES must adhere to the following guidelines to be enforceable:

1.) **SOLE PROPRIETORSHIP** will act or transact business and own business property in their own name and may include a spouse. One person owns the business, thus the term "sole proprietorship."

2.) **PARTNERSHIP** may hold real property in the name of the business partnership—the name of one or all of the partners. Any authorized partner and spouse may contract to transfer title of real property.

3.) **CORPORATIONS** are a **legal entity** and can hold real property in the name of the corporation. A corporation is controlled by the officers who make up a board of directors. Because of this business structure, a corporation is an ongoing entity in perpetuity and therefore a good risk. Depending on the business, individual directors may be liable for the obligations and debts of the corporation.

NOTE

The real estate professional will always verify the responsible party for the transaction of a business. Confirm the authority of the parties involved when working with a business entity by obtaining a copy of the documents that formed the company such as the partnership agreement or the articles of incorporation.

REAL ESTATE CONTRACTS

REAL ESTATE CONTRACTS are currently available in a large number that is used by the **real estate industry**. The ***California Association of Realtors (CAR)*** has more than 150 forms in use by its members.

A. RESIDENTIAL PURCHASE CONTRACT and JOINT ESCROW INSTRUCTIONS is probably the most used and best-known form in the industry today. When a person decides to purchase, they need to write an offer to purchase which includes:

- **Identification** of the subject property—usually the complete address.
- **Price** being offered.
- Deposit amount.
- **Loan terms** as a contingency.
- **Appraised value** equal to the offered price as a contingency.
- Pest inspection.
- Escrow and title companies.
- **Items** to remain with the property.
- Buyers, sellers, and their agent.

When a buyer makes an offer to purchase, it must be accompanied by a deposit in an amount sufficient to show an earnest interest and intention to enter into the contract being presented. The title of the commonly used CAR form is ***"California Residential Purchase Agreement and Joint Escrow Instructions."*** The form is the purchase offer and also provides instructions to escrow on the terms to be met. *Do not confuse this with the escrow instructions as provided by the escrow company.* All parties to the transaction will need a copy of the purchase offer once it has been signed by all parties and the escrow instructions prepared by the escrow company.

NOTE

The selection of the escrow company and the title company used is the buyer's choice per the federal Real Estate Settlement and Procedures Act (RESPA). If the seller chooses the escrow and title companies to be used in a transaction, the seller may be liable to the buyer for three times the buyer's escrow and title fees. The real estate professional is required by federal RESPA law to always provide a minimum of five names of suggested agencies that may be recommended to provide services, such as escrow companies.

The offer to purchase is not an enforceable contract until it has been signed or executed by all parties involved including the agents representing the buyer and the seller. The purchase offer is just an offer until it has been accepted by the offeree and that acceptance is communicated to the offeror. The offeror can withdraw their offer at any time prior to the communication of the acceptance. A counteroffer is actually a rejection of the original offer and a new offer.

A purchase offer contract is a long contract and often becomes quite detailed.

There may be additions and corrections to the contract. Generally, the original offer is typed and will be considered the original. Changes to the purchase offer contract are usually in the form of a counteroffer, which is a separate form. This means that there are rarely handwritten changes to the original unless the changes were added prior to the initial presentation to the seller.

It is important that any **CHANGES** be initialed by all buyers and sellers showing acceptance of any changes.

- **The escrow amendments** take precedence over all others.
- **Escrow instructions** take precedence over the offer.
- **The latest counteroffer** takes precedence over the previous counteroffers and the original offer. There can be any number of counteroffers.
- **Specific information** takes precedence over general information.

- **Handwritten changes** take precedence over the typed insertions.
- **Typed insertions** in a contract take **precedence over the pre-printed** information on the prepared contract form.

The offer to purchase contract must have mutual consent of all parties, capacity, consideration (deposit), and lawful purpose. The contract cannot be enforced without these essential elements.

Persons who want to either sell or buy real property are not required to use a licensed real estate agent. It is, however, advisable. It has been determined in various studies that the majority of *For Sale by Owner (FSBO)* transactions do not close escrow but fall out or are discharged mainly because the parties involved do not know what needs to be done to complete an escrow successfully. The agents have a huge responsibility to oversee the clients' needs in a purchase transaction.

A **REAL ESTATE BROKER/AGENT** or the representative and associate guides the client through the contract giving advice and assisting with filling in the blanks. The decisions and choices are the client's, not the agent's. The real estate professional must be careful to give professional advice and never make the final decision for the client.

The **BUYER'S BROKER/AGENT** presents the prepared offer to the seller in the presence of the seller's broker/agent. It is common practice in some areas to present the offer to the seller's agent who then presents the offer to the seller in private; however, it is beneficial for the buyer's agent to be able to present their client's case in person. The buyer's agent knows the buyer's circumstances and thoughts on the offer to purchase and can best present their case in person. The local customs should be taken into consideration, but the client's interest is always of the utmost importance and must take precedence.

B. LISTING AGREEMENTS are also very well known in the real estate industry based on the frequency of use. A real estate professional must always obtain the listing agreement in writing. Listing agreements or contracts are agreements between a seller of real estate and a real estate agent/broker to list the seller's property for sale to the public.

The **listing agreement** is a **unilateral agreement** because the agent promises to perform actions with due diligence in order to complete the contract by finding a ready, willing, and able buyer for the subject property.

The seller of the property is not making any promises of any actions to the agent other than to pay a commission if the agent performs. Once the agent finds a buyer, a purchase agreement replaces the listing agreement. The purchase offer is a bilateral agreement because all parties to the agreement promise to perform an action or duty in some way.

The **listing agreement** is between the seller/principal and the broker. The associate licensee cannot be the direct representative of the client. (The **broker agent contract** defines the terms of the agreement between the agent/associate licensee and broker.) The agent or associate licensee ***represents*** the broker in a real estate transaction and the broker represents the principal/seller although the principal might never even meet the broker. The agent representing the broker must treat the principal and the transaction with the same principles and laws as the broker.

There are several different types of listing agreements as discussed in *Chapter 9. Forms of Written Real Estate Listing Agreements* are summarized as follows:

1. **EXCLUSIVE AUTHORIZATION AND RIGHT TO SELL LISTING** is currently the most commonly used listing agreement in California. This type of listing agreement allows the exclusive broker to be paid as the listing agent no matter what real estate agency procures the buyer. The total commission stated in the listing agreement is divided accordingly between the listing broker and the selling broker.

   The **Exclusive Authorization and Right to Sell** allows the broker to advertise the listed property for sale in the ***Multiple Listing Service (MLS).*** MLS provides an internet website to be shared with the public and also with other member brokers. The rules for advertising with MLS will vary. MLS may require that all listings be placed on the service within a certain number of days while others may not require that all listings with a member broker be placed in MLS. *The seller/principal has the right to decline listing with the MLS. The listing agreement provides the seller with a space to declare that option.*

2. **EXCLUSIVE AGENCY LISTING** allows the broker to advertise and find a buyer or a cooperating broker to sell the property the same as the Exclusive Authorization and Right to Sell Listing. The main difference between the two types of listings is that the exclusive agency listing allows the seller to find their own buyer without being required to pay commission to a broker.

3. **OPEN LISTING** is also called a **non-exclusive listing**. The open listing derives its name from the fact that the listing is open to any broker who may procure a buyer, and the seller pays only the procuring broker. The open listing is rarely used in residential real estate because there is no assurance of being paid after doing the work. In spite of the lack of use for residential property, the open listing is more commonly used in commercial real estate.

4. **NET LISTING** provides the broker's commission to be any amount in excess of the seller's sales price. The seller sets the price they want for the sale of their property and any amount beyond that figure is the broker's compensation for selling the property. The problem with this type of listing is that it lends itself to fraud on the part of the broker or the impression of fraud on the part of the seller. This type of listing is legal; however, it is not advised. The broker is required to inform the seller of the amount of any anticipated profit as a result of the sale of the property.

5. **OPTION LISTING** is the exclusive listing of the broker that allows the broker to purchase the property. Like the net listing, full disclosure of anticipated profit is required. This type of listing is also legal, but not advised. Using the previous example:

   Example: *Agent Jane decides to purchase the property from Seller Sam for herself. She decides that she will then put it immediately back on the market for sale and make the $100,000 profit.*

NOTE

A definite termination date is required whenever the broker is the exclusive agent for a seller. The Business and Professions Code calls for the revocation or suspension of a real estate license if the licensee receives any compensation under any exclusive listing agreement if the agreement "does not contain a definite, specified date of final and complete termination."

This is not referring to brokers who chose to purchase a home for their own use or to use as rental property; however, the broker must never take unfair advantage. When an agent is discussing the sale of a property with a potential client, they must always be honest and fair about the true value even when desiring the property for their own use.

6. **CANCELED LISTINGS** may often become a refinance transaction because the seller needs the cash from their current residence to purchase their new property. Lenders are reluctant to accept these loans as owner-occupied, cash- out refinance because they know it is common practice to take cash-out to use as a down payment to purchase a new owner-occupied home. Once the loan has been completed, the property owner will put their current home back on the market for sale. The other possibility is that they will rent the current residence even though they got an owner-occupied loan with this transaction. Either way, the lender stands to lose money. If this is a legitimate transaction, the lender will require a listing cancellation and a strong letter of explanation. Many lenders will not consider this scenario at all, but it can be done if the owner's intent to stay and occupy the home is sufficiently proven, or if the owner refinances and takes out cash based on a non-owner-occupied status.

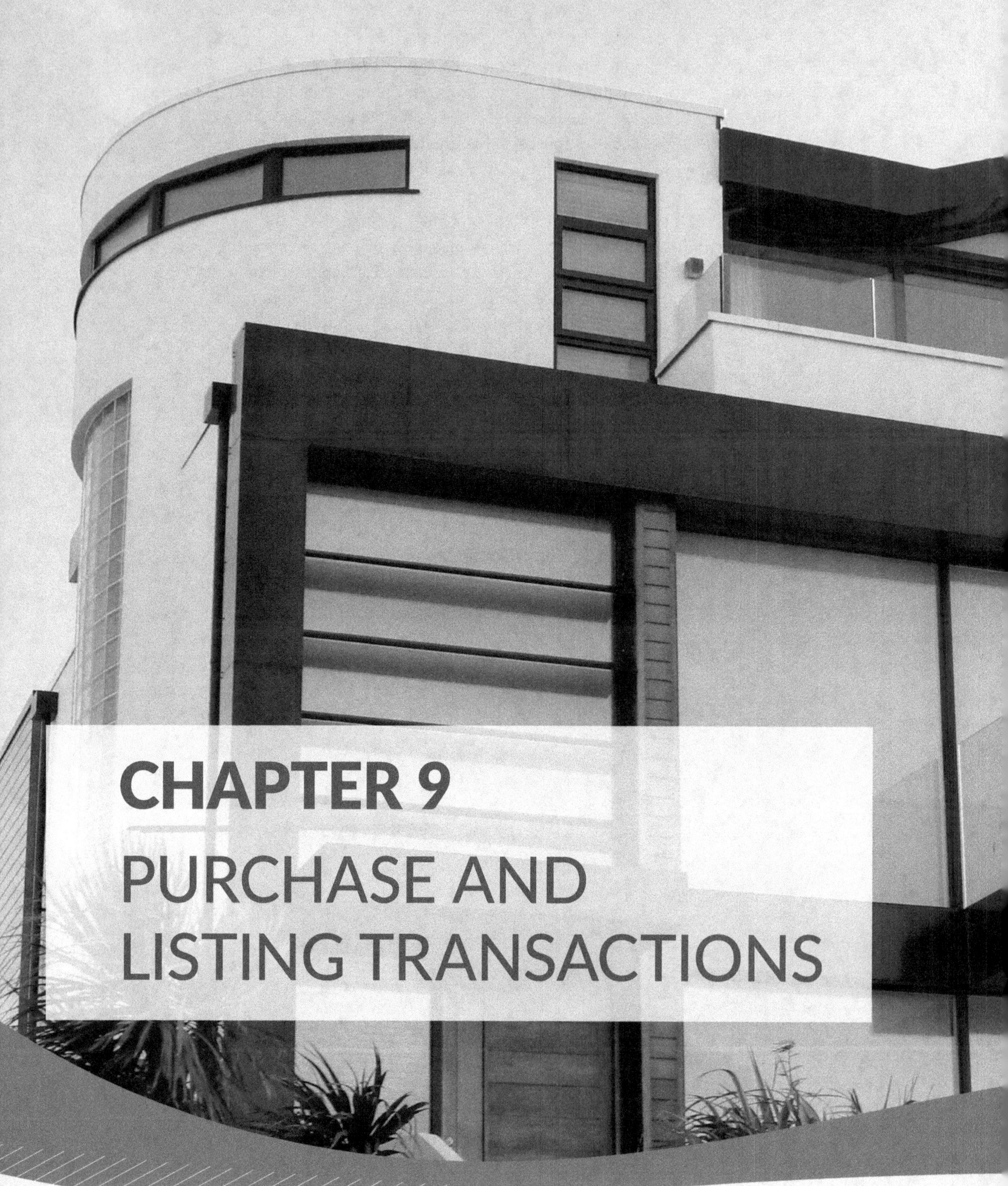

CHAPTER 9
PURCHASE AND LISTING TRANSACTIONS

PURCHASE TRANSACTIONS

PURCHASE TRANSACTIONS AND CONTRACTS, along with the terms of the contract, are different with every contract and every transaction. The details of each separate transaction are negotiated between the individual parties to suit each individual party.

OFFER and OFFER TO PURCHASE, or the PURCHASE CONTRACT are generic terms for the form that is used by real estate agents to determine the terms of the purchase between buyer and seller. The contract is frequently referred to by real estate agents as a **deposit receipt.**

Offer is also the term used to express the amount of money being offered to the seller in a purchase transaction. This is most often a dollar amount, but a party can offer anything of value. A thing of value to be given in exchange for real property can be anything including another piece of property, cars, boats, services, businesses, and love and affection.

The California Association of Realtors (CAR) form is titled *California Residential Purchase Agreement and Joint Escrow Instructions*. This is the current title of the most commonly used purchase offer or contract form in California.

It must be understood that the **DEPOSIT RECEIPT** and the **ESCROW INSTRUCTIONS** also refer to two completely different pieces of documentation when dealing with lending. The purchase agreement includes instructions to escrow regarding the transaction, which is the reason it is often called escrow instructions. It is important to understand and differentiate between the meanings when representing clients in a real estate purchase transaction. Neither is wrong; the terms are merely used differently in various areas of the relating industries.

The **ESCROW INSTRUCTIONS** is also a document which may be prepared by escrow, which summarizes the terms as agreed to by the buyer and seller. In other words, these are the instructions that will be followed by escrow, buyer, seller, agents, and the lender based on the terms of the purchase agreement.

California Residential Purchase Agreement and Joint Escrow Instructions or the **purchase contract** must be included in the client's file once fully executed. Fully executed means that it must have all pages and spaces appropriately signed by both buyers and sellers. A complete copy including any and all counteroffers and addendums should be provided to the escrow officer and a copy in the broker's files. The escrow officer is often the only one involved who actually has a fully executed copy. Brokers should obtain copies of the fully executed documents for their files. The most recent counteroffer should be placed on the top for reference to reflect the most accurate and/or final terms agreed upon.

SELLER'S AGENT or the LISTING AGENT is the real estate agent who lists the property and is the one who works directly with the seller as the seller's agent.

A BUYER'S AGENT or the SELLING AGENT is the real estate agent who sold the property and is the direct contact with the buyer. The loan agent, who works directly with the buyer to arrange for a loan, is responsible for communication with the buyer's agent but will rarely speak with the seller's agent. The buyer's agent is responsible for contacting the seller's agent who in turn contacts the seller. There is an accepted chain to be followed as the various agents and service providers do not have the time to communicate all actions with all parties concerned.

The real estate professional will assist the client with the following items and needs to pay particular attention to them as they will affect the client whether buyer or seller. Some items may become issues that can render the contract invalid.

- **The property address** should be completed as accurately and completely as possible. It will be compared to the prelim for accuracy by escrow and then by the lender. The address on the prelim is considered to be accurate.
- **The purchase price** will be stated on the first page, but if there are any counteroffers included, they should be checked carefully for the final and accurate purchase price.
- **Deposit amount or consideration** is the amount of money that the buyer will be placing in escrow to show their intent to enter into and complete the contract. The law requires that funds must be deposited as earnest money to establish an escrow for a real estate purchase transaction. The purchase offer must be accompanied by the check from the buyer in the amount deposited.

The **deposit receipt required for lending purposes** is the actual receipt from escrow to the buyer for the deposit funds paid to escrow as security as required by law. The real estate professional must remember that consideration must accompany a contract even if it is only $1.00.

CONTINGENCIES are conditions such as particular terms and services that must be met or completed for the contract to continue to a successful completion. The contract is contingent on or subject to these items. Contingencies are not required to be a part of the contract, but it is advisable that they are made a part of a real property purchase contract.

1. **LOAN APPROVAL** is the first contingency that is found in the purchase contract. The contract form provides room for the buyer to make their offer subject to getting a loan for a certain dollar amount, at a stated interest rate, and for a term such as 30 years. Also included are the points, or loan fees, that the buyer will be required to pay to obtain the loan. The terms are stated as the loan that the buyer can afford. If the buyer cannot obtain a loan that they can afford, the purchase contract can be canceled based on the buyer's inability to afford the property.

   Example: *The contract states that the buyer will obtain a 90% loan-to-value (LTV), or a loan that is 90% of the purchase price, and the lender will only approve the borrower for 80%. The borrower has the option to cancel. The borrower may be willing to continue with the transaction; however, they will need to pay the additional funds.*

   The same applies to the **interest rate** as stated in the contract. For example, the contract states that the maximum interest rate will be 6.00% and the only program available for the interest rates have increased to 6.5%. The borrower may choose to accept the higher rate and continue with the transaction or cancel the file. **A rate lock may protect the borrower from this. However, it is essential for the borrower and the loan agent to work closely to avoid the additional fees that will occur if the lock needs to be extended. A lock extension will affect the costs, which will impact the closing.** The borrower may not be able to afford the higher interest rate. The contract also allows for any additional financing terms that the buyer is requesting, such as a 2nd trust deed (TD) or a **seller carry back**, which is a 2nd TD carried by the seller.

These examples indicate that additional terms must be disclosed. There may be other terms that will affect the buyer and should be fully considered.

2. The **NUMBER OF DAYS** that the contract has allowed for loan approval and the acceptance of the terms by the buyer must be strictly adhered to. If that date arrives and loan approval has not been obtained, the real estate agent should request an extension in writing.

   The buyer has the option to waive the **loan contingency**, however, it is *definitely* not advisable because if the loan agent cannot obtain an acceptable loan, the buyer will still be obligated to perform and close escrow. This may be impossible for the buyer to do, and the buyer may be obligated to take a loan that they cannot afford. The buyer can be sued by the seller for **specific performance**. If the loan contingency is not included in the contract, the buyer will be obligated to the terms contract even if they cannot afford the loan that they obtain, which may lead to foreclosure.

3. All possible contingencies that apply to **FINANCING** should be looked at carefully. If the buyer indicates that the offer is **"all cash,"** be certain that the buyer can actually perform with an all-cash offer. **This is the same as waiving any loan contingencies.** Often a buyer will change their mind and apply for a loan instead of tying up all their cash in their home and forfeiting any tax benefits. This is acceptable as long as the buyer is capable of actually paying cash if they need to in order to close escrow in a timely manner. *This does occur frequently with high-end properties, especially in those with a value in excess of one million dollars.*

4. The **APPRAISAL** is a **contingency** that must be met. If the appraised value is less than the purchase price, the buyer has the right to cancel the contract, or they can renegotiate the purchase price with the seller to be equal to the appraised value. Another option is to obtain another appraisal, but the buyer's lender may choose to obtain a **review appraisal**. If this is the case, the lender will use the value determined by their review appraiser. A lender will base the loan amount on the **LESSER of the purchase price OR the appraised value.**

The time period to obtain an acceptable appraisal must be adhered to and the parties to the transaction must be notified if an extension of time is needed for any reason. The buyer can choose to waive this contingency but must be prepared to verify and pay any additional amounts in case the appraised value is less than the purchase price.

If the appraisal contingency is waived, the buyer may need to provide additional cash to cover the difference between the purchase price and the loan that the lender is willing to provide.

Example: *Mike is purchasing a home for $480,000. When the appraisal comes in, the appraised value is $450,000. The lender has approved a loan for Mike for 90% loan-to-value or 90% of the value, which is a loan amount of $432,000 based on the purchase price of $480,000. The appraised value being $450,000 means that the lender will now base the loan amount on the appraised value because it is less than the purchase price. The new loan amount will now be $405,000. Mike has several options:*

- ***Cancel*** *the contract.*
- ***Re-negotiate*** *the purchase price with the seller to match the appraised value of $450,000.*
- ***Pay*** *the additional $27,000 difference between loans, plus the additional down payment for a total of $75,000. Initially Mike planned on a down payment of $48,000.*

If Mike does not have the additional funds, the purchase transaction may need to be canceled. If the appraisal contingency was waived because the buyer was paying cash for the property, Mike may have been locked into purchasing a property for $30,000 more than it was actually worth.

NOTE

It is never a prudent decision to waive the appraisal contingency.

5. **CLOSING and OCCUPANCY** is an important **contingency** because both buyer and seller need to make plans. The buyer needs to vacate their current residence whether it is a rental or a property they are selling. The seller needs to arrange for their new property. If it is a purchase, there are more people that will be affected by this contingency. This all creates a domino effect meaning that there are other people closing escrows and hiring moving vans all depending on this one contract being able to close in a timely manner.

   If there are loans to secure the purchase of the property, the lender needs time to perform their duties. Allowing time for all parties to do what needs to be done is of the utmost importance. With the exception of an all-cash purchase, completing a purchase in less than 45 days is difficult. It can be done, but any problems will delay the scheduled close, which may cause problems for not only the subject transaction, but all the other lives and transactions that are affected by this one transaction.

   - **CLOSING** is the date and time the transaction will close. The date is usually anywhere from 30 to 60 days from the date of acceptance of the offer. There is a blank space on the purchase offer contract to fill in the time and agents will often put the time as 10:00 a.m.; however, the time of closing is actually determined by escrow. The escrow company will send the deeds to be recorded to the county recorder's office with a representative of the title company. The title representative will be at the recorder's office when they open in the morning. The recorder's office does not allow any other recordings ahead of the title representative's deeds.

     The recorder's office receives the documents and stamps, each one with a date and time stamp. Because of the volume of documents to be recorded and the amount of time it takes to process the documents, it may actually be processed later in the day even though it was stamped first thing in the morning.

     Once the documents have been processed by the recorder's office, they contact the escrow company to confirm recording. Escrow does not

NOTE

Every effort must be made to ensure a timely close of escrow. The consequences of not meeting the predetermined closing date can be extremely costly to all parties to the agreement and may even cause cancellation of the transaction.

consider the transaction "closed" and will not release funds or keys to the property until they have received confirmation from the recorder's office. This may happen anywhere from 10:00 a.m. to 4:00 p.m.

- **OCCUPANCY** is the statement by the buyer as to whether they intend to live in the property or not. This affects several aspects of the transaction. The lender for a new loan secured by the property will charge extra, usually to the interest rate, for a property that is not occupied by the owner because the loan becomes a higher risk if non-owner occupied. The lender will usually require more of a down payment for a non- owner-occupied purchase. If the owner gets into financial trouble, they are more likely to allow their non-owner-occupied property to go into default and retain their residence in good standing so they will have a place to live.

  The lender will be concerned with the maintenance of a property when it is occupied by a tenant rather than an owner. A tenant is less concerned with the condition of a house than an owner and the lender is using the property as collateral for the loan and wants the value to be retained.

  Occupancy will also be important if the buyer is purchasing a home that is currently rented. Tenant laws in many California cities such as Los Angeles are strict, and it may not be possible to break a lease or require tenants to vacate the premises unless the buyer will be occupying the subject property as their primary residence.

TERMITE REPORT AND CLEARANCE is the ***Wood Destroying Pests and Organisms Inspection Report.*** This report is prepared by a pest control company and is ordered by the real estate agent. Once the report is completed, it is forwarded directly to escrow. The report will be delivered to escrow and the agent will obtain a copy from escrow. The report discloses wood destroying pests and dry rot damage. The purpose is to locate any issues that will affect the integrity of the structure.

Standard Notice of Work Completed and Not Completed is known as the **TERMITE COMPLETION** and is required to show that all required work and repairs have been completed and will be required prior to the lender funding the loan.

Pest inspection is also a contingency to the contract. The purpose of a pest inspection is to verify that the structures or improvements on real property are free from termites or other destructive pests and that there is no damage which may jeopardize the integrity of the structure. Such damage is capable of actually causing the collapse of a structure if not maintained and repaired.

It is common practice that the buyer request a pest inspection, which is often paid for by the seller, but is negotiable. It is also common practice to request that the seller pay for any repairs required up to a certain dollar amount, which may be in the range of $1,500 to $2,500, depending on the area and the property in question. If the cost of repairs is in excess of the seller's obligation, the buyer will need to pay the difference if they want to continue with the transaction.

In the event that a buyer is expected to pay the costs of repairs, the person may decide that they do not want to pay for the repairs before they own the property. The lender will require that the work be completed prior to funding the loan. The seller will probably not be willing to pay for repairs because if the purchase falls through, they will have lost the money and will need to start the sales process over and may not be in a position to increase the price to cover the expense. The remedy for the situation is to have the buyer place the funds to pay for the repairs in escrow to be paid to the contractor through close of escrow. If escrow falls through, the funds will be refunded to the buyer.

Lenders used to allow the repairs to be made after the close of escrow and there was always a requirement that the repairs be completed within fifteen days of close of escrow. Once escrow closed, buyers rarely worried about completing the work and lenders were left in a precarious position because they loaned against the value of the property.

NOTE

Lenders no longer allow this. All required repairs must be completed before the lender will fund the loan.

When there is either termite or dry rot damage found to a property, the damages are classified as Section I, Section II, or Section III items.

- **Section I items** are damages that jeopardize the integrity of the property and will be required by all lenders to be repaired before funding the loan. Examples of Section I items are termite infestation, termite damage to structure beams, and dry rot, especially if it is found in doorframes and window frames.

- **Section II items** are less serious, but the buyer needs to be made aware that there is damage that will need to be repaired before the effect on the structure worsens. Examples of Section II items may be signs of dry rot and evidence of past infestation without serious damage to supporting beams. Conventional lenders will not require Section II items to be repaired prior to the close of escrow. However, lenders of government-backed loans such as FHA and VA will require all Section II items to be repaired prior to the closing of escrow.
- **Section III items** will not need to be repaired prior to the close of escrow. These items are provided to inform the buyer of potential problems that they need to look for, such as water draining from the roof onto a window frame that will eventually cause dry rot.

The real estate professional will learn to read the termite report and understand the findings. Dry rot is a misnomer as it is actually rot from water or dampness.

The buyer has the right to waive a termite inspection. If this is the case, the lender CANNOT require a termite report UNLESS the appraiser comments on obvious damage. Unless this occurs, there will be no repairs required.

ADDITIONAL REPORTS OR REPAIRS are allowed for things such as a **home inspection**, which is recommended for all transactions. A home inspection does not necessarily prompt or require repairs, but it gives the buyer important information about the condition of the property being purchased. It is negotiable whether the buyer or seller is to pay for the report and any possible damage. In most cases, the seller will pay for these reports. If the buyer is to pay, they need to allow for the additional expense in the closing costs.

Real estate agents should provide an estimate of costs to the buyer so they can be prepared with sufficient funds to close escrow.

Some properties may constitute other reports such as a Geological Report, Mold Report, or an Asbestos Report. Any repairs and costs of any additional reports not included in the original offer are negotiable between the buyer and seller. These

NOTE

A pest inspection is not required by law, but it is advisable, especially for first-time homebuyers. The only time it may be recommended to waive a pest inspection is when the buyer is intentionally purchasing a home to rebuild as a fixer, or when the buyer is planning to destroy the home to build a new structure. Under such circumstances, the buyer would be aware of the condition of the property.

negotiations take place after the transaction has entered escrow so they must be handled carefully as this could cause a transaction to be canceled. If the purchase contract states that the property is being purchased "as is," the buyer will be responsible for any costs incurred for the repairs.

The selection of escrow and title companies and fee division between buyer and seller is negotiable in the purchase contract. Generally, each party to the transaction pays their own fees.

DISCLOSURES of any results and copies of the reports must be provided to the parties of the transaction. The contract also provides for a variety of additional disclosures as prescribed by law.

ITEMS INCLUDED AND EXCLUDED provide any personal items that the buyer would like to be included in the purchase. Commonly included items may be a washer and dryer, refrigerator, or chandeliers. It is common practice to include items that may be listed as "included" in the property listing and items that are attached as a way ensure that the seller leaves the items and also make the seller responsible for the items if they do not remain with the property after close of escrow.

The real estate professional should be aware that the lender has the right to reduce the purchase price by the value of the item, which may affect the loan amount and ultimately the buyer's closing costs. This practice is not always done; however, it is more likely to be done if the personal item is a large or expensive item, such as a car or a piece of expensive furniture. These items are considered unusual and are rarely included in a purchase.

BUYER DISPOSAL OF THEIR CURRENT RESIDENCE can have an effect on the transaction. If the purchase agreement is not contingent on the buyer selling their current residence, provided they own that property, the current housing expenses will be included in the debt ratio for qualifying purposes. Checking this will prepare

NOTE

The selection of the escrow company and the title company is the buyer's choice per federal Real Estate Settlement and Procedures Act (RESPA). If the seller chooses the escrow and title companies, the seller may be liable to the buyer for three times the buyer's escrow and title fees. The real estate professional is required by federal RESPA law to always provide a minimum of five names of suggested agencies that may be recommended to provide services such as escrow companies.

the buyer to ensure that the transaction can close as scheduled even if the current property is not sold.

The buyer may be planning to retain that property as an investment property and rent it. If this is the case, the proposed rent can be included in the buyer's income at 75% of the actual monthly rental amount. If the rental income is required for the buyer to qualify for the new loan, a copy of the rental agreement must be obtained **prior to the close of escrow** to verify the income.

ACTIVE OR PASSIVE refers to the way of responding to the terms of the contract. This clarifies the means of contending with the contingencies of the transaction.

- The **ACTIVE METHOD** provides that the buyer must be aware of the findings, approvals, values, and any other findings regarding the contingencies, reports, and conditions of the contract. The buyer must accept, reject, or request repairs or corrections regarding any and all contingencies in writing. If a written response is not received, the seller has the right to presume the issue has been met and accepted by the buyer or they may have the right to cancel the contract.

- A **PASSIVE** transaction allows for the seller to assume the contingency has been met and is acceptable if there is no response from the buyer within the time limits designated in the contract. If a contingency is not acceptable, the buyer must respond prior to the date. Any unacceptable items may be corrected or repaired as agreed between the buyer and the seller or the contract may be canceled or considered null and void accordingly.

  Example: *The appraised value is less than the sales price. As discussed earlier in this chapter, the buyer has the option to pay any difference if the allowable loan amount is affected. The seller may agree to a reduction of the sales price to an amount equal to the appraised value. If the reduced value is going to cause the transaction to be canceled, the buyer may choose to have another appraisal prepared by another appraiser or they may be able to provide additional information to the appraiser, which will justify the value being increased.*

  The agent may be involved in additional negotiations between the buyer and seller and must be aware of the issues. The loan agent can be helpful with the financing contingencies and issues directly affecting the loan and closing costs and should discuss any of the issues and make suggestions for resolution with the real estate agent and buyer.

"TIME IS OF THE ESSENCE" is important in a real estate transaction and simply means that everything required by the purchase agreement must be done as quickly as possible to meet the times designated in the contract. Dates must be met, if at all possible. If there are any issues that may cause the need for an extension of time, the agents must notify the parties to the transaction as quickly as possible.

ADDITIONAL TERMS to the contract may be included as contingencies to the contract. An example would be when the seller or real estate agent will pay a portion of the buyer's closing costs. Most lenders will allow up to 3% of the loan
amount be paid toward the buyer's closing costs by someone other than the buyer.
Non-recurring closing costs are the costs that will occur for this transaction only such as the appraisal, credit report, lender's fees, escrow fees, and broker's fees.

CARPET ALLOWANCE is another commonly used term in the contract. The real estate professional needs to be aware that the lender may reduce the value of the property by the amount allowed for carpeting, which will reduce the loan amount. This will cause an increase of the amount of money the buyer will need to close escrow.

Interest on a loan, insurance, and property taxes are examples of **RECURRING CLOSING COSTS** and must be paid by the buyer.

COMPLETE SIGNATURES of all buyers and sellers. If there are counteroffers, the seller's signature will be on that form not the original offer. A signature on the original contract by the seller indicates acceptance of the original offer. In the case of counteroffers, the final counteroffer will be the only form with all complete signatures. All buyers and sellers must initial each page of the purchase agreement where indicated at the bottom of each page. The agent obtaining the final acceptance is the one that will have the fully executed contract which will be provided to escrow.

A copy of the complete contract with all signatures can be obtained from that agent or from escrow. A fully executed contract must be in each agent's file.

All borrowers included on the loan application must initial and sign the purchase agreement and all buyers included on the purchase agreement must be included in the loan application.

If there is a buyer who is included in the transaction but will not occupy the property and the transaction is to be owner-occupied, the occupying borrower must qualify for the loan alone. If the occupying borrower does not qualify alone and the non-occupying borrower's income is needed to qualify for the loan, the loan will become a non-owner-occupying transaction. This situation may adversely affect the interest rate and/or closing costs. The closing costs and loan terms will increase and the loan terms in the contingency must be checked for acceptance of the contingency.

EXPIRATION of a purchase offer constitutes discharge or cancellation of the contract. Very few purchase transactions are actually discharged because escrow did not close on the determined date and few transactions actually close by the specified date. The real estate professional will pay attention to all of the dates determined in the contract and do their due diligence to meet all of the dates. If a date or a contingency cannot be handled in a timely manner or a condition cannot be met, the agents should communicate with the other agent and the buyer and seller to find a resolution. Buyers and sellers generally do not want a transaction to fall out of escrow and are usually willing to work out problems such as timeframes that cannot be met.

COMPENSATION to be paid to the agents for their work is determined in the listing agreement. The amount may become a part of the negotiations between the buyer and seller. An example of negotiating the commission amount would occur when the buyer is offering a purchase price considerably less than the list price and the seller agrees to a reduction in price if the agents agree to reduce their commission.
The final commission or fee to be paid to the real estate agents for the transaction will be designated on page 8 of CARs purchase contract. Both agents sign the contract on page 8 and agree to the commission stated on that page by signing.

COMMISSION is not earned until the transaction reaches successful completion. The escrow officer will prepare the commission checks after escrow has closed. The checks will then be delivered to the broker who distributes the commissions as agreed to in the employment contract between the broker and agent.

Commissions will not be distributed and paid until confirmation of recording with the county recorder's office.

COUNTEROFFERS are used to address only the items that the party wants to address. If the buyer makes an offer and the seller agrees with all of the conditions except one, the counteroffer will only address that one item. ***All terms and conditions that are acceptable to the party are considered accepted when not included in the counteroffer.*** Counteroffers are numbered and the highest numbered counteroffer will be considered the final terms.

> ***Example:*** *Joe presents a purchase offer to Mary. He offers her:*
> - *$450,000 purchase price.*
> - *60 days to close escrow.*
> - *Loan conditions with an interest rate of 6.5%.*
> - *Requests that all appliances be included in the sale.*
>
> *Mary does not sign page 8 of 8 because she is going to prepare a counteroffer and is not willing to accept all of the terms as presented. The counteroffer includes a counter to:*
> - *Purchase price $460,000*
> - *45-day escrow*
>
> *Mary is accepting the loan conditions and is agreeable to including the appliances and therefore did not address those items in counteroffer #1. If Joe is agreeable to the new price and the days to close, he will sign counteroffer #1. If Joe is not agreeable, he will prepare counteroffer #2 with his requested changes.*

This process will continue until both parties agree to all terms and conditions. The agents must read the terms carefully to be aware of all the conditions and terms of the agreement. The most frequent issue in the counteroffer is the purchase price. All counteroffers must be read because once a term is entered in the document, it must be addressed. The parties, including the agents, should request clarification of any unusual items and discuss any problems or issues. The loan agent is responsible for relaying any issues or information to the buyer and their agent for resolution and decisions.

CONTRACT FOR DEED or REAL PROPERTY SALES CONTRACT is an installment contract between buyer and seller. The seller is known as the vendor and the buyer is known as the vendee. The purpose of this type of transaction is for the buyer to occupy the property and make payments to the seller. The seller retains the deed or legal ownership until they are paid in full. The buyer has possession of and an equity interest in the property. The deed is delivered to the buyer when the seller has been paid in full.

The **SELLER** does not have a right to sell or dispose the property to anyone else while the contract is in place. The seller also must make any payments that they owe against the property before using the buyers' payment money for any other purpose and cannot secure any new encumbrances against the property. The seller must check the terms of any existing loans against the property to ensure that there is not a "due on sale" clause. A due on sale clause will render a contract for deed situation void because the lender has the right to demand the balance of the loan be paid in full immediately. Lenders may be negotiable on this point if they are consulted prior to entering into such a contract.

The **BUYER** is responsible for maintaining the property in the condition it was in when they received possession. They can improve the property, which will increase its value. This is commonly known as "sweat equity." The buyer is generally responsible for property taxes and homeowner's insurance.

This type of transaction was popular when interest rates were inordinately high, such as in the late 1970s. There was also a time when obtaining a bank loan for a mortgage was considerably more difficult and a contract for deed was a viable option for many buyers who could not otherwise get a loan to purchase a home. A contract for deed can be advantageous to a buyer who does not have a sufficient down payment and needs time to build up cash and equity before obtaining a bank loan. The sale of real property between family members is a commonly used circumstance calling for a contract for deed transaction.

A definite advantage to the seller on a contract for deed transaction is that they only pay capital gains income taxes on the amount of profit that they receive within a tax year.

> ***Example:*** *George owned a rental property that he wanted to sell without reinvesting in another rental property. He also wanted to avoid paying capital gains taxes on the profit. He purchased the property 20 years ago and paid $100,000. The property is now worth $500,000.*

His taxes on $400,000 capital gain is more than he wants to pay within one tax year. By selling the property to his nephew Russ on a contract for deed, George can offset his taxes by paying capital gains taxes only on the amount he collects each year from his nephew's total annual payment amount of $18,000. The taxes went from a range of more than $100,000 to approximately $6,000. The taxes will of course depend on the rest of the income and expenses. This is strictly an estimate for demonstration purposes.

1031 EXCHANGE

1031 EXCHANGE is a transaction that is a purchase of an investment property and the sale of another of the buyer's investment properties of similar property type and value. ***The purpose of doing a 1031 exchange is a tax benefit effecting capital gains.*** By purchasing a property of equal or greater value, the buyer can defer or offset the taxes that would be due on the capital gains income.

A **1031 EXCHANGE** cannot be used for owner-occupied property. This is for investment properties only and must be like properties. Like properties can refer to investments such as residential rental, or properties purchased for speculation and development. The principle of this type of transaction as created by the IRS is that an investor is provided the opportunity to sell an investment property and instead of paying the capital gains on the income from the sale, they are provided the opportunity to defer the gains by reinvesting the gains in another investment property. This is similar to the allowance by the IRS to defer gains from one's residential property to their new residential property except that it is for investment income only.

To exercise the IRS deferment of income, the property owner must reinvest the capital gain from the investment property being sold to an investment property being purchased. This is accomplished by exchanging one property for another of like kind.

The exchange transaction is basically doing a sales transaction and a purchase with a concurrent closing. In other words, the sale of the former property will close at the same time as the purchase of the new property. The buyer of the current property does not need to be the seller of the new property. The buyer of the current property does not need to be the seller of the new property. The property owner is exchanging one property for another. The funds from the sale will be transferred according to the contract and the lender's requirements to purchase the escrow.

The following rules must be adhered to:

- **All funds or profits** from the sale of the current property must be transferred to the purchase or down payment of the new property. Any capital gains that are not used in the purchase of the new property will be taxed as income in that tax year.
- **Any relief taken,** such as by mortgage is referred to as "boot," and will be taxed as income. Boot is the taking of any of the profit of the capital gains. This can be accomplished through cash, a mortgage, or anything of value.
- **Once the property owner opens escrow** on the sale of the currently owned investment property, a replacement property must be named within 45 days of close of escrow of the relinquished property. If that escrow cannot be completed for any reason, another property can be named to replace that property.
- **To qualify as a 1031 exchange,** the transaction must be completed within 180 days of close of escrow of the relinquished property or by the due date for filing income taxes for the year that the relinquished property closed escrow. That date is April 15th of the following calendar year.

Example: *John Is selling his rental property in a 1031 exchange for $500,000. He purchased the property ten years ago and paid $200,000 for the property. His capital gain is $300,000. The total amount of $300,000 must go toward the purchase of the new investment property.*

John is buying the new property for $500,000. $300,000 must transfer to the new property and he can get a mortgage loan for the $200,000 without paying any capital gains taxes.

John is buying a new property for $500,000 and will only transfer $100,000 and get a mortgage loan in the amount of $400,000 to purchase the new property. John will be required to pay capital gains taxes on $200,000 boot that he gained from the mortgage in that tax year.

John is buying the new property for $450,000 and will receive $50,000 in cash at the close of escrow. He will pay capital gains taxes in that tax year on the $50,000 boot. The principle is to transfer profit from one property to another or pay taxes on the capital gains income.

The examples have not taken into consideration any of the property owner's maintenance and other expenses that will affect the capital gains. The real estate agent must take all off-setting expenses into consideration when working with a 1031 exchange. This is a purchase transaction and closing costs cannot be included in the loan amount. The closing costs are to be deducted from the funds from the sale of the former property or the buyer must bring in any additional funds required to close escrow.

The escrow officer is crucial and not all escrow officers perform this type of transaction. There are strict rules determined by the Internal Revenue Service that must be met to qualify for the tax benefit. A potential party to a 1031 exchange should always speak with their tax preparer prior to entering into a binding contract.

NOTE

A real estate agent who wishes to handle this type of transaction should discuss the benefits and consequences with a tax preparer and an escrow officer prior to becoming involved.

DISCLOSURES

DISCLOSURES are required to be delivered to the buyers once a purchase contract becomes binding. The following disclosures are legally required to be provided to the buyer as soon as possible.

1. **AGENCY RELATIONSHIP DISCLOSURE** as discussed in *Chapter 7*, must be provided to both buyer and seller. The disclosure explains to clients the duties and roles of the agents and what an agency means. The client must acknowledge receipt of the disclosure.

2. **TRANSFER DISCLOSURE STATEMENT (TDS)** was discussed in *Chapter 7*. The TDS discloses to the buyer everything that the seller knows about the condition of the property. The ***Real Estate Transfer Disclosure Statement*** is a form that is required by law to be completed by the seller of one-to-four-unit residential dwellings. The disclosure provides for the seller to notify the buyer of real property of any defects or problems that they are aware of with the subject property such as leaking roof or non-working dishwasher. The disclosure also informs the buyer of what is included in the sale such as the appliances, screens for windows and doors, and the type of furnace.

The **seller must complete their designated section**. The **agent cannot complete it for the seller.** The seller must disclose everything they know about the condition of the property. It is assumed that the property owner knows the property better than anyone. The **EXCEPTIONS** to a seller providing a TDS are:

- Sale between co-owners
- Sale between family members
- Probate sale
- Foreclosure sale

All other sales of one-to-four-unit residential dwellings will require a TDS be provided to the buyer by the seller. The term "let the buyer beware" is no longer part of the real estate practice. The agent must also complete a section of the TDS once the seller has completed their section. The **agent must disclose all that they know about the property.**

The **purpose** of this disclosure is to inform the buyer as much as possible about the actual condition and state of the property they are purchasing. This allows the buyer to make an educated decision. The disclosure of defects of a property does not require repairs, it only informs. The disclosure is to be delivered to the buyer as soon as is practical after acceptance of the purchase offer.

The buyer has the right to cancel the transaction within three days of receipt of the Transfer Disclosure Statement (TDS) if it is hand delivered to them and five days to respond if the TDS is mailed to them. If the buyer does not receive a copy of the TDS, they may cancel the transaction at any time prior to the close of escrow.

NOTE

The real estate professional should provide the disclosure to the seller for completion within a day or two of the offer acceptance, then deliver to the buyer immediately.

3. **BUYER'S INSPECTION ADVISORY** is an addendum to the residential purchase agreement. This disclosure advises the buyer of real property to be aware of their rights and duties and those of the seller and the brokers that apply to the contract. It also advises and recommends the use of the various inspections and reports that are available to them in regard to the property and the condition of the property.

4. HUD BOOKLETS entitled ***Closing Costs and You*** and ***Purchasing a Home*** were created by the ***Department of Housing and Urban Development (HUD).*** It is required by federal law that the real estate agent provide these handbooks to the buyers of one-to-four-unit residential properties at the time that they enter into a contract to purchase. The HUD handbooks are manuals prepared according to government regulations disclosing to the borrower information regarding their rights to help protect them from unscrupulous practices. They are categorized according to the transaction.
   - ***Closing Costs and You*** provides the consumer with detailed information about closing costs with a complete breakdown on the closing statement provided by escrow. A line-by-line explanation of possible expenses involved in a real estate purchase transaction is provided to help the consumer understand and prevent fraud.
   - ***Purchasing a Home*** gives the consumer guidance and tips when purchasing a home, including choosing an agent.

   There are additional HUD booklets that apply to the lending process and will be discussed further in Chapter 12, Real Estate Financing. The HUD booklets for loans are categorized according to whether the type of loan is a purchase, refinance, ARM, or home equity line of credit (HELOC).

5. NATURAL HAZARD DISCLOSURE STATEMENT and CARs *Consumers Guide to Disclosures for Buyers* and *Sellers* both provide most of the hazard disclosures that are required to be provided. *The following disclosures must be provided to the buyer of real property.*

   The Natural Hazard Disclosure is provided to the buyer of residential property of potential hazards that affect the property from the area surrounding the property. These disclosures are to be provided to the buyer by the seller or their agent. The following issues are addressed with this disclosure.

   Flood Hazard Zones are areas subject to unusual flood risks. California has a large number of dry riverbeds and other areas that become flooded occasionally as a result of snowmelt in the mountains and from heavy rains. The Federal Emergency Management Agency (FEMA) designates Flood Hazard Zones.

- **Inundation Zones** are areas subject to flooding from the event of a dam failure. The State Office of Emergency Services designates inundation areas.
- **Very High Fire Hazard Severity Zones** are areas that tend to be surrounded by dry brush and scrub that ignites and burns easily. Property owners who are in these areas are required to maintain the areas around their homes to help reduce the possibility of fire. High Fire Hazard Severity Zones are designated by the State Board of Forestry.
- **Wildland Fire Areas,** which are also known **as State Fire Responsibility Areas,** are zones that are the responsibility of the state, rather than local agencies, for fire suppression. Wildland Fire Areas are designated by the State Board of Forestry.
- **Earthquake Fault Zones** are areas located within a certain distance of earthquake fault lines. The State Geologist designates Earthquake Fault Zones.
- **Seismic Hazard Zones** are areas subject to ground movement during earthquakes. The State Geologist designate Seismic hazard Zones.

6. LEAD–BASED PAINT DISCLOSURE informs the consumers of the possibility of paint in the home having lead in its base. It has been determined that lead may cause a number of health issues. In the 1970s, it was discovered that mental impairment among other health issues, including death in children, had been caused by exposure to lead. Children suffered from the effects of lead poisoning through natural childhood behavior, including crawling and exploring their surroundings, or eating paint chips that had flaked from the walls. Lead-based paint was used mainly primarily for trim such as around windows and doors.

   The use of lead-based paint was banned in 1978 by the ***Consumer Product Safety Commission***. Homes built since that time should be free of lead-based paint; however, it is advisable to provide the information in the disclosure. It is always possible that a property owner painted with old paint. Sales of any home built prior to 1978 must include the Lead-Based Paint Disclosure. The disclosure provided to the buyer contains detailed information.

   Additional information can be found on the requirements by calling the National Lead Information Clearinghouse at (800) 424-LEAD (5323), and the Environmental Protection Agency at www.epa.gov/lead, or HUD www.hud.gov/lead.

ENVIRONMENTAL HAZARD DISCLOSURE ADDRESSES MOLD. Molds are simple microscopic organisms that are present virtually everywhere indoors and out. Molds are fungi that are needed to break down dead material to recycle the nutrients back into the environment. They need a food source, which is often found in many household items, and can be caused by certain environmental issues in the average home, such as:

- Flooding
- Plumbing leaks
- Roof leaks
- Sink or sewer overflow
- Dampness in basements and crawlspaces
- Steam from bath usage and cooking
- Wet clothes and fabrics
- Clothes dryers with indoor exhaust.

MOLDS are present in every home and are inhaled and ingested on a regular basis at small levels. Molds are harmful to humans when inhaled in large amounts. An inordinate amount of mold growth and spores inside a house can be considered a health problem, especially to those with breathing problems such as asthma, and needs to be corrected. A home inspection will usually be able to detect a problem, and the inspector will suggest further testing if they feel it is warranted. The disclosure provides more information for the home buyer and additional information is available the California Department of Public Health at https://www.cdph.ca.gov.

RADON is another issue that is addressed in the ***Environmental Hazard Disclosure.*** Radon is a naturally occurring chemically inert radioactive gas that is formed from the decay of radium and uranium. Radon is usually found in rocks containing uranium, such as certain granites and shale. The way that radon enters a home is through cracks and openings to the soil. It generally enters homes when the inside pressure is higher, such as during the cold months when the home is closed and sealed and air vents and ducts draw air into and through the home.

Sealed homes using exhaust fans are also prone to radon presence. Radon can be present in water which enters the home. The Environmental Protection Agency has determined that radon is a carcinogen and is harmful to humans. Long-term exposure to high levels of radon will increase a person's risk of lung cancer. The ***California Department of Health Services*** also provides information pertaining to radon.

HOMEOWNER'S GUIDE TO EARTHQUAKE SAFETY was written and compiled by the California Seismic Safety Commission as required by Assembly Bill 2959. California state law has provisions to help protect homeowners from the damage and devastation that can be the result of an earthquake. Every home in California is subject to the effects of an earthquake. Building codes have been created to help in the strengthening of structures with particular requirements for the construction of residential properties.

The primary legislation went into effect on January 1, 1960. Although all buyers of residential properties are given the disclosure for the purpose of earthquake safety, the homes built prior to January 1960 need additional information to secure their homes and protect themselves based on the construction methods and codes at that time.

WATER HEATER BRACING is of particular importance and the proper bracing will be required prior to the close of escrow of a one-to-four-unit residential property. The lack of proper bracing of a water heater can cause fire when the unit tips over during an earthquake and breaks the gas line. Severe burns have also been caused during and after an earthquake by the unit tipping over and splashing or spilling its contents. The buyer should have a contractor prepare the bracing to ensure its effectiveness. It is not a difficult job, but the precision of the work is vital to the safety of the property and its occupants.

ALQUIST-PRIOLO EARTHQUAKE FAULT ZONING ACT (enacted in 1972) provides for the mapping of known active earthquake faults and the identification of a 1,000-foot-wide zone with the fault zone in the middle. The fault zone is considered to be a quarter mile on either side of the fault. ***Local planning commissions*** are required to provide this information and adhere to building codes specified for these areas.

This act requires that buyers of residential property be provided with ***The Homeowner's Guide to Earthquake Safety***, the bracing of water heaters, and the disclosure by the seller of any known structural weaknesses.

MEGAN'S LAW provides the buyers with the information to access a database either by internet or phone that provides information about the location and addresses of registered sex offenders and child molesters. A potential buyer of residential property has the right to know if there may be a predatory offender within the neighborhood.

SMOKE DETECTOR AND WATER HEATER STATEMENT OF COMPLIANCE
is the seller's statement to the buyer that the state requirements have been met. Water heater strapping or bracing has already been addressed under the Earthquake Disclosure. The state also requires that single family residential properties have smoke detectors installed.

7. **MELLO-ROOS DISTRICT DISCLOSURE** notifies the buyer that the property is or may be in a Mello-Roos Tax District. A Mello-Roos Community Facilities District is an entity formed by a local government district, government, or agency to finance a variety of public services such as school, libraries, police, and fire department expenses. A Mello-Roos District raises funds for the financing of community needs through **special assessment property taxes** which only apply in designated areas. The seller of a property in a designated Mello-Roos District must disclose that fact to any potential buyers.

8. **MILITARY ORDNANCE LOCATIONS** is a disclosure regarding areas that have been used for military ordnance. The area may have been used for the purposes training and may contain explosive munitions.

9. **FHA INSPECTION DISCLOSURE** notifies buyers using FHA financing of the importance of obtaining the appropriate inspections prior to closing a purchase transaction.

10. **FOREIGN INVESTMENT IN REAL PROPERTY TAX ACT (FIRPTA)** is a required tax disclosure which notifies buyers of real property that they are required to withhold 10% of the seller's profit from the sale of real property and forward the funds to the Internal Revenue Service if the seller is a "foreign person" or a non-resident alien. As most buyers would not have knowledge of the seller's status, CAR has developed a form entitled *Seller's Affidavit of Non-Foreign Status.* If the seller has provided this form, the buyer is relieved form any further action.

11. COMPREHENSIVE ENVIRONMENTAL RESPONSE, COMPENSATION, AND **LIABILITY ACT (CERCLA),** or the s***uperfund law,*** imposes liabilities for environmental issues such as a property that once had a gas station on it. The liability or responsibility for cleaning up the problem falls on everyone who has "touched" the property, unlike other disclosure responsibilities that are waived for certain parties:
    - **Owners** and all co-owners
    - Tenants
    - Heirs
    - **Lenders** that have foreclosed

Disclosures are legally required to be delivered to both buyers and sellers. There must be a signature as a form of verification of that delivery. A copy is provided to the client and a copy is retained by each of the brokers.

EXCEPTIONS TO DELIVERY OF DISCLOSURES ARE:

- **Transfer to a spouse:** It is presumed that the receiving spouse is aware of any issues or problems with the property.
- **Transfer to a co-owner:** It is presumed that the receiving co-owner is aware of any issues or problems with the property.
- **Transfer to family members:** It is presumed that the receiving family member is aware of any issues or problems with the property.
- **Probate sale:** The courts and heirs are not required to disclose and probably do not know the property's issues.
- **Foreclosure sale:** The lender would not be aware of the property's issues.

LISTING AGREEMENTS

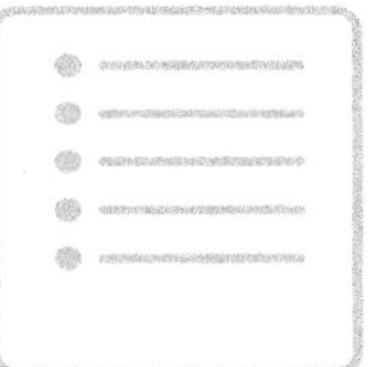

LISTING AGREEMENTS are among the most commonly used contracts in the real estate industry. A real estate professional must always obtain the listing agreement in writing. Listing agreements or contracts are agreements between a seller of real property and a real estate broker to list the seller's property for sale to the public.

The listing agreement is a unilateral agreement because the agent promises to perform actions with due diligence in order to complete the contract by finding a ready, willing, and able buyer for the subject property. The seller of the property is not making a promise to perform an action to the agent other than to pay a commission IF the agent performs. Once the agent finds a buyer, a purchase agreement replaces the listing agreement.

The listing agreement is between the seller/principal and the broker. The associate licensee cannot be the direct representative of the client. The broker agent contract defines the terms of the agreement between the agent and broker. The agent or associate licensee represents the broker in a real estate transaction and the broker represents the principal although the principal might never even meet the broker. The agent represents the broker and must treat the principal and the transaction with the same principles and laws as the broker.

EXCLUSIVE AUTHORIZATION AND RIGHT TO SELL LISTING is currently the most commonly used listing agreement in California. This type of listing agreement allows the exclusive broker to be paid as the listing agent no matter who procures the buyer.

Prior to meeting with a potential seller, the real estate professional will need to prepare for the meeting. ***A comprehensive report on the property value will be important in planning the sale strategy, especially determining the list price.*** The report prepared for presentation to the seller will include the listings and recent sales of the comparable properties (comps) in the immediate area. ***The comparable properties should be in close proximity to the subject property; on the same street is ideal.***

The purpose of presenting comparable properties is to demonstrate the value of the subject property to the seller. It is common for a property owner to have a distorted view of the value of their own property. It is beneficial to have viewed the comps prior to meeting with the seller and viewing their property. It will be easier to give a fully informed opinion and provide when speaking with the seller. If the agent is familiar with the comps, it will be an easy task to establish a good value for the subject property.

While viewing the subject property, the real estate professional will look at walls and ceilings for possible damage, turn on water faucets, and flush toilets. Be certain to be familiar with not only the good things about the property, but also any issues that may need to be addressed. Having a discussion with the seller about any issues at the initial meeting will avoid problems later.

An agent meeting with a potential seller to list their property for sale must take care when completing the listing agreement. The address should be completed as efficiently as possible at this initial meeting. A mistake in the address can and has caused legal problems in the history of real estate. Something as simple as using "Street" instead of "Avenue" can designate a completely different property.

The seller's name should be as complete and accurate as possible. All owners of the property should be on the listing agreement, but do not need to be. The listing agreement is an employment contract and only one owner needs to sign that agreement. The agent needs to confirm all of the owners of the property because even though only one owner needs to sign the listing agreement, all property owners must sign the purchase offer prior to having an executed and binding contract.

The amount of commission or the fee to be charged must be completed. An agent should never allow or request that a client sign a contract with blank spaces. The commission can be charged in the form of a percentage of the sales price or a commission, as a flat fee or a specified dollar amount, or as an hourly rate.

The **total commission** stated in the **listing agreement** is **divided accordingly between the seller's broker and the buyer's broker.** The commission split is not required to be a 50/50 split and often the listing agent will agree to a lower split as a negotiation with the seller. An example would be if the seller's finances are limited, and they can only afford a 3% commission. In order to get other agencies to show the property, the seller's agent will offer to pay the selling office/agent 2% and accept 1% for their office.

It is illegal under the **Sherman Anti-Trust Act** to set pricing by discussing and agreeing between offices to charge a set amount as commission to be charged for a service such as listing a property for sale. A broker may determine a minimum amount of commission to be charged by their own office allowing for room for negotiation with the client.

Commissions are ALWAYS negotiable. The Sherman Anti-Trust Act prevents collusion to set commissions.

LOCK BOX placement on the premises is the seller's choice and the seller must agree to this in the listing agreement. The lock box will contain a key to their home giving access to all members of the Multiple Listing Service (MLS). The purpose of having a lock box is to provide easy access for real estate professionals. When an agent is showing property to potential buyers, they will show the properties that they can get into. The other purpose is to provide access while the seller is not at home. It is advisable that the seller is not home while the property is being shown. Sellers may take offense to buyer comments or otherwise interfere with the agent's job.

MLS is also an option for the seller. The MLS provides a network for real estate agents to access all the listings available through member offices. It provides the seller with expanded advertising of their property. Most sellers agree to an MLS entry for their properties. It is a beneficial organization for all parties to a real estate listing transaction. MLS will require that the listing be placed with them generally within 24 hours.

The **"FOR SALE" SIGN** to go in the front of the property to advertise the listing must also be approved by the seller. The sign can be placed immediately or by a professional sign company.

The seller and agent must both sign the agreement. A copy is left with the seller along with a copy of the Agency Relationship Disclosure.

The listing is now complete, and the real estate professional will begin the work of finding a ready, willing, and able buyer.

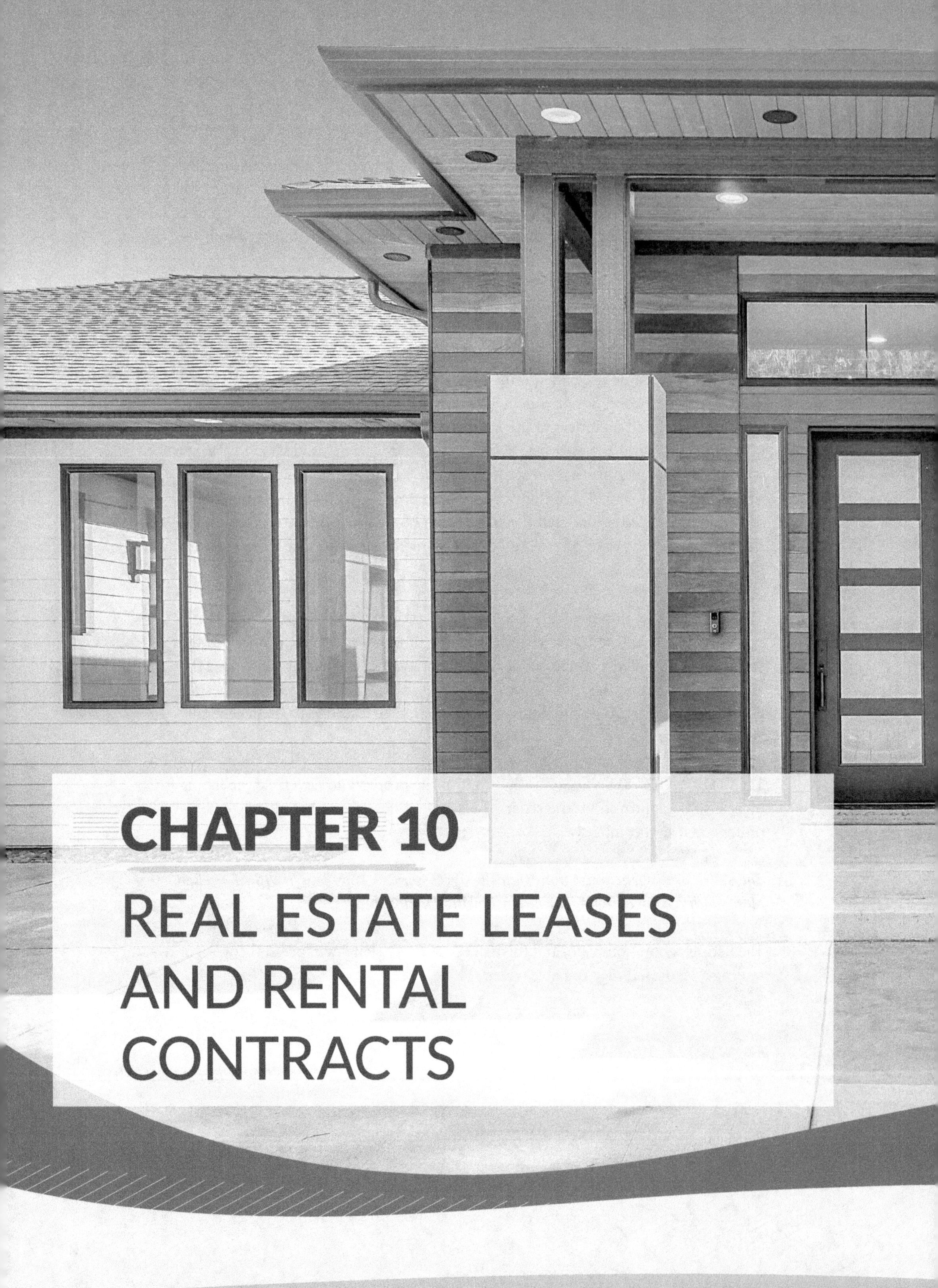

CHAPTER 10

REAL ESTATE LEASES AND RENTAL CONTRACTS

US
Realty School

LEASEHOLD CONTRACTS

Leasehold contracts can be written or oral; however, any lease agreement or any other real estate contract in the state of California that is ***for a period of more than one year must be in writing.*** More than one year means 12 months and one day.

> ***Example:*** *A lease agreement is to begin on January 1 of the current year and will end on December 30 of the same year; the lease is not required to be in writing because it is for a period of one year, not more than one year. Such a lease agreement does not need to be in writing, but it is recommended.*

Many residential leases are for a period of one year and the majority of them are in writing. Commercial leases are usually for a period of three years or more and will always be in writing. Both the landlord and tenant benefit from a lease or rental agreement being in writing. When the terms of the lease are in writing, no matter the length of the lease, there is less chance of misunderstanding and all parties to the lease know what is expected.

The landlord must sign the written lease; however, the tenant does not need to sign because they accept the terms of the lease by taking possession of the property. If the property is being managed by a property manager, the property manager has the authority to sign for the landlord.

LEASE & RENTAL AGREEMENTS There are various prepared forms available as lease or rental agreements. Other forms can be found in office supply stores, online, and to members of the ***California Apartment Association*** at https://caanet.org.

Property leases are legal contracts, whether written or oral, and must be treated as discussed in *Chapter 8*.

Leases have the following legal characteristics:

- **Legal capacity:** All parties to the contract must be 18 years of age, or legally emancipated (such as through marriage, military service, or a court order); sane; sober; not convicted of certain felonies. Leaseholds held by a **person lacking capacity,** such as a minor or one determined to be incompetent, will be established by the courts.
- **Legal purpose:** A legal contract cannot be used to perform an illegal act.
- **Consideration:** Money or something of value must be exchanged to show earnest intent to enter into a contract.
- **Offer and acceptance:** One party must make an offer, such as to rent a property, and another party must accept the offer, such as agreeing to rent the property for the terms offered.
- **Definite terms:** Stated clearly to include:
    - Parties
    - Property
    - Period of time
    - Payment

1. **PARTIES** to a lease agreement must be identified as to who is to have possession of the property, who owns the property, and who has the right to give the use of the subject property. The parties to a lease contract are:
    - Lessor or landlord (OR = Giver)
    - Lessees or tenant (EE = Receiver)

2. **The PROPERTY** must be identified sufficiently to positively identify it in the lease contract.

3. **PERIOD OF TIME** is addressed as the beginning date and the ending date of the lease term. If there is no lease term stated in the agreement, the rent paid will establish the term. For example, if the rent is paid for a one-week period, the term will be established as week-to-week. When there is no lease term stated, it will be presumed to be month-to-month. A lease will often include terms in the event that the lessee wishes to continue the lease of the property after the term of the contract has expired.
   A copy of the rental agreement must be delivered to the tenant within **15 days** of the execution of the agreement. When a tenant remains beyond the term of a one-year lease, they can request the new terms to be provided to them within 15 days of the request.

In the case of an oral agreement, the landlord is required to provide the terms in writing if the tenant requests the written terms. This is not a request for a written lease, but merely the terms of the oral agreement in writing.

- **99 YEAR LEASES** are common practice in California. The term of a lease is not allowed by law for the lease of real property located within the limits of an incorporated city or town to be for a period of more than 99 years. It became a common practice in California in the late 1800s and into the early 1900s to lease land for a period of 99 years. The tenant of a 99-year lease would build their home or other structure on the land without concern of losing their property because 99 years was beyond their lifetime.

  The Wrigley family owns most of Catalina Island with structures having been built on leasehold property. Many of the areas owned by the California Forestry Service or state parks have leasehold properties with private homes. Los Padres National Park had leasehold properties with leases that expired in the 1990s. Interestingly, the tenants did not seem to be aware of the circumstances and were surprised when they were notified that they no longer had a right to occupy the property. In that particular situation, new leases were established allowing the tenants to retain possession of the property. In other situations, the tenants were not as fortunate and had to abandon possession of property that they had bought and paid for.

  Legally, when the lease expires, the possession of the property reverts to the lessor or landlord.

  The real estate professional should always explain the nuances and legalities involved in a leasehold tenancy.

- **AGRICULTURAL LEASES** cannot legally be for a period of more than 51 years.

4. **PAYMENT** of rent must be clearly stated in amount due, and the date and frequency that the payment is due. If rent is being paid in a form other than money, the form of consideration must be stated. A tenant is obligated to pay rent to the landlord once they take possession of the property. Taking possession indicates the tenant's agreement to pay for the use of the property. Rent can be paid at any time and interval that has been agreed to by the parties to the contract.

In most situations the tenant pays the initial rental payment prior to taking possession. If the agreement does not stipulate when the payment is to be made, the State of California has determined that the rent will be due and payable at the end of the lease term if the term is for one year or less. Local governing agencies may have provisions that will override this if they are more stringent.

Residential leases must contain the contact information for the landlord or the entity that the rent will be paid to. The contact information must contain the party's name, address, phone number or other contact information, as necessary. The times of availability or business hours for rent collection must also be provided to the tenant. The landlord does not need to provide personal information as long as they provide information for the tenant to make payments to them in some manner, such as through direct deposit. If the landlord chooses not to provide their personal address, such as when using a P.O. box, the rent is presumed to be paid on the date it is postmarked.

- **SECURITY DEPOSIT** is the amount that the tenant pays as security against possible damage, unpaid rent, cleaning expenses, or any other costs that may arise through the use of the property. The security deposit will be held by the landlord until the tenant has vacated the property. The security deposit can include any processing fees for new tenants. Application fees are not included in the security deposit. Once a tenant has occupied a property for a period in excess of one year, the landlord cannot charge for cleaning, painting, or normal maintenance, which is considered to be normal wear and tear on a property.

  The maximum amount allowed in California as security deposit on a residential property is:
  - **2 month's rent for an unfurnished unit**
  - **3 month's rent for a furnished unit**

Tenants have the option to request an inspection on termination of the lease and has a right to be present when the landlord or their representative inspects the property for damages and cleanliness. *It is also advisable for a tenant to take photographs of the property prior to moving in and after moving out.*

Within three weeks of the tenant vacating the premises, the landlord must provide to the tenant an itemized list of any deductions from the security deposit for repairs to the property or any rent payments that may be owed. If the tenant disagrees with any of the deductions, the burden of proof is on the landlord, and it is assumed that the tenant does not owe until otherwise proven. The landlord is responsible for returning any unused portion of the security deposit to the tenant within that three-week period. The landlord is liable for up to twice the amount of the deposit if the funds are held in bad faith or without verified cause.

security deposits on residential properties are never non-refundable.

When the ownership of a rental property changes hands such as in a sale of the property, the security deposit also transfers hands to the new owner. The tenant is notified of the change of ownership along with the new contact information. In the case of a sale of rental property, the escrow officer will withhold the amount of the security deposit from the seller's proceeds and credit or transfer the funds to the buyer.

Installation of items by the tenant that may destroy or damage the property if removed are considered to be a part of the property and will therefore remain. If the tenant removes any permanently affixed items that they installed, they are responsible for any damage and for restoring the property to its original condition. Installation of items should be addressed, and it is advisable to have a written agreement regarding the improvements in order to avoid conflict.

TRADE FIXTURES are the exception to this rule. A trade fixture is an item that is required for the tenant to conduct business. This rule generally applies to commercial property not to residential property, however, it can apply to either type of property. If a tenant is planning to install a fixture that would be considered permanent, the approval of the landlord should be obtained prior to installation. A tenant has the right to remove trade fixtures prior to vacating the premises or expiration of the lease term.

> ***Example:*** *Mary rented a commercial space for the purpose of opening a beauty shop. Prior to opening her business, she installed plumbing for the shampoo bowls and stations for the stylists were installed against the walls. Extra lighting was also installed.*
>
> *When Mary's lease expired, she decided to move her business to a new location. Mary removed the stations and sinks from the walls. She had the walls repaired to correct the damage done to them. She did not remove the plumbing because it would have caused too much damage to the property. The next tenant would be able to either use the plumbing or seal the walls to hide it.*

Mary did not have time to return to get her light fixtures or sign before the lease expired. She forfeited those items. The landlord had no claim to repairs based on her fixtures because she made repairs and the fact that they were trade fixtures cleared her of further obligation.

COMMERCIAL RENTAL PROPERTIES also have specific provisions for the **security deposit:**

- **The amount of the security deposit** is not limited to the rent of commercial property.
- **All funds held as security deposits** in excess of one-month's rent must be refunded to the tenant within 2 weeks of the tenant vacating the premises.
- **The landlord must refund** the balance of any security deposit within 30 days of the tenant vacating the premises less any deductions for repair of damages, cleaning, or unpaid rents.

Because security deposits are usually substantial amounts, it is in the tenant's best interest to inspect and record any deficiencies or existing damage to the property prior to taking possession. The tenant should prepare a statement regarding any issues and provide a copy to the landlord.

POSSESSION of the property by the tenant and their right to use the property is protected by the **covenant of quiet enjoyment** which is implied by law. The **right to quiet enjoyment** ensures that the tenant can enjoy the property without interference from the landlord; the California Civil Code allows the entrance by the landlord onto the premises only as necessary. The ***landlord is required by law to give adequate notice to the tenant of a need or intention to enter the premises, (24 hours*** is generally considered adequate.) For emergency purposes or for an abandoned tenant, the landlord does not need to notify the tenant immediately after entering. The following situations are allowed:

- **Emergencies,** such as burst water pipes.
- **Abandonment** by the tenant. The property is not considered abandoned while rent is current.
- **Court order** as with an eviction.

- **To perform repairs** as necessary or agreed upon between the landlord and tenant.
- **Showing** the property to potential tenants, lenders, appraisers, potential buyers, workers, or contractors hired to make repairs.

CONSTRUCTIVE EVICTION may be brought by the tenant against the landlord based on the following actions by the landlord:

- **Interference** with the tenant's use of the property.
- **Altering** the property from the condition at the time of leasing, making it less than usable or desirable by the tenant.
- Threats of eviction.
- **Leasing** the property to another party.
- **Failure** to make necessary repairs for the maintenance of the property or as agreed to such as the repair of a furnace or water heater which will affect the use of the property by the tenant.

TRANSFERABILITY of a lease will vary and should be specified in the contract. Circumstances arise that will require a tenant to vacate the premises prior to a lease expiring. Occasionally the landlord and tenant can mutually rescind the contract. The landlord may willingly release the tenant from their commitment for a variety of reasons, the most often being to lease the property for higher rent.

A SUBLEASE of a property is the transfer of possession to another party for a portion of the lease term. Reversionary rights are held by the original tenant, which means that they may choose to reoccupy the property at some time in the future. The original tenant remains responsible for payment of rent and the condition of the property, which means that the original tenant may need to pay the rent or make repairs of damage caused by the sub-lessee if they defaulted on their responsibilities. This is also known as a **sandwich lease** because the original lessee remains in the middle of the contract.

ASSIGNMENT of a lease transfers the right of possession to a new lessee for the remainder of the lease term. The responsibility of the rent payments usually remains with the original tenant if the new tenant defaults on the rent payments. It may be negotiated to release the original tenant from all secondary liability. A sublease or an assignment will both require the approval of the landlord. Any rejection by the landlord must be reasonable and cannot be arbitrary.

RENEWAL or TERMINATION of a lease can be handled in several ways. Remaining in possession of the property is a common way of renewing the rental agreement. The type of lease will have an impact on the way in which the renewal or termination is conducted.

If either party to the contract chooses to terminate the lease, notice must be given in advance for a period equal to a minimum of the lease term or the term that the rental payment covers. In other words, if the tenant is paying rent for a period of one month, the notice to terminate by either party must be for a minimum of one month. If the tenant has been paying for three months at a time, the notice to terminate must be for no less than three months.

There are situations that will require a notice to terminate for a minimum of 60 days. This minimum will generally be required when the tenant is disabled, elderly, or if there are minor children in a residential property. There are a number of internet sites when searching "tenant rights" that should be used to verify on a case-by-case basis.

> ***Example:*** *Sue rents a house from Joe on a month-to-month basis. Sue wants to move out so when she pays her rent for the next month, she gives Joe a written notice that she will vacate the property in 30 days.*
>
> *If Joe wants Sue to move out, he must provide her with a notice to terminate 60-days prior to the day she is to vacate and return possession of the property to Joe because Sue is disabled.*

ESTATE FOR YEARS is a term used to describe a lease that has a **definite termination date**. When that date arrives, the lease is terminated. If the lessee chooses to renew or to remain in possession of the property and the lessor is willing to allow them to continue to possess the property, the lease becomes a month-to-month lease because the original estate for years is no longer a valid contract as it has expired or terminated. The parties to the contract may choose to write a new contract as a form of renewal.

The **estate for years** lease can be for any time period. The name may indicate that it is in terms of years, but that is merely an expression. The time period can be for one week or five years, whatever the lessor and lessee agree to.

> ***Example:*** *Ted leases his rental property to Jim and they execute a lease for the time period of March 1st of the current year to February 28th of the following year. The lease automatically terminates on February 28th of the following year and Jim remains in possession of the property.*
>
> *On March 1st, Jim hands Ted one month's rent for the month of March. Ted accepts the rent. This action creates a new agreement between Ted and Jim, which is now a periodic estate for one month. If Ted and Jim decide to execute a new lease for a predetermined period of time, they will once again have an estate for years.*

PERIODIC ESTATE is a lease or rental agreement that is for a set period of time determined by the amount of rent being paid. This is most commonly a month-to- month lease because the rent is paid in advance for the purpose of possessing the property for that month. At the beginning of each month, the lessee pays the rent to the lessor and if they accept the rent, the lease agreement is renewed.

ESTATE at WILL occurs when there is no written agreement. The parties are continuing the landlord/tenant relationship based on their willingness to do so or at their will. Usually, the written agreement has expired or terminated, and neither party made any attempt to change the circumstances. In other words, the tenant paid rent, and the landlord accepted the rent, and no new written agreement was created. Under an estate at will, termination is by death of either party or a 60-day written notice to terminate.

> ***Example:*** *Mary had a lease agreement which has expired. She pays her rent to the landlord on a monthly basis and the landlord accepts the rent. There is no new written lease and both parties are happy with the arrangement. It is the will of both parties to continue the lessor/lessee relationship.*

ESTATE at SUFFERANCE is the lowest form of a leasehold estate. The term is derived from the word "suffer." The tenant is remaining in the property in spite of the landlord wanting the tenant to vacate for any number of reasons such as non- payment of rent. If rent is the issue and the tenant pays the rent and the landlord accepts it, the situation is no longer an estate at sufferance, but a periodic estate.

> ***Example:*** *Mary had a lease to rent a home, and the lease expired one week ago. She does not have a lease or rental agreement of any kind and has not paid her rent to the landlord. Mary is currently under an estate at sufferance. Mary approaches the landlord and requests a new lease and pays her rent. If the landlord accepts the rental payment, Mary is now under a periodic estate. Once the new lease is drawn with a set expiration date, Mary will have an estate for years.*

Many leases contain verbiage addressing the renewal, which will require specific compliance, or the lease is voidable. Automatic renewal clauses must be:

- **8 point bold type or greater.**
- **Placed directly above the** tenant's signature line.

SURRENDER of a lease can be accomplished by mutual rescission of both parties. Surrender can also be a result of inappropriate actions by one of the parties to the lease such as the landlord not delivering the premises in habitable condition.
Either party may have grounds to cancel the lease without the consent of the other party based on certain actions.

The TENANT may cancel a lease under the following circumstances and actions by the landlord:

- **Violation** of the right to quiet enjoyment.
- **Failure** to repair.
- **Uninhabitable premises.**
- **Eviction.**
- **Breach of terms of the lease.**
- **Destruction of premises.**
- **Eminent domain**- taken by the government.

The **LANDLORD** may terminate a lease based on the following actions by the tenant:

- **Unauthorized use or illegal purpose** of property.
- **Abandonment.**
- **Breach** of terms of the lease.
- **Destruction** of premises.

ABANDONMENT of premises by the tenant is a voluntary act of termination of the lease without the landlord's agreement and with no intent to continue any further obligations of the lease. The landlord can establish abandonment by the tenant if more than 14 days of rent are owed and the landlord has reason to believe that the premises have been abandoned by providing a written Notice of Abandonment to the tenant regarding that belief. The tenant has 15 days to respond and deny the abandonment if the notice was delivered to the tenant personally.

The tenant must respond to the notice within 18 days if the notice was delivered by mail. It is not necessary to provide a Notice of Abandonment if the premises are vacant; however, it is in the landlord's best interest to do this in the event that the tenant returns at a later date to re-occupy the premises within the lease period. If the landlord does not have a forwarding address or other contact information, mailing or personally delivering to the subject property shows intent to notify.

EVICTION is a legal process that requires the tenant to vacate the premises. The landlord must notify the tenant of their intention to evict prior to filing with the courts. The initial notice is given to allow the tenant the opportunity to remedy the situation such as paying the delinquent rent. An eviction can be filed against a tenant for breach of any of the terms of the lease.

If the tenant is in default on their rent, the landlord is required to first provide a ***Three-Day Notice to Quit or Pay Rent.*** This notice allows the tenant an opportunity to remedy the default. A similar notice is provided to the tenant for other breaches of the terms of the contract.

Notices of eviction are given for the period of the lease or the period that the rent is paid for, which is usually 30 days. If the lease period is for less, it can be extended to 30 days at the landlord's discretion. The eviction period can be for no less than a period of seven days. Notice must be in writing and personally delivered to the tenant. In the tenant's absence, an appropriate adult party at the premises can be handed the notice. If there is no one available at the premises to accept the notice, the notice must be posted in an obvious place on the premises to ensure receipt.

UNLAWFUL DETAINER is obtained by the landlord by requesting an Order of Eviction from the courts, which serves as the unlawful detainer. The unlawful detainer is then served to the tenant for failure to comply with the **Notice to Quit or correct the Breach of Contract** by paying rent or otherwise correcting the situation. Once the unlawful detainer is granted by the courts, the lease is canceled, and the tenant is required to vacate the premises. The tenant will be liable for damages and rent through the date of the unlawful detainer or the date that the landlord gains possession of the premises depending on the terms of the lease or the decision of the courts. The tenant's utilities cannot be disrupted by the landlord. An unlawful detainer action is given priority over other civil cases with the exception of criminal cases to provide relief to the landlord, expediently.

The tenant has the right to dispute the unlawful detainer action based on the following actions:

- **Retaliatory actions** on the part of the landlord.
- **Untruthful allegations.**
- **Without good cause.**
- **No proper notice provided.**
- **Violation of civil rights or discriminatory acts or other legal barriers.**

The landlord and tenant will often resolve their issues prior to a court date other than correcting the breach. A landlord may forgive rents owed or agree to a mutual rescission to save court costs and regain possession of the premises quickly and without additional problems and hard feelings.

A WRIT OF POSSESSION may be obtained by the landlord if the tenant still refuses to forfeit possession of the premises. The court clerk issues the writ of possession and directs the sheriff or marshal to proceed with the necessary steps to physically remove the tenant from the property. The authorities serve the writ of possession in person or to an appropriate adult at the premises. If there is no one available to be served, the authorities must post the writ in a conspicuous place at the premises to ensure that the tenant sees it.

Five days after the service, the authorities may physically remove any occupant that remains at the premises unless the occupant is not named in the writ or claims a right to possess from prior to the unlawful detainer action.

STAY OF EXECUTION for the judgment received by the landlord may be obtained for an additional five days for the purpose of paying back rent and to have legal possession restored if any of the following apply:

- **Nonpayment of rent** is the cause for eviction.
- **Termination notice failed** to declare forfeiture of the tenant's rights.
- **Lease term** is not expired.

The tenant's personal possessions left on the premises must be inventoried and stored for a minimum of 15 days from the date of providing the tenant with a copy of the inventory if personally delivered, or 18 days if mailed. The tenant's possessions can be stored, with the tenant being charged the costs of storage if claimed. If the personal possessions are not claimed, they can be sold to pay for damages and costs with the balance, along with unused security deposit, being refunded to the tenant.

GOVERNMENT SUBSIDIZED HOUSING TENANTS must be given a 90-day notice to vacate. Section 8/public housing tenants must be given good cause to evict and are entitled to a private hearing with representation by an attorney. These special notice requirements were established as a result of a California Supreme Court case in 2005, *Wasatch v. Degrate.*

DRUG-RELATED ACTIVITIES, including the sale of illegal or controlled substances, does not require the 3-day notice to correct the situation. Eviction can begin immediately. If the premises are within the city limits of Los Angeles, Long Beach, San Diego, or Oakland, such illegal activities can cause eviction by the city attorney or the district attorney.

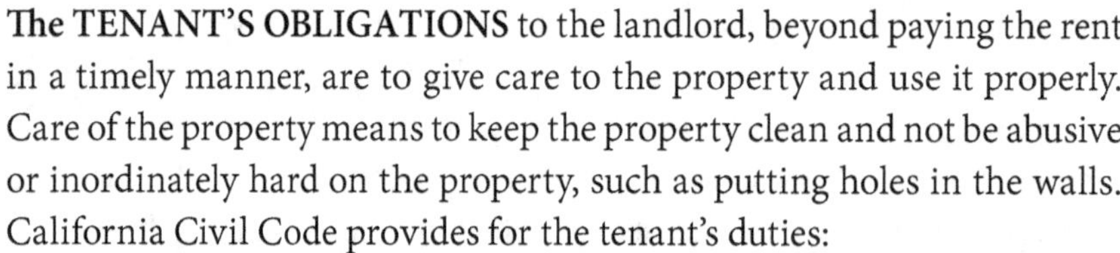

The TENANT'S OBLIGATIONS to the landlord, beyond paying the rent in a timely manner, are to give care to the property and use it properly. Care of the property means to keep the property clean and not be abusive or inordinately hard on the property, such as putting holes in the walls. California Civil Code provides for the tenant's duties:

- The tenant must **keep premises in as clean and sanitary** a condition as possible. Trash and waste must be disposed of properly.
- The tenant must use all utilities and fixtures for electrical, gas, and plumbing properly and maintain it in a clean condition.
- The tenant or any guests of the tenant **may not deface, impair, destroy, or remove any part of the structure or equipment**

belonging to the property.

- **Various portions of the premises must be used by the tenant for the purposes intended.**

If the tenant is in violation of the obligations to use care in maintaining the property, the landlord is not responsible to make the repairs for the tenant's comfort. A lease may contain terms that require damages caused by gross negligence on the part of the tenant to be repaired by the tenant. If the terms of repair are a part of the lease, the landlord may not be able to sue the tenant for excessive repairs.

BREACH OF LEASE TERMS allows the landlord the ability to terminate the lease and evict the tenant.

The LANDLORD'S OBLIGATIONS include the maintenance of the premises to be habitable and tenantable. Communities have building codes and health and safety standards that must be met. Most leases contain provisions and covenants regarding the maintenance and condition of the property. If there is no clause concerning the landlord's obligations as to the condition of the property, the courts will consider the covenant as implied. In other words, the landlord is responsible for maintaining the premises in a manner that is suitable for human habitation as determined by health and safety standards.

CALIFORNIA CIVIL CODE also has provisions with which landlords must comply. A residential dwelling is tenantable or in an acceptable condition to be rented with the following:

- **Dead bolt locks** on entry doors.
- **Locks or some sort of security** on every window that opens.
- **Adequate protection from the weather** to include unbroken windows and doors.
- **Plumbing, electric system, and gas lines** installed in conformance to building codes and maintained in good working order.
- **Hot and cold running water** with all fixture and sewage system meeting health and safety codes.
- **Heating system** that meets building codes and is maintained in a clean workable condition.

- **Electrical lighting** in good working condition.
- **Building structure and grounds to be clean** and sanitary at the time the term of the lease begins to include the grounds to be free of trash and vermin. All areas under the landlord's control are to be maintained in a clean and sanitary condition during the tenancy.
- **Trash receptacles adequate** for the tenant's use are to be provided in good, clean condition and repaired and maintained if under the landlord's control.
- **Floors, stairs, and railings to be maintained** in a secure and solid manner to prevent accidents or injury during use.

If a property is not maintained by the landlord, the tenant has the right to file a complaint with various government agencies, including the local ***Department of Building and Safety, Health Department, and Fire Department.*** The complaints must be in writing and the agency will investigate the complaint for validity. The landlord will be notified of the repairs that must be made to meet the local codes to make the structure habitable.

If the landlord will not make the required repairs, the tenant has the right to notify the landlord in writing or orally that they will make the repairs and deduct the costs from the next month's rent. The tenant must wait 30 days for the landlord to respond or make the repairs. If the landlord has not acted within the 30-day notification period, the tenant can proceed with the repairs and when deducting the amount from the rent, they must include proof of the costs involved. This remedy can only be used twice in a twelve-month period and each incident cannot exceed the amount of one-month rent.

CONSTRUCTIVE NOTICE OF EVICTION is an option the tenant may use when the repairs are excessive and will cost more than the law will allow the tenant to deduct. The lack of maintenance by the landlord does warrant the tenant's right to terminate or cancel the lease for **breach** of the covenant to maintain the property.

The landlord does not have a right to retaliate against a tenant who has filed a complaint or has made repairs then deducted the costs from the rent. Acts of retaliation or penalty by the landlord that are not acceptable include eviction, rent increase, or decreased services.

If the landlord retaliates in any way against a tenant for legitimate complaints and withholding of rent for repairs when the tenant is not delinquent on rent payments, the landlord will not be allowed to regain possession of the property for 180 days from the date of the notice to make repairs. During this time, the landlord cannot remove services or increase rent. In other words, the tenant will have six months unharassed to make any arrangements necessary to alleviate the situation, such as locating a new rental. During this time, the tenant must continue to pay rent per the terms of the lease.

Commercial property does not carry the same provisions for a tenant to repair and deduct from the rent. A tenant of commercial property can sue the landlord for breach of warranty to maintain the premises or use the lack of repairs as a reason to use constructive eviction and vacate the premises.

LIABILITY OF THE LANDLORD AND TENANT to others for injuries or damages to parties who are on the premises either as guests or other reasons, such as a meter reader. Liability will vary with the lease and the circumstances. Generally, the landlord is the party who carries homeowner's insurance on the property and that insurance will cover liability. Injuries sustained on residential property are considered to be the landlord's responsibility based on defective conditions. If the landlord had maintained the property in suitable conditions, there would not have been injuries. The landlord must repair damages or deficiencies to the property when notified. The landlord is not responsible for trespassers if the landlord was not aware of the defects.

The tenant is responsible for notifying the landlord of defects and needed repairs. The tenant is also responsible for injuries caused by their own neglect and lack of care of the premises.

DEMOLITION of a residential property that is rented requires the landlord to provide the tenant with notification of the intention to demolish prior to making an application for the permit to demolish. The landlord must give the notice of their intent to the tenant at the earliest possible date and must give the notice of the intent for future demolition to any prospective tenants prior to signing a lease.

Failure to provide such notice may require the landlord pay the tenant's actual damages and civil penalty, which may be considered or called moving expense, not to exceed $2,500.

DISCRIMINATORY ACTS

DISCRIMINATORY ACTS are of the utmost importance when renting residential property. The ***Fair Employment and Housing Act (FEHA)*** of California prohibits discrimination in housing based on:

- **Race**
- **Color**
- **Religion**
- **Sex**
- **Marital status**
- **Familial status**
- **Age**
- **Disability - physical or mental**
- **Medical condition**
- **Source of income**

The ***Department of Fair Employment and Housing (FEHA)*** enforces the law, which is based on the ***Rumford Act***. Advertising must comply with the ***FEHA*** codes. The discrimination laws and guidelines do not apply to the rental of a single room within an owner-occupied residence.

California's Civil Rights Act of 2006 declares that as of January 1, 2007, all of the protected classifications of the FEHA automatically apply to all other laws and acts protecting the public from discriminatory actions.

The ***Unruh Civil Rights Act*** is part of the ***California Civil Code*** and has become a part of **California's Civil Rights Act of 2006**. The ***Unruh Civil Rights Act*** prohibits arbitrary eviction, rent increase, and withholding services to a tenant by a landlord of any property, including a single-family residence that is rented or sold for profit. The exception to the ***Unruh Civil Rights Act*** is the designation of age for property that is designated for senior citizen housing that has been designed to accommodate the needs of senior citizens. The act forbids discrimination based on the following in both residential and commercial rentals:

- **Race**
- **Color**
- **Religion**
- **Ancestry**
- **National origin**

- **Familial status**
- **Marital status**
- **Sex including gender identity**
- **Sexual orientation**
- **Disability – physical or mental**
- **Medical condition**
- **Source of income**

MOBILE HOME (MANUFACTURED HOME) TENANCIES

MOBILE HOME (MANUFACTURED HOME) TENANCIES vary slightly from rental of other residential properties mainly because the home itself is leased from the owner of the home; however, there is a lease between the park owner/management and the homeowner. This creates a sublease situation between the tenant and the park. The tenant has lease terms that must be abided by with the landlord or the owner of the manufactured home. The landlord has lease terms that must be abided by with the park management. When the tenant agrees to the terms of the lease with the landlord, they are also agreeing to the terms of the lease between the landlord and the park management.

The term mobile home is considered to be antiquated. Manufactured home is the preferred term as the homes are actually not mobile. Following the history of mobile homes tells us that the original mobile homes that were basically mobile are now termed camper trailers. In the 1950s, as a form of low-cost housing, they started being built to be more permanently affixed.

Mobile homes started being built as a "double wide" in the 1960s, which made the permanency of installation necessary. The wheels and axles remained on the undercarriage of most structures, causing the classifications for lending purposes to be established. The guidelines for lending will be discussed further in *Chapter 12, Real Estate Financing.*

Manufacturers began building the homes so the wheels and axles could be removed in the mid-1990s to aid in the viewpoint and attitude toward the integrity of the homes. HUD placed restrictions and building codes on the manufacture of mobile homes in 1976, making the homes substantial and viable additions to the housing industry.

"Manufactured home" also applies to the prefabricated home industry.

Mobile Home Residency Law (MRL) under ***California Civil Code Sections 798 and 799*** regulates the rental agreements used for manufactured homes that are in mobile home parks. The MRL also regulates charges that can be charged to a tenant, grounds for eviction, and the eviction procedure that must be followed within a mobile home park. There are additional civil codes that apply to mobile homes in parks; however, the MRL is the most relevant to the leasing of manufactured homes.

The MRL addresses lease and rental agreements between both the mobile home park management and the resident homeowner and the non-occupying homeowner that is leasing their home. MRL clearly provides for a sublease provision for the non-occupying homeowner. The definition of homeowner, resident, tenancy, mobile home, and mobile home parks are clearly specified in the MRL as the law applies to them. Leasing laws that have already been discussed apply to manufactured homes; however, there are areas of the laws that are particular to mobile homes in parks and, therefore, will prevail over the standard lease laws as they apply to other residential property. Discrimination laws apply to mobile homes and the parks just as they apply to all residential rentals and housing.

There are mobile home parks in California that are owned by the homeowners. The ownership legalities are similar to that of a condo association. When renting a home in such a park, it would be similar to renting a single-family residence and there would be no secondary lease with the park management. The secondary rules would be CC&Rs in compliance with the homeowner's association. It may be advisable to adhere to the lease and regulations as prescribed by the MRL.

Fees that can be charged to the tenant include any fees that are prescribed in the lease and are limited to rent and utilities. Additional and reasonable incidental fees can be added at a later date following a 60-day notice of the additional fee to be charged.

TERMINATION of a lease of a mobile home by the park management can be only for the following reasons:

- Non-payment of rent, utilities, and incidental charges
- Substantial annoyance to other residents
- Failure to comply with park rules
- Failure to comply with laws and ordinances
- Change of use of the park
- Condemnation of the park

Termination proceedings can begin five days after the missed due date for the payment of rent, utilities, or incidental fees. A written ***3-Day Notice to Quit or Pay Rent*** must be personally provided to the tenant to allow 3 days to bring the rent current. A final written ***Notice of Termination*** must be provided to the tenant 60 days prior to the termination date and can accompany the **3-Day Notice to Quit or Pay Rent**. The tenant may set aside the termination by paying the rent and any fees resulting from the delinquency, bringing all past due payments current. A tenant who has been delinquent sufficiently to cause a termination of tenancy action to be initiated more than twice within a twelve-month period will lose the option to bring the delinquent payments current and the termination proceedings will be finalized.

The registered or legal homeowner must also be notified by mail whether for their own default or that of a tenant that is renting their mobile home and will have thirty days from the date the ***Notice of Termination*** was mailed to correct the default. Any lien holders and junior lien holders have the same time as the legal owner to correct any default. None of these claimants will be allowed to remedy a default in payment more than twice within a twelve-month period.

VIOLATION OF PARK RULES will require a written *7-Day Notice to Comply* with a *60-Day Notice to Terminate*. A resident, tenant, or homeowner will not be allowed to remedy a *Notice to Comply* more than three times within a twelve-month period.

LEASE OPTION

LEASE OPTION TO BUY OR LEASE PURCHASE OPTION provides the tenant the option to purchase the property being rented. A lease contract is prepared between the landlord/lessor and the tenant/lessee that includes the terms of the lease with additional terms for the purchase of the property. The purchase is to occur at some time in the future. The most common term for an option is two years, but the term can be for any period of time in which the parties to the contract agree. The terms for the purchase include the usual purchase terms including price and closing date. The lessor/seller is obligated to the terms of the purchase clause;

however, the lessee/buyer is not. The lease purchase option is a unilateral agreement. The seller is bound to sell **IF** the tenant decides to buy.

COMMERCIAL LEASES

COMMERCIAL LEASES are governed by many of the same laws that apply to residential leases, such as the right of quiet enjoyment. Commercial leases do vary considerably as required by the nature of the property usage. There are different types of leases available to lessees and lessors of commercial property.

1. **GROSS LEASES** require that the tenant pays a determined amount of rent, and the landlord pays all of the expenses of property ownership including taxes, insurance, and maintenance. *This type of lease is also the most common type of lease used for residential leasing.* The gross lease is most commonly used in commercial leasing for small commercial properties and small businesses.

   TENANT PAYS
   - **Rent**
   - **Utilities**

   LANDLORD PAYS
   - **Taxes**
   - **Insurance**
   - **Maintenance**

2. **NET LEASES** require that the tenant pay a base amount of rent plus some of the expenses of the property owner, including taxes, insurance, and maintenance. Maintenance usually refers to gardeners, cleaning, walls, and interior carpentry as required by the tenant. What the tenant pays regarding the additional expenses is determined in the lease.

   TENANT PAYS
   - **Rent**
   - **Utilities**
   - **Taxes as determined in the lease**
   - **Insurance as determined in the lease**
   - **Maintenance as determined in the lease**

LANDLORD PAYS

- **Taxes as determined in the lease**
- **Insurance as determined in the lease**
- **Maintenance as determined in the lease**

3. **TRIPLE NET LEASE** is a **net lease** that requires the tenant to pay *all* of the expenses that are normally paid by the property owner. Thus, the term "triple" or three costs of taxes, insurance, and maintenance. Major repairs and maintenance generally remains the responsibility of the property owner.

TENANT PAYS

- **Rent**
- **Utilities**
- **Taxes**
- **Insurance**
- **Maintenance**

LANDLORD PAYS

- **Major repairs**

4. PERCENTAGE LEASE requires a commercial tenant to pay rent based on their monthly income. Depending on the terms of the lease agreement, the tenant may pay a base rent plus a percentage, or they may pay just a percentage of their monthly income. This type of lease is most commonly used in large commercial properties, such as a space in a mall or large shopping centers. Because of the nature of a percentage lease, it can be an excellent negotiation point for a start-up business. The tenant and the landlord both benefit from the success of the business, which is motivation for the landlord to provide support for the business.

TENANT PAYS:

- **Rent**
- **Percentage of gross income for the month**
- **Utilities**
- **Taxes as determined in the lease**
- **Insurance as determined in the lease**
- **Maintenance as determined in the lease**

LANDLORD PAYS

- **Major repairs**
- **Taxes as determined in the lease**
- **Insurance as determined in the lease**
- **Maintenance as determined in the lease**

ESCALATOR CLAUSE allows for an increase in rent at predetermined intervals, usually annually. The rent increases are most often based on a financial index such as the Consumer Price Index (CPI).

ACTS OF TERRORISM since September 11, 2001, have raised concerns about security in everyday life. Leases for many buildings, especially those with a high profile, now include additional security issues. Protection for parking areas and the entrance and escape access may be a point of concern to potential tenants and should be addressed when negotiating a lease.

PROPERTY MANAGEMENT

PROPERTY MANAGEMENT as a viable business venture for the real estate licensee offers a variety of opportunities. A property manager may manage a number of small single-family residences for a variety of property owners, vacation homes, and properties that are rented on a weekly basis, apartment complexes, or commercial and office buildings. Most property managers will specialize in a particular type of property because the duties vary greatly.

A **benefit** of being a property manager is that a regular stream of income is created through the ongoing payment of rent and the continual duties that are required by the property owner. The property manager's income is most commonly based on the income that the property produces on a monthly basis. Payment for the additional duties will vary according to the property and the duties required. *For example, a large commercial building may pay the property manager a percentage of the collected rents, pay a stipend for overseeing the maintenance of the grounds, and pay a percentage for new leases prepared by the property manager.*

Sixteen or more rental units available in residential properties in California are required by law to have a **RESIDENT MANAGER**. The resident manager lives in one of the units on site and therefore is better able to oversee the everyday needs of the property and the tenants. A resident manager also provides an added degree of security for the tenants by virtue of their presence and ability to watch the activities at the site.

The resident manager is required in California to have a minimum of a **real estate sales license and work for a real estate broker** as the property manager and the agent of the property owner.

A PROPERTY MANAGEMENT BUSINESS must have a real estate broker's license, or the business must be operated by a real estate broker. The property manager is the agent of the property owner and owes the principal all the fiduciary duties of a real estate broker.

The most common duties that are required of a property manager are as follows:

- **Show** property to potential tenants.
- **Prepare** leases.
- **Review** applications for creditworthiness.
- **Collect** rent and deposits.
- **Maintain** records and bank accounts.
- **Pay** bills.
- **Provide** reports for the property owner.
- **Prepare** legal documents as required for court needs.
- **Oversee** maintenance and work crews.
- **Work** with security people.

Property management, as with any real estate position, is a highly skilled job and bears a large legal responsibility. Experience should be gained by working for another before assuming the total responsibility as the managing broker.

The property manager will be a contract employee of the property owner. The terms of employment should be specific.

RENT CONTROL

RENT CONTROLS have been a large part of the California housing market for the past 30 to 40 years as a result of rapidly increasing costs and growing populations. Rent controls prohibit the amount and rate that rent may increase on an annual basis for tenants already in a rental property. This allows a certain degree of security for a tenant in knowing that they will be able to afford their current residence in spite of rent increases. Landlords may increase rents annually for current tenants by limited amounts, which are usually percentages of the current rental amount.

Example: Joe has been renting his apartment from ABC Management for one year. He lives in a rent-controlled area which will allow for a maximum increase of 3% over his current rent which is $1,000.

$1,000	*Current rent*
X 3%	*Allowable increase*
= $30	*Allowable dollar amount*
$1,030	*New rent amount*

Joe's rent for the following twelve months cannot be increased to more than $1,030.

In the example, the rent increase will apply to the current tenant only. If Joe decides to move, rent controls in most areas allow the landlord to increase the rent to whatever the going rate is for the area.

***Example:** Joe has decided to move out of the apartment. ABC Management re- rented the apartment at the current rate, which is $1,200.*

The public need to generate affordable housing in a high-cost market encouraged local governments in various cities to create laws to control the rapidly increasing rents. Local governing agencies are responsible for passing the laws and codes for controlling the rate by which rents are allowed to increase and the circumstances under which a property owner is allowed to increase the rents on their residential rental units. Rent controls gained such a hold on the housing market in certain areas that the values of rental properties decreased while other California property values were increasing. The values of real property in areas of strict rent controls have not increased at the same rate as property values in areas without rent controls.

COSTA-HAWKINS RENTAL HOUSING ACT is a state law that overrides any local ordinances regarding rent controls as a way to decrease the impact the rent controls have on the housing market. As result of this act, landlords were allowed to increase rents by the greatest of either 15% of the current rent or 70% of the prevailing rate in the local market. This was allowed **for a period from January 1, 1996, through December 31, 1998, on units that had been VACATED either voluntarily or through eviction for non-payment of rent.**

The ***Costa-Hawkins Rental Housing Act*** applies to the following properties:

- Single family residences and condominiums
- Multi-unit residential units under vacancy controls with the exceptions:
  - Tenancy terminated by change in tenancy terms by the landlord.
  - New units: Certificate of Occupancy issued since February 1, 1995.
  - No limits on allowable rent increases on new tenancies created since January 1, 1996, per decision of January 1, 1999.

RENT CONTROL ORDINANCES WITH VACANCY DECONTROLS are ordinances that contain a decontrol provision which allows for no new limit on new rent when the property has been vacated. The landlord is allowed to increase the rent to market value and once the unit is rented, the **new rent amount becomes the base rent falling under rent control.** California cities that have this type of rent control are Los Angeles, San Francisco, San Jose, and Oakland.

Rent control housing without vacancy decontrol does not allow for the intermediate decontrol on rents when a unit has been vacated. The rent controls remain in place when a unit has been vacated and the rent base remains the same for the new tenant. California cities that use this type of rent controls are Santa Monica, Palm Springs, Berkeley, and East Palo Alto. *Santa Monica has been drastically affected by rent controls. See the city website for the effects on the city. www.santa-monica.org*.

CREDIT REPORTING

CREDIT REPORTING is used by landlords to verify the creditworthiness of potential tenants. Landlords must follow the guidelines and laws as set forth under the ***Fair Credit Reporting Act (FCRA)*** and the ***Fair and Accurate Credit Transactions Act of 2003 (FACTA)*** which amended the FCRA.

A landlord must have a signed authorization from the potential tenant prior to running a credit report on any person. The information received on an application to rent, and the credit report is **personal and confidential** and may not be shared with any parties. All files for tenants and any who applied for tenancy must be retained in a locked and secure place with access limited to those who need access for the purpose of doing business as required for property management. Sharing information, such as selling a list of tenants, is strictly controlled, and should be investigated under the ***FCRA*** and ***FACTA*** prior to actually considering such an act. Landlords must also comply with privacy laws.

IDENTITY THEFT is addressed by FACTA. If a tenant has been a victim of identity theft, the landlord may not report any late payments of rent to the credit reporting agency. A notice of identity theft appearing on a credit report should be confirmed by contacting the party to confirm the action and also positively identify the party.

CHAPTER 11
ESCROW AND TITLE

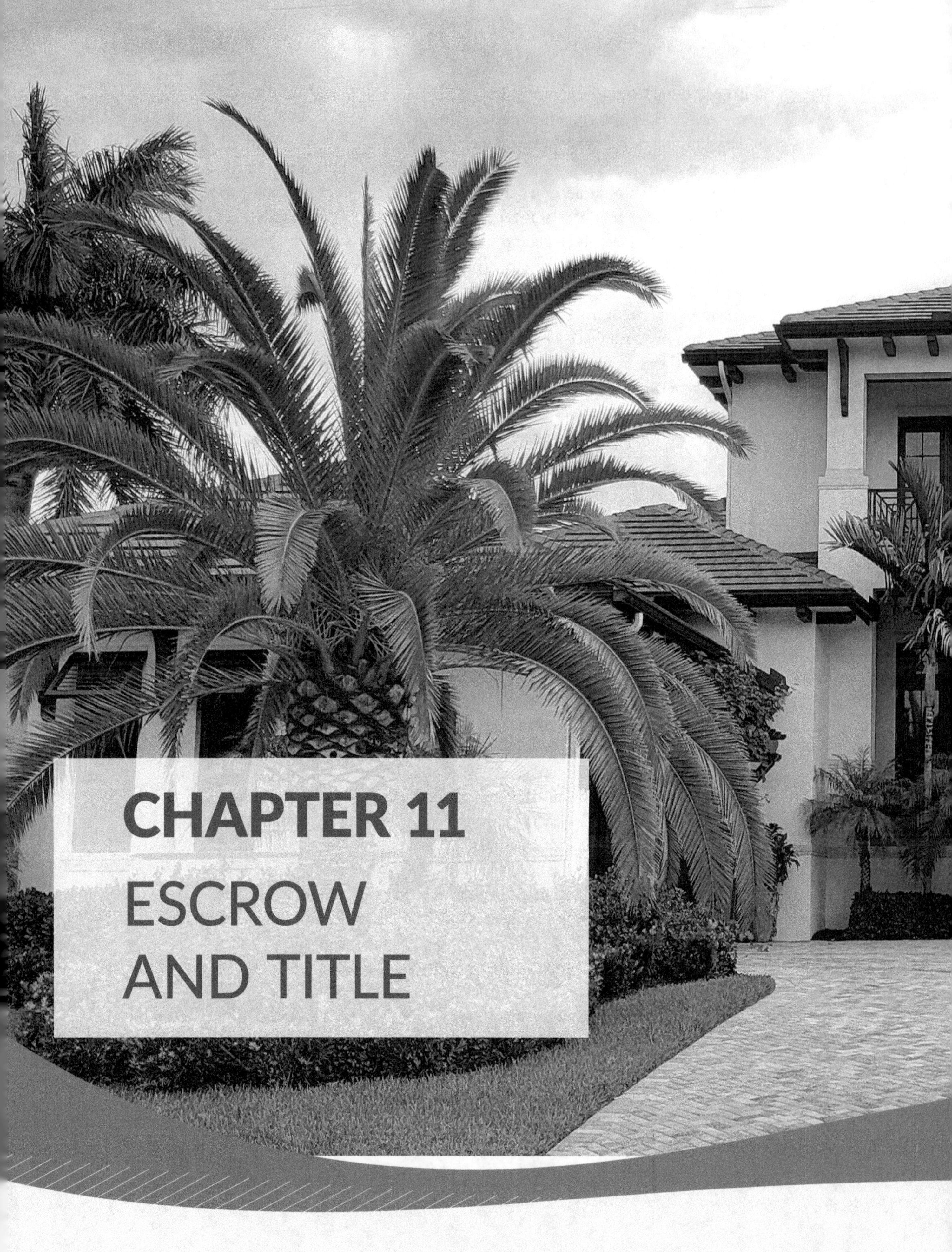

US
Realty School

ESCROW

Escrow companies are a neutral third party to a real estate transaction. They are utilized to provide an unbiased neutral entity that will manage and control the funds, the deeds, and other items of value involved in a real estate transaction to ensure proper distribution and the fair and equitable closing or execution of the transaction.

The escrow company as a neutral third party performs the following duties:

- **Holds the original contract** to track and ensure that the terms of the contract are met.
- **Prepares the escrow instructions** as a summary of the contract.
- **Holds the buyer's deposit funds.**
- **Holds the seller's deed.**
- **Prepares both the loan estimate and closing disclosure** to provide a good faith estimate and final closing costs for both the buyer and seller.
- **Collects the various items** to meet the terms, such as the pest inspection reports and distributes them to the necessary parties, such as the lender.
- **Obtains required information,** such as the pay-off. Demand from the seller's lender to ensure the payment of debts owed by the seller.
- **Reviews the preliminary title report (prelim)** to search for undisclosed liens or debts and to ensure they do carry over to the buyer.
- **Notifies the buyer and the seller** of any issues found on the prelim such as encroachments or easements.
- **Receives loan documents** from the lender, reviews them, and has the borrower sign in their presence for assistance to the borrower, and notarizes the loan documents.
- **Prepares the deeds and arranges for recording** with the county recorder's office.
- **Distributes funds** accordingly and closes escrow or finalizes the transaction.
- **Refunds** unused funds to the appropriate party.

The escrow company must be licensed as a corporation by the Department of Financial Protection and Innovation (DFPI). The California Financial Code contains the laws that govern escrow companies. There are exceptions to the licensing under the DFPI. The exceptions to the licensing of an escrow under DFPI are as follows:

- **Title insurance companies**
- **Attorneys**
- **Banks, and savings and loans**
- **Real estate brokers**
- **Mortgage brokers**

The exception for an escrow that is owned and operated by a real estate broker as a part of the real estate business as either a real estate office or a mortgage brokerage is that they have additional rules and regulations affecting the management of the business.

- **Licensing** can be in the name of the broker of record only. Not an associate licensee.
- **Duties such as clerical** jobs may be delegated to employees of the broker under the broker's supervision.
- **Broker must be a party** to the transaction in some way such as a listing agent or buyer's agent, or mortgage broker. A broker cannot perform escrows for other brokerages without full escrow licensing under the ***DOC***.
- **Escrow** can only be incidental to the main operation of the real estate business.
- **Advertisement** of escrow services can only be as a part of that of their regular business.
- **Cannot use a dba (doing business as)** or a fictitious business name using the words "escrow" or "title."
- **Escrow funds** must be retained in a trust account separate from other brokerage funds and available for audit by the ***DRE.***

An escrow officer acts as a dual agent to both the buyer and seller during the transaction. Once escrow closes, the escrow officer becomes a single agent for each party separately while they finish the remaining details of the transaction. The escrow officer is the person within the escrow company that will handle the individual transactions. The escrow company and its officers are bonded with a $25,000 surety bond. A surety company insures through bonds people who are in positions of handling funds and other items of value on behalf of others.

The escrow officer must remain impartial to the parties to the transaction in order to retain their neutrality.

OPENING ESCROW for a purchase transaction will require:

- **Purchase agreement signed by ALL parties.**
- **Property address.**
- **Buyer's name and vesting,** if known.
- **Loan amount.**
- **Buyer's current** mailing address, phone numbers, and social security numbers.
- **Estimated closing date.**
- **Loan estimate.** (*see Figures 14 – 16*)

  Escrow will provide the buyer with a form requesting a 10-year address history along with former names and spouses, if applicable. The purpose of this form is to help positively identify the true owner of the property if any question of ownership arises in the future. The buyer should complete this form and return it to escrow as soon as possible after receiving the form.

DELIVERY of the signed purchase agreement must be provided to ALL parties to a real estate transaction.

The escrow officer will also require:

- **Seller's name,** address, and contact information.
- **Demand** for pay-off from the existing lender.
- **Accurate information** from the seller for the lender's name, address if available, and the account number.
- **The buyers choose the escrow company** for a purchase transaction.

  federal law states that the choice of escrow and title companies is the buyer's. If the seller or their agent selects the escrow, the seller and their agent may be held liable for three times the buyer's escrow and title fees. RESPA also requires that when a real estate licensee is asked for a referral from a service provider such as escrow, the real estate professional must provide a list of no less than five names of individuals or companies for the client to select from.

PURCHASE TRANSACTION ESCROWS will be opened by the real estate agent on behalf of the clients once the offer to purchase (also known as the **deposit receipt**) has been accepted. The buyer's realtor will provide the loan officer or mortgage broker with the name of the escrow company and the name of the escrow officer along with contact information. The mortgage broker will contact the escrow officer to request the escrow instructions, fully executed purchase contract, and a copy of the receipt for deposit. In this case, the receipt for deposit is a copy of the actual receipt that escrow gave the buyer for their deposit, not a copy of the purchase offer.

REFINANCE TRANSACTIONS by mortgage brokers will be opened by the mortgage broker and the same ***RESPA*** rules apply. The broker must provide the borrower with a list of no less than five names as referrals or use any other escrow company that the borrower may choose. The escrow officer will need the borrower's personal information, pay-off information to acquire a demand from the current lender, if applicable. Any mortgage payoff will be verified by escrow and all other debts being paid through the loan or escrow will be verified with the borrower's most recent statements to be taken with them when they sign loan docs. If statements are not provided, the balances shown on the credit report will be used. An approximate payoff amount and information should be given to the escrow officer when opening the loan.

The escrow officer can accept only written documents that have been signed by all parties to the transaction. Oral instructions must not be followed except for a request to amend the instructions, which will generate written documentation that will be signed by all parties prior to being accepted as a part of the transaction. Any discrepancy must be directed to the real estate agents for clarification. The escrow officer is not responsible for explaining terms of the contract or interceding in disputes and should never become an arbitrator in a transaction dispute.

INTERPLEADER ACTION is a legal action brought by the escrow officer to resolve a disagreement between the parties to the transaction. The courts will determine any disputes and clarify the terms as the law allows. Material facts to the transaction should be disclosed to the parties to the transaction as soon as known; however, the escrow officer should not offer an opinion as to the benefit or harm the material fact may have to the parties to the transaction. *The pest inspection is an example of material information that is pertinent to the transaction as a report of material facts.*

The pest inspection is provided to the escrow officer by the pest inspection company. The escrow officer will be certain that the parties that require a copy, including the buyer, seller, agents, and lender. The escrow officer will oversee the distribution of the funds for any work required and the payment of the report and the repairs per the terms of the contract but will not pass judgment or opinion as to the effects of the reported issues. Likewise, it is unethical and not the job of the escrow officer to pass a determination on the quality of the loan being obtained against the property.

NOTE

The escrow officer must remain neutral.

RESPONSIBILITIES of each party to the transaction must be met to attain a successful escrow. The escrow officer keeps a checklist of all duties that must be met to successfully complete the escrow. Certain portions of the escrow officer's checklist will be the same on every file, however, every transaction is different and must be treated as such by being sure that all details are recognized.

THE ESCROW OFFICER RESPONSIBILITIES and **transaction checklist** will have the following basic needs plus others that are peculiar to the individual transaction:

- Date of contract.
- Date of opening escrow.
- Scheduled closing date and time.
- Order title report.
- Buyer/borrower (refi) Info: Full name and correct spelling, contact info, address.
- Vesting for new title/deed.
- Seller info: Full name and spelling, contact info, address.
- Property address.
- Purchase price.
- Terms of contract.
- Loan contingency: amount and approval date.
- Deposit amount and receipt.

- Appraisal contingency and approval date.
- All cash offer.
- Pest inspection report and distribution.
- Other reports: home inspection, mold test, geological report.
- Items remaining with property.
- Passive or active removal of contingencies.
- Additional conditions or terms.
- Names and contact info for buyer's agent.
- Names and contact info for seller's agent.
- Prepare deeds: grant deed, quit claim deed.
- Seller to sign deed and documents.
- Buyer to sign loan documents.
- Record deed.
- Disperse funds.
- Close file.
- Calculate pro-rations such as taxes and rents.

SELLER'S RESPONSIBILITIES consist of the following:

- **Execute deed.**
- **Lease agreements** if property is rented.
- **Contact info for tenants** if property is rented.
- **Amount and proof** of tenant's security deposit credited to buyer.
- **Lender's info** for mortgage pay-off.
- **HOA and Condo or PUD** info and CC&Rs.
- **Lien releases** for mechanics liens and any other debts showing on prelim.
- **Subordination agreement** if carrying 2nd TD.
- **Note** for 2nd TD.
- **Pay for:**
    - **Reports and inspections** as required per the terms of the contract.
    - **Share of escrow fees.**
    - **Termite report, repairs, clearance.**
    - **Beneficiary statement.**
    - **Property taxes** to close of escrow.
    - **Maintain property** in the condition determined by the terms of the contract.
    - **All closing fees in a VA transaction.**
    - **Notary fees for seller's documentation.**

BUYER'S RESPONSIBILITIES consist of:

- **Complete** escrow identification form.
- **Sign escrow instructions.**
- **Deposit funds** into escrow.
- **Apply for loan.**
- **Order appraisal.**
- **Obtain homeowner's insurance.**
- **Review prelim.**
- **Review pest inspection report.**
- **Perform final walk-through inspection.**
- **Sign loan documents.**
- **Provide** required closing costs in form of a cashier's check.
- **Pay for:**
    - **Share of escrow fees.**
    - **Notary fees for buyer's documentation.**

RECORDKEEPING

RECORDKEEPING must be maintained in an efficient and accurate manner. Recording of any information whether financial or otherwise pertinent to the transaction must be recorded immediately. Financial recordings are of absolute priority. The escrow officer is responsible for the accurate recordkeeping of the funds for all parties to the transaction.

CLOSING DISCLOSURES are a detailed disclosure of estimated closing costs that must be provided to the parties to the transaction. As of October 3, 2015, TRID rules mandated that the former **HUD1** form be used ONLY for **reverse mortgages.** All other transactions utilize the **loan estimate** *(Figure 14–16)* and the **closing disclosures** *(Figure 17–21).* At the close of escrow, the **closing disclosure** will provide the final accounting of all funds dispersed per the terms of the contract including the commissions paid the real estate agents and mortgage brokers. The closing disclosure must be as clear and concise as possible. Clarification of expenditures is not only detailed in amount but should also clearly spell out the recipient of all funds. For example, it should not say: real estate commissions $12,000. The proper disclosure of disbursement of funds should show: RE Commissions ABC Realty $6,000 and Joe's Realty $6,000.

PRORATIONS are calculations of items that will be carried over to the buyer whether as a cost or as an expense. These are called **date items** as they are calculated based on the closing date. Such items include rent and property taxes. The escrow officer must calculate the items based on the date the item was due and the date the escrow will close. *As discussed in Chapter 5, Government Rights in Land,* property taxes are prorated according to the date of closing. The seller owes taxes up to the close of escrow and the buyer will owe taxes from the day escrow closes.

Unless otherwise agreed to in the contract for a date item, the buyer is responsible for the day escrow closes forward, and the seller is responsible through the day before escrow closes. The escrow officer will determine the date that escrow will close then determine which party will be debited or credited for the item.

Property tax calculations are based on the fiscal tax year which is July 1 through the following June 30. If the escrow closes on June 30, the seller owes the entire previous year's property taxes, and the buyer will owe the entire new year's property taxes.

When counting calendar days do not merely subtract the number 15 from 30 to derive at 15. The 15th is also included for a total of 16 days. **Escrow uses 364 days in a year and 30 days in a month** unless instructed to do otherwise by the parties to the transaction.

> ***Example:*** *John is in escrow for the sale of his home. Escrow is scheduled to close on May 15. John has already paid his property taxes of $3,000 for the year. The escrow officer will calculate that buyer Linda must reimburse John the taxes that he has already paid for the period of the tax Year that she will own the property which is from May 15 through June 30. It must be remembered that* ***the buyer is responsible for the day of closing.*** *Buyer Linda will owe John for 16 days in May and 30 days in June for a total of 46 days.*

$3,000	*Annual property taxes*
÷ 364	*Days in escrow year*
= $8.24	*Daily tax amount*
x 46	*Days owned by Linda*
=$379.12	*Property taxes owed by Linda*

Buyer Linda will be charged $379.12 at close of escrow which will be credited to John as reimbursement for property taxes he has already paid.

If John had not paid his property taxes, the total amount of $3,000 would have been calculated by determining John's share:

364	*Days in the year*
– 46	*Days Linda owes*
= 318	*Days John owes*
x $8.24	*Daily tax amount*
= $2,620.32	*Taxes John owes*

The escrow officer would collect these amounts and forward the total property taxes collected to the county tax collector. The escrow officer builds into the buyer's estimated closing costs a "pad" or "cushion" usually for a dollar amount of $300 to $500. This cushion is used to cover any miscalculations caused by escrow closing on a day different from the day that the estimates were based upon.

RENT CALCULATIONS are calculated the same way except that a 30-day base is used for calculations.

Example 1: *John's property is rented, and he collected $1,000 rent on May 1. When escrow closes on May 15, he will owe Linda rent from the 15th through the 30th.*

$1,000	*Month rent collected*
÷ 30	*Days in an escrow month of 30 days not actual 31 days in May*
= $33.33	*Daily rent*
x 16	*Days owned by Linda (the buyer is entitled to the day escrow closes)*
= $533.33	*John owes Linda*

Example 2: *John has not collected the rent on the 1st. Linda will collect the rent after the close of escrow. Linda will be charged the amount of rent that is owed to John for the period of the amount that John owned the property.*

$1,000	*Month rent collected*
÷ 30	*Days in an escrow month of 30 days not actual 31 days in May*
= $33.33	*Daily rent*
X 14	*Days owned by John (Because Linda in entitled to the day escrow closes)*
=$466.62	*Linda owes John*

LENDER'S INSTRUCTIONS TO ESCROW

LENDER'S INSTRUCTIONS TO ESCROW is part of the loan documents. They instruct escrow to the terms of the loan and the lender's requirements. The lender's instructions provide the terms of the loan being obtained by the buyer/borrower whether it is a purchase or refinance transaction. The costs accrued as a part of the loan are included in the instructions including any rebate or a premium that is paid back to the broker or borrower by the lender when obtaining a loan with a higher interest rate. The rebate can be credited toward the borrower's nonrecurring closing costs or pay the mortgage broker or loan officer their commission.

REBATES are used as a way to offset costs, including paying the loan agent. Lenders will only allow the rebate or seller paid closing costs to pay for a percentage of the loan amount usually not to exceed 3%. (Some lenders will allow up to 6% of the loan amount to be paid by rebate or seller paid closing costs.) The lender will allow any outside contribution to the buyer's closing costs not to be applied to any fees other than nonrecurring fees.

NONRECURRING FEES are fees charged to the buyer/borrower for this transaction only. Typical nonrecurring fees include:

- **Appraisal fee**
- **Credit report**
- **Loan processing fee**
- **Mortgage broker or loan commission**
- **Lender's fees**
- **Underwriting**

- Flood cert
- Tax service fee
- Doc drawing
- Wire transfer
- Escrow fees
- Notary fees
- Recording fee

Fees that will occur again that CANNOT be paid by outside contribution are:

- Interest
- Taxes
- Insurance

These items will be paid repeatedly and are not fees resulting from this loan transaction in particular.

A person other than the borrower may sign loan docs if they have a properly prepared **specific power of attorney.** An attorney must have prepared the power of attorney for this particular transaction. A general power of attorney is rarely accepted.

CLOSING A REAL ESTATE TRANSACTION

CLOSING a real estate transaction involves several different duties or actions. The escrow officer will receive the loan documents, including the lender's instructions to escrow from the lender. Once the escrow officer has prepared the deeds and all other pieces of documentation that will be included in the transaction, the escrow officer will arrange meetings with the buyer and seller to sign the necessary items. The buyer or borrower for a refinance transaction will sign loan documents except for a purchase transaction that will be all cash. The buyer is instructed on the amount of cash they need to close the transaction. The seller will sign the grant deed.

The escrow officer returns the loan documents to the lender and allows the lender 2 to 3 days to review the documents to ensure that everything is executed properly and confirms that the buyer has brought their funds into escrow. **The lender wires funds to the escrow company which constitutes funding.** The escrow officer prepares all the documentation to go to the county recorder's office to be recorded the day after funding.

This is called a **COMPLETE ESCROW** because all conditions and contingencies have been met and the escrow is ready to close.

The day after funding, the title company representative is at the county recorder's office when it opens for business in the morning to record all of the documentation such as deeds prior to any other recordings that may affect the property such as with a mechanic's lien. The county recorder's office will time and date stamp all documentation. It may take into the afternoon to confirm the recording of the deeds depending on how busy the county recorder's office is on any given day. Escrow cannot close and ownership does not legally transfer until the county recorder's office has confirmed that the documentation has recorded.

At this point, the escrow is classified as a **PERFECT ESCROW** as it is now completed and closed.

DRY FUNDING is the term used to describe the way escrows are closed in California. In a dry-funding state, the ink has had time to dry by the time escrow closes based on the process followed. It is several days from the time that the buyer/borrower signs the documents until it funds and escrow closes. This gives the lender an opportunity to make sure that everything has been handled properly.

WET FUNDING is a term used to describe the closing of a transaction when the ink has not had time to dry before the closing and the ownership transfers. Many states use the wet funding method whereby the parties to the transactions all meet in one place such as the escrow office or attorney's office. All parties sign the required documentation including deeds and loan documents. The funds change hands and the transfer of ownership changes hands. The buyer is handed the keys at this meeting, closing the transaction.

DEEDS PREPARED BY ESCROW

GRANT DEED is a deed that is used to transfer or grant interest from the current property owner to others. This may be a new owner as in a purchase transaction or granting a lien interest to a new lender as in a refinance transaction. A grant deed must be prepared by the escrow officer and signed with loan documents. A new grant deed is prepared for all real estate transactions, even for a refinance transaction that will not change ownership but will change the lien holder's interest. The grant deed will include the information for a new owner of a purchase transaction and confirm the lien holder or lender for either a purchase or refinance transactions.

QUIT CLAIM DEEDS are used to remove a party's interest in property ownership. The party signing the quit claim deed is quitting any claim that they may have in the property such as a party releasing their interest in another's property by quit claiming an easement. With a purchase transaction, an escrow officer will prepare a quit claim deed if the buyer is married, and the spouse will not be on title or will not claim ownership of the property. The non-buying spouse will sign the quit claim deed when the buying spouse signs their loan documents. **California is a community property state which means that any property purchased during marriage is owned by both spouses as community property.**

A **lender** cannot provide a loan using real property as security unless **all** owners are on the loan. If a lender does provide such financing and a party on the loan dies, the loan is uncollectable from the remaining co-owners. A **quit claim deed** eliminates this lending issue.

A quit claim deed also relieves a purchasing spouse's obligation to the non-purchasing spouse. One spouse may choose to invest money in a property to be held separately from the spouse. A quit claim deed will ensure that the property belongs only to the investing spouse. When a couple divorces, one spouse will "quit claim" their interest in the marital property. In a divorce, the releasing spouse needs to be aware that a quit claim deed does not release them from any loan obligations that they were a party to when originally financing the property.

Escrow may prepare a quit claim deed for a current owner of a refinance transaction who is forfeiting ownership rights or any claim to the property. The purpose of the quit claim deed is to legally relinquish ownership or claim to the property. The escrow officer should be notified as soon as the possibility is known.

TITLE SEARCH

A TITLE SEARCH is a search performed by the title insurance company to provide the **preliminary title report (prelim).** The prelim provides a complete report of all information that is recorded with the county recorder's office against the subject property. *See Figure 13: Preliminary Title Report.*

The PRELIM Is ordered by the escrow officer and will forward to the processor along with escrow instructions within a few days. When the prelim is received, the buyer and seller and their agents should all review the contents of the prelim.

The buyer and their agent want to ascertain that there are no items that will affect their interest in the property such as when the neighbor's fence is over the property line and infringing on the subject property by several feet.

The seller and their agent need to review the prelim to be certain that there are no liens against the property that have previously been paid in full or are erroneous. It is common for previous mortgages not to be released or reconveyed once paid in full. Most refinance transactions performed through escrow have been removed because escrow provides the reconveyance deed to the lender to be paid and records the document at close of escrow. Occasionally, a reconveyance deed may be overlooked but most frequently an unreleased lien was a private money loan and the private party that loaned the funds did not know about reconveyance deeds to reconvey their interest back to the borrower once paid in full.

Another common error on a prelim is a result of a party who owes child support. In California, when a district attorney is trying to collect unpaid child support, they will file a blanket claim against any property owned by everybody in the state with the same name as the perpetrator and will file the claim in every county in the State of California. This obviously creates a large amount of erroneous claims, but it is effective. If the seller claims that it is not their responsibility, the title company will contact the DA's office that filed the lien and once the seller's social security number is compared against the perpetrator's, the lien will be released.

The **prelim** will be checked for seller's or borrower's name, vesting, property tax amount owed or delinquent, and the accurate and complete property address. These items must be corrected in other documentation, such as the escrow instructions or the appraisal, if necessary.

The name and vesting of the current owner are usually found on the first page with the address found on the "**note**" page at the end of the report. The property tax figures are found approximately three pages into the prelim.

NOTE

The prelim is assumed to be accurate as this information is as it is recorded with the county recorder's office.

FLAG POLICY is a shortened form of a prelim used for second trust deeds and VA refinance transactions and is less expensive. It is assumed that there has been little or no activity against the title if a flag policy is used.

PROPERTY TAX amount appears in the prelim as Item #1 and shows the amount of taxes to be paid on the subject property. The tax amount is divided by two to derive a biannual payment for a refinance transaction. A monthly tax amount for qualifying purposes is derived by dividing the taxes by 6 (6 months). The amount of property taxes for a purchase transaction will be different as a new tax amount will be determined by the county tax assessor based on the purchase price of the property.

If there is an additional name appearing in the prelim as a current owner that is not a party to the transaction, the escrow officer will need to:

- **Add that person to the transaction** for a purchase by amending the contract or escrow instructions. All owners must agree to and sign the purchase offer for the contract to be valid.
- **Complete a loan application** for a refinance transaction.
- **Prepare a quit claim deed** for a refinance transaction.

The **prelim** will disclose any additional liens to be paid, including mechanic's liens, judgments, mortgages, delinquent taxes, easements and encumbrances.

Delinquent taxes must be brought current through escrow. In the case of a refinance transaction, the amount will be collected through the loan proceeds. The escrow officer will prepare the ***final closing statement*** to disclose to the borrower and the lender whether there will be sufficient loan proceeds to pay any delinquent taxes. A letter of explanation will be required from the borrower for any delinquent taxes or for any liens not disclosed.

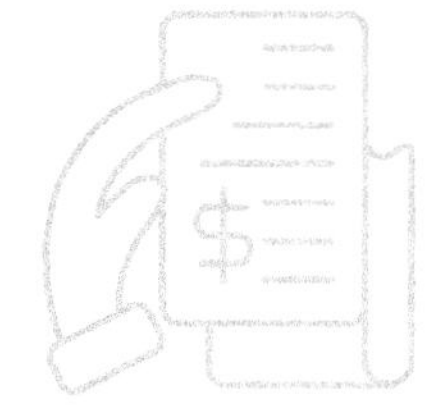

ENCUMBRANCES will include such items as utilities crossing the property or roads and driveways crossing the property. A private road crossing the property with ownership rights of the owner along with others or those other than the owners will require a ***road maintenance agreement***. Request this document immediately from the property owner or escrow can order the document from the title officer. These items will not affect the loan, but the title company will insure against damage and loss due to these encumbrances.

ROAD MAINTENANCE AGREEMENT is an agreement between property owners to share the responsibility of maintaining a shared road or driveway that crosses more than one property. The situation will occur when there are several adjoining properties and only one property has direct access to a main road or a public access. The buyer and the lender should review the document to confirm that the subject property does not have excessive responsibility or liability to the other property owners or adjoining properties.

TRUST OR A CORPORATION is acceptable and are common forms of property ownership. Few lenders will fund into a trust or a corporation because they are not an individual, which makes it difficult legally for a lender to act against these entities, such as to file a default or foreclosure procedure against a trust or corporation. Lenders will require the owner's quit claim deed from the trust or corporation to the individuals prior to funding. Once the loan has been funded and recorded, the owners/borrowers can, and usually do, grant deed ownership back into the trust. There are some lenders who will fund into a trust, but it is usually easier for the borrower to change ownership if they are willing to do so. Some title companies will not ensure funding to a trust, so this must also be confirmed early in the process.

LOW INCOME ASSISTANCE PROGRAMS are sponsored by municipalities for the purpose of helping families buy homes. Generally, this is done by assisting contractors with loans or other incentives to complete housing projects and new subdivisions. In exchange for the help from the local government, the builder reserves a set number of homes for special assistance programs, usually in the form of municipal or county bonds which create the funds to loan the down payment.

This agreement stays with the land and the entire project and will control the maximum value for resale purposes.

This agreement becomes an attachment of sorts and is called **INCLUSIONARY ZONING.**

TITLE INSURANCE

TITLE INSURANCE is insurance for the homeowners' protection against current and prior claims against the title or ownership of the property. The **title company** provides insurance on the property's title or guarantees that everything recorded with county recorder's office is accurate and all those on title or claiming a right to the property, actually have that right. There is an information form sent to the buyer prior to the close of escrow requesting complete information for the buyer covering a 10-year period. This must be completed and returned to escrow prior to closing as this assists the title company in verifying the buyer and therefore the rightful owner of the property. They also ensure the rights of those who have a right to use the property, such as utility companies that have access across the property and all other easements.

When escrow is ready to close, the title company will provide a **title insurance policy** for both the seller and the buyer.

CLTA Preliminary Report Form
(Rev. 11/06)

Order Number:
Page Number: 1

XYZ Title Company

Order Number:	11-23456
Title Officer:	
Phone:	(866)
Fax No.:	(866)
E-Mail:	
Escrow Officer:	
Phone:	
Fax No.:	
E-Mail:	
E-Mail Loan Documents to:	
Borrower:	Samuel A. Smith
Property:	Sally A. Smith

PRELIMINARY REPORT

In response to the above referenced application for a policy of title insurance, this company hereby reports that it is prepared to issue, or cause to be issued, as of the date hereof, a Policy or Policies of Title Insurance describing the land and the estate or interest therein hereinafter set forth, insuring against loss which may be sustained by reason of any defect, lien or encumbrance not shown or referred to as an Exception below or not excluded from coverage pursuant to the printed Schedules, Conditions and Stipulations of said Policy forms.

The printed Exceptions and Exclusions from the coverage and Limitations on Covered Risks of said policy or policies are set forth in Exhibit A attached. *The policy to be issued may contain an arbitration clause. When the Amount of Insurance is less than that set forth in the arbitration clause, all arbitrable matters shall be arbitrated at the option of either the Company or the Insured as the exclusive remedy of the parties.* Limitations on Covered Risks applicable to the CLTA and ALTA Homeowner's Policies of Title Insurance which establish a Deductible Amount and a Maximum Dollar Limit of Liability for certain coverages are also set forth in Exhibit A. Copies of the policy forms should be read. They are available from the office which issued this report.

Please read the exceptions shown or referred to below and the exceptions and exclusions set forth in Exhibit A of this report carefully. The exceptions and exclusions are meant to provide you with notice of matters which are not covered under the terms of the title insurance policy and should be carefully considered.

It is important to note that this preliminary report is not a written representation as to the condition of title and may not list all liens, defects, and encumbrances affecting title to the land.

This report (and any supplements or amendments hereto) is issued solely for the purpose of facilitating the issuance of a policy of title insurance and no liability is assumed hereby. If it is desired that liability be assumed prior to the issuance of a policy of title insurance, a Binder or Commitment should be requested.

Figure 13: Preliminary Title Report Page 1 of 7

Order Number: 11-23456
Page Number: 2

Dated as of December 30, 2008 at 7:30 A.M.

The form of Policy of title insurance contemplated by this report is:

ALTA Loan Policy 1056.06 (6-17-06)

A specific request should be made if another form or additional coverage is desired.

Title to said estate or interest at the date hereof is vested in:

Samuel A. Smith and Sally A. Smith Husband and Wife as Joint Tenants

The estate or interest in the land hereinafter described or referred to covered by this Report is:

A fee.

The Land referred to herein is described as follows:

(See attached Legal Description)

At the date hereof exceptions to coverage in addition to the printed Exceptions and Exclusions in said policy form would be as follows:

1. General and special taxes and assessments for the fiscal year 2009-2010, a lien not yet due (payable.

2. General and special taxes and assessments for the fiscal year 2008-2009.

First Installment:	$1,063.91, PAID
Penalty:	$0.00
Second Installment:	$1,063.91, PAYABLE
Penalty:	$0.00
Tax Rate Area:	05011
A. P. No.:	136-0-

3. The lien of supplemental taxes, if any, assessed pursuant to Chapter 3.5 commencing with Section 75 of the California Revenue and Taxation Code.

Figure 13: Preliminary Title Report Page 2 of 7

Order Number: **11-23456**
Page Number: 6

LEGAL DESCRIPTION

Real property in the City of Los Angeles County of Los Angeles State of California, described as follows:

LOT 7 , TRACT NO. 19 AS PER MAP RECORDED IN BOOK 53, PAGES 1 THROUGH 5 OF MAPS, IN THE OFFICE OF THE COUNTY RECORDER OF VENTURA COUNTY STATE OF CALIFORNIA.

APN: 136-0-

Figure 13: Preliminary Title Report.
Page 3 of 7

Order Number: **11-23456**
Page Number: 6

LEGAL DESCRIPTION

Real property in the City of Los Angeles County of Los Angeles State of California, described as follows:

LOT 7 . TRACT NO. 19: AS PER MAP RECORDED IN BOOK 53, PAGES 1 THROUGH 5 OF MAPS, IN THE OFFICE OF THE COUNTY RECORDER OF VENTURA COUNTY STATE OF CALIFORNIA.

APN: 136-0-:

Figure 13: Preliminary Title Report.
Page 4 of 7

Order Number: 11-23456
Page Number: 5

WIRE INSTRUCTIONS
for

XYZ Title Company

ABA 122

Credit to

Account No. 300

Reference Escrow Order Number 11-23456 and Escrow Officer

Please wire the day before recording. Also, notify the Escrow Officer of your intent to wi

Funds for other loans being insured by ***XYZ Title Company*** must not be combin into one wire or funds may be returned.

Figure 13: Preliminary Title Report.
Page 5 of 7

Order Number: **11-23456**
Page Number: 6

LEGAL DESCRIPTION

Real property in the City of Los Angeles County of Los Angeles State of California, described as follows:

LOT 7 , TRACT NO. 19: AS PER MAP RECORDED IN BOOK 53, PAGES 1 THROUGH 5 OF MAPS, IN THE OFFICE OF THE COUNTY RECORDER OF VENTURA COUNTY STATE OF CALIFORNIA.

APN: 136-0-:

Figure 13: Preliminary Title Report.
Page 6 of 7

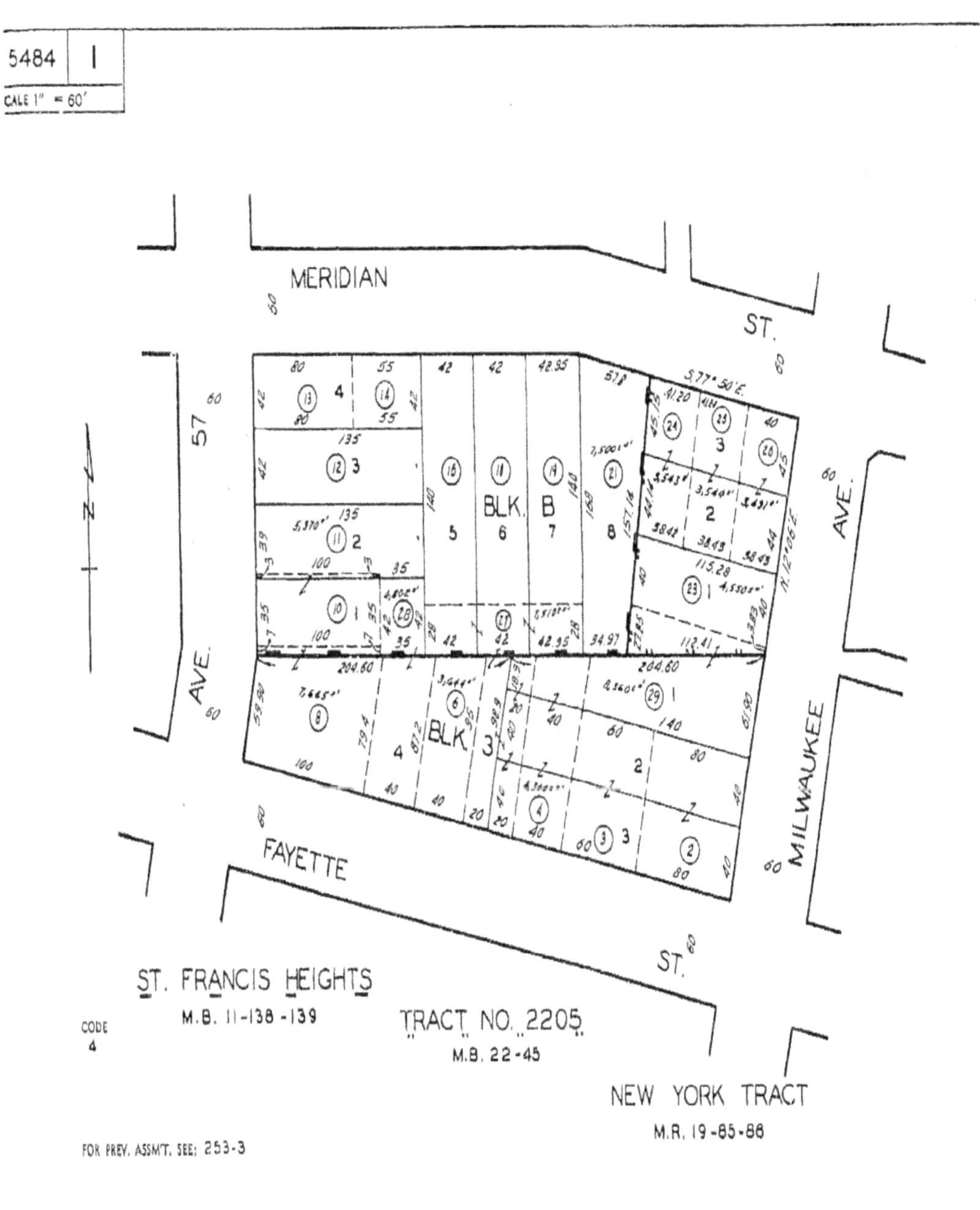

Figure 13: Preliminary Title Report.
Page 7 of 7

The **SELLER'S TITLE INSURANCE POLICY** insures against items resulting from or occurring during their tenure as the owner of the property. This also ensures that the party who sold the property is the actual owner of the property and has the right to transfer title and receive the funds derived from the sale of the property.

The **BUYER'S TITLE INSURANCE POLICY** ensures that they have purchased a property free of any undisclosed encumbrances, liens, and has good and merchantable title.

The California Insurance Commissioner regulates TITLE INSURANCE COMPANIES. As an insurance company, it is regulated as such and is required to uphold the laws, rules, and regulations as required by the ***Insurance Commissioner***, including retaining a **title insurance surplus fund** to guarantee the cash and the ability to pay any claims and be able to fulfill any needs of the insured. A title insurance policy and company are available to correct issues that may arise such as:

- **A party claims ownership** that was not granted.
- Unpaid mechanic's liens.
- **Unpaid property taxes** by a previous owner.

These are examples of issues that may arise in the future. The title company does research and reviews county records and documentation, including the escrow files to determine the legitimacy of any claim. Claims are either released by proving them to be invalid or correcting them. Payment for items such as an overlooked mechanic's lien that was legally recorded is paid by either the title insurance or the escrow company if they were at fault. **The property owner will not be liable for the debt.**

PRIOR TO TITLE INSURANCE

Historically, the record ownership and claims against a property were kept in a permanent record with the county recorder's office. Prior to the introduction of title insurance, a purchaser of real property wanted to know that they were purchasing a property with good, marketable title meaning that they wanted to know that they would be the legitimate owners of the property. In order to ensure this, a search of the history of the title needed to be performed. This was performed in several different ways and varied in different areas of the country.

The following are ways that this title search was dealt with. Some are still in use in other states; however, **California uses title insurance**.

- **THE CHAIN OF TITLE** is the history of a property and its owners. The abstract of title provides the data, and the title insurance guarantees it.

- **ABSTRACT OF TITLE** is a report that contains all recorded history of a specified property. The abstract of title is similar to reading a book giving all the details from the time the property was recorded. The report is usually quite thick as the record will show all owners, transfers, liens, and building permits that may go back as far as the 1700s. An abstract company prepares the report or gathers the records. An attorney reviews the records and provides a lawyer's opinion of title commenting on the apparent marketability of title. This method provides a clear picture, and the buyer can be confident of the marketability of title as there is not likely to be anything hidden. Fraud by a previous owner or person with an interest may not be as easily identifiable and there is no insurance or guarantee.

- **CERTIFICATE OF TITLE** began to be used by abstract companies as a result of the records that they had accumulated. The filing systems had become so complete and accurate that the abstract companies were able to research the history of the title and prepare a certificate of title without the need for an attorney's opinion. The abstract company certified that the title was marketable. This certification also made the abstract company liable for errors. This method provides a clear picture, and the buyer can be confident of the marketability of title as there is not likely to be anything hidden. Fraud by a previous owner or person with an interest may not be as easily identifiable and there is no insurance or guarantee.

- **GUARANTEE OF TITLE** was the result of the work and compilation of the records held by abstract companies. Abstract companies began to guarantee the title, acting much the same as a title insurance company.

- **TITLE INSURANCE was the ultimate step** in the process of verifying and guaranteeing that title to a property was marketable. Several attorneys in Chicago, Illinois, created the first title insurance company and worked closely with abstract companies that continued to research the records. **title companies have assumed the abstract company's role in most of the country.**

CALIFORNIA LAND TITLE ASSOCIATION (CLTA) is the standard policy of title insurance. The policy assumes that the purchaser of real property has had the opportunity to inspect the property and reasonably determine the proper use and condition of the property, and the apparent ownership.

The CLTA insures the property owner against:
- **Matters of record**
- **Forgery and fraud**
- **Lack of capacity**
- **Improper delivery**
- **Legal description**
- **Encumbrances**

AMERICAN LAND TITLE ASSOCIATION (ALTA) is an extended insurance coverage policy. This policy is most often used for the benefit of the lender and is *rarely used when there is no mortgage against the property.* Just as the CLTA assumes that the buyer has inspected the property, the ALTA allows the lender to inspect the property; however, that is rarely possible as the lender is probably some distance from the property. The assumption of property inspection was implemented as part of the insurance process during a time when the mortgage was obtained through a local bank, which inspected the property.

Because this has changed so dramatically since the mid-to late twentieth century, the lender will now require the extended policy as it insures the following:
- **Unrecorded easements**
- **Unrecorded liens**
- **Mining claims**
- **Water rights**
- **Rights or claims of persons in possession**

- **Reservations**
- **Survey claims**
- **Forgeries occurring after the issuance of the policy**
- **Removal of a for lack of building permits or violation structure**

The ALTA policy will not cover any title defects that are known to the buyer of real property at the time of the purchase.

Neither the CLTA nor the ALTA will insure against zoning changes or any effect that a zoning change has on real property. It is illegal for a title company to pay a referral fee to any party in exchange for business or for the purpose of generating business in the future.

Fees charged for a title insurance policy must be posted and available to the public and will be charged as one fee. The cost of a title insurance policy can be negotiated as part of the purchase offer; however, the buyer usually pays for the ALTA policy as it benefits them and is required by their lender. The payment or the CLTA policy is commonly negotiated between the buyer and seller. The manner in which this negotiation is handled varies in different communities.

CHAPTER 12
REAL ESTATE FINANCING

US
Realty School

PURPOSE OF REAL ESTATE FINANCING

REAL ESTATE FINANCING has undergone many changes over the years. Prior to the Depression of the 1930s, a homebuyer would go to the local bank or savings and loan and obtain a term loan, also known as a straight loan or mortgage. The borrower would make one annual interest payment for usually a five-year term. At the end of the five years, the balance of the loan was due and payable in full, in one balloon payment. When so many banks failed and the economy was bad, many homeowners lost their homes because they were unable to make the balloon payment or find a bank that was able to refinance the existing mortgage.

Another option to home lending was to obtain a land contract or contract for deed. The seller would carry the financing. The buyer or vendee gained possession of the property, and the seller or vendor retained legal title until the mortgage was paid in full. The buyer held an equitable interest in the property during the term of the contract, which meant that the seller could not sell to another or make any changes to the property.

NOTE

A mortgage and a trust deed are both instruments that are used as security on real property when lending money. The terms are used synonymously; however, trust deeds are the commonly used form of security in California. The differences will be explained later in this Chapter.

TYPES OF MORTGAGES

TYPES OF MORTGAGES come in a variety of terms and options with many lenders offering terms that are designed to help as many people as possible to attain the American dream of home ownership. Loans are available in many forms, are redesigned, and changed regularly according to the economic climate. Terminology also changes with many of the loan changes.

1. **FIXED-RATE LOANS** are the most popular and are considered by most to be the most secure. A fixed-rate mortgage loan (or a trust deed, as is used in California) is one where the interest rate will not change, and therefore the payment amount will not change, for the life of the loan.

This loan is referred to as a **fully amortized loan,** which means that when the end of the loan term is reached, the loan will be paid in full. As each monthly payment is made, a portion is applied to the interest and a portion is applied to the principal. With each payment, the interest balance will decrease, which allows a steadily increasing amount to be applied to the principal.

Currently most fixed-rate loans are amortized for 15 years (180 months) or 30 years (360 months). Some lenders have programs for 20 years (240 months) or 40 years (480 months).

2. **ADJUSTABLE-RATE MORTGAGE LOANS (ARM)** are amortized over a set period of time, but the interest rate and payment will adjust on preset dates according to a predetermined margin in relation to a pre-determined index. The programs currently available are monthly adjustable, cost of funds index (**COFI**) or monthly treasury average (**MTA**) index, 6-month adjustable or **LIBOR**, and 1 year adjustable or **T-Bill**. The adjustment period is determined by the index used.

   - **INDEX** is the actual rate that these funds cost the investor or the interest rate that a bank pays another bank to borrow funds. The indices change daily and are also printed in the business section of the newspaper. They vary according to the economy.

   - **MARGIN** is the investor's profit and the amount over the index that the borrower is charged for use of the funds. The margin is established at the time of locking the loan and will vary according to the borrower's creditworthiness and the desired interest rate. For instance, a higher loan- to-value (LTV) such as a loan that is 90% of the total value of the property constitutes a higher margin. The margin establishes the amount the interest rate and payment will adjust at the given date of adjustment. Margins are usually about 2.50% to 3.5%.

   - **CAP** is the maximum amount the interest rate can adjust within any given adjustment period.
     There is an **adjustment cap, annual cap,** and a **life cap.**
     - **ADJUSTMENT CAP** is the maximum amount the rate can adjust at each adjustment date. The adjustment cap is usually 1% if the adjustment period is less than 1 year such as for a COFI or a LIBOR loan program.

- ◦ **ANNUAL CAP** is the maximum amount the interest rate can adjust within a one-year period. The annual cap is usually 2% and the life cap is usually 6% on conforming loans and is disclosed by the lender as 2/6 loan documents.
- ◦ **LIFE CAP** is the maximum amount the interest can adjust to over the entire term or life of the loan. Some loans, such as the COFI loans, have a **payment cap** or the maximum amount the payment can adjust over the current payment, which is usually 7.5% annually.

- **FLOOR** establishes the lowest amount the interest rate is for the life of the loan. This amount is usually the start rate or the starting index.

__Example:__ A six-month or __LIBOR__ will be used for a loan amount of $486,000 for a 30-year amortization:

Start Rate	*4.75%*
Adjustment Cap	*1.00%*
Life Cap	*6.00%*
Margin	*2.25%*
Index	*3.79%*

Payment for the first six months of the loan will be $2,535.21 at an interest rate of 4.75%.

First sixth month adjustment will be the __LESSER__ of -

4.25%	*Index (current)*
+2.25%	*Margin*
6.04%	*Possible New Rate*
$2926.33	*Payment*

OR

The maximum the interest can increase is 2.00% per year; however, on most LIBOR loans, the interest rate will generally adjust 1% at each 6-month adjustment period.

4.75%	*Current rate*
+1.00%	*6 Month adjustment*
= 5.75%	*New rate*
$2838.16	*New payment*

The new interest rate will be 5.75% with a new payment amount of $2,843.16. The note will clarify the terms for the borrower.

The **loan estimate** will show the amortization and will calculate adjustments based on the original index.

- **T-BILL** or treasury bill (bond) loans adjust annually based on the bond market. The caps control the maximum the rate can adjust.

- **LIBOR (London Inter-Bank Offered Rate)** loans adjust every six months, and the index historically does not move very much as it is based on interest paid on savings accounts or is money borrowed from banks investing money from their depositors' savings accounts.

- **COFI (cost of funds index)** is a **monthly adjustable** program, and many lenders may offer COFIs with a 3-month fixed start rate meaning that the first three payments will not adjust. These loans have been called **negative amortization or neg am** and are currently called **OPTION ARMS.** The term option arm is preferred because of the negative connotations of the term cost of funds index. Option ARM loans are often negatively amortized (neg am) meaning the actual rate owed the lender is greater than the amount of the monthly payment.

Example: *based on a $450,000 loan amount:*

$1,499.63	*Initial payment based on 1.25% interest*
$1,698.75	*Actual interest based on 4.25% index*
$199.12	*Negative amortization ($1,698.75 - $1,499.63)*

The payment amount is short $199.12 of covering the actual interest being charged. The shortage amount will be added to the balance of the loan amount making the new balance $450,199.12.

3. **BALLOON LOAN** is defined as a loan that will receive a payment in excess of twice the minimum payment due in any payment period. Balloon loans are loans that are not amortized over for the actual term of the loan. A balloon mortgage is a loan that has the payments based on a term that is longer that the actual term of the loan. A balloon loan may have payments amortized over a period of 30 years, but the balance of the principal will be due in 15 years. Thus, the term "balloon" as the principal balance will be considerably more than any one payment. This is commonly used for 2nd TD or as a way to receive a lower interest rate on a 1st TD.

Example: *Tom has a balloon mortgage with ABC Bank for $100,000 at 6.0% interest. The loan is amortized for 30 years requiring a payment from him in the monthly amount of $622.88. The loan will be due and payable in 15 years meaning that the 180th payment will be for a total amount of $71,671.85. Tom plans to refinance the property prior to that last payment coming due and payable so he will never actually make the one large payment out of his personal cash.*

If Tom had gotten a 15-year loan, his payment would have been $867.19. The shortened term would have made the monthly payment more than $200 higher. He was able to obtain a loan for the same period of time but with a lower payment.

A lender will consider that the borrower is requesting a loan of a considerable amount of money for a long term. However, if the loan will be paid back in half the time, it is a more appealing loan to the lender, even though they are making a lower interest rate reasonable.

4. **BUY-DOWN LOANS** are basically fixed-rate loans. The difference is that with a buy-down, the beginning rate is for a set interest rate less than the final or actual note rate and can adjust according to the original agreement.

Buy-downs are referred to as a 2/1 buy-down or a 3/1 buy-down. Additional terms may be offered. A 2/1 buy-down will adjust twice before reaching the actual interest rate for the remaining term of the loan. The adjustment is generally made on an annual basis.

Example:

8.50%	*Interest rate 30-year fixed (actual note rate)*
6.50%	*Rate for the 1st year (2% difference)*
7.50%	*Rate for the 2nd year (1% difference)*
3.00%	*Cost to borrower for 2/1 buy-down*

2% 1st year + 1% 2nd year = 3% Total Charge to Borrower

The borrower "bought down" the interest rate for a total of 3.00% of the loan amount. The amortization is not negative and there are no shortages to add-on to the balance of the loan because the borrower paid for the difference upfront.

Buy-down loans are often used by builders of subdivisions as an incentive to buyers, especially when interest rates are high. ***This loan program is rarely offered by developers during periods of low interest rates.***

NOTE

The lender charges an upfront fee, which is the difference in the interest rates, at close of escrow to compensate for the decreased interest rate. The borrower actually buys the rate down for a temporary period of time. The fee can be paid by the seller, which is commonly done when buying in a new development as an incentive from the developer.

The term "buy-down" can also be used in reference to a borrower choosing an interest rate below par or a lower interest rate that the lender will charge for versus a higher interest rate, which will provide a rebate. This is referred to as a one-time buy-down.

5. **GRADUATED PAYMENT MORTGAGE (GPM)** is a fixed rate mortgage that starts at a lower interest rate like a buy-down. A GPM will adjust at a predetermined amount for a period of either three years or five years. There is no margin or cap. The purpose of these loans is to help qualify a borrower who can look forward to their income increasing over the period, such as someone who has recently finished college. These loans are also commonly used when interest rates are high. The borrower may choose this type of loan in anticipation of rates lowering during the GPM period. They are not often available during periods of low interest rates.

6. **INTEREST-ONLY LOANS** require that the borrower pay only the interest due for a preset term. At the end of that term, which is usually about five years, the full principal amount will still be owed. This means that the fully amortized payment at the end of the interest-only period will be for a period of 25 years instead of the usual 30-years, making the payment considerably higher.

   These terms are often suggested and used to acquire a higher loan amount for a borrower who will likely have an increase in income in the future and most borrowers will refinance at the end of the interest-only period to reduce the payment. These loans are also useful for investors and investment property as a way to keep the payment at a lower amount.

7. **CONVENTIONAL LOANS** are standard 1st trust deeds with a mortgage lender and of any loan amount. A conventional loan is one that can be procured with a conventional lender or bank.

8. **CONFORMING LOANS** refers to loans up to a maximum amount established by FNMA and FHLMC. Minimum amounts vary with lenders, but are rarely less than $20,000 per FNMA/FHLMC guidelines. Many lenders will not accept a loan of less than $40,000 because of the guidelines set forth by the predatory lending laws. A conforming loan can be fixed, adjustable, convertible, or balloon as long as it is no more than the current FNMA/FHLMC limit and will be underwritten to FNMA/FHLMC guidelines.

The best or lowest rates are available for conforming loans, and these are generally the easiest loans to procure for a borrower.

9. **PORTFOLIO LOANS** are loans issued by financial institutions and normally do not meet FNMA and FHLMC guidelines. They are *not* sold on the secondary market; instead, portfolio lenders assume the risk, create their own underwriting guidelines, and charge a high rate and closing fee. Portfolio loans accommodate the real estate investment market. Since portfolio loans are *nonconforming* and are not sold on the secondary market, such lenders can offer more flexible rates, terms, and qualifications, making them an excellent tool for real estate investors.

10. **JUMBO LOANS** are any loans of an amount greater than the maximum loan amount allowed by FNMA/FHLMC guidelines. FNMA/FHLMC will not purchase or guarantee these loans, so they are underwritten according to the investors' guidelines. Investors in the secondary market can set their own guidelines and will generally conform to other investor's guidelines, including FNMA and FHLMC. These loans are conventional and are packaged the same as a FNMA/FHLMC loan.

11. **ALL INCLUSIVE TRUST DEED (AITD)** or a land contract, or a contract for deed, is a method of purchasing a home whereby the seller becomes the lender. The buyer makes payments to the seller and the seller retains title in most situations. When the buyer applies for a new loan to "take-out" or to pay off the seller and obtain title, it may be considered a refinance; however, many lenders will consider this a purchase.

NOTE

Leveraging. *A noteworthy idea to discuss related to mortgages is the concept that sets real estate apart from other investments - leverage. To leverage means to invest a small amount of your own money and borrow the rest from a lender to reduce your own liability for any loss and gain a high return in relation to your investment. Real estate leveraging, when used properly, can be an efficient tool for real estate investors in increasing their return on investment. While leverage is a remarkable tool, it can work against you. If real estate values decrease several years in a row, you could find that you owe more than the property is worth. The key is to find your personal balance between leverage and your tolerance for debt.*

A rule-of-thumb establishing ownership is if all payments have been applied to principal, interest, and the down payment. If the seller has retained part of the payments received for other than toward the purchase, it may be considered rent and determines that the transaction is a purchase. Possession by the borrower establishes intent.

12. **ALT-A LOANS** are loans that do not fit into an A-paper program for a variety of reasons such as property issues, lack of reserves, or excessive debt ratio.

13. **SUB-PRIME LOANS** are loans that have various issues that are not A-paper or alt-A. In addition to the issues listed under alt-A, sub-prime loans are used for credit scores that are not acceptable to A-paper lenders. The actual credit score will determine the grade and, therefore, the interest rate, and the terms. Sub-prime loans, like alt-A loans, are used when either the borrower or the property do not fit the guidelines of A-paper lenders.

14. **SECOND TRUST DEEDS or JUNIOR LIENS** are smaller loans that may be used for a variety of reasons. Often on a purchase money loan, the lender on the 1st trust deed (TD) will not allow the borrower a high enough LTV to meet the borrower's needs or the borrower may not have enough cash to close. A purchase money 2nd TD will be used to obtain the additional cash needed. When the borrower has a good 1st TD but wants additional cash for personal needs such as remodeling, they will request a 2nd TD to acquire the funds. Lenders look at the combined loan to value (CLTV). They may put a maximum on the LTV and allow an additional percentage or a higher CLTV. This may be shown as or referred to as an 80/10/10. This means that they will allow an 80% 1st, a 10% 2nd, and a 10% down payment from the buyer.

    Lenders do not like to place small 2^{nds} behind a large 1st because if the borrower defaults on the 1st, they will have to bring the 1st current in order to be able to file a notice of default and collect their own funds through a foreclosure proceeding. The holder of a junior lien is in a weaker position because they are subordinate to the 1st TD. In a foreclosure proceeding, the lien position that filed the foreclosure will collect along with any lien holder in a priority position. Second TDs are a riskier position for the lender. Lenders also do not like to place a large 2nd TD behind a 1st TD that is smaller than their 2nd for basically the same reasons. It is because of the weaker or lesser position that 2nd TDs have a higher interest rate and fees than for a 1st TD.

15. **SUBORDINATION AGREEMENT**
In a situation where a borrower is refinancing their 1st TD and does not want to pay off the existing 2nd, the borrower must acquire a **SUBORDINATION AGREEMENT**. In other words, the holder of the 2nd agrees to allow the new 1st to take a priority lien position although the new lien is filed at a later date than their lien. The priority of any lien against a property is established by the date that the lien is filed unless otherwise subordinated. Tax liens may also be subordinated in this manner if acceptable to the lender. The IRS is generally easy to work with if the borrower has been making regular payments on their IRS debt, but lenders rarely will agree.

Second TDs are generally amortized for a period of 15 years or 180 monthly payments and 20 years or 240 monthly payments. **Fixed 2^{nds}** are fully amortized for that period, but lenders commonly offer a variety of amortization choices such as 30 due in 15 or 30/15. 30/15 means that the payment amount will be based on a 30-year amortization and the balance at the 15-year anniversary date will be due at that time. This is known as a **balloon payment**.

16. **HOME EQUITY LINES OF CREDIT (HELOC)** work much like a credit card, and the rate is adjustable monthly. The borrower may draw the entire amount at time of funding, or they can draw on the funds using checks provided by the lender. When borrowers are deciding how much to draw at close of escrow, they need to know that they will not be able to draw additional funds for a set period from the date of closing to be disclosed in the Note, anywhere from 15 to 45 days. A disbursement schedule is provided by the lender asking the amount of the initial draw when docs are ordered. Be sure the borrower understands the process before completing this form.

When the borrower is refinancing to pay-off a 2nd TD when the 2nd is an equity line, the loan is considered **cash-out** if the borrower has drawn funds from the equity line in the last 12 months, generally in excess of $2,000 or 1% of the loan amount.

On the pay-off of any 2nd TD that is being refinanced, the new loan will be considered cash-out unless the 2nd TD was a purchase money loan. Lenders used to consider the pay-off of a 2nd TD to be a rate & term loan if there had been 12-months seasoning. FNMA and FHLMC changed the ruling in 2002 and all 2nd TD pay-offs that were not part of the purchase money are now cash-out loans and will incur additional costs.

MORTGAGE INSURANCE

MORTGAGE INSURANCE (MI) or PRIVATE MORTGAGE INSURANCE **(PMI)** is insurance that insures the loan if the borrower defaults. MI is used by lenders as a way to protect their investment when lending. mortgage insurance is required on loans greater than 80% of the value of the property or 80% loan-to- value (LTV).

When the loan amount is greater than 80% LTV, the lender is at a higher risk of losing a portion of the money they have invested in making the loan. If the borrower defaults on the loan or otherwise does not fulfill the contract, the costs that will be incurred in collecting by foreclosure or any other course will be costly. By the time the lender has undergone foreclosure and is selling the property, they may actually have lost money on the transaction. If a property does not sell at the foreclosure sale, the lender then needs to hire a real estate agent and list the property for sale which will cost even more.

The mortgage insurance insures the loan down to 75% LTV. This means that any amount of the original loan amount that is lost will be reimbursed to the lender by the insurance company down to an amount equal to but no less than 75% of the original loan amount.

Example:	*$100,000*	*Value of property*
	90,000	*Loan amount*
	90%	*Loan-to-value (LTV)*
	$10,000	*Equity*

If the lender forecloses on the loan. The following costs are incurred by the lender:

$4,000	*Foreclosure filing*
$3,000	*Lost interest from the time of last payment made*
$3,500	*Delinquent property taxes*
$1,500	*Foreclosure sale and sheriff's costs*
$12,000	*Total costs*
$2,000	*Loss after foreclosure sale*

The lender will be paid $2,000 by the mortgage insurance company.

The higher the LTV, the more a borrower will pay for the mortgage insurance because the risk is greater. A loan that has an 85% LTV may require .35% MI based on the loan amount whereas a loan that has a 95% LTV may require .65% MI based on the loan amount. The borrower pays for the mortgage insurance that will protect the lender based on the risk assessment.

The insurance and the insurance company charges based on the risk is the same as a driver with a history of accidents and tickets will pay more than a driver who does not have tickets or accidents.

MORTGAGE TERMS

MORTGAGE TERMS that are a regular part of language when working with mortgages are as follows:

LOAN-TO-VALUE (LTV): The percentage of the value that is the loan amount.

Example 1: *A lender will loan a particular borrower 90% of the value of the property or a 90% LTV.*

$350,000	*Purchase price*
X 90%	*Maximum LTV*
=$315,000	*Loan amount*

Example 2: *A borrower is refinancing their home, and they are looking for a loan of $360,000. The lender has approved them for an LTV of 85%.*

$360,000	*Loan amount needed.*
÷ 85%	*Maximum LTV*
$423,530	*Needed appraised value to obtain the loan desired.*

COMBINED LOAN-TO-VALUE (CLTV) is the combination of the 1st and 2nd TDs. HELOC combined loan-to-value (HCLTV) is the percentage of the value that is a home equity line of credit (HELOC).

DEBT RATIO or QUALIFYING RATIOS: The percentage of debt in relation to the income. Lenders will qualify a borrower by calculating this information against the maximum allowable.

FRONT-END RATIO is the primary housing expense/income which is the percentage of the borrower's income that is dedicated to the basic housing expenses. The percentage is derived by totaling the monthly payment and the insurance and taxes broken down to a monthly amount. Divide that amount by the total income.

Example:

$1,500	*Monthly mortgage payment*
200	*Monthly property taxes ($2,400÷12=$200)*
+ 50	*Monthly insurance ($600÷12=$50)*
$1,750	*Total monthly housing expense*
÷$4,700	*Gross monthly income*
= 37.23%	*Front-end debt ratio (FNMA guideline 38%)*

BACK-END DEBT RATIO is the total of all housing expenses included in the Front- End ration plus all other consumer debt. The borrower's total debt ratio will appear as 37/48 debt ratio or total obligation.

Example:

$1,750	*Total monthly housing expense*
350	*Car payment*
+ 150	*Credit card payments*
$2,250	*Total monthly expense*
÷ $4,700	*Monthly income*
= 47.87%	*Back-end debt ratio (FNMA guideline 48%)*

NOTE RATE is the actual interest rate the borrower will be paying on the loan. The mortgage interest rate is **Simple interest** meaning that the interest due is calculated on the balance due. **Fully amortized interest** is calculated for the full term of the loan based on what the balance will be at each payment date.

QUALIFYING RATE is the interest rate that will be used to qualify the borrower, which is used when obtaining an adjustable-rate loan. The qualifying rate is usually a rate higher than the start rate and is based on an estimated rate after the first adjustment. The purpose is to verify that the borrower will be able to make a higher payment.

% ABOVE NOTE RATE is the higher rate used for qualifying based on what the note rate may adjust to by the end of the first year or one full adjustment period. This amount is generally 2%.

The lender wants to be certain, especially in a period of increasing interest rates, that the borrower will in fact be able to meet any increasing payments.

IMPOUND ACCOUNT: A trust account held by the lender on behalf of the borrower to hold funds collected as part of the monthly payment that is for the purpose of **paying the taxes and insurance** when the bill comes due.

LOAN OPERATING SYSTEM (LOS): Computer program used by the agent/broker to process loans.

AUTOMATED UNDERWRITING SYSTEM (AUS): A computerized system of underwriting. Many lenders now offer an AUS on their websites. Most can be populated from the LOS used by brokers for processing loan applications, or the information can be entered directly into the AUS. By using an AUS, it can be determined in a short period of time whether the loan fits the lender's guidelines, which program will work, and rates and costs. Approval and conditions are obtained immediately but may be subject to underwriting review on receipt of the file by the lender and additional conditions may be required. This can all be done while the client waits.

DESKTOP UNDERWRITING (DU): An AUS developed by FNMA for the purpose of providing approval on a loan which is acceptable for purchase by FNMA.

LOAN PROSPECTOR (LP): The AUS designed and used by FHLMC.

MONEY SOURCES AND LENDERS

MONEY SOURCES have changed drastically since the 1970s. The Federal Reserve System was created in 1913 by Congress to operate as the central bank for the United States.

A. **FEDERAL RESERVE SYSTEM** is also known as the **Fed** and controls the flow of money in the American economy and regulates the cost of money and of credit. The ***Federal Reserve Board (FRB)*** is the governing body of the Federal Reserve System. Some of the main duties of the Fed are to perform and otherwise oversee the following:

   A. **Establish the interest rate**, which is also called the **discount rate**, that member banks must pay when they borrow money from the Fed.

   B. **Control the reserve rate** that a bank is required to maintain.

   C. **Buy and sell government securities** to generate cash flow or available funds.

1. The Fed establishes **INTEREST RATES,** which **is** the amount that is charged to member banks when they borrow money from the FED. The member bank in turn may lend money to other member banks within their district by adding a small profit to the rate that they paid, thus creating income or profit for the bank. The bank also determines their **prime rate** based on what they pay for their money plus the amount added on for profit or income for the bank.

   Example: *ABC Bank will be funding a number of mortgage loans by the end of the month and need to increase their cash reserves, so they borrow money from the Fed. The Fed charges ABC Bank 3.5% interest for the loan.*

   XYZ Bank needs to borrow funds to increase their reserves, so they get a loan from ABC Bank who charges them 4.0%. ABC Bank is making .50% profit on the money they have loaned XYZ Bank over the 3.5% they are paying the FED for the money.

   Mr. Smith wants to buy a new car and approaches ABC Bank for a car loan. He is a good customer with a good credit rating. The bank will make the loan to Mr. Smith at their prime interest rate of 6.5%. The bank is now making 3.0% profit on the money loaned to Mr. Smith from the money they borrowed from the Fed for 3.5%.

   The bank will also make money by loaning funds that are on deposit with either CDs or savings accounts. If the bank is paying Mr. Jones 4.5% into his savings account, they can loan the same funds to another bank customer for 7.5%, making a profit of 2.0%. When the Fed chairman makes an announcement that they are changing the interest rate, it affects everybody, from what they pay to borrow money to what they make on investments.

2. **The RESERVE RATE** is the percentage of deposits held by the bank that must be available for customer withdrawal. Many bank failures during the Depression of the 1930s occurred because the individual banks did not hold enough of their cash reserves to cover customer withdrawal of their savings accounts. When bank customers became scared that the banks were going to close, they made what was called a "run on the bank." In other words, more customers panicked and withdrew their money. The banks had not

anticipated so many withdrawals and therefore did not have sufficient funds or reserves. The result was that the banks had to close their doors.

The Fed now regulates the amount of cash that banks must hold in reserve. This control not only protects customer money, but it also helps control the cash flow into the economy. When the Fed decides the economy needs a boost, they will reduce the percentage of cash to deposit that they are required to have in reserve.

> ***Example:*** *ABC Bank has $1,000,000 in savings account deposits. (In other words, their customers have $1,000,000 in savings accounts.) The Fed notifies ABC Bank that the deposit reserve needs to be no less than 65% of the funds in deposits. This means that ABC Bank can loan $350,000 of the $1,000,000 in savings accounts and keep $650,000 available for their customers who may choose to withdraw their money.*
>
> *Several months later, the Fed contacts ABC Bank and informs them that they need to increase their deposit reserve to a reserve rate of 75%. The Fed has made this decision* ***as a way to slow spending to help prevent inflation****. This means that now ABC Bank can loan $250,000 of available cash deposits and must retain $750,000 in reserve to have available to its depositors. The reserve rate is a direct percentage of the funds on the deposit.*

3. **GOVERNMENT SECURITIES** help generate cash flow by the sale of the securities and slows spending or cash flow by withdrawing the sale of securities. This works in much the same as increasing or decreasing the reserve rate.

   The Fed banks are divided into twelve regional Federal Reserve banks that are governed by the Board of Governors. The Board consists of seven members who are appointed by the President of the United States and confirmed by the U.S. Senate for a term of 14 years. The 12th Federal Reserve District is in San Francisco and includes California, Nevada, Arizona, Idaho, Washington, and Oregon. Most banks are members of the Federal Reserve, and as of 1980, even the banks that are not members must adhere to the rules, regulations, and laws as established and set forth by the Federal Reserve Board and Bank.

B. **FEDERAL HOME LOAN BANK SYSTEM or THE FHL BANK SYSTEM** was established by Congress in 1932. The FHL Bank System established banking districts similar to the regions established by the Fed. California, Nevada, and Arizona are in the FHL Bank System's 11th District.

The organization and purpose are much the same as that of the Fed; however, it originally applied to savings and loans. Since 1989, commercial banks and federally insured credit unions became eligible for membership. Congress made membership in the FHL Bank System available to all eligible banking institutions.

C. **ELEVENTH DISTRICT COST OF FUNDS** is a commonly heard term and is responsible for the **cofi** or **cost of funds index** which is the index that is usually used to establish the interest rate for option ARMs or neg am loans.

D. **FEDERAL DEPOSIT INSURANCE CORPORATION (FDIC)** was also a result of the Great Depression. It was established in 1933 by Congress as a way to protect bank depositors from losing their money as a result of a bank failure. The FDIC insures consumer bank deposits in an amount not to exceed $100,000 per account. Certain types of accounts are insured to a maximum amount of $250,000, such as IRAs.

The Financial Institutions Reform, Recovery, and Enforcement Act (FIRREA) was put in place in 1989 as a way to prevent the fraud and abuses that occurred in the 1980s as a result of the Depository Institutions Deregulation and Monetary Control Act of 1980. The purpose of the deregulation was to give thrifts and savings and loans the same benefits as commercial banks. The FDIC assumed the insuring of thrifts and savings and loans when the Federal Savings and Loan Insurance Corporation (FSLIC) ceased to exist.

LENDERS

LENDERS in the primary mortgage lending market include:

- Commercial banks
- Savings and loans
- Credit unions

A. **RETAIL LENDERS** are the most frequently used sources for real estate financing. These sources are referred to as retail because they work directly with the public or the consumer. Banks, savings and loans, and other lenders loan mortgage money directly to the consumer using their own money. Many of these lenders will retain the mortgages, or "paper," and generate income from the collection of interest and the fees charged for servicing of the loan.

Servicing a loan consists of the various duties performed in the collecting of payments and otherwise managing the accounts. When a lender funds a loan with their own funds and keeps the paper and retains the servicing of the loan, they are called a portfolio lender.

B. **SECONDARY MARKET** is an arena of funds for mortgages and loans using real property as security. Deregulations allowed many of these new sources using investments such as creating mortgage-backed securities.

When a lender chooses to generate more cash in order to enable the business to fund more mortgages, they sell some of the mortgages or paper that they hold in the secondary market. The secondary market is not available to the consumer. It is a marketplace only for retail lenders, which are the banks or other entities funding mortgage loans.

MAIN SOURCES or entities in the secondary market are:

- **Wall Street mortgage-backed securities:** Pools of securities sold on Wall Street to investors. The pools generate a steady stream of income from the interest earned on the paper. The pools also generate large pools of funds to be used to buy paper.

- **Mortgage bankers**: Institutions that are licensed as banks by the Department of Financial Protection and Innovation (DFPI) under the California Residential Mortgage Lending Act (CRMLA) and perform the same duties that a mortgage division of a regular bank would perform, but the only banking duties performed are those associated with mortgage loans or lending money secured by real estate.

- **Federal National Mortgage Association (FNMA)** FANNIE MAE: Privately owned corporation that purchases loans on the secondary market and is backed by and works closely with the Federal Reserve Bank. Control of FNMA was assumed by the Fed in mid-2008 as a result of failed mortgages and excessive losses due to foreclosures. *See www.fanniemae.com*

- **Federal Home Loan Mortgage Corporation (FHLMC)** FREDDIE MAC: A federally backed private corporation created by Congress in 1970 and supervised by the federal government. Freddie Mac serves the same purpose as Fannie Mae. *See www.freddiemac.com*

- **Insurance companies:** Investment funds from insurance companies are used as funds for funding mortgages. It has become a common practice for large companies to invest funds such as retirement funds in real estate investments of some sort, especially financing mortgages.

GOVERNMENT LOANS

GOVERNMENT LOANS or government-backed loans are either through the Veteran's Administration (VA) or through the Federal Housing Administration (FHA). California also offers a VA loan through the **Cal Vet Program**.

A. **VA LOANS (Veteran's Administration)** are loans guaranteed by the federal government for the benefit of **all veterans of the United States Military Services.** The maximum loan amount has historically been 75% of the FNMA/FHLMC maximum loan amount. This was changed January 1, 2002, to be equal to the FNMA/FHLMC guidelines for maximum loan amount. These amounts also now apply to FHA loans.

A VA loan is obtained through the usual banking entities that the broker is approved with. The VA then guarantees the loan to the bank. This means that if the veteran defaults on the loan, the VA will assume the loan and handle the servicing of the loan.

The VA was created following World War II as a way to help reintroduce returning veterans into civilian life by offering education benefits, loans, and other compensation for their service. The idea of offering home lending opportunities was to see all Americans enjoy owning their own home.

VA loans allow **100% financing** plus the closing costs up to 104% of the purchase price or appraised value, whichever is less. VA loans must be fully documented or verify all income and all assets.

VA allows a **streamline refinance** for borrowers who currently have a VA loan for the purpose of reducing the payment. The required documentation is minimal as long as the payments have been made in a timely manner. An appraisal is generally required as verification that the value is still there.

The VA will not allow the borrower to pay the non-recurring closing costs (NRCC) consisting of the broker's fees, lender's fees, appraisal, credit report, and escrow fees. A purchase offer transaction to be completed using a VA loan must always specify that the **seller will pay these costs.** Rebate pricing may be used to compensate or pay some of the costs and the lender pays a yield-spread premium to the broker for their commission.

All eligible veterans must provide a copy of a **certificate of eligibility or the DD214, which is issued by the VA.** This form is provided to veterans at the time of discharge or is available on request for veterans and those currently active in the military.

Disclosures concerning issues, including lead paint poisoning, is initially provided by the real estate agent and the lender with the loan docs. When the mortgage broker has completed inputting the usual information into the computer processing program or loan operating system (LOS), the information will carry over to the appropriate places in the additional forms required for a VA loan. The broker will have additional information to input, most of which will be found on the discharge papers.

Some of the additional information required for VA loans will include:

- **Date of birth**
- **Date of discharge** from military service
- **Branch of military service**
- **Date of entry and current rank status** if currently active in the service
- **Breakdown of withholding taxes** on pay stub
- **Service number**

VA underwriters must have completed training and testing to be approved to underwrite a VA loan, receiving a certificate called a **designated endorsement**. VA underwriters are referred to as **DE underwriters**. This designation also applies to FHA loans. VA, FHA, and HUD all offer seminars offering thorough training on government loans.

Each mortgage broker must obtain approval to do VA loans separately from the usual broker approval. Brokers will generally be approved by only one VA lender but may be approved by more than one if they choose to do so.

B. **FHA LOANS** are similar to VA loans except instead of being guaranteed by the government, they are insured by the government. A DE underwriter must underwrite them. The loan package must be full doc, and the loan amount must be equal to but not exceed the FNMA/FHLMC maximum loan limit.

The broker must be approved by HUD in order to broker FHA loans. The broker approval by HUD for FHA is a more expensive and a lengthier process than for VA. HUD used to require a fully audited profit & loss statement (P&L) from the broker to obtain FHA approval, which can be costly. Now instead of the fully audited P&L, HUD will accept a broker if they have a net worth of $75,000.

The FHA loans were created as a way to help all citizens enjoy home ownership. FHA loans were created **for lower income families** and will allow a loan amount of 97.3% of the purchase price plus non-recurring closing costs in most situations. Gifts up to 100% of down payment and closing costs are acceptable from an immediate family member only.

There may be maximum income limits based on the number of people in the household and the county of residence. These guidelines generally apply to variations or clones of FHA loan programs such as a CHAFA program. The specifications and county limits can be obtained from the lender. FHA borrowers are required to complete a homebuyer's course and answer questions relating to debt management and homeowner's responsibilities. This may be given by a phone interview or online.

The forms are similar to those required by VA with the exception of the military information. The basic mortgage loan application is used along with the FHA forms. An estimate of living expenses is also used in qualifying including the utilities.

FHA allows streamline refinancing for borrowers who currently have an FHA loan. The purpose is to reduce the payment. The required documentation is minimal as long as the payments have been made in a timely manner. An appraisal is generally required as verification that the property value is there.

SECURITY INSTRUMENTS

MORTGAGES AND TRUST DEEDS are terms for lending Instruments that use real estate as security for the repayment of the loan. The process of securing real property to guarantee payment of a debt is called **HYPOTHECATION**.

By hypothecating the debt, the borrower retains possession of the property while making a pledge of payment to the lender. This process allows for the lender to take the property if the borrower defaults on the debt through the foreclosure process.

The terms "mortgage" and "trust deed" are used synonymously; however, they are two different types of legal documents. They are both used to secure a debt obligation on real estate, however, with different legal effects which apply mostly in the event of a default on the loan and the resulting foreclosure process. California uses trust deeds instead of mortgages.

MORTGAGES are legal instruments that use real property as security for a loan. Mortgages are the most commonly used loan instrument used in the United Sates for financing real property; in California, **notes secured by a deed of trust** are used instead. The significant difference between a mortgage and a trust deed is that the trust deed does not contain a **deficiency clause,** the trustee cannot go after the trustor's (borrower's) other assets. The borrower becomes the mortgagor by giving the lender the interest or the hypothecation in their property in the form of a mortgage making the lender the mortgagee by receiving the mortgage.

The mortgage, as a legal document provides the terms of the loan in clauses. Some of the clauses included in a mortgage are as follows:

- **IN CASE OF DEFAULT**: If the borrower defaults on the terms of the mortgage, the mortgagee has the right to claim the property through a judicial or court-ordered foreclosure. Causes of foreclosure may include violation of the following covenants:
    - Lack of payment
    - Non-payment of property taxes
    - Lack of homeowners' insurance
    - Waste or lack of care for the property

- **ACCELERATION CLAUSE**: Allows the mortgagee to demand payment of the remaining balance of the loan in full if the loan is in default.

- **POWER OF SALE CLAUSE**: Allows the mortgagee to claim the property through a foreclosure sale process similar to the process used by trust deeds rather than the lengthier judicial foreclosure.
  - **ALIENATION/DUE ON SALE CLAUSE**: Allows the mortgagee to demand payment in full or call the loan due and payable for the balance of the loan if the mortgagor allows a purchaser of the property to assume the loan without approval of the mortgagee.
  - Sells the property on a **CONTRACT FOR DEED**
  - When **PAID IN FULL,** a mortgage is referred to as being **"DEAD."** The lender/mortgagee provides the mortgagor with a **SATISFACTION OF MORTGAGE** which the mortgagor then records with the county recorder's office to give constructive notice that there are no mortgage liens against the property.

- PREPAYMENT PENALTY CLAUSE: **A *prepayment penalty* is a fee the borrower must pay if they pay off their mortgage loan sooner than the agreed upon terms.** In general, the prepayment penalty fee applies only during the first three years of the loan. Certain prepayment penalty clauses also require that a borrower cannot pay off more than 20% of the loan balance each year. In California, lenders can use prepayment penalty provisions if the assessed penalties apply to the first five years of their mortgage loans; after five years, lenders are restricted from assessing prepayment penalties.

FORECLOSURE PROCESS begins when the mortgagor fails to make a payment per the terms of the mortgage. Payments are usually made on a monthly basis; however, the terms can be whatever the parties agree. When the mortgagor's missed payments have reached ninety days since the first delinquent payment was due, the process begins with a notice of default and the legal proceedings of the foreclosure process begin.

- **JUDICIAL FORECLOSURE** can take any length of time, often taking many months just to procure a court hearing. As the term indicates, a judicial foreclosure must be heard by the courts and the courts will pass the judgment on the right of the mortgagee to move forward and hold a foreclosure sale.

- **LAWSUIT TO FORECLOSE** on the subject property is initiated by the mortgagee. During this time while waiting for the court action, the mortgagor/borrower has the right to **reinstate the loan**.

- **REINSTATEMENT** allows the mortgagor/borrower to bring the mortgage payments current by paying all past due payments and any fees and costs incurred by the mortgagee/lender including:
  - » **Accrued interest**
  - » **Late fees**
  - » **Court costs**
  - » **Filing fees**

  Reinstatement returns both parties to a mortgage to their position prior to the default. The right of reinstatement ends once the court issues the foreclosure decree.

- **RIGHT OF REDEMPTION** is the mortgagor's right to redeem the property by paying the entire loan obligation including:
  - **Principal balance**
  - **Accrued interest**
  - **Late fees**
  - **Court costs**
  - **Foreclosure sale costs**
  - **Filing fees**

  Right of redemption is available to the mortgagor/borrower from the time the court gives the foreclosure decree until either:
    - » **Three months after foreclosure sale if no deficiency** as a result of the sale or the sale produced sufficient funds to pay the debt.
    - » **Twelve months after foreclosure sale if a deficiency judgment** is available or the property did not sell for enough money to pay the mortgagee/lender in full.

- The ***foreclosure decree*** allows the mortgagee/lender to schedule the property to be sold to the highest bidder at the foreclosure sale which is held at a public auction. The foreclosure sale is carried out by either a court–appointed commissioner or a sheriff who ensures that the statutory requirements of the foreclosure are met. The highest bidder on the subject property is given a ***certificate of sale.***

- The successful bidder on the property is generally expected to pay for the purchase of the property in full at the time of the auction. If the purchase price is greater than $5,000, the buyer has the option to pay the entire price at the time or pay only 10% of the purchase price with the remaining balance to be paid within ten days of the foreclosure sale. If the buyer has chosen to pay only 10% of the purchase price at the sale, they will be liable for costs and expenses that accrue at the time of making the total payment.

  Failure of the successful bidder to pay for the property within the ten days allowed will result in the property being resold at auction and the defaulting buyer being responsible for the costs of the original sale, any other resultant costs and fees involved the new sale, and interest and expenses caused by the default of that buyer. A sale can be postponed to another sale date in the future if there are no adequate bids on the property.

  The funds from the foreclosure sale are distributed first to the mortgagee that filed the foreclosure suit. Residual funds are then used to pay any other taxes or liens against the property in the order of recordings until the funds are depleted. The remaining funds after all liens have been paid will be paid to the original mortgagor/borrower.

- **DEFICIENT SALE PRECEDES** means that the sale did not generate enough cash to pay the party that filed the foreclosure suit. This can result in the mortgagee/lender obtaining a ***deficiency judgment*** against the mortgagor/borrower. A deficiency judgment allows the mortgagee/lender to collect the remaining balance owed from the mortgagor/borrower.

  Example 1: *Mary financed her home with ABC Bank for $200,000 and has defaulted on her loan payments. ABC Bank filed foreclosure proceedings against her and the court awarded a foreclosure decree. ABC Bank had a foreclosure sale, and the property sold for $180,000, which is $20,000 less than the principal balance owed. ABC Bank also* *spent $10,000 on foreclosure costs and there is an additional $6,000 of accrued interest. The foreclosure sale caused a deficiency of $36,000 that ABC Bank is still owed if they choose to file a deficiency judgment against Mary.*

Judgments are good for 10 years and can be renewed for an additional 10 years, which means that Mary still owes this debt and may be collectable for the next 20 years.

Mary has 12 months from the date of the sale to redeem the property. In order to exercise that right, Mary will need to pay to ABC Bank a total of $236,000 plus any additional interests and fees that have accrued to the date of redemption. Mary retains possession of the property during her redemption period.

***Example 2**: Mary financed her home with ABC Bank for $200,000 and has defaulted on her loan payments. ABC Bank filed foreclosure proceedings against her and the court awarded a foreclosure decree. ABC Bank had a foreclosure sale, and the property sold for $250,000, which is $50,000 more than the principal balance owed. ABC Bank also spent $10,000 on foreclosure costs and there is an additional $6,000 of accrued interest. The foreclosure sale paid ABC Bank in full with a balance of $14,000. The past due property taxes were $3,000 and she had a mechanic's lien against the property for $2,000. Those debts were paid and the balance of $9,000 was forwarded to Mary.*

Because there was no deficiency available to the lender, Mary has only 3 months to redeem the property. Mary retains possession of the property during her redemption period.

A **Deficiency Judgment** may not be allowed under the following circumstances:

- The mortgage was all or part of purchase money for an owner-occupied, 1-to-4-unit residential dwelling.
- The mortgage was for the purchase and mortgagee is the seller of the subject property.
- Trust deeds

California has initiated guidelines to protect homeowners from deficiency judgments through the ***Homeowner's Safety Net, California Code Procedure 580b.*** This code disallows a deficiency judgment if the loan was for the purchase of the property including any chattel mortgage which included personal property such as furniture in the purchase price.

The code does not protect a loan that was acquired as a refinance on property already owed or a second trust deed or mortgage that was acquired after the purchase transaction and was not a part of the purchase money.

- **SUBORDINATE LIEN HOLDER** against the property or a lien that was recorded after the lien held by the party that is foreclosing may lose their opportunity to collect on the debt that is owed to them if the foreclosing party continues with the action. A party that holds a 2nd mortgage may not be paid the balance of their debt. The solution to this dilemma is for the holder of any subordinate liens to pay current the past due debt owed to the foreclosing party.

  The secondary lien holder then files foreclosure against the debtor and then when the foreclosure sale is held, the primary lien holder is paid, and the secondary lien holder is paid because they will control the outcome of the sale by rejecting bids that are insufficient to pay all debts owed.

  > ***Example 3:*** *Mary financed her home with ABC Bank for $200,000 and has defaulted on her loan payments. ABC Bank also spent $10,000 on foreclosure costs and there is an additional $6,000 of accrued interest ABC Bank filed foreclosure proceedings against her and the court awarded a foreclosure Decree. Mary owes ABC Bank a total of $16,000 to reinstate her mortgage. Mary also gave a mortgage to XYZ Bank for a 2nd or Junior Lien for $20,000. XYZ Bank pays ABC Bank $16,000 to stop the foreclosure proceedings.*
  >
  > *XYZ Bank then files foreclosure against Mary. The foreclosure sale procures a high bid of $230,000, which is short $6,000 of the total amount needed to pay the debts in full. XYZ Bank has the option to not accept the highest bid and offer the property at a later sale or to accept the $6,000 deficiency and get a deficiency judgment against Mary.*

- **SHERIFF'S DEED** is issued to the successful bidder from the judicial foreclosure sale if the mortgagor/borrower does not redeem the property within the redemption time limits. At that point, the original mortgagor surrenders possession of the property.

TRUST DEEDS

TRUST DEEDS are the preferred financing instrument in California. A trust deed does not contain the terms of the loan like the mortgage does. A trust deed is accompanied by a ***note,*** which provides all of the pertinent terms and agreements between the parties to the loan transaction.

The formation of a trust deed is the same as for any type of trust with the same parties performing basically the same jobs just for a different purpose. The parties to a trust deed are:

- **Trustor or borrower:** The party giving a trust interest in the property as security for a loan.
- **Trustee or third party**: The party who manages and oversees the trust for the beneficiary.
- **Beneficiary or lender**: The party who will benefit from the trust, in this case by earning interest on the money that they have lent to the trustor.

The **trustor/borrower hypothecates an interest** in their property in exchange for a monetary loan. A trustee is named or hired to manage the account on behalf of the beneficiary/lender. The trustee may or may not service the loan by accepting payments and handling the bookkeeping, but the trustee is responsible for filing and managing the foreclosure proceedings if the trustor/borrower defaults on their loan.

The trustee is notified and instructed to **record a notice of default** once the first missed payment is ninety days old. It is filed with the county recorder's office and the trustor must be notified by certified mail. It must be posted in a conspicuous place on the property and in public such as at the county courthouse.

Three months must pass from the date the notice of default is recorded until advertising the **notice of sale** can commence. Once the three months has passed, a notice of sale must be recorded at the county recorder's office and the trustee can begin advertising the notice of sale. A minimum of twenty days is required to pass from the date of recording to the date of foreclosure sale. The sale must be advertised once a week for three weeks. The sale is advertised by posting in a public place including the courthouse and under "public notices" in the local newspaper.

Foreclosure under a deed of trust will result in the issuance of a TRUSTEE'S DEED to the successful bidder at the sale.

SUBORDINATE LIEN HOLDERS and any others who have recorded a notification request are notified to be provided with the opportunity to make claims or to pay the loan current in order to be able to file their own foreclosure proceeding. This, as with the judicial foreclosure proceedings of a mortgage, is the only way for a subordinate lien holder to ensure a sale sufficient to collect the debt they are owed. In the event of a foreclosure sale all lien holders in lien positions in front of the party filing the foreclosure will be paid through the proceeds of the sale before that filing lien holder is paid. Any lien holders behind the filing lien holder will not be paid unless the sale generates enough cash to pay them. The orders of the foreclosure sale may state that the property must generate a predetermined amount of money to cover the debts, and the costs incurred as a result of the foreclosure proceedings and resultant sale. A **deficiency judgment** is not available under a private foreclosure sale.

The trustor/borrower has a **RIGHT OF REDEMPTION** up to **five business days prior** to the date of the sale to the time of sale. Once the foreclosure sale has taken place, the trustor/borrower has no further claim to the property and the successful bidder gains immediate possession. If the trustor/borrower refuses to vacate the property, the new buyer of the property may need to have the Sheriff serve them with a notice of eviction.

The **FORECLOSURE PROCESS** may take approximately 117 days from the date of recording the notice of default until the foreclosure sale. The new owner's rights of possession are immediate, and the defaulting trustor/borrower has no residual right of redemption or possessory rights following the foreclosure sale.

The private sale rights that are available in a trust deed transaction versus a mortgage make the trust deed favored over mortgages in California. A judicial foreclosure is an available option with a trust deed; however, the trustee would generally not benefit from requesting a judicial foreclosure.

MORTGAGE BROKERS

MORTGAGE BROKERS are responsible for taking a loan application for a borrower and negotiating with lenders to locate the one that best suits the borrower's needs. A mortgage broker then brokers the loan to that lender. *This is done in a similar way as a stockbroker finds an investment that matches the needs of their investors.*

Licensing is required in California to act as a mortgage broker. The ***California Department of Real Estate*** provides for the licensing needs under the ***real property loan laws*** as part of real estate law. The licensing allows a mortgage broker to solicit borrowers and to negotiate loans using 1- to 4-unit residential real property as security.

A mortgage broker is allowed to loan their personal funds and funds that they are in control of, but this must be disclosed to the borrower prior to becoming committed to the loan. The broker has a number of disclosures that are required to be provided to the borrower.

USURY LAWS are laws that limit the excessive use of charges or interest rates. The usury laws were originally federal laws and in 1979 California voters passed ***Proposition 2***, which exempts all loans secured by real property except loans secured through the use of a mortgage broker; however, the mortgage broker is limited on the amount of commissions that can be charged. The limitations are affected by several separate controls.

- **SECTION 32** is a federal guideline that limits mortgage broker commissions plus the non-recurring closing costs to no more than 8% of the loan amount. This restriction was created in the late 1990s as a result of predatory lending acts. Originally the predatory lending laws only required the disclosure as a 'high-cost loan." The laws were directed at loans in an amount of $20,000 or less. These loans were subject to violation of **Section 32**, which requires that closing costs in excess of 8% must be disclosed to the borrower as a high-cost loan. Lenders and mortgage brokers cannot make the normal commission on small loans, but they require the same amount of work and cost.

There are also issues on smaller loans that may qualify such loans to be done under consumer lending laws, which require a finance lending license under the Department of Financial Protection and Innovation (DFPI). ***The stricter law always prevails.***

Example:	*$20,000*	*Loan amount*
	X 8%	*Maximum non-recurring closing costs*
	= $1,600	*Maximum dollar amount allowed by RESPA*

Example:	*$20,000*	*Loan amount*
	X 5.99%	*Maximum non-recurring closing costs*
	= $1,199.80	*Maximum dollar amount allowed by DRE*

NOTE

California has a stricter predatory lending law which will not allow NRCC's (nonrecurring closing costs) in excess of 5.99% of the loan amount.

- **CALIFORNIA LAWS** provide for the following limits to protect the consumer from acts of predatory lending:

  1st TRUST DEED
  - **less than $30,000** for a period of **3 years** or more=maximum
  - **commission of 10%** of the loan amount
  - **$30,000 or more** for less than **3 years**= maximum **commission of 5%** of the loan amount
  - **$30,000 or more for any number of years** or term= no maximum commission

  2nd TRUST DEED
  - **less than $20,000** for a period of **3 years** or more=maximum
  - **commission of 15%** of the loan amount
  - $20,000 or more for less than 3 years= maximum commission of 10% of the loan amount
  - $20,000 or more for less than 2 years= maximum commission of 5% of the loan amount
  - $20,000 or more for any number of years or term= no maximum commission
  - The following limits the amount of charges for the broker's costs and expenses on loan amounts:
    - Up to $7,800- lesser of actual costs or $390
    - $7,800 to $14,000- lesser of 5% or actual costs

MORTGAGE LOAN DISCLOSURES

Mortgage loan disclosures are a result and requirement of several different state and federal laws. For more than three decades, federal law required lenders to provide two different *disclosure forms* to consumers applying for a home loan.

Additionally, the law required two different forms, at or before, closing on the loan. These forms were developed separately by two different federal agencies, under two federal statutes: The Truth in Lending Act (TILA) and the Real Estate Settlement Procedures Act (RESPA). Unfortunately, the information on these forms was overlapping and the language inconsistent. As expected, consumers often found the forms confusing; it is also understandable that lenders and settlement agents found the forms burdensome to provide and explain.

The Dodd-Frank Wall Street Reform and Consumer Protection Act (Dodd- Frank Act) created the Consumer Financial Protection Bureau (CFPB), whose main objective is to protect consumers by carrying out federal consumer financial laws. The Dodd-Frank Act mandated the CFPB to integrate the mortgage loan disclosures under TILA and RESPA and instructed that the CFPB to propose for public comment rules and model disclosures that integrate the TILA and RESPA disclosures by July 21, 2012. On December 31, 2013, the CFPB issued a final rule with new, integrated disclosures— "Integrated Mortgage Disclosures under the Real Estate Settlement Procedures Act and the Truth in Lending Act," or the TILA-RESPA Final Rule. On January 20, 2015, and July 21, 2015, the CFPB published amendments to the TILA- RESPA Final Rule. Moreover, the CFPB issued technical corrections on December 24, 2015, and a correction to supplementary information on February 10, 2016. On July 7, 2017, the CFPB published further amendments to ratify guidance, and provide greater clarity and certainty about the TILA-RESPA Final Rule. These amendments were published in the Federal Register on August 11, 2017.

The CFPB Final Rule new integrated disclosures—the TILA-RESPA Integrated Disclosures, also known as TRID, is designed to help mortgage loan applicants understand the terms of their home financing transaction. The TRID rule became effective on October 3, 2015.

This new rule applies to most closed-end consumer mortgage loans; it does not apply to home-equity lines of credit, reverse mortgage loans, mortgage loans secured by a mobile home, or to creditors that write five or lesser mortgages a year.

The TRID rule aims to simplify the mortgage process by streamlining and encapsulating certain loan disclosures and changing the timing of certain mortgage processes. First, applicants will see consumer disclosures that are easy to read—the new TRID documents have the most important information in more prominent places. The *loan estimate* (which replaced the good faith estimate) forms will clearly set forth the terms of the proposed transaction to help the applicant determine whether they would like to proceed with the transaction. Next, applicants will be given their *closing disclosures* early (the closing disclosure replaced the HUD-1 statement). Before closing on a home purchase or refinance, applicants should receive a copy of their closing disclosure at least three business days before closing so if they have questions, their lenders can provide them with additional information. The format of the closing disclosure will also mirror the loan estimate to make comparison easy.

Specific benefits of the new forms and rules include:

- **Combining several forms** and additional statutory disclosure requirements into two forms. This will reduce paperwork and consumer confusion.

- **Using clear language** and design will help consumers understand complicated mortgage loan and real estate transactions.

- **Highlighting the information** that has proven to be most important to consumers. On the new forms, the interest rate, monthly payments, and the total closing costs will be clearly presented on the first page. This will make it easier for consumers to compare mortgage loans and choose the one that is right for them.

- **Providing more information** about the costs of taxes and insurance and how the interest rate and payments may change in the future. This information will help consumers decide whether they can afford the mortgage loan and the home, now and in the future.

- **Warning consumers about features** they may want to avoid, like penalties for paying off the loan early or increases to the mortgage loan balance even if payments are made on time.

- **Making the cost estimates consumers receive** for services required to close a mortgage loan more reliable, such as appraisal or pest inspection fees.

The rule prohibits increases in charges from lenders, their affiliates, and for services for which the lender does not permit the consumer to shop unless a specific exception applies.

> *Examples of the specific exceptions include when information provided by a consumer at application was inaccurate or becomes inaccurate, or when the consumer asks for a change in the services.*

- **Requiring that consumers receive** the closing disclosure at least three business days before closing on the mortgage loan. Currently, consumers often receive this information at closing or shortly before closing.

  This additional time will allow consumers to compare the final terms and costs to the terms and costs they received in the estimate. That will better equip them to raise any questions before they go to the closing table.
  Source: Consumer Financial Protection Bureau (CFPB)

WHAT HAS AND HAS NOT CHANGED ABOUT THE MORTGAGE LOAN PROCESS

- ***Preapprovals* and *prequalifications* are unchanged by the new rule.**

- **The application process starts with a *loan estimate*.** The application process generally starts after the applicant has identified a property. A lender must provide a *loan estimate* within three business days after the applicant has provided such lender with:

  - Their name
  - Their income
  - Their social security number
  - The property's address
  - The property's estimated value
  - The mortgage loan amount the applicant seeks

NOTE

The lender must provide the loan estimate within three business days, but there is no set timeframe for the applicant to receive it. If the lender mails the loan estimate, the applicant may receive the loan estimate more than three days after their application.

In the past, comparing multiple loans could be burdensome because each lender may have had different requirements. Now, while lenders may accept and consider income verification documents and other information provided voluntarily, they cannot require this documentation as a condition of providing a *loan estimate.*

As a result, applicants should have a much easier time getting and comparing loan estimates from various lenders; and by comparing the same type of loan among various lenders, applicants are more likely to find their best deal.

- **Applicants must indicate their intent to proceed.** After applicants have compared loan estimates and determined which loan best meets their needs, they must let the lender know; if the applicant is silent, the lender must not assume an intent to proceed. In general, lenders will not move forward with an application without a strong indication from the applicant that they intend to proceed. However, after 10 business days without such indication, the lender is no longer obligated to honor the terms initially offered in the loan estimate.

- **After an applicant indicates their intent to proceed, lenders can start charging fees.** Until applicants indicate their intent to proceed, lenders cannot charge any fees related to a mortgage application, including the mortgage application or appraisal fee. The *only exception* is a reasonable fee for the credit report. In the past, lenders may request credit card information or a post-dated check to be charged or cashed later, after a required estimate was sent; such is not allowed under the *new rule.* Payment information can only be obtained after the lender provides the *loan estimate* and the applicant has expressed their intent to proceed.

NOTE

Issuing a loan estimate does not mean the lender approved or denied the loan. By issuing the loan estimate, the lender has pledged to honor the fees described in the loan estimate—as long as the loan is approved later without any changes in circumstance affecting the loan application.

NOTE

If the lender closes an application because the application remains incomplete, the applicant will most likely have to start the application process from the beginning.

- **Since lenders cannot collect payment information in advance,** lenders may require the applicants to provide payment for an appraisal, mortgage application, or other loan processing fee immediately after, or as part of confirming the intent to proceed with the application. Lenders may require payment before beginning the processing, verification, appraisal, or underwriting processes.

- **A *changed circumstance* may signify a revised *loan estimate* or a revised *closing disclosure.*** The lender is responsible for providing accurate information about the loan requested based on the data available to the lender when the disclosure is provided.

  - **But if the information about the applicant, the proposed mortgage loan, or the property was incorrect or *changes*,** a revised loan estimate may be issued. This is referred to as a *changed circumstance.*

  A new *loan estimate* may indicate changed rates and terms affected by the new information. However, not all changes require the lender to issue a revised loan estimate; minor changes do not require the lender to issue a revised loan estimate, but significant ones most likely do.

  The common reasons why a loan estimate may be revised include:
  - ***The applicant decided to change loan programs or the amount of the down payment.***
  - ***The appraisal came in higher or lower than expected.***
  - ***The applicant's credit status changed.***
  - ***The lender could not verify the applicant's overtime, bonus, or other income provided on the application.***

- **The applicant must receive the *closing disclosure* at least three business days before closing.** A lender needs to make sure that the applicant receives the closing disclosure at least three business days before closing. This gives the applicant time to go over the summary of the final loan terms. Applicants should no longer face significant changes from the lender and be pressured to sign on the same day. Adaptability has been built into the rule to accommodate small, last-minute changes common to purchase transactions. However, when such transaction changes are significant, a *new* three-business-day review period is required. Because substantial, last-minute changes would be unusual, an additional review period would be unusual as well.

In providing a closing disclosure three business days before the closing that confirms all the terms of the transaction, settlement agents and creditors need as much information from all the parties involved regarding the transaction as far in advance of closing as possible.

- **Additional three-day reviews are unlikely.** Applicants should not encounter major changes to their loan terms on the day of closing and be required to make a very important decision under duress. Although most changes that come up in the last few days before settlement typically would not delay a closing, there are three crucial changes to loan terms that would require the lender to issue a revised closing disclosure and would cause a new three-business-day review period.

  Primary changes that would cause a new three-business-day review period are:

  - The Annual Percentage Rate (APR) increases by more than 1/8 of a percent for regular loans (fixed-rate loans), or 1/4 of a percent for irregular loans (adjustable loans). A decrease in APR will not require a new three-day review if it is based on changes to the interest rate or other fees.

  - A prepayment penalty is added, making it expensive to refinance or sell.

  - The basic loan product changes, such as a switch from fixed rate to adjustable interest rate, or to a loan with interest-only payments.

NOTE

The closing disclosure must contain the buyer's and seller's real estate brokers' and agents' names, addresses, license ID numbers, email addresses, and phone numbers. If this information is not established, the form cannot be completed.

NOTE

In general, applicants may not waive their right to this new three-business-day review period.

NOTE

Lenders have been required to provide a three-day review for such changes in APR since 2009.

ENFORCEMENT OF THE TILA-RESPA FINAL RULE/TRID

The CFPB can levy considerable penalties so lenders can be very vigilant:

- Up to $5,000 per day for any violation of a law, rule, or final order or condition imposed in writing by the CFPB.
- Up to $25,000 per day for any person who recklessly engages in a violation of a federal consumer financial law.
- Up to $1,000,000 per day for any person who knowingly violates a federal consumer financial law.

NOTE

Resources to help consumers understand and comply with the Dodd-Frank Act mortgage reforms and the CFPB regulations, including downloadable guides, are available through the CFPB's website at consumerfinance.gov/policy-compliance/ guidance/ implementation-guidance.

THE LOAN ESTIMATE FORM EXPLAINED

The loan estimate (LE) is an estimate that is a three-page form, which includes a list of all costs and fees that will arise during the processing of the loan.

It provides the applicant with important details about their loan, including the estimated interest rate, monthly payment, total closing costs, estimated costs of taxes and insurance, and how the interest rates and payments may change in the future; these estimates are not legally binding, but the final costs of the loan cannot have more than a 10 percent difference from any third-party fees associated with the loan.

The LE is expounded more below. This is according to the CFPB:

- "Either a mortgage broker or creditor is required to provide the loan estimate form upon receipt of an application by a mortgage broker. However, even if the mortgage broker provides the loan estimate, the creditor remains responsible for complying with the all requirements concerning provision of the form."

- "The creditor or mortgage broker must provide the form to the consumer no later than three business days after the consumer applies for a mortgage loan. The final rule contains a definition of what constitutes an "application" for these purposes, which consists of the consumer's name, income, social security number to obtain a credit report, the property address, an estimate of the value of the property, and the mortgage loan amount sought."

- "Consistent with current law, the creditor generally cannot charge consumers any fees until after the consumers have been given the loan estimate form and the consumers have communicated their intent to proceed with the transaction. There is an exception that allows creditors to charge fees to obtain consumers' credit reports."

- "Creditors and other persons may provide consumers with written estimates prior to application. The rule requires that any such written estimates contain a disclaimer to prevent confusion with the loan estimate form. This disclaimer is required for advertisements."

THE CONSUMER FINANCIAL PROTECTION BUREAU'S GUIDE TO PAGE 1 OF THE LOAN ESTIMATE FORM

DATE

The *Date Issued* is the date the loan estimate is placed in the mail or delivered to the consumer (not the date the form is actually printed).

APPLICANTS

Applicants include the name and mailing address(es) of the consumer(s) applying for the loan. Use each applicant's name and mailing address if there are multiple applicants. The mailing address disclosed must be the U.S. postal mailing address of the consumer applying for credit. The mailing address cannot be any other type of address, such as an applicant's email address. An additional page may be added to the loan estimate if the space provided is insufficient to list all of the applicants.

If credit is extended to a trust established for tax or estate planning purposes, the loan estimate may be provided to the trustee on behalf of the trust. If the loan estimate is delivered to the trustee on behalf of the trust (and to no other consumer), a creditor may opt to disclose the name and mailing address of the trust only, although nothing in the TILA-RESPA rule prohibits the creditor from additionally disclosing the names of the trustee or other consumers applying for the credit.

PROPERTY

Property is the address of the property (which must include the zip code) that will secure the transaction. If the address of the property is unavailable, use a description of the location of the property—a lot number, for example. Always use a zip code. Personal property such as furniture or appliances that also secures the credit transaction may be, but is not required to be, included as property. An additional page may not be appended to the loan estimate to disclose a description of personal property.

SALE PRICE

Sale price or appraised value or estimated value. If the loan is for a purchase money mortgage, use the contract sale price for the property and label it as sale price. If personal property is included in the sale price of the property, use that price without any reduction for the appraised or estimated value of the personal property. If the sale price is not yet known, disclose the estimated value of the property, using the label "sale price." For a transaction without a seller, disclose an appraised value or an estimated value, as applicable, and use the label "prop. value."

The disclosed value must be based on the best information reasonably available to the creditor at the time that the loan estimate is provided to the consumer. If the creditor has obtained an appraisal of the property at the time the loan estimate is provided to the consumer, disclose the appraised value stated in the appraisal that the creditor will use during the underwriting of the loan.

If the creditor does not know which appraisal it will use to underwrite the loan at the time the loan estimate is provided to the consumer, disclose the value set forth in any appraisal that the creditor reasonably believes it will use in the underwriting.

If the creditor has not obtained an appraisal but has prepared its own estimate of value, use the creditor's estimate of value rather than an estimate of value received from a consumer.

If the creditor has not obtained an appraisal or prepared its own estimate of value, it may disclose an estimate of value provided by a consumer. When disclosing an appraised value or an estimated value for a construction loan without a seller, the creditor has the option to include the estimated value of improvements to be made on the property. Alternatively, the creditor may disclose a value that does not include the estimated value of the improvements.

A loan term is the term of the debt obligation. Describe the loan term as "years" when the loan term is in whole years. For a loan term that is more than 24 months but is not whole years, describe using years and months with the abbreviations "yr." and "mo.," respectively. For a loan term that is less than 24 months and not whole years, use months only with the abbreviation "mo."

For a construction-permanent loan disclosed as a single transaction, the loan term is the total combined term of both phases. If the construction-permanent loan is disclosed as two separate transactions, the loan term for the permanent phase is counted from the date interest for the permanent phase's periodic payment begins to accrue.

LOAN TERM PURPOSE

Describe the consumer's intended use for the loan. Purpose is disclosed using one of four descriptions:

- *Purchase* is disclosed if the loan will be used to finance the property's acquisition.
- The purpose of a simultaneous subordinate lien loan is disclosed as "purchase" if the loan will be used to finance the property's acquisition and will be secured by the property.
- *Refinance* is disclosed if the loan will be used for the refinance of an existing obligation that is secured by the property (even if the creditor is not the holder or servicer of the original obligation).
- *Construction* is disclosed if the loan will be used to finance the initial construction of a dwelling on the property.
- *Home equity loan* is disclosed if the loan will be used for any other purpose.

FICUS BANK

4321 Random Boulevard • Somecity, ST 12340

Save this Loan Estimate to compare with your Closing Disclosure.

Loan Estimate

Date disclosure mailed/delivered to Borrower

DATE ISSUED	2/15/2013
APPLICANTS	Michael Jones and Mary Stone 123 Anywhere Street Anytown, ST 12345
PROPERTY	456 Somewhere Avenue Anytown, ST 12345
SALE PRICE	$180,000

LOAN TERM	30 years
PURPOSE	Purchase
PRODUCT	Fixed Rate
LOAN TYPE	☒ Conventional ☐ FHA ☐ VA ☐ ___________
LOAN ID #	123456789
RATE LOCK	☐ NO ☒ YES, until 4/16/2013 at 5:00 p.m. EDT *Before closing, your interest rate, points, and lender credits can change unless you lock the interest rate. All other estimated closing costs expire on* ***3/4/2013*** *at 5:00 p.m. EDT*

Transaction Type: Purchase, Refinance, Construction, or Home Equity Loan

Not rounded but truncated at decimal point when loan is an even dollar amount

Loan Terms		Can this amount increase after closing?
Loan Amount	$162,000	**NO** *If YES, the loan has a negative amortization feature*
Interest Rate	3.875%	**NO**
Monthly Principal & Interest *See Projected Payments below for your Estimated Total Monthly Payment*	$761.78	**NO**
		Does the loan have these features?
Prepayment Penalty		**YES** • **As high as $3,240** if you pay off the loan during the first 2 years *A YES shows information specific to loan program*
Balloon Payment		**NO**

Loans with adjustable payments may show up to four projected payment columns

Projected Payments		
Payment Calculation	**Years 1-7**	**Years 8-30**
Principal & Interest	$761.78	$761.78
Mortgage Insurance	+ 82	+ —
Estimated Escrow *Amount can increase over time*	+ 206	+ 206
Estimated Total Monthly Payment	$1,050	$968

Estimated Taxes, Insurance & Assessments *Amount can increase over time*	$206 a month	**This estimate includes** ☒ Property Taxes ☒ Homeowner's Insurance ☐ Other:	**In escrow?** YES YES

If NO, this item is not included in the Estimated Total Monthly Payment

See Section G on page 2 for escrowed property costs. You must pay for other property costs separately.

Includes items paid at and before closing

Costs at Closing		
Estimated Closing Costs	$8,054	Includes $5,672 in Loan Costs + $2,382 in Other Costs – $0 in Lender Credits. *See page 2 for details.*
Estimated Cash to Close	$16,054	Includes Closing Costs. *See Calculating Cash to Close on page 2 for details.*

Visit **www.consumerfinance.gov/mortgage-estimate** for general information and tools.

LOAN ESTIMATE PAGE 1 OF 3 • LOAN ID # 123456789

Figure 14: Loan Estimate, Page 1 of 3 (with some item detailing)

PRODUCT

Provide a description of the loan. You are required to include two pieces of information in this disclosure.

The first piece of information is any payment feature that may change the periodic payment, which includes:

- ***Negative amortization*** is when the principal balance of the loan may increase due to the addition of accrued interest to the principal balance.
- ***Interest only*** is when one or more regular periodic payments may be applied only to interest accrued and not to the principal of the loan.
- ***Step payment*** is when the scheduled variations in regular periodic payment amounts occur that are not caused by changes to the interest rate during the loan term.
- ***Balloon payment*** is when the terms of the legal obligation include a payment that is more than two times that of a regular periodic payment.
- ***Seasonal payment*** is when the terms of the legal obligation expressly provide that regular periodic payments are not scheduled between specified unit-periods on a regular basis.

The second piece of information disclosed is whether the loan uses an adjustable rate, step rate, or fixed rate to determine the interest rate applied to the principal balance.

- An interest rate is an adjustable rate if the interest rate may increase after consummation, but the rates that will apply or the periods for which they will apply are not known at consummation.
    - Each description must be preceded by the duration of any introductory rate or payment period, and the first adjustment period, as applicable.
    - When there is no introductory period for an adjustable rate, disclose "0."

- An interest rate is a step rate if the interest rate changes after consummation and the rates that will apply and the periods for which they apply are known at consummation.
    - Each description must be preceded by the duration of any introductory rate or payment period, and the first adjustment period, as applicable.
    - When there is no introductory rate for a step rate, disclose "0" and then the applicable time period until the first adjustment.

- An interest rate is a fixed rate if the interest rate is not an adjustable rate or step rate.

- If the loan product consists of a combination of product types, only one product type is used.
    - If a loan has a step rate for a set period of time followed by an adjustable rate for the remaining term, only the adjustable rate is disclosed. Here, there will be periods of the loan where the rate is not known at consummation, and, as a result, the product cannot be disclosed as step rate.
    - If a loan has a fixed rate for a set period of time followed by an adjustable rate for the remaining term, only the adjustable rate is disclosed. Here, there will be periods where an adjustable rate applies, and as a result, it would not meet the requirements of a fixed rate disclosure.

The following are examples of product with both pieces of information included:

- Year 7 balloon payment, 3/1 step rate: a step rate with an introductory interest rate that lasts for three years and adjusts each year thereafter until a balloon payment is due in the seventh year of the loan term.
- 2 Year Negative Amortization, fixed rate: a fixed rate product with a step-payment feature for the first two years of the legal obligation that may negatively amortize.

When the time periods disclosed in the product are not in whole years, for time periods of 24 months or more, disclose the applicable fraction of a year by use of decimals rounded to two places. For time periods of 24 months or less, disclose the number of months with the abbreviation "mo."

- An adjustable-rate product with an introductory interest rate for 31 months that adjusts every year thereafter is a 2.58/1 adjustable rate.
- An adjustable-rate product with an introductory interest rate for 18 months that adjusts every 18 months thereafter is an 18 mo./18 mo. adjustable rate.

LOAN TYPE

Loan type is the type of the loan, such as conventional or Federal Housing Administration (FHA). For loan type, disclose:

- Conventional-- if the loan is not guaranteed or insured by a federal or state government agency.
- FHA-- if the loan is insured by the FHA.
- VA-- if the loan is guaranteed by the U.S. Department of Veterans Affairs.
- Other-- with a brief description, if the loan is insured or guaranteed by another federal or a state agency.

LOAN ID

Loan ID # is the creditor's loan identification number that may be used by a creditor, consumer, and other parties to identify the transaction.

The loan ID # may contain alphanumeric characters and must be unique to the particular transaction. The same loan ID # may not be used for different, but related, loan transactions. When a revised loan estimate is issued, the loan ID # must be sufficient for the purpose of identifying the transaction associated with the initial loan estimate.

When the loan estimate is completed by a mortgage broker:

- If the creditor is known, the loan ID # must be completed. The creditor can outsource the generation and assignment of the loan ID # to the mortgage broker or the creditor can provide the loan ID # in advance of the disclosures for inclusion.

- If the creditor is unknown and the loan ID # is not reasonably available, the mortgage broker may leave that disclosure blank.

RATE LOCK

Indicate the rate is locked with "yes;" indicate the rate is not locked with "no." When the interest rate is locked at the time of the loan estimate's delivery, the date and time when the lock period ends must be disclosed. The date and time at which the estimated closing costs expire are disclosed on the loan estimate. However, the date and time are left blank on any revised loan estimate provided after a consumer has indicated an intent to proceed with the transaction.

LOAN AMOUNT

Use the total amount the consumer will borrow as set forth on the face of the note. If the amount is in whole dollars, do not disclose cents.

INTEREST RATE AND MONTHLY PRINCIPAL & INTEREST

The interest rate disclosed is the initial rate at consummation. If the initial interest rate is not known at consummation, the fully indexed rate is disclosed; a fully-indexed rate is the interest rate calculated using the index value and margin at the time of consummation. The initial principal and interest payment amount also would be calculated using the same fully indexed rate, if the initial interest rate is not known at consummation.

PREPAYMENT PENALTY

A prepayment penalty is a charge imposed for paying all or part of a transaction's principal before the date on which the principal is due. It does not include a waived third-party charge that the creditor imposes if the consumer prepays the loan's entire principal sooner than 36 months after closing.

BALLOON PAYMENT

A balloon payment is a payment that is more than two times a regular periodic payment.

Under the subheading "Does the loan have these features?", when the loan has a prepayment penalty, or a balloon payment disclose "Yes" as applicable. When the answer is "Yes" to either, also disclose, as applicable:

- The maximum amount of the prepayment penalty and the date when the period during which the penalty may be imposed terminates.
- The maximum amount of the balloon payment and the due date of such payment.

PAYMENT CALCULATION

Payment calculation column headings. To the right of the payment calculation label, as column headings, use the years of the loan during the payments, or ranges of payments shown in that column will apply.

- Use a sequence of whole years, counting from the due date of the initial periodic payment.
- For periodic payments that may increase based on an adjustment of the interest rate, use the maximum loan term possible under the terms of the legal obligation. To calculate the maximum loan term, assume that the interest rate rises as rapidly as is possible under the terms of the legal obligation, considering any applicable interest rate caps.
- For a balloon payment scheduled as a final payment, use "final payment" as the column heading.

PRINCIPAL & INTEREST

Use the amount due for principal & interest for the period shown in the column heading. If the payment or range of payments includes any payments of interest only, use the phrase "only interest" under the amount of the payment or range of payments.

MORTGAGE INSURANCE

Disclose the maximum amount payable as mortgage insurance that corresponds to the principal & interest payment shown in the same column. Disclosed as a rounded number, mortgage insurance includes any mortgage guarantee that provides coverage similar to mortgage insurance, even if not technically considered insurance under state or other applicable law.

Calculate mortgage insurance premiums based on the principal balance that will exist after changes to the interest rate and payment amounts pursuant to the legal obligation. The calculations should consider any initial discounted or premium interest rate. If mortgage insurance is not required, disclose "0."

Disclose the mortgage insurance amount that corresponds with the principal & interest amount shown in the same column, even if mortgage insurance is paid on a different schedule than principal & interest.

ESTIMATED ESCROW

Disclose the amount the consumer will pay into an escrow account each month under the terms of the legal obligation. Use a rounded number. If an escrow account will not be established, disclose "0." Disclose "—" if there will be an escrow account, but the escrow account will be closed during the timeframe attributable to the applicable periodic payment.

ESTIMATED TOTAL MONTHLY PAYMENT

For each column, disclose the sum of the principal & interest, mortgage insurance, and estimated escrow as estimated total monthly payment. The amount is rounded if any of the component amounts are rounded.

ESTIMATED TAXES, INSURANCE & ASSESSMENTS

As estimated taxes, insurance & assessments, disclose the total monthly amount due for property taxes, homeowner's insurance, charges imposed by a cooperative, condominium or homeowners' association, ground rent, leasehold payments, and certain insurance premiums or charges if required by the lender. Disclose estimated taxes, insurance & assessments as a rounded number.

ESTIMATED CLOSING COSTS

Estimated closing costs are calculated in the same manner as the total closing costs disclosed on page 2 of the loan estimate. The estimated closing costs are also itemized to show from page 2 of the loan estimate:

- The total of the loan costs table.
- The total of the other costs table.
- Lender credits in the total closing costs subheading.

ESTIMATED CASH TO CLOSE

The estimated amount of cash the consumer will be expected to pay at closing is also shown as estimated cash to close. This amount is the same as the estimated cash to close, from the calculating cash to close table on page 2 of the loan estimate.

Loan Estimate Page 1 Definition of Terms

- **Monthly principal & interest.** Principal (the amount the borrower borrows), and interest (the lender's charge for lending money to the borrower) usually make up the main components of the borrower's monthly mortgage payment. The borrower's total monthly payment will typically be more than this amount due to taxes and insurance.

- **Prepayment penalty.** A prepayment penalty means that the lender can charge the borrower a fee if the borrower pays off their mortgage early.

- **Balloon payment.** A balloon payment means that the final mortgage payment is a lump sum much larger than the regular monthly payments

- **Principal & interest.** Principal is the amount the borrower will borrow; interest is the lender's charge for lending money to the borrower.

- **Mortgage insurance.** Mortgage insurance is typically required if the borrower's down payment is less than 20 percent of the price of the home.

- **Estimated escrow.** Additional charges related to homeownership, such as property taxes and homeowners' insurance, which are bundled in the borrower's monthly payment.

- **Estimated total monthly payment.** The total payment the borrower will make each month, including mortgage insurance and escrow, if applicable.

- **Estimated closing costs.** Upfront costs the borrower will be charged to get their loan and transfer ownership of the property. Also sometimes referred to as "settlement costs."

- **Estimated cash to close.** The total amount the borrower will have to pay at closing, in addition to any money they have already paid.

THE CONSUMER FINANCIAL PROTECTION BUREAU'S GUIDE TO PAGE 2 OF THE LOAN ESTIMATE FORM

ORIGINATION CHARGES

Origination charges are items the consumer will pay to each creditor and loan originator for originating and extending credit. First, include the amount paid, if any, by the consumer to the creditor to reduce the interest rate (sometimes referred to as "points") as both a percentage of the loan amount and a dollar amount. If no points are charged, then leave both the percentage of points stated in the label and the dollar amount blank. Any other items that the consumer will pay to the creditor and loan originator may also be disclosed, up to 13 individual items. If there are more than 13 origination charges, disclose the total amount of the items that exceed 12 as additional charges. Describe the items, other than for points paid, using terminology that clearly and conspicuously describes the service that is disclosed.

The following items should be itemized separately in the origination charges subheading:

- Compensation paid directly by a consumer to a loan originator that is not also the creditor.

- Any charge imposed to pay for a loan level pricing adjustment (LLPA) assessed on the creditor that is passed on to the consumer as a cost at consummation and not as an adjustment to the interest rate.

Only items paid directly by the consumer to compensate a loan originator are origination charges. Do not disclose compensation to a loan originator paid indirectly by a creditor through the interest rate on the loan estimate. Also, if the LLPA is accounted for through the rate but not charged as a direct up-front fee, do not disclose the LLPA as a separately itemized origination charge.

SERVICES YOU CANNOT SHOP FOR

Services You Cannot Shop For are items provided by persons other than the creditor or mortgage broker that the consumer cannot shop for and will pay for at settlement.

Items listed as Services You Cannot Shop For must use terminology that describes each item and disclose them in alphabetical order.

Services You Cannot Shop For might include:

- Appraisal fee
- Appraisal management company fee
- Credit report fee
- Flood determination fee
- Government funding fee (such as a VA or USDA guarantee fee, or any other fee paid to a government entity as part of a governmental loan program)
- Homeowner's association certification fee
- Lender's attorney fee
- Tax status search fee
- Third party subordination fee
- Title – closing protection letter fee
- Title – lender's title insurance Policy
- An upfront mortgage insurance fee (unless the fee is a prepayment of future premiums or a payment into an escrow account).

Closing Cost Details

Loan Costs

A. Origination Charges		$1,802
.25 % of Loan Amount (Points)	*All charges are listed alphabetically with the exception of the % of Loan Amount (Points)*	$405
Application Fee		$300
Underwriting Fee		$1,097

B. Services You Cannot Shop For	$672
Appraisal Fee	$405
Credit Report Fee	$30
Flood Determination Fee	$20
Flood Monitoring Fee	$32
Tax Monitoring Fee	$75
Tax Status Research Fee	$110

C. Services You Can Shop For	$3,198
Pest Inspection Fee	$135
Survey Fee	$65
Title – Insurance Binder	$700
Title – Lender's Title Policy	$535
Title – Settlement Agent Fee	$502
Title – Title Search	$1,261

D. TOTAL LOAN COSTS (A + B + C)	$5,672

Other Costs

E. Taxes and Other Government Fees	$85
Recording Fees and Other Taxes *These are in the 10% variation/tolerance category*	$85
Transfer Taxes *These are in the zero variation/tolerance category*	

F. Prepaids	$867
Homeowner's Insurance Premium (6 months)	$605
Mortgage Insurance Premium (months)	
Prepaid Interest ($17.44 per day for 15 days @ 3.875%)	$262
Property Taxes (months)	

G. Initial Escrow Payment at Closing		$413
Homeowner's Insurance	$100.83 per month for 2 mo.	$202
Mortgage Insurance	per month for mo.	
Property Taxes	$105.30 per month for 2 mo.	$211

These totals are rounded and truncated at the decimal

H. Other	$1,017
Title – Owner's Title Policy (optional)	$1,017

"Optional" indicates premium not required by Lender and purchased by Borrower

I. TOTAL OTHER COSTS (E + F + G + H)	$2,382

J. TOTAL CLOSING COSTS	$8,054
D + I	$8,054
Lender Credits	

Calculating Cash to Close

Total Closing Costs (J)	$8,054
Closing Costs Financed (Paid from your Loan Amount)	$0
Down Payment/Funds from Borrower	$18,000
Deposit	– $10,000
Funds for Borrower	$0
Seller Credits	$0
Adjustments and Other Credits	$0
Estimated Cash to Close	$16,054

Additional Tables appear here if loan program includes Adjustable Payment (AP) or Adjustable Interest Rate (AIR) features

LOAN ESTIMATE PAGE 2 OF 3 • LOAN ID # 123456789

Figure 15: Loan Estimate, Page 2 of 3, Closing Cost Details (with some item detailing)

Describe services related to the issuance of title insurance policies with the word "title" at the beginning of the item.

Items that are required for the issuance of title insurance policies may include:

- Examination and evaluation of title evidence to determine the insurability of the title being examined and what items to include or exclude in any title commitment and policy to be issued.
- Preparation and issuance of the title commitment or other document that discloses the status of title, identifies the conditions that must be met before the policy will be issued, and obligates the insurer to issue a policy of title insurance if such conditions are met.
- Resolution of title underwriting issues and taking steps needed to satisfy any conditions for the issuance of title insurance policies.
- Preparation and issuance of the title insurance policies.
- Payment of premiums for any lender's title insurance coverage.

The amount of the premium for the lender's title insurance coverage must be disclosed without any adjustment to the premium that might be made for the simultaneous purchase of an owner's title insurance policy.

Disclose no more than 13 Services You Cannot Shop For. If there are more than 13 Services You Cannot Shop For, disclose the total amount of the items that exceed 12 with the label "additional charges." An addendum to the loan estimate cannot be used to disclose the additional items.

SERVICES YOU CAN SHOP FOR

Services You Can Shop For are services that the creditor requires but that are provided by people other than the creditor or mortgage broker. They are services that the consumer can shop for and will pay for at settlement. Items listed as Services You Can Shop For must use terminology that describes each item and disclose them in alphabetical order.

A creditor permits a consumer to shop for an item if the creditor permits the consumer to select the provider of that item, subject to reasonable requirements. Whether a creditor permits a consumer to shop is determined by the relevant facts and circumstances.

Services You Can Shop For might include:

- Pest inspection fee
- Survey fee
- Title – closing agent fee
- Title – closing protection letter fee

When disclosing services related to the issuance of title insurance policies, use the word "title" at the beginning of the item. Items that are related to the issuance of title insurance policies may include:

- Examination and evaluation of title evidence to determine the insurability of the title being examined and what items to include or exclude in any title commitment and policy to be issued.

- Preparation and issuance of the title commitment or other document that discloses the status of title, identifies the conditions that must be met before the policy will be issued, and obligates the insurer to issue a policy of title insurance if such conditions are met.

- Resolution of title underwriting issues and taking steps needed to satisfy any conditions for the issuance of title insurance policies.

- Preparation and issuance of the title insurance policies.

- Payment of premiums for any lender's title insurance coverage.

The creditor must disclose the amount of the premium for the lender's title insurance coverage without any adjustment to the premium that might be made for the simultaneous purchase of an owner's title insurance policy.

Disclose no more than 14 Services You Can Shop For. If there are more than 14 Services You Can Shop For, disclose the total amount of the items that exceed 13 with the label "additional charges." An addendum to the loan estimate can be used to disclose the additional items.

TOTAL LOAN COSTS

Total loan costs is the sum of the subtotals of origination charges, services you cannot shop for, and services you can shop ror.

TAXES AND OTHER GOVERNMENT FEES

Under *Taxes and Other Government Fees*, disclose recording fees and other taxes first and transfer taxes second.

RECORDING FEES AND OTHER TAXES

Recording Fees and Other Taxes are fees assessed by a government authority to record and index the loan and title documents as required under state or local law, together with any charges or fees imposed by a state or local government that are not transfer taxes. Recording fees and other taxes do not include fees that are based on the sale price of the property or loan amount.

TRANSFER TAXES

Transfer taxes are state and local government fees on mortgages and home sales that are based on the loan amount or sale price of the property. The name that is used under state or local law to refer to these amounts is not determinative of whether or not they are disclosed as transfer taxes on the loan estimate.

> Disclose only transfer taxes paid by the consumer on the loan estimate. Whether the consumer pays the transfer tax is based on applicable state or local law.
>
> Transfer taxes to be paid by the seller are not disclosed on the loan estimate as transfer taxes.
>
> The amount of transfer taxes disclosed could be modified to the extent the creditor has knowledge of the apportionment of transfer taxes in the contract for sale between the consumer and a seller when it issues the loan estimate. When a creditor does not have the contract of sale when it issues the loan estimate, the creditor must use the apportionment of transfer taxes provided for by state or local law, or common practice when state or local law is unclear.

Disclose the sum of all transfer taxes paid by the consumer as transfer taxes. No additional items may be listed or deleted in the taxes and other government fees category.

PREPAIDS

Pre-paid are items to be paid by the consumer in advance of the first scheduled payment of the loan.

Pre-paids are:

- Homeowner's insurance premium
- Mortgage insurance premium
- Prepaid interest
- Property taxes
- A maximum of three additional items

Each item must include the applicable time period covered by the amount to be paid by the consumer and the total amount to be paid.

INITIAL ESCROW PAYMENT AT CLOSING

Initial Escrow Payment at Closing includes items that the consumer will be expected to place into a reserve or escrow account at consummation to be applied to recurring periodic payments.

Initial escrow payment at closing includes:

- Homeowner's insurance
- Mortgage insurance
- Property taxes
- A maximum of five other items

Also disclose the amount escrowed per month for each item, the number of months collected at consummation, and the total amount paid.

OTHER

"Other" includes items in connection with the transaction that the consumer is likely to pay or has contracted with a person other than the creditor or loan originator to pay at closing and of which the creditor is aware at the time of issuing the loan estimate.

Separate insurance, warranty, guarantee, or event coverage products include, for example:

- Owner's title insurance
- Credit life insurance
- Debt suspension coverage
- Debt cancellation coverage
- Warranties of home appliances and systems

- Similar products

These items are disclosed when coverage is written in connection with the mortgage loan. These examples would not include additional coverage and endorsements on insurance otherwise required by the creditor.
Items that disclose any premiums paid for separate insurance, warranty, guarantee, or event coverage products not required by the creditor must include the parenthetical description (optional) at the end of the label. A maximum of five items can be disclosed as "other."

Describe services related to the issuance of title insurance policies with the word "title" at the beginning of the item. When the owner's title insurance premium includes a simultaneous issuance premium, the premium is calculated by taking the full owner's title insurance premium, adding the simultaneous issuance premium for the lender's
coverage (if any), and then deducting the full premium for lender's coverage.

When the creditor is aware of those items, "other" includes, for example:

- Commissions of real estate brokers or agents
- Additional payments to the seller to purchase personal property pursuant to the contract of sale
- Homeowner's association and condominium charges associated with the transfer of ownership
- Fees for inspections not required by the creditor but paid by the consumer pursuant to the contract of sale

Other does not include construction costs, payoffs of existing liens, or payoffs of other secured debt or unsecured debt

TOTAL CLOSING COSTS

Total Closing Costs is the sum of *Total Loan Costs*, *Total Other Costs*, and *Lender Credits.*

LENDER CREDITS

Lender credits is the amount of any payments from the creditor to the consumer that do not pay for a particular fee on the loan estimate and is disclosed as a negative number. Lender credits include specific lender credits (if any) that pay for a particular fee disclosed on the loan estimate and general or non-specific lender credits (if any) that do not pay for a particular fee on the loan estimate.

For loans where all or a portion of closing costs are offset by a credit or rebate provided by the creditor (sometimes referred to as "no cost" loans), disclose such credit or rebate as lender credits.

The creditor should ensure that lender credits is sufficient to cover the estimated items the creditor represented to the consumer as not being paid by the consumer at consummation, regardless of whether such representations pertained to specific items.

TOTAL CLOSING COSTS

Total Closing Costs is the same amount disclosed as total closing costs in the other costs table.

CLOSING COSTS FINANCED (PAID FROM YOUR LOAN AMOUNT)

Closing costs financed (paid from your loan amount) is calculated by subtracting the estimated total amount of payments to third parties not otherwise disclosed in the loan costs and other costs tables from the loan amount disclosed on page 1 of the loan estimate.

For a purchase loan other than a simultaneous subordinate lien loan, the sale price is included in the closing costs financed calculation as a payment to a third party. The sale price is not included in the closing costs financed disclosure for a simultaneous subordinate lien loan, even if it is a purchase transaction. Other examples of payments to third parties not otherwise disclosed in the loan costs or other costs tables include the amount of construction costs for transactions that involve improvements to be made on the property and payoffs of secured or unsecured debt.

- If the result of the calculation is a positive number, closing costs financed (paid from your loan amount) is that amount, disclosed as a negative number. However, only disclose the amount to the extent that it (as a positive number) does not exceed the amount of total closing costs.
- If the result of the calculation is zero or negative, then closing costs financed (paid from your loan amount) is $0.

DOWN PAYMENT/FUNDS FROM BORROWER

- In a purchase loan other than a simultaneous subordinate lien loan or a loan that involves improvements to be made on the property, subtract the sum of:
    - The loan amount
    - Any existing loans the borrower will assume
    - Any loans subject to which the borrower will take title to the property, from the sale price. The calculation is sale price less loan amount less the amount that will be disclosed as existing loans assumed or taken subject to on the Closing Disclosure's Summaries of Transactions table. If the result is $0 or a positive number, disclose that result as down payment/funds from the borrower. However, when the sum of the loan amount and the amount to be disclosed as existing loans assumed or taken subject to exceed the sale price, the result will be negative. In such cases, the creditor must perform another calculation, as discussed below, to determine what number to disclose as down payment/funds from the borrower.
- For a purchase loan that is a simultaneous subordinate lien loan, a purchase loan that involves improvements to be made on the property, or a purchase loan where the sum of the loan amount and the amount to be disclosed as existing loans assumed or taken subject to exceeds the sale price, subtract the sum of the loan amount and the amount that will be disclosed as existing loans assumed or taken subject to (excluding any amount disclosed as closing costs financed (paid from your loan amount) from the total amount of all existing debt being satisfied in the transaction.
    - If this calculation yields an amount that is positive, disclose that amount as the down payment/funds from the borrower.
    - If this calculation yields a negative amount or $0, disclose $0 as the down payment/funds from the borrower.

For purposes of calculating the down payment/funds from the borrower, "the total amount of all existing debt being satisfied in the transaction" is the sum of amounts that will be disclosed on the closing disclosure in the summaries of transactions, as applicable. Generally, this includes the sale price of property, the sale price of any personal property included in the sale as well as the adjustments and the other consumer charges that may be disclosed on Line K.04.

- In all other transactions, subtract the sum of the loan amount and the amount that will be disclosed as existing loans assumed or taken subject to (excluding any amount disclosed as closing costs financed (paid from your loan amount) from the total amount of all existing debt being satisfied in the transaction.
    - If this calculation yields an amount that is positive, disclose that amount as the down payment/funds from borrower.
    - If this calculation yields a negative amount or $0, disclose $0 as the down payment/funds from borrower.

DEPOSIT

- In a purchase transaction, the deposit is the amount disclosed as a negative number that is paid to the seller or held in trust or escrow by an attorney or other party under the terms of the contract for sale of the property.
- In all other transactions, the deposit is $0.

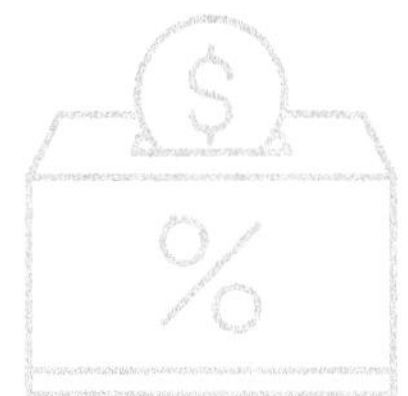

FUNDS FOR BORROWER

- In a purchase loan (other than a simultaneous subordinate lien loan, a purchase loan that involves improvements to be made on the property, or a loan where the sum of the loan amount and the amount to be disclosed as existing loans assumed or taken subject to exceeds the sale price), disclose $0 as funds for the borrower.

- In all other transactions, subtract the sum of the loan amount and the amount to be disclosed as existing loans assumed or taken subject to (excluding any amount disclosed as closing costs financed (paid from your loan amount) from the total amount of all existing debt being satisfied in the transaction.
    - If this calculation yields a negative amount, disclose that amount as funds for the borrower.
    - If the calculation yields a positive amount or $0, disclose $0 as funds for the borrower.

For purposes of calculating the funds for the borrower, "the total amount of all existing debt being satisfied in the transaction" is the sum of amounts that will be disclosed on the closing disclosure in the summaries of transactions, as applicable. Generally, this includes the sale price of property, the sale price of any personal property included in the sale as well as the adjustments and the other consumer charges that may be disclosed on Line K.04.

SELLER CREDITS

Seller credits is the sum of the amounts that the seller will pay for items included in the loan costs and other costs table, to the extent known. The amount disclosed as seller credits in the calculating cash to close table includes non-specific or general seller credits and any specific seller credits not disclosed in the loan costs or other costs table. Non-specific or general seller credits are payments from the seller to the consumer that do not pay for a particular fee. Specific seller credits are payments from the seller to the consumer to pay for a listing agreement or a specific fee. The seller credit amount in the calculating cash to close table is disclosed as a negative number.

ADJUSTMENTS AND OTHER CREDITS

Adjustments and other credits is the sum of adjustments requiring additional funds from the consumer, calculated as a positive amount, and other credits for certain items expected to be paid at closing by persons other than the loan originator, creditor, consumer, or seller, calculated as negative amounts.

The calculation includes:

- The total of all items in the loan costs and other costs tables that are expected to be paid at closing by persons other than the loan originator, creditor, consumer, or seller. A creditor is not required to include such amounts if they are expected to be paid in advance of closing. Examples of items that are paid by persons other than the loan originator, creditor, consumer, or seller include:

    - Gifts from family members expected to be paid at closing. Gifts expected to be paid in advance of closing are not included.

    - Credits from a developer or home builder to be applied to items in the loan costs and other costs tables.

- Funds provided to the consumer from the proceeds of subordinate financing, local or state housing assistance grants, or other similar sources. For a purchase transaction that involves both a first lien loan and a simultaneous subordinate lien loan, these amounts are included in the loan estimate for the first lien loan only.

- Any other amounts that are required to be paid by the consumer at closing or pursuant to the contract of sale (if any) as long as they are not already included in the calculation for down payment/funds from the borrower or funds for the borrower as debt that is being satisfied in the transaction. Examples of amounts to be paid by the consumer at closing pursuant to the contract of sale include:

    - Charges for personal property to be acquired by the consumer

    - Prorations for property taxes

    - Prorations for homeowner's association dues

ESTIMATED CASH TO CLOSE

Estimated cash to close is calculated as the sum of the seven other amounts disclosed in the loan estimate's calculating cash to close table.

Loan Estimate Page 2 Definition of Terms

- **Origination charges.** Upfront charges from the borrower's lender for making the loan.
- **Points.** An upfront fee that the borrower pays the lender in exchange for a lower interest rate than the borrower would have paid otherwise.
- **Closing services.** Third-party services required by the lender in order to get a loan. These services are also sometimes referred to as "settlement services." The borrower can shop separately for services listed in section C.
- **Other costs.** Costs associated with the real estate transaction transferring the property to the borrower and costs associated with owning the home.
- **Lender credits**. A rebate from the lender that offsets some of the borrower's closing costs. Lender credits are typically provided in exchange for the borrower agreeing to pay a higher interest rate than the borrower would have paid otherwise.

THE CONSUMER FINANCIAL PROTECTION BUREAU'S GUIDE TO PAGE 3 OF THE LOAN ESTIMATE FORM

CONTACT INFORMATION

Disclose the name and NMLS/_License ID number for the creditor and mortgage broker, if any, and the individual loan officer of both. The NMLS/_ License ID number should be the same as that identified on the note and other documents. Also, disclose the email and/or phone number of the individual loan officer. The person identified as the individual loan officer must be the primary contact for the consumer.

COMPARISONS

IN 5 YEARS

In 5 Years **includes the following information:**

- The total amount the consumer will have paid in principal, interest, mortgage insurance, and loan costs paid through the end of the 60th month after the due date of the first periodic payment

- The amount of principal paid through the end of the 60th month after the due date of the first periodic payment

ANNUAL PERCENTAGE RATE (APR)

Disclose the APR, together with a brief descriptive statement, in the comparisons table on page 3.

TOTAL INTEREST PERCENTAGE (TIP)

The TIP is the total amount of interest that the consumer will pay over the loan term, expressed as a percentage of the loan amount. The TIP includes prepaid interest that the consumer will pay but does not include prepaid interest that someone other than the consumer will pay. If prepaid interest is disclosed as a negative number, the negative value of the prepaid interest must be included in the calculation of the TIP.

Additional Information About This Loan

LENDER	Ficus Bank	MORTGAGE BROKER	
NMLS/__ LICENSE ID		NMLS/__ LICENSE ID	
LOAN OFFICER	Joe Smith	LOAN OFFICER	
NMLS/__ LICENSE ID	12345	NMLS/__ LICENSE ID	
EMAIL	joesmith@ficusbank.com	EMAIL	
PHONE	123-456-7890	PHONE	

Comparisons	Use these measures to compare this loan with other loans.
In 5 Years	$56,582 Total you will have paid in principal, interest, mortgage insurance, and loan costs. $15,773 Principal you will have paid off.
Annual Percentage Rate (APR)	4.274% Your costs over the loan term expressed as a rate. This is not your interest rate.
Total Interest Percentage (TIP)	69.45% The total amount of interest that you will pay over the loan term as a percentage of your loan amount.

Other Considerations

Appraisal	We may order an appraisal to determine the property's value and charge you for this appraisal. We will promptly give you a copy of any appraisal, even if your loan does not close. You can pay for an additional appraisal for your own use at your own cost.
Assumption	If you sell or transfer this property to another person, we ☐ will allow, under certain conditions, this person to assume this loan on the original terms. ☒ will not allow assumption of this loan on the original terms.
Homeowner's Insurance	This loan requires homeowner's insurance on the property, which you may obtain from a company of your choice that we find acceptable.
Late Payment	If your payment is more than *15* days late, we will charge a late fee of *5% of the monthly principal and interest payment.*
Refinance	Refinancing this loan will depend on your future financial situation, the property value, and market conditions. You may not be able to refinance this loan.
Servicing	We intend ☐ to service your loan. If so, you will make your payments to us. ☒ to transfer servicing of your loan.

Confirm Receipt

Consumer is not required to sign; signature is acknowledgement of receipt, NOT acceptance of the loan

By signing, you are only confirming that you have received this form. You do not have to accept this loan because you have signed or received this form.

Applicant Signature	Date	Co-Applicant Signature	Date

LOAN ESTIMATE PAGE 3 OF 3 • LOAN ID #123456789

Figure 16: Loan Estimate, Page 3 of 3, Additional Information About This Loan (with some item detailing)

OTHER CONSIDERATIONS

Other considerations includes the following information:

- **Appraisal.**
- As to an **assumption**, whether the subsequent purchaser of the property can assume the loan on its original terms.
- At the option of the creditor, a statement that **homeowner's insurance** is required and that the consumer may choose the provider.
- A statement detailing any amount that may be imposed for a **late payment.**
- A statement about the nature of a **refinance** of the loan in the future.
- A statement whether the creditor intends to **service** the loan or transfer it to another servicer.
- For **refinance** transactions, a statement relating to state law protections against liability after foreclosure.
- At the option of the creditor, for transactions involving new construction, where the creditor reasonably expects that settlement will occur 60 days or more after the provision of the loan estimate, a clear and conspicuous statement that the creditor may issue a revised disclosure any time prior to 60 days before consummation.

CONFIRM RECEIPT

The consumer is not required to sign the loan estimate. The creditor may add a signature statement and have the consumer sign page 3 of the loan estimate in order to confirm receipt of the loan estimate by the consumer. If used by the creditor, the signature statement must contain the exact language from the model form. If the confirm receipt table is not used by a creditor, a statement about loan acceptance must be included at the end of the other consideration table that states, "You do not have to accept this loan because you have received this form or signed a loan application."

Loan Estimate Page 3 Definition of Terms

- **Annual percentage rate (APR).** The APR is one measure of the borrower's cost of the loan.

- **Total interest percentage (TIP)** - This number helps the borrower understand how much interest they will pay over the life of the loan and lets them make comparisons between loans.

- **Appraisal** - The lender uses an appraisal to decide how much the borrower's home is worth. The appraisal is conducted by an independent, professional appraiser. The borrower has a right to receive a copy.

- **Assumption** - If the borrower's loan allows assumptions, that means that if the borrower sells the home, the buyer may be allowed to take over the borrower's loan on the same terms, instead of having to get a new loan. If the borrower's loan does not allow assumptions, the buyer will not be allowed to take over the borrower's loan. Most loans do not allow assumptions.

- **Servicing** - Servicing means handling the loan on a day-to-day basis once the loan is made; for example, accepting payments and answering questions from borrowers. The lender can choose to service the borrower's loan itself or transfer that responsibility to a different company.

NOTE

Revised loan estimate - When there is a changed circumstance after the loan estimate has been provided, the creditor can revise the loan estimate within three business days of receiving information sufficient to establish that there has been a changed circumstance. Revised loan estimates generally can be provided no later than four business days before consummation.

THE CLOSING DISCLOSURE FORM EXPLAINED

On October 3, 2015, after the Consumer Financial Protection Bureau (CFPB) took over the Real Estate Settlement Procedures Act (RESPA), homebuyers begun receiving ***closing disclosures***, in lieu of the previously used HUD-1 Settlement Statement (used while RESPA was under HUD administration). Out of the several documents that the homebuyer will encounter during the mortgage process, the *closing disclosure* is one of the most important.

The ***closing disclosure*** is a five-page form that summaries the final details of the borrower's home loan when they obtain an official offer for a mortgage. This standard form, which the CFPB requires lenders to provide to borrowers three business days before closing, lets the borrower compare their final loan offer to the *loan estimate* that was provided to them at the time of application.

The three days also gives the borrower time to ask the lender any questions before the borrower go to the closing table.

The CD includes the loan terms, the borrower's projected monthly payments, and how much they will pay in fees and other costs to get their mortgage. Aside from comparing the costs, there are other information on the CD that the borrower needs to validate. Borrowers can check if the loan has a prepayment penalty or a balloon payment. Are there items that are not in the borrower's escrow account? It is vital that the borrower take the three days before closing to go over the information on the CD with the loan officer.

The Closing Disclosure at a glance:

- This new form consists of 5 pages
- This new form replaces the TILA and HUD-1
- One closing disclosure is required for each loan
- Charge descriptions used on both the loan estimate and closing disclosure must be similar

Closing Disclosure

This form is a statement of final loan terms and closing costs. Compare this document with your Loan Estimate.

Closing Information *Date mailed/delivered to Borrower*		Transaction Information *Borrower & Seller names/addresses are required*		Loan Information	
Date Issued	4/15/2013	**Borrower**	Michael Jones and Mary Stone	**Loan Term**	30 years
Closing Date	4/15/2013 *Consummation Date; often the signing date, but is determined by Lender*		123 Anywhere Street	**Purpose**	Purchase *Transaction type: Purchase, etc.*
Disbursement Date	4/15/2013		Anytown, ST 12345	**Product**	Fixed Rate
Settlement Agent	Epsilon Title Co.	**Seller**	Steve Cole and Amy Doe		
File #	12-3456		321 Somewhere Drive	**Loan Type**	☒ Conventional ☐ FHA ☐ VA ☐ ______
Property	456 Somewhere Ave Anytown, ST 12345		Anytown, ST 12345		
		Lender	Ficus Bank	**Loan ID #**	123456789
Sale Price	$180,000			**MIC #**	000654321

Not rounded but truncated at decimal point when loan is an even dollar amount

Loan Terms		**Can this amount increase after closing?**
Loan Amount	$162,000	**NO** *If YES, the loan has a negative amortization feature*
Interest Rate	3.875%	**NO**
Monthly Principal & Interest *See Projected Payments below for your Estimated Total Monthly Payment*	$761.78	**NO**
		Does the loan have these features?
Prepayment Penalty		**YES** • **As high as $3,240** if you pay off the loan during the first 2 years *A YES shows information specific to loan program*
Balloon Payment		**NO**

Loans with adjustable payments may show up to four projected payment columns

Projected Payments		
Payment Calculation	**Years 1-7**	**Years 8-30**
Principal & Interest	$761.78	$761.78
Mortgage Insurance	+ 82.35	+ —
Estimated Escrow *Amount can increase over time*	+ 206.13	+ 206.13
Estimated Total Monthly Payment *"Estimated" is used because the Escrow amount can change over time*	$1,050.26	$967.91

		This estimate includes	In escrow?
Estimated Taxes, Insurance & Assessments *Amount can increase over time* *See page 4 for details*	$356.13 a month	☒ Property Taxes	**YES**
		☒ Homeowner's Insurance	**YES**
		☒ Other: Homeowner's Association Dues	**NO** *If NO, this item is not included in the Estimated Total Monthly Payment*
		See Escrow Account on page 4 for details. You must pay for other property costs separately.	

Costs at Closing		
Closing Costs *Includes items paid at and before closing*	$9,712.10	Includes $4,694.05 in Loan Costs + $5,018.05 in Other Costs – $0 in Lender Credits. *See page 2 for details.*
Cash to Close	$14,147.26	Includes Closing Costs. *See Calculating Cash to Close on page 3 for details.*

The actual amount required for closing may differ from this Cash to Close amount if the Lender does not allow a title premium adjustment on Page 3, Sections L and N

CLOSING DISCLOSURE PAGE 1 OF 5 • LOAN ID # 123456789

Figure 17: Closing Disclosure, Page 1 of 5 (with some item detailing)

THE CONSUMER FINANCIAL PROTECTION BUREAU'S GUIDE TO PAGE 1 OF THE CLOSING DISCLOSURE FORM

CLOSING INFORMATION

For *closing information*, disclose the following information:

- The date issued, which is the date the closing disclosure is delivered or placed in the mail to the consumer (not the date the form is actually printed).

- The closing date, which is the date of consummation.

- The disbursement date, which is the date funds are disbursed.
  - In a purchase other than a simultaneous subordinate lien transaction, the disbursement date is the date that the cash to close amount is expected to be paid to the consumer or seller, as applicable.
  - In a simultaneous subordinate lien transaction or in a non-purchase transaction, the disbursement date is the date that some of all of the loan amount is expected to be paid to the consumer or a third party other than the settlement agent.

- The name of the settlement agent, which is the name of the entity, not the individual agent conducting the closing

- The File #, which is the file number assigned to the transaction by the settlement agent (the TILA-RESPA Rule does not prescribe how the settlement agent creates the file number; the file number, for example, may be alphanumeric)

- The property address or location

- For the property:
  - Sale price
  - Appraised prop. value
  - Estimated prop. value

The Appraised Prop. Value of the property is disclosed for transactions without a seller if a creditor has obtained an appraisal of the property. If a creditor has obtained more than one appraisal of the property, the creditor discloses the value set forth in the appraisal that the creditor used to approve the loan. The estimated for a transaction without a seller. If the creditor has prepared its own estimate of value for purposes of approving the credit transaction, it must use that value when disclosing the Estimated Prop. Value, rather than an estimate of value from a consumer.

If the creditor has prepared more than one estimate of value, it discloses the value in the estimate it used to approve the transaction. If a creditor considers the value of improvements to the property when approving a construction loan where there is no seller, it must include the value of the improvements when disclosing the Appraised Prop. Value or Estimated Prop. Value.

TRANSACTION INFORMATION

For *transaction information*, disclose the name of the seller (if any) as seller, and the name of the creditor as lender. Disclose the name(s) and address(es) of the person(s) to whom credit is extended as the borrower. Do not disclose the names or addresses of other consumers. The name and address of each person who is a seller in the transaction and each person to whom credit is extended must be disclosed, except that the name and address for seller may be left blank on the closing disclosure for a simultaneous subordinate lien loan if the closing disclosure for the first lien loan will disclose the entirety of the seller's transaction. The name and address of the seller is also left blank for transactions without a seller. If there is not enough space to show the name and address of all such people, an additional page may be used and appended to the end of the closing disclosure.

LOAN INFORMATION

For *loan information*, disclose the loan term, purpose, product, loan type, the creditor's loan identification number as Loan ID #, and mortgage insurance case number, if required by the creditor, as MIC # under the loan information subheading. The information disclosed for loan term, purpose, product, loan type, and Loan ID # are determined by the same definitions for those items on the loan estimate. These items should be updated to reflect the terms of the legal obligation at consummation.

LOAN TERMS

The *loan terms* table on the closing disclosure discloses the same information required to be disclosed on the loan estimate, updated to reflect the terms of the legal obligation at consummation.

PROJECTED PAYMENTS

The *projected payments* table on the closing disclosure discloses the same information required to be disclosed on the projected payments table disclosed on the loan estimate, updated to reflect the terms of the legal obligation at consummation.

However, there are two differences in the closing disclosure:

- For loans subject to RESPA, the amounts disclosed under the estimated escrow and estimated taxes, insurance, and assessments sections on the closing disclosure must be determined under the escrow account analysis described in Regulation X. Loans not subject to RESPA also have this option on the closing disclosure.

- The closing disclosure refers the consumer to page 4 of the closing disclosure, instead of the reference to page 2 that is on the loan estimate.

COSTS AT CLOSING

The *costs at closing* table discloses:

- The total amount disclosed as total closing costs in the other costs table disclosed on page 2 of the closing disclosure. Total closing costs are also itemized to show the total loan costs, the total other costs, and lender credits from the total closing costs subheading disclosed on page 2 of the closing disclosure.

- The estimated amount of cash the consumer will pay at, or receive from, closing as cash to close. This amount is the same as the cash to close calculated in the calculating cash to close table on page 3 of the closing disclosure.

Closing Cost Details

Unlike the HUD-1, Borrower subtotals are shown at the TOP of each section

Loan Costs	Borrower-Paid At Closing	Borrower-Paid Before Closing	Seller-Paid At Closing	Seller-Paid Before Closing	Paid by Others
A. Origination Charges *All items in this section are zero variation/tolerance charges*	**$1,802.00**				*Payor not specified in this column*
01 0.25 % of Loan Amount (Points)	$405.00				
02 Application Fee	$300.00				
03 Underwriting Fee	$1,097.00				
04					
05 *Except for Line A.01, all charges are listed alphabetically*					
06 *in each section*					
07					
08					
B. Services Borrower Did Not Shop For	**$236.55**				
01 Appraisal Fee to John Smith Appraisers Inc.					$405.00
02 Credit Report Fee to Information Inc.		$29.80			
03 Flood Determination Fee to Info Co.	$20.00				
04 Flood Monitoring Fee to Info Co.	$31.75				
05 Tax Monitoring Fee to Info Co.	$75.00				
06 Tax Status Research Fee to Info Co.	$80.00				
07					
08 *Items in this section are zero or 10% variation/tolerance*					
09 *charges, as determined by the Lender*					
10					
C. Services Borrower Did Shop For *All items in this section are unlimited variation/tolerance charges*	**$2,655.50**				
01 Pest Inspection Fee to Pests Co.	$120.50				
02 Survey Fee to Surveys Co.	$85.00				
03 Title – Insurance Binder to Epsilon Title Co.	$650.00				
04 Title – Lender's Title Insurance to Epsilon Title Co.	$500.00				
05 Title – Settlement Agent Fee to Epsilon Title Co.	$500.00				
06 Title – Title Search to Epsilon Title Co.	$800.00				
07 *Any item that is a component of/related to title insurance or*					
08 *settlement must contain description that begins with the word "Title"*					
D. TOTAL LOAN COSTS (Borrower-Paid)	**$4,694.05**				
Loan Costs Subtotals (A + B + C)	$4,664.25	$29.80			

Recording Fees: 10% variation/tolerance category if paid by Borrower
Transfer Tax: Zero variation/tolerance category, if paid by Borrower

Other Costs	Borrower-Paid At Closing	Borrower-Paid Before Closing	Seller-Paid At Closing	Seller-Paid Before Closing	Paid by Others
E. Taxes and Other Government Fees	**$85.00**				
01 Recording Fees Deed: $40.00 Mortgage: $45.00	$85.00				
02 Transfer Tax to Any State			$950.00		
F. Prepaids	**$2,120.80**				
01 Homeowner's Insurance Premium (12 mo.) to Insurance Co.	$1,209.96				
02 Mortgage Insurance Premium (mo.)					
03 Prepaid Interest ($17.44 per day from 4/15/13 to 5/1/13)	$279.04				
04 Property Taxes (6 mo.) to Any County USA	$631.80				
05			*Charges in sections F, G, and H are in the unlimited variation/tolerance category*		
G. Initial Escrow Payment at Closing	**$412.25**				
01 Homeowner's Insurance $100.83 per month for 2 mo.	$201.66				
02 Mortgage Insurance per month for mo.					
03 Property Taxes $105.30 per month for 2 mo.	$210.60				
04					
05					
06					
07					
08 Aggregate Adjustment	- 0.01				
H. Other	**$2,400.00**				
01 HOA Capital Contribution to HOA Acre Inc. *If paid by Borrower, it*	$500.00		*However, if paid by Seller, 'Optional'*		
02 HOA Processing Fee to HOA Acre Inc. *must include 'Optional'*	$150.00		*may be indicated but is not required*		
03 Home Inspection Fee to Engineers Inc. *at end of description*	$750.00			$750.00	
04 Home Warranty Fee to XYZ Warranty Inc.			$450.00		
05 Real Estate Commission to Alpha Real Estate Broker *Full commission is shown regardless of*			$5,700.00	*Additional charges for services*	
06 Real Estate Commission to Omega Real Estate Broker *who holds the earnest money deposit*			$5,700.00	*provided are itemized separately*	
07 Title – Owner's Title Insurance (optional) to Epsilon Title Co.	$1,000.00				
If Lender allows title premium adjustment between Borrower & Seller, it will show on Page 5, Sections L & N; if Lender does not allow title premium adjustment, Cash To/From Borrower & Seller will not be accurate					
I. TOTAL OTHER COSTS (Borrower-Paid)	**$5,018.05**				
Other Costs Subtotals (E + F + G + H)	$5,018.05				
J. TOTAL CLOSING COSTS (Borrower-Paid)	**$9,712.10**				
Closing Costs Subtotals (D + I)	$9,682.30	$29.80	$12,800.00	$750.00	$405.00
Lender Credits					

CLOSING DISCLOSURE PAGE 2 OF 5 • LOAN ID # 123456789

Figure 18: Closing Disclosure, Page 2 of 5, Closing Cost Details (with some item detailing)

THE CONSUMER FINANCIAL PROTECTION BUREAU'S GUIDE TO PAGE 2 OF THE CLOSING DISCLOSURE FORM

ORIGINATION CHARGES

Origination charges - loan originator compensation. Loan originator compensation is disclosed as origination charges, even though loan originator compensation is not disclosed on the loan estimate. Compensation from the consumer to a third-party loan originator is designated as the borrower-paid at closing or before closing on the closing disclosure. Compensation from the creditor to a third-party loan originator is designated as paid by others on the closing disclosure. A designation of (L) can be listed with the amount to indicate that the creditor pays the compensation at consummation. The amount of compensation from the creditor to the third-party loan originator is the dollar value of salaries, commissions, and any financial or similar compensation provided by the creditor and considered to be points and fees. Compensation to individual loan originators is not calculated or disclosed on the closing disclosure.

SERVICES THE CONSUMER (BORROWER) DID AND DID NOT SHOP FOR

Services the Consumer (Borrower) Did and Did Not Shop For. Items that the consumer could have shopped for, but did not, are disclosed in the Services Borrower Did Not Shop For subheading, regardless of where the item was disclosed on the loan estimate. When a consumer chooses a provider that was on the written list of providers for a service, that service is listed as Services Borrower Did Not Shop for in the closing disclosure loan costs table. For example, if the consumer could have shopped for the flood determination fee on the loan estimate but chose a provider that was on the creditor's written list of providers, that charge is listed as Services Borrower Did Not Shop For even though the creditor did not require that service provider. Items disclosed as Services Borrower Did Shop for and Services Borrower Did Not Shop For are re-alphabetized when an item is added to or removed from the closing disclosure, when compared to the loan estimate.

TOTAL LOAN COSTS (BORROWER-PAID)

Total Loan Costs. The amounts that are designated as borrower-paid at or before closing are subtotaled as total loan costs (borrower-paid). The amounts that are designated seller-paid at or before closing and paid by others are not subtotaled as total loan costs (borrower-paid).

TAXES AND OTHER GOVERNMENT FEES

In the shaded column of the line with the subheading *Taxes and Other Government Fees*, disclose the total amount expected to be paid by the consumer to state or local governments for recording fees and transfer taxes at or before closing. In the appropriate columns of the next line, disclose the total amount expected to be paid to state or local governments for recording the deed, security instruments, and any other instrument or document recorded to preserve marketable title or to perfect

the creditor's security interest in the property. Also, on this line (which includes the label recording fees), disclose the total fees expected to be paid to the state or local government for recording deeds after the word "deed" and, separately, disclose the total fees expected to be paid to state or local government for recording security instruments after the word "mortgage." An itemization of transfer taxes paid by the consumer and the seller is disclosed under the heading taxes and other government fees, instead of the sum total of transfer taxes to be paid by the consumer. This itemization is disclosed after the disclosure of the recording fees.

The name of the government entity assessing the fee (which may not necessarily be the payee of the check cut by the settlement agent) is provided on the closing disclosure, unlike on the loan estimate. Itemize each transfer tax and each government entity, because multiple taxes may be assessed by each governmental entity.

PREPAIDS

Prepaids are items to be paid by the consumer in advance of the first scheduled payment of the loan. Prepaids include:

- Homeowner's insurance premium
- Mortgage insurance premium
- Prepaid interest
- Property taxes
- A maximum of three additional items

Each item must include the applicable time period covered by the amount to be paid by the consumer and the total amount to be paid. If homeowner's insurance premiums, mortgage insurance premiums, prepaid interest, or property taxes are not applicable to the loan, the inapplicable lines should not be deleted.

Instead:

- If there are no prepaid homeowner's insurance premiums, mortgage insurance premiums, or property taxes associated with the loan, the time period, daily amount, and percentage used in the labels should be left blank.

If no prepaid interest will be collected at consummation, the amount should be disclosed as "$0.00."

INITIAL ESCROW PAYMENT AT CLOSING

Property taxes paid during different time periods can be disclosed as separate items. For example, general property taxes assessed for January 1 to December 31 and property taxes to fund schools for November 1 to October 31 can be disclosed as separate items. The last item disclosed in the *Initial Escrow Payment at Closing* is the aggregate adjustment. The aggregate adjustment is calculated under Regulation X.

OTHER

Items are disclosed as *other* to reflect costs incurred by the consumer or seller that were not required to be disclosed on the loan estimate. These costs include:

- Real estate brokerage fees.
- Homeowner or condominium association fees paid at consummation.
- Home warranties.
- Inspection fees.
- Other fees paid at closing that are not required by the creditor or otherwise required to be disclosed elsewhere on the closing disclosure.

The amount of an earnest money deposit does not affect the amount of real estate commissions paid by the consumer or seller on the closing disclosure, even if the earnest money deposit is held by the real estate brokerage.

TOTAL OTHER COSTS (BORROWER-PAID) AND TOTAL CLOSING COSTS (BORROWER-PAID)

Total Other Costs and Total Closing Costs. The total of all closing costs paid by the consumer, reduced by the lender credit, is disclosed as total closing costs (borrower-paid). The total of items designated as borrower-paid at or before closing, seller-paid at or before closing, and paid by others are disclosed as closing cost subtotals. Lastly, the total amount of lender credits, if any, are disclosed and designated as the borrower-paid at closing.

Amounts shown in LE column are rounded; amounts shown in Final column are not rounded; Final column may appear larger due to rounding

Calculating Cash to Close

Use this table to see what has changed from your Loan Estimate.

	Loan Estimate	Final	Did this change?	
Total Closing Costs (J)	$8,054.00	$9,712.10	YES	• See **Total Loan Costs (D)** and **Total Other Costs (I)**
Closing Costs Paid Before Closing	$0	– $29.80	YES	• You paid these Closing Costs **before closing**
Closing Costs Financed (Paid from your Loan Amount)	$0	$0	NO	
Down Payment/Funds from Borrower	$18,000.00	$18,000.00	NO	
Deposit	– $10,000.00	– $10,000.00	NO	
Funds for Borrower	$0	$0	NO	
Seller Credits	$0	– $2,500.00	YES	• See Seller Credits in **Section L**
Adjustments and Other Credits	$0	– $1,035.04	YES	• See details in **Sections K and L** *This figure is an aggregate of debits and credits shown in Sections K and L; it may also include subordinate financing, gift funds, prorations & generalized credits*
Cash to Close	$16,054.00	$14,147.26		

Summaries of Transactions

Use this table to see a summary of your transaction.

BORROWER'S TRANSACTION

K. Due from Borrower at Closing		**$189,762.30**
01 Sale Price of Property		$180,000.00
02 Sale Price of Any Personal Property Included in Sale		
03 Closing Costs Paid at Closing (J)		$9,682.30
04		
Adjustments		
05		
06		
07		
Adjustments for Items Paid by Seller in Advance		
08 City/Town Taxes	to	
09 County Taxes	to	
10 Assessments	to	
11 HOA Dues	4/15/13 to 4/30/13	$80.00
12		
13		
14		
15		
L. Paid Already by or on Behalf of Borrower at Closing		**$175,615.04**
01 Deposit		$10,000.00
02 Loan Amount		$162,000.00
03 Existing Loan(s) Assumed or Taken Subject to		
04		
05 Seller Credit		$2,500.00
Other Credits		
06 Rebate from Epsilon Title Co.		$750.00
07		
Adjustments		
08 *If Lender allows title premium adjustment between Borrower &*		
09 *Seller, it will show on Page 3, Sections L & N; if Lender does*		
10 *not allow title premium adjustment, Cash To/From Borrower &*		
11 *Seller will not be accurate*		
Adjustments for Items Unpaid by Seller		
12 City/Town Taxes	1/1/13 to 4/14/13	$365.04
13 County Taxes	to	
14 Assessments	to	
15		
16		
17		
CALCULATION		
Total Due from Borrower at Closing (K)		$189,762.30
Total Paid Already by or on Behalf of Borrower at Closing (L)		– $175,615.04
Cash to Close ☒ **From** ☐ **To Borrower**		**$14,147.26**

SELLER'S TRANSACTION

M. Due to Seller at Closing		**$180,080.00**
01 Sale Price of Property		$180,000.00
02 Sale Price of Any Personal Property Included in Sale		
03		
04		
05		
06		
07		
08		
Adjustments for Items Paid by Seller in Advance		
09 City/Town Taxes	to	
10 County Taxes	to	
11 Assessments	to	
12 HOA Dues	4/15/13 to 4/30/13	$80.00
13		
14		
15		
16		
N. Due from Seller at Closing		**$115,665.04**
01 Excess Deposit		
02 Closing Costs Paid at Closing (J)		$12,800.00
03 Existing Loan(s) Assumed or Taken Subject to		
04 Payoff of First Mortgage Loan		$100,000.00
05 Payoff of Second Mortgage Loan		
06		
07		
08 Seller Credit		$2,500.00
09 *If Lender allows title premium adjustment between Borrower*		
10 *& Seller, it will show on Page 3, Sections L & N; if Lender does*		
11 *not allow title premium adjustment, Cash To/From Borrower*		
12 *& Seller will not be accurate*		
13		
Adjustments for Items Unpaid by Seller		
14 City/Town Taxes	1/1/13 to 4/14/13	$365.04
15 County Taxes	to	
16 Assessments	to	
17		
18		
19		
CALCULATION		
Total Due to Seller at Closing (M)		$180,080.00
Total Due from Seller at Closing (N)		– $115,665.04
Cash ☐ **From** ☒ **To Seller**		**$64,414.96**

If Lender does not allow title premium adjustment, Cash To/From Borrower & Seller will not be accurate on the CD; Borrowers & Sellers must refer to the Settlement Statement for the final figures

CLOSING DISCLOSURE PAGE 3 OF 5 • LOAN ID # 123456789

Figure 19: Closing Disclosure, Page 3 of 5 (with some item detailing)

Closing Disclosure Page 2 Definition of Terms

- **Borrower-paid** - This column lists the costs that are charged to the borrower.

- **Taxes and other government fees** - Costs associated with transferring the property to the borrower and registering the borrower's mortgage with the county records office.

- **Prepaids** - This category includes interest on the borrower's loan between the time they close and the end of that month. It is also common to pay the borrower's first year's homeowner's insurance premium in advance at closing.

- **Initial escrow payment at closing** - This payment will establish an initial balance in the borrower's escrow account.

- **Total closing costs** - Total upfront costs associated with the borrower's loan and real estate transaction, excluding the borrower's down payment. This is different from the actual amount of money the borrower had to bring to closing, which is called "cash to close" on page 3.

THE CONSUMER FINANCIAL PROTECTION BUREAU'S GUIDE TO PAGE 3 OF THE CLOSING DISCLOSURE FORM

CALCULATING CASH TO CLOSE

The *Calculating Cash to Close* table has nine items listed in the table:

- **Total closing costs**
- **Closing costs paid before closing**
- **Closing costs financed (paid from your loan amount)**
- **Down payment/funds from borrower**
- **Deposit**
- **Funds for borrower**
- **Seller credits**
- **Adjustments and other credits**
- **Cash to close**

The table has three columns to disclose the amount for each item as it was disclosed on the loan estimate, the final amount for the item, and an answer to the question:

Did this change? The amounts disclosed in the loan estimate column are the same as the amounts disclosed in the most recent loan estimate provided to the consumer. The amounts disclosed in the loan estimate column are rounded to the nearest dollar in order to match the corresponding amount disclosed on the loan estimate's calculating cash to close table. Generally, the amounts in the final column are calculated using the same methods that were used for the calculating cash to close table on the loan estimate and must be based on the best information reasonably available to the creditor at the time that the closing disclosure is provided to the consumer.

When the answer to the question *Did this change?* is Yes, indicate where the consumer can find the amounts that have changed on the loan estimate. If the seller credit amount changed and the change is attributable only to general seller credits, the
creditor may disclose "See Seller Credits in Section L." Examples of language for disclosing changes to other items are found in example form H-25(B) in appendix H of Regulation Z.

BORROWER'S TRANSACTION

A creditor can work with a settlement agent, and the settlement agent can disclose the *borrower's transaction* column of the summaries of transactions table. Any references to the creditor would apply to the settlement agent when the settlement agent
discloses the borrower's transaction column.

DUE FROM BORROWER AT CLOSING

Generally, in a purchase transaction, the amount *due from the borrower at closing* includes:

- *Sale price of property*
- *Sale price of any personal property Included in sale*
- *Closing costs paid at closing*
- *Adjustments*
- *Adjustments for items paid by the seller in advance*, pursuant to the terms of the real estate sale contract
- Other consumer charges disclosed in Section K, such as those that may be disclosed on Line K.04

However, the sale price is not disclosed in the summaries of transactions table for a simultaneous subordinate lien loan in a purchase transaction. For purposes of disclosing the sale price of any personal property included in the sale, personal property is defined by state law, but could include such items as carpets, drapes, and appliances. Manufactured homes are not considered personal property for the closing disclosure. Closing costs paid at closing is the amount of closing costs designated as the borrower-paid at closing minus any lender credits on page 2 of the closing disclosures.

Under the heading *adjustments,* disclose a description and amount for each of the following:

- Items not otherwise disclosed in Section K of the closing disclosure that the seller has paid prior to the real estate closing but that will be reimbursed by the consumer at closing.
- Items not otherwise disclosed in Section K of the closing disclosure are owed to the seller but payable to the consumer after the closing.

Examples of items that are disclosed as Adjustments include:

- A balance in a seller's reserve account transferred to the consumer in connection with an assumed loan
- Rent that the consumer will collect after closing for a period of time prior to the closing
- A tenant security deposit

Under *Adjustments for Items Paid by the Seller in Advance*, disclose the prorated amounts for prepaid city/town taxes, county taxes, and other assessments due from the consumer to reimburse the seller and the time period corresponding to that amount. Also, disclose a description and amount for any item paid for by the seller prior to the real estate closing that is due from the consumer at the closing.

Examples of these items include:

- Taxes (other than county or city/town taxes) paid in advance for an entire year when the closing occurs prior to the expiration of the year.
- Flood or hazard insurance premiums when the consumer is being substituted as an insured under the same policy.
- Mortgage insurance in connection with an assumed loan.
- Planned unit development or condominium association assessments paid for in advance.
- Fuel or other supplies on hand purchased by the seller which the consumer will use when the consumer takes possession of the property.
- Ground rent paid in advance by the seller.

Disclose other consumer charges owed by the consumer in the real estate closing not otherwise disclosed in the loan costs table, other costs table, or Section K of the closing disclosure. Generally, these amounts may be disclosed on Line K.04.

Examples include:

- Amounts paid to any existing holders of liens on the property in a refinance transaction.
- Payoffs of other secured or unsecured debt.
- Any outstanding real estate property taxes.
- Construction costs that the consumer will be obligated to pay in connection with the transaction.
- Principal reductions.
- For a simultaneous subordinate lien loan, the proceeds of the simultaneous subordinate lien loan are applied to the first-lien loan.

These amounts are disclosed without a corresponding credit in the seller's transaction column.

PAID ALREADY BY OR ON BEHALF OF BORROWER AT CLOSING

The amount ***paid already by or on behalf of the borrower at closing*** is the sum of:

- Deposit
- Loan amount
- Existing loan(s) assumed or taken subject to
- Seller credits
- Other credits
- Adjustments for items unpaid by seller pursuant to the terms of the real estate sale contract

A deposit is the amount paid into a trust account by the consumer pursuant to a contract of sale. If the deposit has been applied toward a closing cost paid by the consumer, the amount so applied should be deducted from the amount of the deposit. No deduction in the amount of the deposit is to be made for the payment of any real estate commission disclosed on page 2 of the closing disclosure.

Existing Loan(s) Assumed or Taken Subject *to* is the total amount of all loans that the consumer is assuming in the transaction, even if more than one loan is being assumed, and all loans subject to which the consumer is taking title to the property.

Seller credits include any general or non-specific seller credits. However, if the seller credit is attributable to a charge listed on *closing disclosure page* 2, then the amount should be listed with the item and designated as *seller paid at closing or seller-paid before closing on the closing disclosure* page 2. *Seller credits* include any seller credits for issues identified at a walk-through of the property.

Other credits include a general credit from any party other than the seller or creditor. One example is a credit a consumer receives from a real estate agent. A description of the credit and the name of the party giving the credit must also be included. However, if the credit or rebate is attributable to a charge listed on page 2 of the *closing disclosure*, then the amount should be listed with the item and designated as *paid by others on closing disclosure* page 2. *Other credits* include any transferred escrow balance in a refinance transaction. *Other credits* also include a credit for any money or other payments made at closing by third parties (including gifts from family members) not otherwise associated with the transaction, along with a description of the nature of the funds. Amounts provided in advance of the real estate closing to consumers by third parties (including gifts from family members) not otherwise associated with the transaction are not required to be disclosed.

Any financing arrangements or other new loans not otherwise disclosed in the *borrower's transaction* column table as part of the *loan amount or existing loans assumed or taken subject to* must be disclosed under the subheading other credits (or on line L.04) for the first lien loan. If the net proceeds of the subordinate lien loan are less than its principal amount, the net proceeds must also be disclosed. The net proceeds may be disclosed on the same line as the principal amount of the subordinate lien loan. Disclosure of any amount paid with funds other than closing funds by a consumer in connection with the payoff of an existing subordinate loan are disclosed with a statement that such amounts were paid outside of closing.

Under *Adjustments for Items Unpaid by Seller*, disclose the prorated amounts for any unpaid city/town taxes, county taxes and other assessments due from the seller to reimburse the consumer at the real estate closing and the time period corresponding to that amount. Also, disclose a description and amount for any additional items which have not been paid for and which the consumer is expected to pay after the real estate closing but are attributable to a period of time prior to the closing.

Examples of these items include:

- Utilities used but not paid for by the seller
- Interest on loan assumptions

CASH TO CLOSE FROM OR TO BORROWER

Under a subheading of calculation:

- Disclose total due from the borrower at closing as a positive number.
- Disclose total paid already by or on behalf of the borrower at closing as a negative number.
- Disclose the sum of total due from the borrower at closing and total paid already by or on behalf of the borrower at closing as cash to close from borrower when the sum is a positive number, or as cash to close to borrower when the sum is a negative number. The sum is disclosed as a positive number in either event.

SELLER'S TRANSACTIONS

The settlement agent completes and discloses the *seller's transaction* column of the summaries of transactions table.

The requirement to complete the seller's transaction column of the summaries of transactions table does not apply to a simultaneous subordinate lien loan if the closing disclosure for the first lien loan discloses the entirety of the seller's transaction. If the requirement to complete the seller's transaction column applies to a simultaneous subordinate lien loan, complete the disclosures based only on the terms and conditions of the subordinate lien loan and do not include the sale price.

DUE TO SELLER AT CLOSING

Generally, the amount *due to seller at closing* includes:

- The sale price of the property
- Sale price of any personal property included in the sale
- Adjustments for items paid by seller in advance due to the seller pursuant to the terms of the real estate sales contract
- Other items owed by the consumer and disclosed in Section M of the closing disclosure

For purposes of disclosing the sale price of any personal property included in sale, personal property is defined by state law, but could include such items as carpets, drapes, and appliances. Manufactured homes are not considered personal property for the closing disclosure. Under adjustments for items paid by the seller in advance disclose the prorated amounts for prepaid city/town taxes, county taxes and other assessments due from the consumer to reimburse the seller and the time period corresponding to that amount. Also, disclose a description and amount for any additional items paid for by the seller prior to the real estate closing that are due from the consumer at the closing.

Examples of these items include:

- Taxes paid in advance for an entire year when the closing occurs prior to the expiration of the year.
- Flood or hazard insurance premiums when the consumer is being substituted as an insured under the same policy.
- Mortgage insurance in connection with an assumed loan.
- Planned unit development or condominium association assessments paid for in advance.
- Fuel or other supplies on hand purchased by the seller which the consumer will use when the consumer takes possession of the property.
- Ground rent paid in advance by the seller.

Also, disclose in Section M, such as on lines M.03 to M.08, a description and amount for any other items paid to the seller by the consumer pursuant to the contract of sale or other agreement.

Examples of these amounts include:

- A balance in a seller's reserve account transferred to the consumer in connection with an assumed loan.
- Rent that the consumer will collect after closing for a period of time prior to the closing.
- The treatment of any tenant security deposit.

DUE FROM SELLER AT CLOSING

Disclose the amount *due from seller at closing* as the sum of:

- Any excess deposit
- Closing costs paid at closing by the seller
- Existing loan(s) assumed or taken subject to by the consumer
- Payoff of first mortgage loan
- Payoff of second mortgage loan
- Seller credit
- Payment of other seller obligations
- Adjustments for items unpaid by seller due to the consumer pursuant to the terms of the real estate sale contract

If a simultaneous subordinate lien loan is disclosed using the alternative tables, the *closing disclosure* for the first lien loan must include any contributions from the seller that are disclosed in the *payoffs and payments* table as amounts contributed to the simultaneous subordinate lien loan.

Excess deposit is the amount of any deposit made by the consumer that has been disbursed to the seller prior to closing. Note that the calculation of the excess deposit does not include any deposits held by the real estate brokerage.

Seller credit is an amount the seller is giving as a general credit not tied to a specific charge on page 2 or is making as an allowance to the consumer for items to purchase separately. The amount of seller credit would include any credits to the consumer as the result of a walk-through of the property prior to the closing.

However, if the amount of a credit is attributable to a charge listed on page 2, then the amount should be listed with the applicable item on page 2 and designated as ***seller-paid at closing or seller-paid before closing***, as appropriate.

Disclose the *payoff of the first mortgage loan*, if any, and then the *payoff of the second mortgage loan*, if any. Disclose the payoff or satisfaction amounts for any additional seller obligations as separately itemized amounts.

Examples of these seller obligations include, but are not limited to:

- Satisfaction of outstanding liens imposed due to federal, state or local income taxes, real estate property tax liens.
- Judgments against the seller reduced to a lien upon the property.
- Other obligations the seller wishes the *settlement agent* to pay from the seller's proceeds at closing.
- Funds to be held by the *settlement agent* for repairs or the payment of water, fuel, or other utility bills that cannot be prorated between the parties at closing because the amounts used by the seller prior to closing are not yet known at closing. Subsequent disclosure of a corrected *closing disclosure* after the repairs are made or the utility bill is received is optional.

Disclose any amount paid with funds other than closing funds in connection with a subordinate loan payoff with a statement that such amounts were paid from outside of closing funds.

Adjustments for items unpaid by seller due to the consumer to be paid by the seller pursuant to the real estate sales contract has two components:

- First, disclose amounts owed by the seller with the time period associated with the adjustments. Examples include:
  - Taxes paid in arrears for an entire year when the closing occurs prior to the start of the year.
  - Flood or hazard insurance premiums when the consumer is being substituted as an assured under the same policy.
  - Mortgage insurance in connection with an assumed loan.
  - Planned unit development or condominium assessments not yet paid.
  - Ground rent not yet paid by the seller.

- Second, disclose amounts owed by the seller that are neither disclosed on page 2 nor specifically disclosed as *due from seller at closing*. Examples of these amounts include:
  - Utilities used but not paid for by the seller.
  - Rent collected in advance by the seller from a tenant for a period of extending beyond the closing date.
  - Interest on loan assumptions.

CASH TO CLOSE DUE TO OR FROM SELLER

Under a subheading of calculation:

- Disclose *total due to the seller at closing*, as a positive number.
- Disclose *total due from seller at closing*, as a negative number.
- Disclose the sum of *total due to the seller at closing* and *total due from seller at closing* as a positive number. When the result is a positive number, disclose the amount as *cash to the seller.* When the result is a negative number, disclose the amount as *cash from the seller.* The sum is disclosed as a positive number in either event.

Closing Disclosure Page 3 Definition of Terms

- **Due from borrower at closing**. Total amount charged to the borrower at closing. It includes the borrower's house price and closing costs. It does not include any credits or rebates that lower the borrower's closing costs. (Those are below in Section L).
- **Adjustments for items paid by seller in advance**. Costs that have been prepaid by the seller that the borrower are now reimbursing the seller for.

- **Paid already by or on behalf of borrower at closing.** This section details how the borrower will pay for the items in Section K. It includes the amount they are borrowing, the amount of their deposit, and any rebates or credits paid by the seller or third-party service providers. It does not include the amount the borrower had to bring to closing - that is below in "cash to close."
- **Adjustments for items unpaid by seller.** Prior taxes and other fees owed by the seller that the borrower will pay in the future. The seller is reimbursing the borrower now to cover these expenses.
- **Cash to close**. The actual amount the borrower will have to pay at closing. They will typically need a cashier's check or wire transfer for this amount. Ask the closing agent about how to make this payment. Depending on the borrower's location, this person may be known as a settlement agent, escrow agent, or closing attorney.

THE CONSUMER FINANCIAL PROTECTION BUREAU'S GUIDE TO PAGE 4 OF THE CLOSING DISCLOSURE FORM

LOAN DISCLOSURES - In the loan disclosures table, disclose:

- Information concerning future **assumption** of the loan by a subsequent purchaser
- Whether the legal obligation contains a **demand feature** that can require early payment of the loan
- The terms of the legal obligation that impose a fee for a **late payment** including the amount of time that passes before a fee is imposed and the amount of such fee or how it is calculated
- Whether the regular periodic payments can cause the principal balance of the loan to increase, creating **negative amortization**
- The creditor's policy in relation to **partial payments** by the consumer
- A statement that the consumer is granting a **security interest** in the property (along with an identification of the property)
- Information related to any **escrow account** held by the servicer (or a statement that an escrow account has not been established with a description of estimated property costs during the first year)

Additional Information About This Loan

Loan Disclosures

Assumption
If you sell or transfer this property to another person, your lender
☐ will allow, under certain conditions, this person to assume this loan on the original terms.
☒ will not allow assumption of this loan on the original terms.

Demand Feature
Your loan
☐ has a demand feature, which permits your lender to require early repayment of the loan. You should review your note for details.
☒ does not have a demand feature.

Late Payment
If your payment is more than *15* days late, your lender will charge a late fee of *5% of the monthly principal and interest payment.*

Negative Amortization (Increase in Loan Amount) *These are new disclosures*
Under your loan terms, you
☐ are scheduled to make monthly payments that do not pay all of the interest due that month. As a result, your loan amount will increase (negatively amortize), and your loan amount will likely become larger than your original loan amount. Increases in your loan amount lower the equity you have in this property.
☐ may have monthly payments that do not pay all of the interest due that month. If you do, your loan amount will increase (negatively amortize), and, as a result, your loan amount may become larger than your original loan amount. Increases in your loan amount lower the equity you have in this property.
☒ do not have a negative amortization feature.

Partial Payments *These are new disclosures*
Your lender
☒ may accept payments that are less than the full amount due (partial payments) and apply them to your loan.
☐ may hold them in a separate account until you pay the rest of the payment, and then apply the full payment to your loan.
☐ does not accept any partial payments.
If this loan is sold, your new lender may have a different policy.

Security Interest
You are granting a security interest in
456 Somewhere Ave., Anytown, ST 12345

You may lose this property if you do not make your payments or satisfy other obligations for this loan.

Escrow Account
For now, your loan
☒ will have an escrow account (also called an "impound" or "trust" account) to pay the property costs listed below. Without an escrow account, you would pay them directly, possibly in one or two large payments a year. Your lender may be liable for penalties and interest for failing to make a payment.

Escrow		
Escrowed Property Costs over Year 1	$2,473.56	Estimated total amount over year 1 for your escrowed property costs: *Homeowner's Insurance* *Property Taxes*
Non-Escrowed Property Costs over Year 1	$1,800.00 *These are new disclosures*	Estimated total amount over year 1 for your non-escrowed property costs: *Homeowner's Association Dues* You may have other property costs.
Initial Escrow Payment	$412.25	A cushion for the escrow account you pay at closing. See Section G on page 2.
Monthly Escrow Payment	$206.13	The amount included in your total monthly payment.

☐ will not have an escrow account because ☐ you declined it ☐ your lender does not offer one. You must directly pay your property costs, such as taxes and homeowner's insurance. Contact your lender to ask if your loan can have an escrow account.

No Escrow		
Estimated Property Costs over Year 1		Estimated total amount over year 1. You must pay these costs directly, possibly in one or two large payments a year.
Escrow Waiver Fee		

In the future,
Your property costs may change and, as a result, your escrow payment may change. You may be able to cancel your escrow account, but if you do, you must pay your property costs directly. If you fail to pay your property taxes, your state or local government may (1) impose fines and penalties or (2) place a tax lien on this property. If you fail to pay any of your property costs, your lender may (1) add the amounts to your loan balance, (2) add an escrow account to your loan, or (3) require you to pay for property insurance that the lender buys on your behalf, which likely would cost more and provide fewer benefits than what you could buy on your own.

Additional Tables appear here if loan program includes Adjustable Payment (AP) or Adjustable Interest Rate (AIR) features

CLOSING DISCLOSURE   PAGE 4 OF 5 • LOAN ID # 123456789

Figure 20: Closing Disclosure, Page 4 of 5, Additional Information About This Loan (with some item detailing)

Closing Disclosure Page 4 Definition of Terms

- **Demand Feature.** A demand feature allows the lender to demand immediate payment of the entire loan at any time.
- **Negative Amortization.** Negative amortization means the borrower's loan balance can increase even if they make their payments on time and in full. Most loans do not have negative amortization.
- **Security Interest.** The security interest allows the lender to foreclose on the borrower's home if the borrower does not pay back the money they borrowed.
- **Escrow Account.** An escrow account lets you pay your homeowner's insurance and property taxes monthly as part of your mortgage payment, instead of in a large lump sum.

THE CONSUMER FINANCIAL PROTECTION BUREAU'S GUIDE TO PAGE 5 OF THE CLOSING DISCLOSURE FORM

LOAN CALCULATIONS

Disclose *Loan Calculations, Other Disclosures, Questions, Contact Information,* and, if desired by the creditor, *Confirm Receipt* tables on page 5 of the closing disclosure.

Disclose the *total of Payments*, the *Finance Charge*, the *Amount Financed*, the *APR*, and the *total Interest Percentage (TIP)* in the loan calculations table.

The **total of Payments** is the amount a consumer will have paid after making all payments of principal, interest, mortgage insurance, and loan costs, as scheduled. The amount disclosed as the total of payments excludes any portion of the principal, interest, mortgage insurance, or loan costs that is offset by a specific credit from another party. However, non- specific or general credits do not pay for a specific fee or amount. Therefore, they do not offset amounts used to calculate the total of payments.

The **APR** and **TIP** amounts should be updated from the amounts disclosed on the loan estimate to reflect the terms of the legal obligation at consummation.

Loan Calculations

Total of Payments. Total you will have paid after you make all payments of principal, interest, mortgage insurance, and loan costs, as scheduled.	$285,803.36
Finance Charge. The dollar amount the loan will cost you.	$118,830.27
Amount Financed. The loan amount available after paying your upfront finance charge.	$162,000.00
Annual Percentage Rate (APR). Your costs over the loan term expressed as a rate. This is not your interest rate.	4.174%
Total Interest Percentage (TIP). The total amount of interest that you will pay over the loan term as a percentage of your loan amount.	69.46%

Questions? If you have questions about the loan terms or costs on this form, use the contact information below. To get more information or make a complaint, contact the Consumer Financial Protection Bureau at **www.consumerfinance.gov/mortgage-closing**

Other Disclosures

Contains required disclosure language

Appraisal
If the property was appraised for your loan, your lender is required to give you a copy at no additional cost at least 3 days before closing. If you have not yet received it, please contact your lender at the information listed below.

Contract Details
See your note and security instrument for information about
- what happens if you fail to make your payments,
- what is a default on the loan,
- situations in which your lender can require early repayment of the loan, and
- the rules for making payments before they are due.

Liability after Foreclosure
If your lender forecloses on this property and the foreclosure does not cover the amount of unpaid balance on this loan,

☒ state law may protect you from liability for the unpaid balance. If you refinance or take on any additional debt on this property, you may lose this protection and have to pay any debt remaining even after foreclosure. You may want to consult a lawyer for more information.

☐ state law does not protect you from liability for the unpaid balance.

Refinance
Refinancing this loan will depend on your future financial situation, the property value, and market conditions. You may not be able to refinance this loan.

Tax Deductions
If you borrow more than this property is worth, the interest on the loan amount above this property's fair market value is not deductible from your federal income taxes. You should consult a tax advisor for more information.

Contact Information

	Lender	Mortgage Broker	Real Estate Broker (B)	Real Estate Broker (S)	Settlement Agent
Name	Ficus Bank		Omega Real Estate Broker Inc.	Alpha Real Estate Broker Co.	Epsilon Title Co.
Address	4321 Random Blvd. Somecity, ST 12340		789 Local Lane Sometown, ST 12345	987 Suburb Ct. Someplace, ST 12340	123 Commerce Pl. Somecity, ST 12344
NMLS ID	*Nationwide Mortgage Licensing System ID*				
ST License ID			Z765416	Z61456	Z61616
Contact	Joe Smith		Samuel Green	Joseph Cain	Sarah Arnold
Contact NMLS ID	12345				
Contact ST License ID			P16415	P51461	PT1234
Email	joesmith@ficusbank.com		sam@omegare.biz	joe@alphare.biz	sarah@epsilontitle.com
Phone	123-456-7890		123-555-1717	321-555-7171	987-555-4321

Confirm Receipt

By signing, you are only confirming that you have received this form. You do not have to accept this loan because you have signed or received this form.

Consumer is not required to sign; signature is acknowledgment of receipt, NOT acceptance of the loan

Applicant Signature Date Co-Applicant Signature Date

CLOSING DISCLOSURE PAGE 5 OF 5 • LOAN ID # 123456789

Figure 21: Closing Disclosure, Page 5 of 5 (with some item detailing)

OTHER DISCLOSURES

The creditor discloses in the *other disclosures* table:

- A statement related to the consumer's rights in relation to any **appraisal** conducted for the property.
- A statement informing the consumer of consequences of nonpayment, what constitutes default, when a creditor can accelerate maturity, and prepayment rebates and penalties pursuant to **contract details.**
- A statement, among other things, of whether state law provides for continued consumer responsibility for any **liability after foreclosure.**
- A statement concerning the consumer's ability to **refinance** the loan.
- A statement concerning the extent that interest on the loan can be included as a **tax deduction** by the consumer.

CONTACT INFORMATION

In the *contact information* table, disclose the following information for the lender: the *mortgage broker*, the consumer's *real estate brokerage*, the seller's *real estate brokerage*, and the *settlement agent* in a columnar format:

- Name
- Address
- The NMLS or state license ID, as applicable
- The contact name of an individual (and the NMLS or state license ID)
- Email
- Phone number

Unused columns may be removed, and columns may be added for additional parties. For example:

- If there are two real estate brokers representing the seller, a column may be added to identify that party and a column for a party not involved in the transaction may be deleted.

CONFIRM RECEIPT

The creditor, at its option, may include a line for the signatures of the consumers to *confirm receipt*. Although the creditor only lists persons to whom credit is extended as *borrowers* on the first page of the *closing disclosure*, in rescindable transactions, the creditor may add signature lines for other consumers who have the right to rescind. If the creditor includes a signature line to *confirm receipt*, the creditor must also include a statement that the signature only signifies receipt of the *closing disclosure*.

If the creditor does not include a statement line or the consumer's signature, add a statement to the *other disclosures* concerning *loan acceptance* that states: "You do not have to accept this loan because you have received this form or signed a loan application."

Closing Disclosure Page 5 Definition of Terms

Total of payments. The total of payments tells the borrower the total amount of money they will pay over the life of their loan, if they make all payments as scheduled.

Finance charge. The finance charge tells the borrower the total amount of interest and loan fees they will pay over the life of their loan, if they make all payments as scheduled.

Amount financed. The amount financed is the net amount of money the borrower is borrowing from the lender, minus most of the upfront fees the lender is charging the borrower.

NOTE

Corrected closing disclosure - Prior to consummation, an additional three-business-day waiting period applies when there are changes to the closing disclosure that result in an increase to the APR that becomes inaccurate, the addition of a prepayment penalty, or the change of a loan product. For other changes prior to consummation, provide the consumer the updated information in a corrected closing disclosure no later than consummation. Upon the consumer's request, by the business day before consummation, a creditor must permit the consumer to inspect the closing disclosure, although the creditor may omit items related only to the seller's transaction. In addition, provide a corrected closing disclosure if an event related to the settlement occurs during the 30- calendar-day period after consummation that causes the closing disclosure to become inaccurate and results in a change to an amount paid by the consumer from what was previously disclosed. Deliver or place in the mail the corrected closing disclosure no later than 30 calendar days after receiving information sufficient to establish changes to the amount paid by the consumer.

Other Disclosures

STATE AND FEDERAL DISCLOSURES are required to be given to all borrowers of mortgage loans by either state or federal laws. A signed copy for the file is required by law and verifies that the borrower has been given a copy of each and notified of the various rights and laws designed to protect them on a mortgage loan transaction.

The following disclosures are required to be provided to all the borrowers of a mortgage loan:

1. Borrowers Signature Authorization
2. ECOA (Equal Credit Opportunity Act)
3. (California) Fair Lending
4. Credit Score Information Disclosure
5. Right to Receive Appraisal and Request for Appraisal
6. Patriot Act
7. Privacy Policy Disclosure
8. Servicing Disclosure Statement
9. Loan Origination Agreement
10. California Real Estate Agency Disclosure
11. PMI and Adjustable-Rate Mortgage Disclosure.

1. **BORROWERS SIGNATURE AUTHORIZATION** gives the broker authorization to acquire a credit report and other necessary documentation, such as the Verification of Assets. A copy will accompany each request for verification and will also be required before talking to any necessary parties, such as the the borrower's tax preparer. *See Figure 22, Borrower Signature Authorization.*

2. **EQUAL CREDIT OPPORTUNITY ACT (ECOA)** explains the federal law prohibiting discriminatory lending and includes the address for the borrower to write if they have a complaint or feel that their civil rights have been violated.

3. **CALIFORNIA FAIR LENDING NOTICE DISCLOSURE** is the State of California's equivalent to the ECOA prohibiting discrimination in lending practices.

4. **CREDIT SCORE INFORMATION DISCLOSURE** is a relatively new disclosure that is required in all loan packages dated July 1, 2001, or later. In the past, the information on a borrower's credit report was not disclosed. As of July 1, 2001, the information must be disclosed in a form that explains the way the credit score works, the borrower's credit score, and the information that has directly affected their own credit score. Also included are the addresses of the credit agency for the borrower to contact to correct any errors in the report.

5. **RIGHT TO RECEIVE APPRAISAL** lets the borrower know that they have a right to receive a copy of the appraisal on completion of the loan based on the premise that they paid for the appraisal. Borrowers were not provided with a copy until the late 1990s; the law made it clear that the borrower has a right to receive it. The form provides a space for the complete the address where the borrower would like the appraisal to be delivered. *See Figure 23, Right to Receive Appraisal.*

6. **PATRIOT ACT** is a requirement of the federal government as a result of the creation of Homeland Security as a way of tracking any potential terrorist and any questionable activities. The purpose of the forms is to verify the borrower's identification. There are three pages to the form. Page 1 requires the mortgage broker or lender to complete the information obtained from the borrower's two required forms of identification, which are usually the driver's license and the Social Security card. Pages 2 and 3 are for completion by the borrower and co- borrower. *See Figure 24: Patriot Act.*

7. **PRIVACY POLICY DISCLOSURE** is required to notify the borrower that, per Title V of the Gramm-Leach-Bliley Act, financial institutions and their affiliates are generally prohibited from sharing non-public personal information concerning their clients. A client has the right to "opt out" if they so choose. There are businesses that sell "lists" of their clients to other businesses for the purpose of advertising. Brokers must disclose to the borrowers whether they normally share or intend to share any contact information that they have on their clients with other businesses.

8. **SERVICING DISCLOSURE STATEMENT** informs the borrower that lenders sell loans, and that brokers and lenders do retain for servicing, which is the job of collecting the payments and any other duties required to manage the account. The statement also discloses what percentage of loans the lender or broker sells as a normal course of business.

9. **MORTGAGE LOAN ORIGINATION AGREEMENT** is required by the federal government to explain to the borrower the relationship between the consumer and the mortgage broker/agent. The **mortgage loan origination agreement states that the mortgage originator is not an agent per federal definition.**

10. **CALIFORNIA REAL ESTATE AGENCY DISCLOSURE** is similar to the mortgage loan origination agreement; however, this form is required by the California Department of Real Estate because it states that the **mortgage originator is an agent according to California law.**

11. **PMI DISCLOSURES (private mortgage insurance)** are available for adjustable- rate, fixed-rate, and high-risk loans. The disclosures explain to the consumer the reason for Private mortgage insurance (PMI), how it works, and the benefits. The potential problems that may occur as a result of adjusting interest rates are also disclosed. *See Figure 27 and 28: PMI Disclosures.*

    PMI ARM disclosures provide the borrower with information about adjustable-rate mortgages and how they work and the potential changes that may occur to the interest rate and payment. All disclosures not shown here are available in *Chapter 15, Anti-Discrimination Laws and Disclosures.*

Borrower Signature Authorization

Privacy Act Notice: This information is to be used by the agency collecting it or its assignees in determining whether you qualify as a prospective mortgagor under its program. It will not be disclosed outside the agency except as required and permitted by law. You do not have to provide this information, but if you do not your application for approval as a prospective mortgagor or borrower may be delayed or rejected. The information requested in this form is authorized by Title 38, USC, Chapter 37 (if VA); by 12 USC, Section 1701 et. seq. (if HUD/FHA); by 42 USC, Section 1452b (if HUD/CPD); and Title 42 USC, 1471 et. seq., or 7 USC, 1921 et. seq. (if USDA/FmHA).

Part I - General Information

1. Borrower(s)	2. Name and address of Lender/Broker **ABC Mortgage** **1212 Main St.** **Oxnard, CA 93030** **TEL: 805-555-6666 FAX: 805-555-0000**

3. Date	4. Loan Number	

Part II - Borrower Authorization

I hereby authorize the Lender/Broker to verify my past and present employment earnings records, bank accounts, stock holdings, and any other asset balances that are needed to process my mortgage loan application. I further authorize the Lender/Broker to order a consumer credit report and verify other credit information, including past and present mortgage and landlord references. It is understood that a copy of this form will also serve as authorization.

The information the Lender/Broker obtains is only to be used in the processing of my application for a mortgage loan.

Borrower ____________________ Date ____________

Borrower ____________________ Date ____________

Figure 22: Borrower Signature Authorization

NOTICE TO APPLICANT OF RIGHT TO RECEIVE COPY OF APPRAISAL REPORT

APPLICATION NO.

PROPERTY ADDRESS

You have the right to receive a copy of the appraisal report to be obtained in connection with the loan for which you are applying, provided that you have paid for the appraisal. We must receive your written request no later than __90__ days after we notify you about the action taken on your application or you withdraw your application.

If you would like a copy of the appraisal report, contact

ABC Mortgage
1212 Main St.
Oxnard, CA 93030

Applicant	Date	Applicant	Date
Applicant	Date	Applicant	Date

Figure 23: Right to Receive Appraisal

PATRIOT ACT
INFORMATION DISCLOSURE

Applicant Name ____________________

Co-Applicant Name ____________________

Present Address ____________________

Mailing Address ____________________

To help the government fight the funding of terrorism and money laundering activities, Federal law requires all financial institutions to obtain, verify, and record information that identifies each person who opens an account.

What this means for you: When you open an account, we will ask for your name, address, date of birth, and other information that will allow us to identify you. We may also ask to see your driver's license or other identifying documents.

I/we acknowledge that I/we received a copy of this disclosure.

____________________	____________________
Applicant	Date
____________________	____________________
Applicant	Date

Figure 24: Patriot Act Information Disclosure Page 1 of 2

Customer Identification Documentation
Patriot Act

The USA Patriot Act requires all financial institutions to obtain, verify and record information that identifies every customer. Completion of this documentation is required in order to comply with the USA Patriot Act. A completed copy of this information must be retained with the loan file.

Application Number ______________________ Date ______________________

Name of Applicant ____

Social Security # ______________________ Date of Birth ______________________

Present Address ____

Mailing Address ____

Primary Identification Documentation

Document Type ______________________ Other Document Type ______________________

Document Number ____

Issue Date ______________________ Expiration Date ______________________

Issued by ____

Secondary Identification Documentation

Document Type ______________________ Other Document Type ______________________

Document Number ____

Issue Date ______________________ Expiration Date ______________________

Issued by ____

Discrepancies and Resolution

Completed by ____

Figure 24: Patriot Act Information Disclosure Page 2 of 2

MORTGAGE LOAN ORIGINATION AGREEMENT

(Warning to Broker: The content of this form may vary depending upon the state in which it is used.)

You agree to enter into this Mortgage Loan Origination Agreement with ABC Mortgage as an independent contractor to apply for a residential mortgage loan from a participating lender with which we from time to time contract upon such terms and conditions as you may request or a lender may require. You inquired into mortgage financing with ABC Mortgage on

We are licensed as a "Mortgage Broker" under

SECTION 1. NATURE OF RELATIONSHIP. In connection with this mortgage loan:

* We are acting as an independent contractor and not as your agent.
* We will enter into separate independent contractor agreements with various lenders.
* While we seek to assist you in meeting your financial needs, we do not distribute the products of all lenders or investors in the market and cannot guarantee the lowest price or best terms available in the market.

SECTION 2. OUR COMPENSATION. The lenders whose loan products we distribute generally provide their loan products to us at a wholesale rate.

* The retail price we offer you - your interest rate, total points and fees - will include our compensation.
* In some cases, we may be paid all of our compensation by either you or the lender.
* Alternatively, we may be paid a portion of our compensation by both you and the lender. For example, in some cases, if you would rather pay a lower interest rate, you may pay higher up-front points and fees.
* Also, in some cases, if you would rather pay less up front, you may be able to pay some or all of our compensation indirectly through a higher interest rate in which case we will be paid directly by the lender.

We also may be paid by the lender based on (i) the value of the Mortgage Loan or related servicing rights in the market place or (ii) other services, goods or facilities performed or provided by us to the lender.

By signing below, the mortgage loan originator and mortgage loan applicant(s) acknowledge receipt of a copy of this signed Agreement.

MORTGAGE LOAN ORIGINATOR		APPLICANT(S)	
ABC Mortgage Company Name		Applicant Name(s)	
1212 Main St. Address		Address	
Oxnard, CA 93030 City, State, Zip		City, State, Zip	
805-555-6666 / 805-555-0000 Phone/Fax		Borrower Signature	Date
Broker or Authorized Agent Signature	Date	Co-Borrower Signature	Date

Figure 25: Mortgage Loan Origination Agreement

Real Estate Agency Disclosure

When you begin discussions with a California Department of Real Estate License Agent regarding a real estate mortgage lending transaction, you should understand what type of agency relationship you have with that agent. A Mortgage Broker acts as the agent for the borrower in the mortgage loan transaction and may act as the limited agent of the lender for certain purposes including, but not limited to, making disclosures, ordering appraisal and credit reports, and assembling underwriting information. The brokerage has the following affirmative obligations:

To the Borrower:

1. Fiduciary responsibility of the utmost care, integrity, honesty, and loyalty in dealing with the borrower.

To the Borrower and the Lender:

1. Fiduciary responsibility of the utmost care, integrity, honesty, and loyalty in dealing with the borrower and the lender.
2. Diligent exercise of reasonable skill and care in performances of the agent's duties.
3. A duty of honesty and fair dealing and good faith.
4. A duty to disclose all facts known to the agent materially affecting the value or desirability of the property and/or credit risk of the transaction that are not known to or within the diligent attention and observation of the parties.

The above duties of the agent in this transaction do not relieve you from the responsibility to protect your own interests. You should carefully read all agreements to assure that they adequately express your understanding of this transaction. A Mortgage Broker is a person qualified to advise about real estate loan transactions. If legal or tax advice is desired, consult a professional in those fields.

ABC Mortgage is a California Department of Real Estate Licensed Brokerage, license number . The California Department of Real Estate license information phone number is 916-227-0770 and Fax number is 916-227-0777.

ABC Mortgage
1212 Main St.
Oxnard, CA, 93030
(P) 805-555-6666
(F) 805-555-0000

I/We acknowledge receipt of a copy of this agency disclosure statement.

____________________ ________
Signature Date

____________________ ________
Signature Date

Figure 26: California Real Estate Agency Disclosure

Private Mortgage Insurance - Initial Disclosure - High Risk Loans

Borrower(s) : ____________________ Date : ____________________

____________________ Property Address :

____

Loan Number : ____________________ ____________________

You are obtaining a mortgage loan that requires private mortgage insurance ("PMI"). PMI protects lenders and others against financial loss when borrowers default, and charges for the insurance are added to your loan payments.

Lender-Defined High Risk Loans. PMI will not be required on your mortgage loan beyond the date the principal balance of your loan is first **scheduled** to reach 77% of the original value of the property. If PMI is not sooner terminated in accordance with the foregoing sentence, PMI will not be required on your mortgage loan beyond the date that is the midpoint of the amortization period for the loan, if you are current on your loan payments on that date. "Original value" means the lesser of (a) the contract sales price of the property or (b) the appraised value of the property at the time the loan was closed.

Fannie Mae / Freddie Mac. PMI will not be required on your mortgage loan beyond the date that is the midpoint of the amortization period for the loan, provided you are current on your loan payments on that date.

Please note that PMI is **not** the same as property/casualty insurance -- such as homeowner's or flood insurance -- which protects you against damage to the property. Termination of PMI does **not** affect any obligation you may have to maintain other types of insurance.

I/we have received a copy of this disclosure.

____________________ ____________________

Borrower Date

____________________ ____________________

Borrower Date

Figure 27: Private mortgage Insurance Disclosure – High Risk

Private Mortgage Insurance Disclosure - Adjustable Rate Mortgages

Borrower(s) : ____________ Date : ____________

____________ Property Address : ____________

Loan Number : ____________ ____________

You are obtaining a mortgage loan that requires private mortgage insurance ("PMI"). PMI protects lenders and others against financial loss when borrowers default. Charges for the insurance are added to your loan payments.

Under certain circumstances, federal law gives you the right to cancel PMI or requires that PMI automatically terminate. This disclosure describes when cancellation and termination may occur. Please note that PMI is not the same as property/casualty insurance -- such as homeowner's or flood insurance - which protects you against damage to the property. Cancellation or termination of PMI does not affect any obligation you may have to maintain other types of insurance. In this disclosure, "loan" means the mortgage loan you are obtaining; "you" means the original borrower (or his or her successors or assigns); and "property" means the property securing the mortgage loan.

Borrower Requested Cancellation of PMI

You have the right to request that PMI be canceled on or after the following dates:

(1) The date the principal balance of your loan is first **scheduled** to reach 80% of the original value of the property. **For balloon loans with either an adjustable interest rate or a conditional right to refinance, if applicable, this date will not be reached before the loan matures.**

(2) The date the principal balance **actually** reaches 80% of the original value of the property.

"Original value" means the lesser of the contract sales price of the property or the appraised value of the property at the time the loan was closed. **If this loan refinances an existing loan secured by the property "original value" means the appraised value relied on by the lender to approve this loan.**

You will be notified when these dates are reached.

PMI will only be canceled if all the following conditions are satisfied:

(1) you submit a written request for cancellation;

(2) you have a good payment history;

(3) you are current on the payments required by your loan; and

(4) we receive, if requested and at your expense, evidence that the value of the property has not declined below its original value, and certification that there are no subordinate liens on the property.

For purposes of PMI Cancellation, a good payment history means no payments 60 or more days past due within two years and nopayments 30 or more days past due within one year of the later of (a) the cancellation date, or (b) the date you submit a request for cancellation.

Automatic Termination of PMI

If you are current on your loan payments, PMI will automatically terminate on the date the principal balance of your loan is first **scheduled** to reach 78% of the original value of the property. **For balloon loans with either an adjustable interest rate or a conditional right to refinance, if applicable, this date will not be reached before the loan matures.** This date is called the "termination date." If you are **not** current on your loan payments as of the termination date, PMI will automatically terminate on the first day of the month immediately following the date you thereafter become current on your payments. On or about the termination date, you will be notified that the PMI has been terminated or will be terminated when you become current on on your loan payments.

Exceptions to Cancellation and Automatic Termination

The cancellation and automatic termination requirements described above do not apply to certain loans that may present a higher risk of default. Your loan, however, does not fall into this category. Accordingly, the cancellation and automatic termination provisions described above apply to your loan.

I/we have received a copy of this disclosure.

____________ ____________

Borrower Date

____________ ____________

Borrower Date

Figure 28: Private mortgage Insurance – Adjustable Rate

HUD PAMPHLETS must be provided on all loans accordingly. The first three pamphlets mentioned are provided for both purchase and refinance transactions. They are designed by HUD to explain the borrowers' rights, costs, and laws regarding the transaction. Providing the appropriate pamphlet is a federal law.

These pamphlets may be purchased from a variety of companies that sell real estate-related forms and documents. HUD used to provide them but has discontinued that practice.

1.) **"Settlement Costs and You"** is to be given with **all** loan applications and real estate sales transactions. The disclosure provides information regarding potential costs.

2.) **"When Your House is on the Line"** is to be given with applications for home equity lines of credit. The disclosure provides information regarding the way an equity line of credit works, including rate and payment changes and the potential problems that may arise from the unusual terms of this loan type.

3.) **"Adjustable-Rate Mortgages"** is to be given when an adjustable-rate loan is to be obtained for the borrower to explain the information about the intricacies of the workings of adjustable-rate mortgages.

4.) **"Refinancing Your Home"** is provided when the borrower is applying for a loan to refinance their property whether owner-occupied or not.

NOTE

The booklets can be copied or retyped; however, it is against federal law to change the wording in any way. A broker or lender is, however, allowed to add their business name and address.

The ***Consumer Financial Protection Bureau*** has issued an updated version of the home buying information booklets (also known as the special information or settlement cost booklet) required under RESPA and TILA. These have been designed to be used with the new TILA/RESPA integrated disclosures.

1.) ***Your Home Loan Toolkit – A step-by-step guide.*** Lenders are required to deliver or mail the Toolkit not later than 3 days after receipt of an application. The goals of the Toolkit are to:
- inform consumers of the steps they need to take to get the best mortgage for their individual situation

- help consumers understand their closing costs and what it takes to buy a home
- give consumers tips on how to be a successful homeowner

2.) ***Consumer Handbook on Adjustable-Rate Mortgages (CHARM Booklet)*** this handbook gives you an overview of adjustable-rate mortgages (ARMs), explains how ARMs work, and discusses some of the issues you might face as a borrower. It includes:
- ways to reduce the risks associated with ARMs.
- pointers about advertising and other sources of information, such as lenders and trusted advisers.
- a glossary of important ARM terms.
- a worksheet that can help you ask the right questions and figure out whether an ARM is right for you.

3.) ***What You Should Know About Home Equity Lines of Credit (HELOC Brochure)*** a home equity line of credit is a form of revolving credit in which your home serves as collateral. If you decide to apply for a home equity line of credit, this brochure may assist you in choosing the plan that best meets your particular needs.

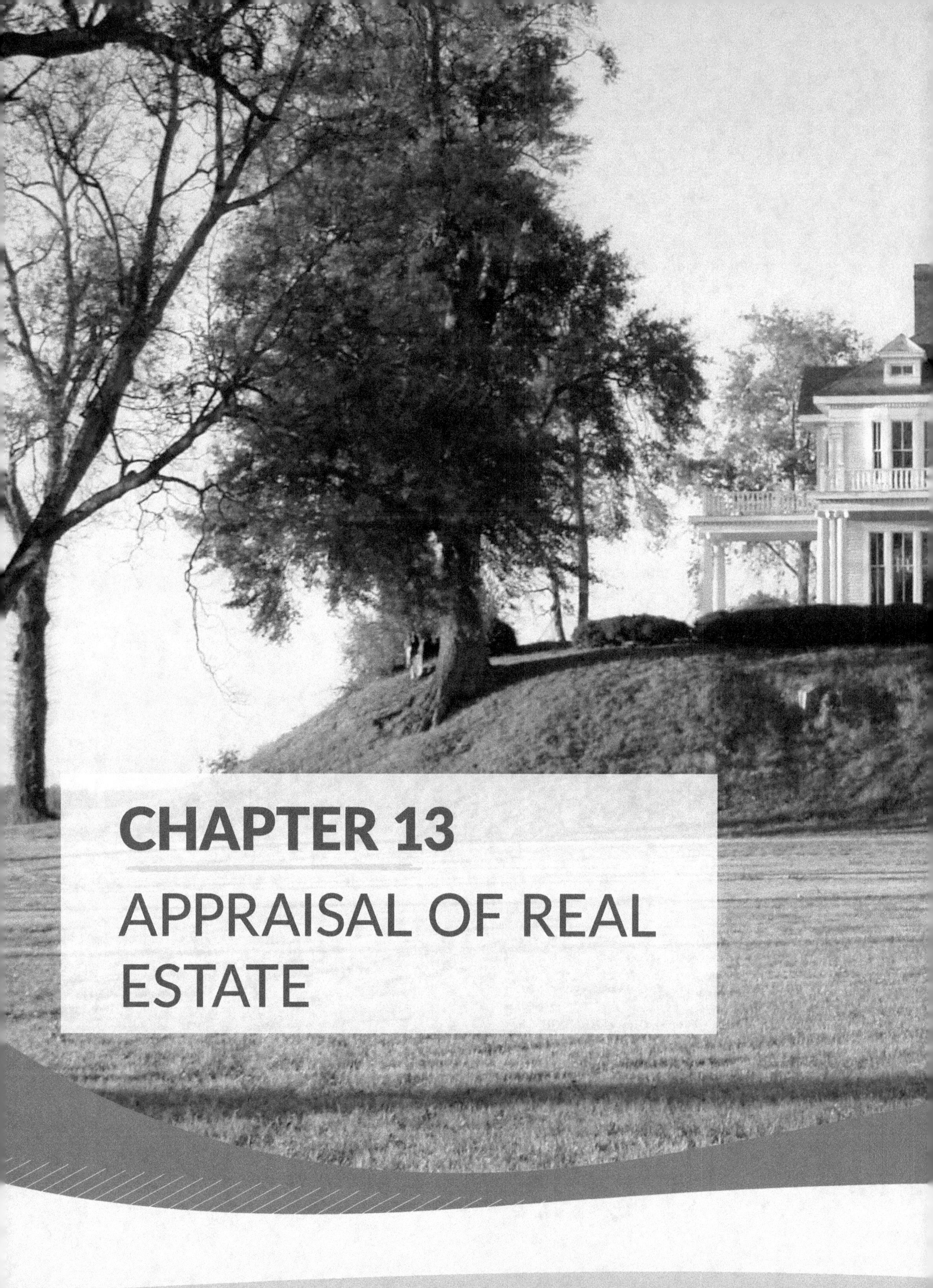

CHAPTER 13

APPRAISAL OF REAL ESTATE

US
Realty School

PURPOSE AND FUNCTION OF AN APPRAISAL

PURPOSE AND FUNCTION OF AN APPRAISAL is to estimate the value of a given property on the day of the evaluation. A real estate appraisal may be performed to serve several purposes.

FUNCTION is the intended use of the appraisal. The appraisal serves the function of providing the information as required. The following are the most common reasons that a property owner may have to want to know the value of their property. Appraisals are often prepared for the following uses:

- **Sell** at a good/fair price
- **Buy** at a good/fair price
- Refinance
- Tax purposes
- Potential improvements
- Development
- Insurance replacement value
- **Condemnation action,** such as through eminent domain
- **Distribution or disposal,** such as in a court action of probate or divorce

The PURPOSE of an appraisal is the reason that the appraisal is being done. What is the homeowner looking for? Do they want a high value to establish a good sales price or are they looking for a lower value to have property taxes reduced? What is the party ordering the appraisal looking for? The appraiser must determine the purpose of the appraisal in order to collect the correct data and develop the correct process of calculating the value.

The DEFINITION OF AN APPRAISAL is ***a written report providing the determination of the value of a specified parcel of real estate on a given date prepared by a licensed, certified, and impartial appraiser.*** An appraised value is good for the date that the value was determined only because values change regularly.

COMPONENTS OF AN APPRAISAL

COMPONENTS OF AN APPRAISAL provide all the various areas of information that affect or make up the total report and influence the appraiser's opinion as to the value of a property.

PRICE AND VALUE are affected by any number of influences that can change the value of a property at any moment in time. The closing of a sale of another comparable property in the subject property's neighborhood could increase the value of the subject if it sold for more than its market price; it could decrease the value by selling for less. Social and political changes affect the value, such as when the Fed raises interest rates to slow inflation. This typically causes property values to decrease. Recession decreases property values because there are fewer buyers in the market.

A. **PRICE** is established by the amount that a buyer pays for a property. The market price is the amount actually paid when escrow closes. The logic is that a property owner can ask any price they choose, but until a buyer offers an amount, the appraiser establishes value, and the lender agrees to loan the requested or needed amount to close escrow the actual market price is not determined. The market price is the amount that a ready, willing, and able buyer is paying a ready, willing, and able seller will accept under any circumstances.

B. **VALUE** is what a particular item or thing is worth.

1) **MARKET VALUE** is the value that the property will generate when there is a ready, willing, and able buyer and a ready, willing, and able seller when available on the market for a reasonable amount of time. What the buyer is ready to buy, willing to buy, and able to pay the amount agreed upon; and the seller is ready sell, willing sell, and able to accept. If there is no agreement about the value between the buyer and seller, the value is not what the market will bear. Both parties must be aware of the property's uses, advantages, and defects. Neither party can be under an inordinate amount of pressure to sell.

2) **UTILITY VALUE** is a subjective value based on the use or utility that the property's use has to an individual purchaser. This aspect of property value generally applies to a property that is not the usual property or one that has unusual amenities. A one-bedroom home is an example of a property that would be valued based on its utility because the average home buyer would not want a one-bedroom home. Only a particular homebuyer would want a one-bedroom home, which will affect the property's utility value.

3) **FOUR ESSENTIAL ELEMENTS OF VALUE** that must be considered when appraising real property are as follows:
   1) **Demand:** There must be a demand or buyers that are buying. The more people that are in the market to buy a home, the more valuable the property.
   2) **Utility:** There must be a practical use for the property. The more a property suits the needs of the buying public, the more valuable the property will be.
   3) **Scarcity:** The more unusual or the more amenities a property has, the scarcer and therefore the more desirable the property is, increasing the value of the property.
   4) **Transferability:** If the owner of a property is unable to transfer ownership easily, the value of the property will decrease. The cleaner the title, the higher the value.

4) **LOCATION! LOCATION! LOCATION!** Environmental and physical aspects outside of the property also influence and have an effect on the value of real property. This is the mantra of the real estate industry.

5) **SOCIAL IDEALS, LIFESTYLES, AND CUSTOMS** all influence a neighborhood through social changes that occur as parties move into a neighborhood, change their home in any way, and move out of the neighborhood.

6) **ECONOMIC INFLUENCES** affect the value of real property as inflationary and then recessionary periods go in and out. The established or older neighborhoods will experience the greatest fluctuation of values.

   During an inflationary period, new homes and developments are being built and established. Even though all properties increase during these economic times, they will not increase as quickly as when they were new because the new homes and developments are in greater demand for those who can afford them. The established neighborhoods become available to the lower income range of potential home buyers. When the inflationary period ends, the older established neighborhoods will have undergone a change from higher income owners to a lower income range of homeowners.

7) **GOVERNMENT AND POLITICAL REGULATIONS** always have an effect and influence on property through several means. Local zoning laws are the most obvious and frequent influence on areas and the surrounding neighborhoods. A change in the zoning for the immediate neighborhood may be as drastic a change as converting a neighborhood, or portion of one, from residential to commercial. The adjacent neighborhood will also be affected, although obviously not as drastically. The change to an adjacent neighborhood may be positive if that neighborhood's values will increase, such as by adding upscale shopping. The values may decrease if the change to the adjacent neighborhood is less desirable, such as would happen if a commercial area became more of an industrial area.

8) **PHYSICAL FORCES.** One of the great factors that influence the value of real property is physical forces. Physical and environmental forces on property values consist of easily identifiable factors, such as location, transportation availability, the local climate, topography, availability of schools, shopping, churches, and parks.

Physical forces describe the differences to the abovementioned factors. For example:

- ***Location.*** The property's location is of primary importance in defining value; a piece of land in an adjacent neighborhood may have an immense discrepancy in value.
- ***Transportation and roads.*** Commuters want to be close to interstate highways or public transportation. Proximity to transportation can have a positive impact on value.
- ***Climate.*** A population shift from the northern states to the southern states due to a more inviting climate.
- ***Topography.*** A rolling wooded piece of land is perfect for residential construction, while a steep lot is usually undesirable and has less value.

9) **PRINCIPLES OF VALUE** that an appraiser will consider when inspecting a property in preparation to determine the values are as follows:

a. **THE HIGHEST AND BEST USE** of the property is the starting point for an appraisal. This term refers to the best use for a particular piece of property that will generate the highest value. The highest and best use is not necessarily the current use of the property.

Example 1: *A single-family residence in a residential neighborhood.*

Example 2: *A single-family residence in a commercial neighborhood would not be the highest and best use for that particular piece of property. The use must be feasible, legal, and the use of the adjacent property must be taken into consideration.*

b. **SUBSTITUTION** is an important principle when appraising real property. Substitution is the basis for the sales comparison approach and is used for all three approaches to appraisal. A property that is similar to the subject property in desirability, size, room count, and location is used to determine the value or price of the subject. The comparable property must have closed escrow within a reasonable amount of time prior to the comparison in order to have established a usable market value.

When the subject is an income producing property, the comparables must be income-producing in establishing the value and the rental income.

When identical properties are for sale simultaneously, the property with the lower price will sell first.

c. **SUPPLY AND DEMAND** is in reference to the number of properties of a certain type that are available for purchase in a certain area, and the demand or desire for that type of property. The more potential buyers who want this type of property create a demand. The number of properties in relation to the number of potential buyers is the supply.

NOTE

The greater the demand, the more valuable the property. The greater the supply, the less valuable the property.

When a greater number of properties are available on the market, there is a large supply. If there are not as many buyers as there are available properties, the result is that the values will decrease, creating a ***buyer's market*** where buyers have the favorable position.

Conversely, when a lesser number of properties are on the market for sale and there is a greater number of buyers or an increase in demand, the values will increase as the buyers will be bidding to be able to purchase a property. This creates a ***seller's market,*** and the sellers are in a favorable position.

d. **CONTRIBUTION** is a principle concerned with the value that any particular item or amenity adds to a property. An extra bathroom, a fireplace, or swimming pools are all examples of amenities that will increase the value of a property over comparable properties that do not have the amenities.

e. **INCREASING RETURNS** are improvements that add more value to the property than the improvement cost.

> ***Example:*** *Sam is renovating his kitchen with new cabinets, countertops, flooring, and appliances. The total cost was $30,000. The improvement is an increasing return because the overall value of his property increased by $45,000, which is $15,000 more than the cost of the investment.*

f. **DECREASING RETURNS** are improvements that cost more than the value that will be gained in the overall property value. Decreasing returns are items or improvements that are generally made for the enjoyment of the property owner for long term use and occupancy.

> ***Example:*** *Sam installs a swimming pool in his yard. The costs of the improvements are $45,000. The overall value of the property has increased in value by $15,000 by virtue of the swimming pool improvement. The overall increased property value is $30,000 less than the cost of the improvement.*

g. **CONFORMITY** occurs when a reasonable degree of economic and social similarity exists in an area, creating the maximum value for the properties within the area or neighborhood. When the socio-economic makeup is similar, the residents have a comfort level, and the stability of the area is established because the properties are not often sold.

   Conformity also exists when there is uniformity in architectural style and similar properties. This is a desirable attribute of a neighborhood; however, an overly conforming neighborhood can become mundane and boring, resulting in decreasing values.

h. **PROGRESSION** is when a property of lesser value through size, quality, and amenities becomes more valuable as the surrounding properties increase in value through improvements. The subject property is said to be "under-improved" for the neighborhood.

   Progression can occur as the property owners begin to improve properties in a neighborhood improving the value of the neighborhood, but the few that do not improve their properties benefit from the owners that do improve by virtue of being in a neighborhood of **increasing values**. The under-improved properties increase in value strictly based on the location being surrounded by improved properties.

i. **REGRESSION** occurs when a property of greater value loses value or is valued for less based on the surrounding properties and neighborhood being lesser in size, quality, and amenities. A property is said to be "overbuilt" for the neighborhood. This usually occurs when one property owner begins to improve their property, and it is improved beyond the other properties in the neighborhood.

   Regression can also occur when the neighboring properties become rundown through lack of maintenance. This may occur when a neighborhood becomes predominantly non-owner-occupied or rental properties, which generally show less pride of ownership. The improved property decreases in value because it is in a neighborhood of **decreasing value**.

j. **LIFE-CYCLES** are typical neighborhood changes involving progression and regression. These changes occur in most areas, especially low-to-mid range housing, however, it affects all neighborhoods to some extent.

__Example:__ A neighborhood begins as new housing, whether as a subdivision or development, or as individual homes built over a period of time. The new homes are typically owned by occupying homeowners showing pride in ownership and of similar social and economic stature to each other. After a period of time, the houses begin to show wear.

Some of the property owners experience an increase in income and choose to move up to another neighborhood. They may choose to rent the property once they have moved on.

A rented property typically is not maintained as well as it would be if owner occupied which means that the property will experience deferred maintenance and lose value. If the previous owners chose to sell the property, it may sell to one who cannot afford a new home and perhaps cannot afford the maintenance. The neighborhood is on a downward trend in values or a period of regression.

Eventually, the neighborhood will begin to attract potential homeowners that are looking for homes that need renovation or a "fixer" as a means of making a profit through speculation. The properties may also be purchased by potential homeowners that cannot afford more and view such a neighborhood as a way to attain home ownership. Once one property owner begins to fix a property in an otherwise run-down neighborhood, many of the surrounding homeowners will begin to repair their properties. Once one home begins, it usually does not take long for others to follow. Progression has begun and the neighborhood is now in a period of increasing values.

A typical life cycle of a neighborhood will generally be over a period of 20 to 50 years. Progression and regression do not usually occur quickly but are slow processes.

k. **SPECULATION** creates anticipation as a part of this process of progression and regression. The anticipation of making a profit by investing in real property has been a part of the real estate industry since the beginning. Many people make a living by buying and selling real property.

Some of the ways of investing in real property in anticipation of making a profit include:

- **Fixing** or improving a property for resale to gain profit.
- **Speculation** of increase in values to sell at a later date for profit once values have increased.
- **Development** through building or construction to sell for profit.
- **Rental investment** to generate long-term income.

l. **CHANGE.** This principle explains that no physical or economic condition remains constant, that change is mostly the result of cause and effect, and that existence occurs in three stages: integration, equilibrium, and degeneration. *(Sourced from Appraisal)*

APPRAISAL PROCESS

APPRAISAL PROCESS is made up of several steps and processes. The appraiser must determine the purpose of the appraisal in order to collect the correct data and develop the correct process of calculating the value.

1. **SALES COMPARISON** is the most commonly used method of establishing a value. The sales comparison approach is a method of using comparable properties, referred to as comps, as discussed previously. The appraiser locates properties in the subject property's area that are as similar to the subject as is possible. The appraiser is looking for properties that are similar in size, style, condition, room count, and amenities.

   Three comps are the norm unless the comps are not closely similar to the subject. It is preferred that the comps bracket the subject, meaning that at least one comp should have greater square footage and at least one comp should have lesser square footage. This principle of bracketing the subject property carries through to all of the amenities being compared, including the sales price of all the comps.

All of the comps must have closed escrow. The true value is not established until the sale is closed. Any number of issues can cause a real estate sale to fall through, such as the buyer determining that the value is not equal to the price, or the seller may determine that the purchase price is too low. Occasionally an appraiser will use a sale that has not yet closed escrow because it helps establish the property value. The lender will usually require that comp close escrow prior allowing the subject to close escrow.

2. **The COST APPROACH** is a method of determining the value by establishing the cost to build the subject improvements new. The cost approach works well for newer properties; however, it can be very difficult and inaccurate on older properties. This method is used to appraise new properties or unusual properties that do not have available comps. An unusual property that the cost approach may be used for would be a church or a post office.

   The upper end of the value is reached by using the cost approach because it uses the value of new materials and current construction costs. The formula used to determine value by using the cost approach is:

   Cost to build new
   – Accrued depreciation (based on age and condition of the structure)
   + Land value
   = Value

   This section looks at the replacement cost of the subject if it has to be rebuilt. The value of the improvements or structures to the value of the land is a consideration. Depending on the area and the property, especially for property in rural areas with acreage, the value of the land may be too excessive for the structure.

3. **REPRODUCTION COST** as a method of the "cost to build new" that establishes the replication of the building exactly as it stands based on current construction costs and current costs of materials using the same quality of workmanship. This establishes the costs of building an exact replica.

4. **ACCRUED DEPRECIATION** is the amount of depreciation or wear and tear, all buildings may decline in value because of the aging of the materials and use of the structure.

5. **LAND VALUE** determines the value of the land if it were vacant with no improvements. The value of land can be determined by establishing comparable vacant lots in the subject property's neighborhood. Land value is determined on all appraisals.

6. **REPLACEMENT COST NEW** is a method of using the cost approach that is more practical of older buildings. Buildings with older and outdated building methods and materials may not be conducive to appraising a reproduction cost method. To appraise the value of a house, such as a 1900 Victorian, using the reproduction method would not create a fair value because the reproduction cost of expensive items, such as stained-glass windows and elaborate moldings, could overinflate the value.

   Replacement cost new allows for the cost of building an equivalent replacement of the subject property instead of replicating the property exactly. The replacement cost new method determines the value of a property that serves the same function and utility as the subject using current materials and methods.

   FIVE METHODS OF DETERMINING COST of the building materials and the construction costs are used whether using the replacement or reproduction method to determine value by use of the cost approach.

   a. **QUANTITY SURVEY** is the most accurate method of determining the cost of replacing a building. The costs of the materials and labor are determined using a book that provides a breakdown of the materials and often costs to build various styles of houses. The books allow for items, such as the amount of stucco required to build a Spanish style home of a designated square footage. Appraisers refer to these handbooks as a means of determining the quantity of the required building supplies. They are then able to determine the cost to build by multiplying the cost of material by the square footage of the house. One of the most commonly used books is the ***Marshall and Swift Manual***.

b. **UNIT COST-IN-PLACE** is the second most accurate method which establishes the costs to rebuild by adding the various units once installed by each of the various contractors. An example is the total cost the drywall contractor will charge for the job of putting the drywall in place including the drywall, mud, tape, and labor. This will include the complete cost for each contractor separately and totaled as a complete project or structure.

c. **SQUARE FOOTAGE** is a very common and quick method of determining value based on the construction cost per square foot of the completed building. ***Marshall and Swift*** and other available handbooks provide the amount of materials per square foot according to style and the appraiser can then determine the cost per square foot based on current costs. Building contractors will quite often provide a bid to build based on the square footage method as they are familiar with the costs at any given date in time. This method is often used for single-family residences. The formula for square footage is:

Length x Width= Square Footage

NOTE

To determine the size of a triangle, the total square footage must then be divided by two.

d. **CUBIC FOOTAGE** is similar to the square foot method and is commonly used for large industrial buildings such as factories or warehouses where the value is not based on just the length and width, but also the height. The formula for cubic footage is:

Length x Width x Height = Cubic footage

e. **The INDEX METHOD** is not a very accurate method of determining the cost of construction but may work well for properties that are not very old. The appraiser can determine the cost of the subject when it was built then multiply the total cost by the percentage of change in the cost of building from the time of construction to the current market whether it is higher or lower.

> ***Example:*** *Appraiser Jones determines the value of a property that was built 5 years ago. At that time the building cost for the quality of construction was $250 per square foot. He knows that the current cost for similar quality construction is $350 per square foot.*

$250 ÷ $300 = 20%	*the cost of construction has increased by 20% since the subject property was built. The factor or index is 20%.*
$375,000	*Cost to build property 5 years ago*
x 20%	*Index/% Costs Increase*
=) + $75,000	*Increase in $*
= $450,000	*Cost to build new today ($375,000 + $75,000)*

7. **The SALES COMPARISON APPROACH,** or the **market data approach,** is the method used for residential appraisals. The principle of this method is to locate properties similar in location, size, amenities, condition, and quality. Comparison is made to the similar properties by adjusting value of the changes to a comp to make the comp an identical property to the subject.

> ***Example:*** *Comp 1 has a swimming pool, but the subject property does not. The value of Comp 1 will be reduced by $15,000 to make it equivalent to the subject property.*

Sales comparison analysis lists the main amenities and features taken into consideration in evaluating the value of any given property. This section will provide the attributes of the subject property with additional properties that sold recently thereby establishing a fair market value. Three properties are generally used as comparables (comps), but additional comps may be requested based on several issues, such as the sale dates of the comps and how similar the properties are.

The following guidelines are used to determine the similarities in properties. The comps should be:

- Within a ten-block radius of the subject.
- COE (close of escrow) date of the comp should be within 6 months of the appraisal date.
- Line adjustments should not exceed 8% of the value of the property.
- Total line adjustments, or the net adjustments, should not exceed 17% of the value of the property.

See page 2 of Figure 29: Residential Appraisal Report for the following calculations to determine adjustments and similarities:

> ***Example:*** *Comparable No. 2, sales price is $295,000. Comp is 0.35 miles from the subject property. In this case, the distance is acceptable because it is in the neighborhood. See the location map in the appraisal.*
>
> *The comp is in inferior condition to the subject, so the appraiser increased the value of the comp by $20,000 to equalize the value to match the subject more closely.*
>
> *$20,000 Line adjustment*
> *÷$295,000 property value*
> *= .0677 or 7% of property value*
>
> *This is an acceptable line adjustment. The net adjustment is $20,000, which is less than 10% and there is no need to be concerned.*
>
> *The total of all adjustments is:*

$20,000	*Line adjustment*
+ 3,000	*Line adjustment*
=$23,000	*Gross line adjustment*
÷ $295,000	*property value*
= 7.797%	*of property value*

> *The maximum acceptable gross adjustment is 15%. This is an acceptable gross adjustment.*

In situations where the adjustments are excessive, the appraiser may offer explanations or provide additional comps to verify the properties being acceptable based on what is typical for the area. "Typical for the area" is one of the most important issues to the lender, especially in terms of resale. The lender is always concerned about the ability to sell the property quickly in the event of foreclosure.

Comments on sales comparisons immediately follows the comps and should be reviewed for any adverse comments that may affect the lending ability of the property.

Indicated value by sales comparison approach will be the last item in this section. This figure represents the total of the figures used to make the properties of equal value. The appraiser totals each column for an adjusted value of the individual comps. This figure represents the value of the property once the adjustments make it identical to the subject. The figures are reviewed from a subjective point of view and reconciled to determine the value of the subject property. The figures are not averaged.

1. **DEPRECIATION or PHYSICAL DEPRECIATION** of the properties and the amenities must be considered when determining the value. A roof generally has an estimated life of 20 years. If the roof is 15 years old, the value of the property will be reduced to depreciate or accommodate for the wear of that component of the property. A new roof would not be depreciated because there is minimal wear or usage to the component. Depreciation applies to all aspects of a structure and other improvements such as fencing.

NOTE

The comps are always adjusted to match the subject, and the figures are Reconciled not averaged.

NOTE

Land is never DEPRECIATED. Values may change with the economy; however, land itself is never considered in the depreciation factors.

- **FUNCTIONAL OBSOLESCENCE** refers to the functionality of a structure that is functional or works, but it is obsolete to current standards. Older homes may have floor plans that were common when built, but the function of the floor plan is no longer acceptable. Small or no closet space is another form of functional obsolescence. Functional obsolescence can be cured or corrected.

  Example: *In Simi Valley, near Los Angeles, was a large ranch built in the early 1900s. During that time there were small, one-bedroom houses built for the ranch hands that would come from their homes in Los Angeles or other places to work on the ranch for a couple weeks at a time then go home. The ranch hands lived in these houses only while they were at the ranch to work. The houses had a typical floor plan that allowed access to the only bathroom in the house through the bedroom. This was an acceptable floor plan for ranch hands on a temporary basis.*

  As the ranch was parceled out and sold, these houses were sold and many still exists today. The bathroom is functional; however, the floor plan is obsolete or not an acceptable floor plan in today's market.

- **EXTERNAL OBSOLESCENCE** refers to things outside of the property that will render a property obsolete or not up to current standards and expectations. ***External obsolescence is not curable.*** These are issues that the property owner does not have control over. Some examples of external obsolescence are as follows:
  - » Zoning
  - » Neighborhood change
  - » Airport creation
  - » Freeway expansion
  - » Street rerouting

COMPUTATION of the value will be discussed in the following section. There are several websites that can be used to obtain an estimated value of a property as a guideline for a real estate professional while waiting for an appraisal to be prepared. One such site is www.zillow.com

RECONCILIATION AND REPORT PREPARATION

REPORT PREPARATION will generate a report of approximately fifteen pages, with the most pertinent information on the first three to four pages. The real estate professional should review the appraisal prior to submission to the lender to be certain the property is acceptable. If there are any issues with the property, the appraiser's comments should be reviewed to be certain they have been properly explained, and to be competent to discuss the property with the client who may be the buyer or the seller. Many transactions have been declined or cancelled because the property was unacceptable. *See Figure 29: Uniform Residential Appraisal Report.*

An appraisal is good for 6 months at which time a new appraisal must be provided. Once an appraisal is 4 months old, a re-certification of value will be required from the appraiser. This is a one-page document generally in the form of a letter stating the value is still valid.

- **SUBJECT:** The subject address must match the complete address on the prelim. The prelim is the correct address. Request a correction from the appraiser if there are any discrepancies.
- **LEGAL DESCRIPTION** and the **ASSESSOR'S PARCEL NUMBER (APN)** must be compared to the plat map in the prelim. Different numbers may indicate fraud, and any errors must be corrected.
- **BORROWER** must match the name of the primary borrower on the loan application or the buyer of the property.
- **CURRENT OWNER** must match the name of the borrower for a refinance or the seller for a purchase transaction.
- **OCCUPANT** must match the "occupancy status" of the purchase contract or the loan application. If the loan is being done as an owner occupied, the borrower's name must be in this space.

NOTE

The words road, street, avenue, etc., must match the prelim exactly and are important to ascertain that the subject is the correct property.

If it states another person's name or states "tenant," the issue must be addressed to establish the accurate occupancy and prevent fraud.

- **THE PROPERTY RIGHTS APPRAISED** indicates the type of ownership. Most property is owned as **"fee simple,"** which is the term used indicating full ownership with no contingencies on that ownership.

- **LEASEHOLD** indicates that someone other than the borrower owns the land, and the borrower owns only the improvements or house and pays rent on the land the house is on.

- **PROJECT TYPE** will most commonly be an SFR, PUD, or condo. If the property is a PUD or condo, the name of the project will be included.

- **SALES PRICE** will indicate the purchase price for a sales transaction. If the loan is a refi, the last date of transfer may be indicated in this space, or it may be left blank.

  If the sales date for a refi is indicated and it has sold less than a year prior to the current closing date, the lender will use **the lesser of the purchase price or the current appraised value**. If this is an issue, the closing can be scheduled to be after the one-year anniversary date of the purchase.

- **LENDER/CLIENT** must be the name of the broker/company. If the borrower has an appraisal that was prepared for another mortgage company, the appraiser can change the name to the current brokerage providing the borrower has paid for the appraisal. The borrower may pay for the appraisal at this point to release any obligation by the former broker in which case the broker will release the appraisal to the new broker.

- **NEIGHBORHOOD: Location, etc.** the preferred responses will appear in the first or the middle columns starting with the property being "urban" or "suburban." When items are marked in the third column, "rural," the appraiser should address these at the bottom of this page in the "COMMENT" section or in detail in the addendum, which will be found on pages 3, 4, or 5 in most appraisals.

- **RURAL PROPERTY** indicates to the lender that comparable properties will not be nearby, the subject property may be zoned agricultural, and the marketing time will probably be longer than for an urban property.

- **MARKETING TIME** is the biggest issue to a lender if it is "Over 6 Mos." This will indicate to the lender that if the property goes into default, there may be additional losses due to extended marketing time or it will take approximately 6 months or more to sell the property if the lender has to foreclose.

- **PREDOMINANT OCCUPANCY** indicates whether the value of the property will be continuing as it would with a predominantly owner-occupied neighborhood or decreasing value as it would with non-owner-occupied neighborhood.

- **SINGLE-FAMILY HOUSING** should bracket the value of the subject property in dollar amount representing recent sales within the neighborhood. The main concern would be if the value of the subject was greater than the rest of the neighborhood suggesting that it would not be easily sold at its highest value. If the subject is worth less than most of the other properties in the neighborhood, it indicates to the lender that there is much room for improvement or the subject is being sold below value, which places the buyer and their lender in a strong position and the house could be sold quickly if necessary.

- **PRESENT LAND USE** and **LAND USE CHANGE** are also indicators of future value. If the appraiser indicates that the present use of land is likely to continue, values are likely to remain the same or increase with the economy. Land use change indicates that there may be dramatic changes. The changes may be in many different ways, but the appraiser must clarify, or the Appraisal/subject property may be unacceptable. Some changes occurring may be from single family to multi-family, or condos and PUDS (acceptable); residential to commercial (unacceptable); or agricultural to residential (acceptable). Some of the possible changes may also indicate a change in zoning affecting the value in use.

- **NEIGHBORHOOD AND MARKET CONDITIONS** contain appraiser's notes that should be read for any comments affecting the marketability of the subject property. The appraiser should explain any adverse comments. Negative comments can cause the loan to be declined due to unacceptable property.

- **PUD:** Project information for PUDs applies to both PUDs and condos. The information should be checked with that on the prelim. The name of the project is at the top of the page. The number of units is stated in this section. Complexes with fewer than 10 units are difficult to find lenders willing to finance, complexes with fewer than 4 units are financed by still fewer lenders.

- **SITE:** Zoning is of the utmost importance to the use and future of the property. The zoning on a residential property must be for residential use. The designation will vary in different communities.

  Examples of typical zoning designations are:
    - **R1**- residential, single family
    - **R2**- residential, up to 2 units
    - **R3**- residential, up to 3 units
    - **R4**- residential, up to 4 units
    - **MR**- multiple family
    - **C1**- small commercial
    - **C2**- large commercial

  These are commonly used zoning designations, but it is wise to verify the local classifications as they will vary.

- **"LEGAL"** means that it is zoned according to the current use. For residential use, an "R" zoning will apply, and the number of units allowed for that lot is indicated by the number following the "R." For example, an SFR with an R-1 zoning complies because it is one unit. An SFR in an R-4 zone is still in compliance, although it is 1 unit in an area zoned for 4 residential units. An SFR in a C-1 zoning is not in compliance or is "not legal."

- **LEGAL NONCONFORMING** is also referred to as **grandfathered use** and indicates that the subject does not conform such as a 2-unit property located in an area that is zoned R1 or one unit per lot.

  Grandfathered use indicates that the subject was built and in use prior to the zoning being established to its current use. A lender will require the Building and Planning Department of the local jurisdiction to provide a "rebuild letter" stating that the property can be rebuilt for its current use if damaged by natural causes. These are not always obtainable and will require contacting the local Department of Building and Development. The local governing agency may merely fax a copy of the building codes with the pertinent information.

- **HIGHEST & BEST USE** as improved should be marked "present use." If not, look for related comments at the end of this section. Highest & best use means the best purpose or usage of the property, which is not always its current use.

- **PUBLIC UTILITIES** indicate whether the property has utilities provided by the local government or if the property is self-contained by using a septic tank, well, or a generator. Septic tanks may require a septic cert (certification) from a qualified/licensed company unless the tank is less than five years old, which will require proof, generally in the form of a receipt for the installation of a new septic tank. ***A well for water may require a cert from a qualified/licensed company and may require a perc (percolation) test.***

- **FEDERAL EMERGENCY MANAGEMENT AGENCY (FEMA)** A Special Flood Hazard Area will require flood insurance if the appraiser has marked this "Yes." A flood cert will be obtained from FEMA if there is financing involved in the transaction.

- **FEMA ZONE** indicates if there is a need for flood insurance. Zones "C" and "B" generally will not require flood insurance. The lender will run a flood cert to verify the appraiser's findings. A flood zone which is classified "A" will generally require flood insurance.

- **DESCRIPTION OF IMPROVEMENTS:** A general description does just that. It is good to review this section and read the "comment" section immediately following it. The age of the subject/the year built will be found in the first column. Legally free-standing appliances that are not built-in are personal property, or **chattel**, and the sales price on a purchase transaction can be reduced by the estimated value of the item at the lender's discretion for a purchase transaction.

- **COMMENTS:** Additional features, condition of the improvements etc., and adverse environmental conditions should always be read thoroughly for consideration of any adverse comments, which may indicate that the subject is unacceptable property.

RECONCILIATION will provide the date of the appraisal or the date of determination of the value, the property's value as determined by the appraiser on that date, the appraiser's signature, and state certification/license number. The pages immediately following the comps will contain various comments the appraiser may wish to make concerning the property and the decisions made in reaching the value.

Also included in this area will be a statement regarding the **chain of title** and states whether the subject has been listed for sale or sold within the last 12 months. If the loan is a refi and the appraiser states the property is currently listed or has been listed for sale in the last 12-month period, a listing cancellation and a letter of explanation will be required. If the property was purchased within the last twelve-month period and the loan is a refinance, the property value will be the lesser of the purchase price or the appraised value.

If the loan is a cash-out refi and the property has been listed for sale recently, it is an indication that the borrower is taking money out of the property's equity to purchase another home. This is done quite often with the intent of moving to a new home and renting the subject home, which is being refinanced as an owner-occupied property. This may be an indication of fraud, and the real estate professional must not be a party to fraud. The photos of the subject property should be looked at closely at this point to see if there are any telling indicators such as a "for sale" sign on the property. To avoid fraud, the loan application and appraisal must be properly represented.

THE SKETCH ADDENDUM: This page is a diagram of the subject property's floor plan. The floor plan should be checked for obsolescence. This means that the floor plan may be functional, but the floor plan is obsolete or no longer used or accepted. The most frequently seen form of functional obsolescence would be a floor plan requiring that a bedroom or a bathroom is accessed through another room. These issues usually only exist in older homes.

SITE PLAN ADDENDUM: This is a copy of the plat map and should be compared to the plat map in the prelim. The appraiser takes the map directly from the prelim and may occasionally request a copy when the appraisal is ordered.

LOCATION MAP ADDENDUM: The location map is an area street map that shows the location of the subject property and the comparable properties. Comparing the distance between the subject property and the comps may be helpful if there are any issues.

PHOTOGRAPH ADDENDUM: Photos for the front, back, and street scene are required for the subject property. Occasionally the appraiser will provide additional photos if the property is exceptional, or if the additional photos are needed to validate decisions made on the value. Photos will also be provided for the front of each comp.

The appraiser is liable for anything disclosed or intentionally omitted from the appraisal. They will work to explain any problems, but they are obligated by law to disclose any problems or issues that they are aware of. They cannot make changes without good cause or justification. Usually, a more thorough explanation will suffice.

COMPARATIVE MARKET ANALYSIS (CMA)

COMPARATIVE MARKET ANALYSIS (CMA) is a report that shows the properties that are comparable to the subject property. The report merely shows the price of currently marketed properties in the same area as the subject property. The purpose of the CMA is to help determine the price range the subject property may bring if placed on the market within a reasonable time frame from the sale date of the comparable properties (comps).

A comparative market analysis is a report that can be prepared by a real estate agent for their selling clients to aid in determining a fair price at which to list the property.

NOTE

The CMA is not an appraisal and should not be presented as one.

The Appraisal Office (707) 964-5800

Main File No. 15-0365g Page #1

Uniform Residential Appraisal Report

20
File # 15-0365g

The purpose of this summary appraisal report is to provide the lender/client with an accurate, and adequately supported, opinion of the market value of the subject property.

SUBJECT

Property Address | City Cazadero | State CA | Zip Code 95421
Borrower | Owner of Public Record | County
Legal Description
Assessor's Parcel # | Tax Year 2015 | R.E. Taxes $ 2,203
Neighborhood Name Magic Mountain | Map Reference County Fold Out | Census Tract 1543.04
Occupant ☒ Owner ☐ Tenant ☐ Vacant | Special Assessments $ 0 | ☒ PUD HOA $ 1,297 ☒ per year ☐ per month
Property Rights Appraised ☒ Fee Simple ☐ Leasehold ☐ Other (describe)
Assignment Type ☐ Purchase Transaction ☒ Refinance Transaction ☐ Other (describe)
Lender/Client W.J. Bradley Mortgage Capital, LLC | Address 100 West Towne Ridge Parkway, Suite 300, Sandy, UT 84070
Is the subject property currently offered for sale or has it been offered for sale in the twelve months prior to the effective date of this appraisal? ☐ Yes ☒ No
Report data source(s) used, offering price(s), and date(s). **Bay Area Real Estate Information Service (BAREIS) checked indicates the subject property has not been listed in the past 12 months.**

CONTRACT

I ☐ did ☐ did not analyze the contract for sale for the subject purchase transaction. Explain the results of the analysis of the contract for sale or why the analysis was not performed.

Contract Price $ | Date of Contract | Is the property seller the owner of public record? ☐ Yes ☐ No Data Source(s)
Is there any financial assistance (loan charges, sale concessions, gift or downpayment assistance, etc.) to be paid by any party on behalf of the borrower? ☐ Yes ☐ No
If Yes, report the total dollar amount and describe the items to be paid.

NEIGHBORHOOD

Note: Race and the racial composition of the neighborhood are not appraisal factors.

Neighborhood Characteristics				One-Unit Housing Trends				One-Unit Housing			Present Land Use %	
Location	☐ Urban	☐ Suburban	☒ Rural	Property Values	☐ Increasing	☒ Stable	☐ Declining	PRICE		AGE	One-Unit	95 %
Built-Up	☐ Over 75%	☒ 25-75%	☐ Under 25%	Demand/Supply	☐ Shortage	☒ In Balance	☐ Over Supply	$ (000)		(yrs)	2-4 Unit	2 %
Growth	☐ Rapid	☒ Stable	☐ Slow	Marketing Time	☐ Under 3 mths	☒ 3-6 mths	☐ Over 6 mths	415	Low	10	Multi-Family	1 %
Neighborhood Boundaries	Austin Creek State Recreation Area to the North, Freezeout Road to the South,							550	High	65	Commercial	2 %
Highway 1 to the West, and The Russian River to the East.								512	Pred.	40	Other	%

Neighborhood Description The Subject is in the Cazadero/Russian River area, a popular area on the Pacific Coast approximately 1.0 hour from Santa Rosa with regional shopping and within 15 minutes from Guerneville for grocery, pharmacy, and banking. The subject is a strong second home and retirement area. Many State Parks in the area/abalone diving is popular.

Market Conditions (including support for the above conclusions) Property values have shown a marked decrease over the past several years. More recently the market appears to be stabilizing with supply and demand more in balance. Some properties have increased in the stabilization process. However not enough data for supportable trend.

SITE

Dimensions 58X839X60X839 | Area 1.15 ac | Shape Rectangular | View N;Mtn;
Specific Zoning Classification AR2 | Zoning Description Rural Residential
Zoning Compliance ☒ Legal ☐ Legal Nonconforming (Grandfathered Use) ☐ No Zoning ☐ Illegal (describe)
Is the highest and best use of subject property as improved (or as proposed per plans and specifications) the present use? ☒ Yes ☐ No If No, describe

Utilities	Public	Other (describe)		Public	Other (describe)	Off-site Improvements – Type	Public	Private
Electricity	☒	☐ PG&E	Water	☒	☐	Street Asphalt	☒	☐
Gas	☐	☒ Delivered Propane	Sanitary Sewer	☐	☒ Septic	Alley None	☐	☐

FEMA Special Flood Hazard Area ☐ Yes ☒ No | FEMA Flood Zone X | FEMA Map # 06097C0050E | FEMA Map Date 12/02/2000
Are the utilities and off-site improvements typical for the market area? ☒ Yes ☐ No If No, describe
Are there any adverse site conditions or external factors (easements, encroachments, environmental conditions, land uses, etc.)? ☐ Yes ☒ No If Yes, describe
The preliminary title report should be reviewed by interested parties for for any unapparent easements, encroachments or any other possible unapparent matters of record. Septic and delivered propane are the only services available with no impact on value or marketability.

IMPROVEMENTS

General Description		Foundation		Exterior Description	materials/condition	Interior	materials/condition
Units ☒ One ☐ One with Accessory Unit		☐ Concrete Slab	☒ Crawl Space	Foundation Walls	CC Perim/Gd	Floors	HW/WW/Tile/Gd
# of Stories	2	☐ Full Basement	☒ Partial Basement	Exterior Walls	Wd/Stone/Gd	Walls	Dry Wall/Gd
Type ☒ Det. ☐ Att. ☐ S-Det./End Unit		Basement Area	288 sq.ft.	Roof Surface	Comp Shg/Gd	Trim/Finish	Wood/Gd
☒ Existing ☐ Proposed ☐ Under Const.		Basement Finish	0 %	Gutters & Downspouts	Metal/Gd	Bath Floor	Tile/HW/Gd
Design (Style)	Craftsman	☒ Outside Entry/Exit	☐ Sump Pump	Window Type	Dual Pane/Gd	Bath Wainscot	Tile/Gd
Year Built	1975	Evidence of ☐ Infestation		Storm Sash/Insulated	None/Typ	Car Storage	☐ None
Effective Age (Yrs)	10	☐ Dampness	☐ Settlement	Screens	Alum Wire/Gd	☒ Driveway # of Cars	2
Attic	☒ None	Heating ☒ FWA ☐ HWBB	☐ Radiant	Amenities	☒ Woodstove(s) # 1	Driveway Surface	Gravel
☐ Drop Stair	☐ Stairs	☐ Other	Fuel Del Propane	☒ Fireplace(s) # 1	☒ Fence Partial	☐ Garage # of Cars	0
☐ Floor	☐ Scuttle	Cooling ☐ Central Air Conditioning		☐ Patio/Deck None	☒ Porch Front	☐ Carport # of Cars	0
☐ Finished	☐ Heated	☐ Individual	☒ Other None	☐ Pool None	☐ Other None	☐ Att. ☐ Det.	☐ Built-in

Appliances ☐ Refrigerator ☒ Range/Oven ☒ Dishwasher ☐ Disposal ☒ Microwave ☐ Washer/Dryer ☐ Other (describe)
Finished area above grade contains: 6 Rooms 2 Bedrooms 2.0 Bath(s) 1,806 Square Feet of Gross Living Area Above Grade
Additional features (special energy efficient items, etc.). Standard energy saving features required by code.

Describe the condition of the property (including needed repairs, deterioration, renovations, remodeling, etc.). C4;No updates in the prior 15 years;See attached addenda.

Are there any physical deficiencies or adverse conditions that affect the livability, soundness, or structural integrity of the property? ☐ Yes ☒ No If Yes, describe
Scope of Work is for a walk thru inspection only and it is assumed that there are no structural defects hidden by floor or wall coverings or any other hidden or unapparent conditions of the property; that all mechanical equipment and appliances are in good working condition, and that all electrical components and the roofing are in good condition. Utilities were on and working at the time of inspection.
Does the property generally conform to the neighborhood (functional utility, style, condition, use, construction, etc.)? ☒ Yes ☐ No If No, describe

Freddie Mac Form 70 March 2005 | UAD Version 9/2011 | Page 1 of 6 | Fannie Mae Form 1004 March 2005

Form 1004UAD — "WinTOTAL" appraisal software by a la mode, inc. — 1-800-ALAMODE

Figure 29: Uniform Residential Appraisal Report 1 of 14

Uniform Residential Appraisal Report

20
File # 15-0365g

There are 2 comparable properties currently offered for sale in the subject neighborhood ranging in price from $ 350,000 to $ 358,000

There are 4 comparable sales in the subject neighborhood within the past twelve months ranging in sale price from $ 362,000 to $ 750,000

FEATURE	SUBJECT	COMPARABLE SALE # 1		COMPARABLE SALE # 2		COMPARABLE SALE # 3	
Address	Cazadero, CA 95421	18015 Bei Rd Cazadero, CA 95421		4225 Austiin Creek Rd Cazadero, CA 95421		1605 Austin Creek Rd Cazadero, CA 95421	
Proximity to Subject		4.17 miles NW		2.62 miles NW		0.53 miles N	
Sale Price	$		$ 515,000		$ 540,000		$ 520,000
Sale Price/Gross Liv. Area	$ sq.ft.	$ 309.50 sq.ft.		$ 257.39 sq.ft.		$ 442.18 sq.ft.	
Data Source(s)		BareisMLS#21519862;DOM 70		BareisMLS#21500572;DOM 40		BareisMLS#21510582;DOM 102	
Verification Source(s)		DOC#92180		DOC#24621		DOC#76584	
VALUE ADJUSTMENTS	DESCRIPTION	DESCRIPTION	+(-) $ Adjustment	DESCRIPTION	+(-) $ Adjustment	DESCRIPTION	+(-) $ Adjustment
Sales or Financing Concessions		ArmLth Conv;5000	-5,000	ArmLth Conv;0		ArmLth Conv;3750	
Date of Sale/Time		s10/15;c10/15		s03/15;c03/15		s08/15;c07/15	
Location	N;Rural;	N;Rural;		N;Rural;		N;Rural;	
Leasehold/Fee Simple	Fee Simple	Fee Simple		Fee Simple		Fee Simple	
Site	1.15 ac	6,534 sf	0	3.20 ac	-2,050	1.49 ac	0
View	N;Mtn;	N;Mtn;		B;Wtr;	-6,750	B;Wtr;	-13,000
Design (Style)	DT2;Modern	DT1;Contemp	0	DT2;Custom	0	DT1;Bungalow	0
Quality of Construction	Q4	Q4		Q4		Q4	
Actual Age	40	50	0	46	0	63	0
Condition	C4	C4		C4		C4	
Above Grade	Total / Bdrms. / Baths	Total / Bdrms. / Baths	0	Total / Bdrms. / Baths		Total / Bdrms. / Baths	0
Room Count	6 / 2 / 2.0	6 / 3 / 2.0	0	5 / 2 / 2.0	0	4 / 1 / 1.0	+10,000
Gross Living Area	1,806 sq.ft.	1,664 sq.ft.	+4,615	2,098 sq.ft.	-9,490	1,176 sq.ft.	+20,475
Basement & Finished Rooms Below Grade	288sf0sfwo	0sf	0	0sf	0	0sf	0
Functional Utility	Good	Good		Good		Good	
Heating/Cooling	FAU/None	EBB/None	0	EBB/None	0	FAU/None	
Energy Efficient Items	Code	Code		Code		Code	
Garage/Carport	2dw	2gd	-2,000	2ga	-2,000	1cp10dw	+1,000
Porch/Patio/Deck	Patio/Deck	Deck	0	Deck	0	Deck	0
Amenities	None	Shop	-2,500	Outbuildings	-5,000	None	
Amenities	None	Storage	-2,500	None		None	
Assessor's Parcel #	097-250-019	106-080-004	0	105-180-015	0	097-050-046	0
Net Adjustment (Total)		☐ + ☒ -	$ -7,385	☐ + ☒ -	$ -25,290	☒ + ☐ -	$ 18,475
Adjusted Sale Price of Comparables		Net Adj. 1.4 % Gross Adj. 3.2 %	$ 507,615	Net Adj. 4.7 % Gross Adj. 4.7 %	$ 514,710	Net Adj. 3.6 % Gross Adj. 8.6 %	$ 538,475

I ☒ did ☐ did not research the sale or transfer history of the subject property and comparable sales. If not, explain

My research ☐ did ☒ did not reveal any prior sales or transfers of the subject property for the three years prior to the effective date of this appraisal.

Data Source(s) REALIST, effective date of data source 12/01/2015

My research ☐ did ☒ did not reveal any prior sales or transfers of the comparable sales for the year prior to the date of sale of the comparable sale.

Data Source(s) Realist, effective date of data source 12/01/2015

Report the results of the research and analysis of the prior sale or transfer history of the subject property and comparable sales (report additional prior sales on page 3).

ITEM	SUBJECT	COMPARABLE SALE #1	COMPARABLE SALE #2	COMPARABLE SALE #3
Date of Prior Sale/Transfer				
Price of Prior Sale/Transfer				
Data Source(s)	REALIST	REALIST	REALIST	REALIST
Effective Date of Data Source(s)	12/01/2015	12/01/2015	12/01/2015	12/01/2015

Analysis of prior sale or transfer history of the subject property and comparable sales See Above.

Summary of Sales Comparison Approach See attached addenda.

Indicated Value by Sales Comparison Approach $

SALES COMPARISON APPROACH

Indicated Value by: Sales Comparison Approach $ Cost Approach (if developed) $ 533,867 Income Approach (if developed) $

Sales Comparison Approach [$487,000(r)-$535,000(r)Closed Sales] best reflects interaction of buyers and sellers in the open market and bears most weight. Cost Approach [$534,000(r)] supports the range of value indicated by the Sales Comparison Approach. The subject is in an area of primarily owner occupied residences with few rentals. Therefore, there is not enough data available to develop a reliable Gross Rent Multiplier.

This appraisal is made ☒ "as is", ☐ subject to completion per plans and specifications on the basis of a hypothetical condition that the improvements have been completed, ☐ subject to the following repairs or alterations on the basis of a hypothetical condition that the repairs or alterations have been completed, or ☐ subject to the following required inspection based on the extraordinary assumption that the condition or deficiency does not require alteration or repair:

Based on a complete visual inspection of the interior and exterior areas of the subject property, defined scope of work, statement of assumptions and limiting conditions, and appraiser's certification, my (our) opinion of the market value, as defined, of the real property that is the subject of this report is $, as of , which is the date of inspection and the effective date of this appraisal.

RECONCILIATION

Freddie Mac Form 70 March 2005 UAD Version 9/2011 Page 2 of 6 Fannie Mae Form 1004 March 2005

Form 1004UAD — "WinTOTAL" appraisal software by a la mode, inc. — 1-800-ALAMODE

Figure 29: Uniform Residential Appraisal Report Page 2 of 14

Main File No. 15-0365g Page #3

Uniform Residential Appraisal Report

20
File # 15-0365g

USPAP Standards Rules 1-5 (a) and (b) require an appraiser, when the value opinion to be developed is market value, and if such information is available to the appraiser in the normal course of business, to analyze(1) all agreements of sale, option, or listings of the subject property current as of the effective date of the appraisal and (2) all sales of the subject property that occurred within three(3) years prior to the effective date of the appraisal. USPAP Standards Rules 2-2(a)(ix), (b)(xi), and (c)(ix) call for the written report to contain sufficient information to indicate compliance with the sales history requirement. This appraiser is not aware of any supplemental standards developed by Fannie Mae to expand the scope of this requirement. Owner transfers (ie., transfers which do not alienate title) and transfers for finance purposes are not considered by this appraiser to be applicable and therefore are not included within this report.

The existence of termites, beetles, fungus and dry rot which may, or may not, be present on the property, was not observed by me nor do I have any knowledge of the existence of such in or on the property other than as noted in this appraisal.
The value estimated in this report is based upon the assumption that the property is not negatively impacted by the existence of hazardous substances or detrimental environmental conditions. I am not an expert in identification of hazardous substances or detrimental environmental conditions. My routine inspection of and inquiries about the subject property did not develop any information that indicated any apparent significant hazardous substances or detrimental environmental conditions which would affect the subject property negatively. It is possible that tests and inspections made by a qualified hazardous substance and environmental expert would reveal the existence of hazardous materials and environmental conditions on or around the property that would negatively affect its value. If the client has any questions regarding these items, is the client's responsibility to order the appropriate inspections. The appraiser does not have the skill or expertise needed to make such inspections. The appraiser assumes no responsibility for these items.

Various "submarkets" can exist within the same neighborhood. These intertwined "submarkets" can have different predominant price ranges, age ranges, land use, and housing mix. The neighborhood generally has compatible social, economic, government, and environmental forces on property values.

Scope of Work is for a walk thru inspection only and it is assumed that there are no structural defects hidden by floor or wall coverings or any other hidden or unapparent conditions of the property; that all mechanical equipment, well, septic and appliances are in good working condition, and that all electrical components and the roofing are in good condition.

Supplement to Certification Statement # 23. The Intended User of this appraisal report is the Lender Client. The Intended Use is to evaluate the property that is the subject of this appraisal for a mortgage finance transaction, subject to stated Scope of Work, purpose of the appraisal reporting requirements of this appraisal report form, and Definition of Market Value. No additional Intended Users are identified by the appraiser.
Note: This supplement to Certification Statement #23 has been developed by Fannie Mae in cooperation with the Appraisal Institute and is acceptable to Fannie Mae

I have performed no services, as an appraiser or in any other capacity, regarding the property that is the subject of this report within the three-year period immediately preceding acceptance of this assignment.

ADDITIONAL COMMENTS

COST APPROACH TO VALUE (not required by Fannie Mae)

Provide adequate information for the lender/client to replicate the below cost figures and calculations.
Support for the opinion of site value (summary of comparable land sales or other methods for estimating site value) Land value from abstraction. NO CURRENT LAND SALES EXIST TO USE FOR COMPARABLES. THEREFORE, SITE VALUE WAS ABSTRACTED FROM CURRENT SALES AND LISTINGS. BUILDING COSTS HAVE NOT DECREASED SINCE THE MARKET HAS STABILIZED WHICH RESULTS IN SUBSTANTIAL REDUCTIONS IN LAND VALUE.

ESTIMATED ☐ REPRODUCTION OR ☒ REPLACEMENT COST NEW	OPINION OF SITE VALUE	=$ 135,000
Source of cost data Building-Cost.Net Estimator	DWELLING 1,806 Sq.Ft. @ $ 196.70	=$ 355,240
Quality rating from cost service C4 Effective date of cost data 12/2015	Basement 288 Sq.Ft. @ $ 50.00	=$ 14,400
Comments on Cost Approach (gross living area calculations, depreciation, etc.)		=$
Land/improvement ratios typical for area. The Cost Approach is	Garage/Carport Sq.Ft. @ $	=$
developed to assist the underwriter in processing the loan and is not	Total Estimate of Cost-New	=$ 369,640
intended for fire insurance underwriting purposes.	Less Physical / Functional / External	
	Depreciation 49,273	=$(49,273)
	Depreciated Cost of Improvements	=$ 320,367
	"As-is" Value of Site Improvements	=$ 78,500
Estimated Remaining Economic Life (HUD and VA only) 65 Years	INDICATED VALUE BY COST APPROACH	=$ 533,867

COST APPROACH

INCOME APPROACH TO VALUE (not required by Fannie Mae)

Estimated Monthly Market Rent $ X Gross Rent Multiplier = $ Indicated Value by Income Approach
Summary of Income Approach (including support for market rent and GRM) The subject is in an area of primarily owner occupied residences with few rentals. Therefore, there is not enough data available to develop a reliable Gross Rent Multiplier.

INCOME

PROJECT INFORMATION FOR PUDs (if applicable)

Is the developer/builder in control of the Homeowners' Association (HOA)? ☐ Yes ☒ No Unit type(s) ☒ Detached ☐ Attached
Provide the following information for PUDs ONLY if the developer/builder is in control of the HOA and the subject property is an attached dwelling unit.
Legal Name of Project
Total number of phases Total number of units Total number of units sold
Total number of units rented Total number of units for sale Data source(s)
Was the project created by the conversion of existing building(s) into a PUD? ☐ Yes ☐ No If Yes, date of conversion.
Does the project contain any multi-dwelling units? ☐ Yes ☐ No Data Source
Are the units, common elements, and recreation facilities complete? ☐ Yes ☐ No If No, describe the status of completion.

Are the common elements leased to or by the Homeowners' Association? ☐ Yes ☐ No If Yes, describe the rental terms and options.

Describe common elements and recreational facilities.

PUD INFORMATION

Freddie Mac Form 70 March 2005 UAD Version 9/2011 Page 3 of 6 Fannie Mae Form 1004 March 2005

Form 1004UAD — "WinTOTAL" appraisal software by a la mode, inc. — 1-800-ALAMODE

Figure 29: Uniform Residential Appraisal Report Page 3 of 14

Main File No. 15-0365g Page #4

Uniform Residential Appraisal Report

20
File # 15-0365g

This report form is designed to report an appraisal of a one-unit property or a one-unit property with an accessory unit; including a unit in a planned unit development (PUD). This report form is not designed to report an appraisal of a manufactured home or a unit in a condominium or cooperative project.

This appraisal report is subject to the following scope of work, intended use, intended user, definition of market value, statement of assumptions and limiting conditions, and certifications. Modifications, additions, or deletions to the intended use, intended user, definition of market value, or assumptions and limiting conditions are not permitted. The appraiser may expand the scope of work to include any additional research or analysis necessary based on the complexity of this appraisal assignment. Modifications or deletions to the certifications are also not permitted. However, additional certifications that do not constitute material alterations to this appraisal report, such as those required by law or those related to the appraiser's continuing education or membership in an appraisal organization, are permitted.

SCOPE OF WORK: The scope of work for this appraisal is defined by the complexity of this appraisal assignment and the reporting requirements of this appraisal report form, including the following definition of market value, statement of assumptions and limiting conditions, and certifications. The appraiser must, at a minimum: (1) perform a complete visual inspection of the interior and exterior areas of the subject property, (2) inspect the neighborhood, (3) inspect each of the comparable sales from at least the street, (4) research, verify, and analyze data from reliable public and/or private sources, and (5) report his or her analysis, opinions, and conclusions in this appraisal report.

INTENDED USE: The intended use of this appraisal report is for the lender/client to evaluate the property that is the subject of this appraisal for a mortgage finance transaction.

INTENDED USER: The intended user of this appraisal report is the lender/client.

DEFINITION OF MARKET VALUE: The most probable price which a property should bring in a competitive and open market under all conditions requisite to a fair sale, the buyer and seller, each acting prudently, knowledgeably and assuming the price is not affected by undue stimulus. Implicit in this definition is the consummation of a sale as of a specified date and the passing of title from seller to buyer under conditions whereby: (1) buyer and seller are typically motivated; (2) both parties are well informed or well advised, and each acting in what he or she considers his or her own best interest; (3) a reasonable time is allowed for exposure in the open market; (4) payment is made in terms of cash in U. S. dollars or in terms of financial arrangements comparable thereto; and (5) the price represents the normal consideration for the property sold unaffected by special or creative financing or sales concessions* granted by anyone associated with the sale.

*Adjustments to the comparables must be made for special or creative financing or sales concessions. No adjustments are necessary for those costs which are normally paid by sellers as a result of tradition or law in a market area; these costs are readily identifiable since the seller pays these costs in virtually all sales transactions. Special or creative financing adjustments can be made to the comparable property by comparisons to financing terms offered by a third party institutional lender that is not already involved in the property or transaction. Any adjustment should not be calculated on a mechanical dollar for dollar cost of the financing or concession but the dollar amount of any adjustment should approximate the market's reaction to the financing or concessions based on the appraiser's judgment.

STATEMENT OF ASSUMPTIONS AND LIMITING CONDITIONS: The appraiser's certification in this report is subject to the following assumptions and limiting conditions:

1. The appraiser will not be responsible for matters of a legal nature that affect either the property being appraised or the title to it, except for information that he or she became aware of during the research involved in performing this appraisal. The appraiser assumes that the title is good and marketable and will not render any opinions about the title.

2. The appraiser has provided a sketch in this appraisal report to show the approximate dimensions of the improvements. The sketch is included only to assist the reader in visualizing the property and understanding the appraiser's determination of its size.

3. The appraiser has examined the available flood maps that are provided by the Federal Emergency Management Agency (or other data sources) and has noted in this appraisal report whether any portion of the subject site is located in an identified Special Flood Hazard Area. Because the appraiser is not a surveyor, he or she makes no guarantees, express or implied, regarding this determination.

4. The appraiser will not give testimony or appear in court because he or she made an appraisal of the property in question, unless specific arrangements to do so have been made beforehand, or as otherwise required by law.

5. The appraiser has noted in this appraisal report any adverse conditions (such as needed repairs, deterioration, the presence of hazardous wastes, toxic substances, etc.) observed during the inspection of the subject property or that he or she became aware of during the research involved in performing the appraisal. Unless otherwise stated in this appraisal report, the appraiser has no knowledge of any hidden or unapparent physical deficiencies or adverse conditions of the property (such as, but not limited to, needed repairs, deterioration, the presence of hazardous wastes, toxic substances, adverse environmental conditions, etc.) that would make the property less valuable, and has assumed that there are no such conditions and makes no guarantees or warranties, express or implied. The appraiser will not be responsible for any such conditions that do exist or for any engineering or testing that might be required to discover whether such conditions exist. Because the appraiser is not an expert in the field of environmental hazards, this appraisal report must not be considered as an environmental assessment of the property.

6. The appraiser has based his or her appraisal report and valuation conclusion for an appraisal that is subject to satisfactory completion, repairs, or alterations on the assumption that the completion, repairs, or alterations of the subject property will be performed in a professional manner.

Freddie Mac Form 70 March 2005 UAD Version 9/2011 Page 4 of 6 Fannie Mae Form 1004 March 2005

Form 1004UAD — "WinTOTAL" appraisal software by a la mode, inc. — 1-800-ALAMODE

Figure 29: Uniform Residential Appraisal Report Page 4 of 14

Main File No. 15-0365g Page #5

Uniform Residential Appraisal Report

20
File # 15-0365g

APPRAISER'S CERTIFICATION: The Appraiser certifies and agrees that:

1. I have, at a minimum, developed and reported this appraisal in accordance with the scope of work requirements stated in this appraisal report.

2. I performed a complete visual inspection of the interior and exterior areas of the subject property. I reported the condition of the improvements in factual, specific terms. I identified and reported the physical deficiencies that could affect the livability, soundness, or structural integrity of the property.

3. I performed this appraisal in accordance with the requirements of the Uniform Standards of Professional Appraisal Practice that were adopted and promulgated by the Appraisal Standards Board of The Appraisal Foundation and that were in place at the time this appraisal report was prepared.

4. I developed my opinion of the market value of the real property that is the subject of this report based on the sales comparison approach to value. I have adequate comparable market data to develop a reliable sales comparison approach for this appraisal assignment. I further certify that I considered the cost and income approaches to value but did not develop them, unless otherwise indicated in this report.

5. I researched, verified, analyzed, and reported on any current agreement for sale for the subject property, any offering for sale of the subject property in the twelve months prior to the effective date of this appraisal, and the prior sales of the subject property for a minimum of three years prior to the effective date of this appraisal, unless otherwise indicated in this report.

6. I researched, verified, analyzed, and reported on the prior sales of the comparable sales for a minimum of one year prior to the date of sale of the comparable sale, unless otherwise indicated in this report.

7. I selected and used comparable sales that are locationally, physically, and functionally the most similar to the subject property.

8. I have not used comparable sales that were the result of combining a land sale with the contract purchase price of a home that has been built or will be built on the land.

9. I have reported adjustments to the comparable sales that reflect the market's reaction to the differences between the subject property and the comparable sales.

10. I verified, from a disinterested source, all information in this report that was provided by parties who have a financial interest in the sale or financing of the subject property.

11. I have knowledge and experience in appraising this type of property in this market area.

12. I am aware of, and have access to, the necessary and appropriate public and private data sources, such as multiple listing services, tax assessment records, public land records and other such data sources for the area in which the property is located.

13. I obtained the information, estimates, and opinions furnished by other parties and expressed in this appraisal report from reliable sources that I believe to be true and correct.

14. I have taken into consideration the factors that have an impact on value with respect to the subject neighborhood, subject property, and the proximity of the subject property to adverse influences in the development of my opinion of market value. I have noted in this appraisal report any adverse conditions (such as, but not limited to, needed repairs, deterioration, the presence of hazardous wastes, toxic substances, adverse environmental conditions, etc.) observed during the inspection of the subject property or that I became aware of during the research involved in performing this appraisal. I have considered these adverse conditions in my analysis of the property value, and have reported on the effect of the conditions on the value and marketability of the subject property.

15. I have not knowingly withheld any significant information from this appraisal report and, to the best of my knowledge, all statements and information in this appraisal report are true and correct.

16. I stated in this appraisal report my own personal, unbiased, and professional analysis, opinions, and conclusions, which are subject only to the assumptions and limiting conditions in this appraisal report.

17. I have no present or prospective interest in the property that is the subject of this report, and I have no present or prospective personal interest or bias with respect to the participants in the transaction. I did not base, either partially or completely, my analysis and/or opinion of market value in this appraisal report on the race, color, religion, sex, age, marital status, handicap, familial status, or national origin of either the prospective owners or occupants of the subject property or of the present owners or occupants of the properties in the vicinity of the subject property or on any other basis prohibited by law.

18. My employment and/or compensation for performing this appraisal or any future or anticipated appraisals was not conditioned on any agreement or understanding, written or otherwise, that I would report (or present analysis supporting) a predetermined specific value, a predetermined minimum value, a range or direction in value, a value that favors the cause of any party, or the attainment of a specific result or occurrence of a specific subsequent event (such as approval of a pending mortgage loan application).

19. I personally prepared all conclusions and opinions about the real estate that were set forth in this appraisal report. If I relied on significant real property appraisal assistance from any individual or individuals in the performance of this appraisal or the preparation of this appraisal report, I have named such individual(s) and disclosed the specific tasks performed in this appraisal report. I certify that any individual so named is qualified to perform the tasks. I have not authorized anyone to make a change to any item in this appraisal report; therefore, any change made to this appraisal is unauthorized and I will take no responsibility for it.

20. I identified the lender/client in this appraisal report who is the individual, organization, or agent for the organization that ordered and will receive this appraisal report.

Freddie Mac Form 70 March 2005 UAD Version 9/2011 Page 5 of 6 Fannie Mae Form 1004 March 2005

Form 1004UAD — "WinTOTAL" appraisal software by a la mode, inc. — 1-800-ALAMODE

Figure 29: Uniform Residential Appraisal Report Page 5 of 14

Main File No. 15-0365gl Page #6

Uniform Residential Appraisal Report

20
File # 15-0365g

21. The lender/client may disclose or distribute this appraisal report to: the borrower; another lender at the request of the borrower; the mortgagee or its successors and assigns; mortgage insurers; government sponsored enterprises; other secondary market participants; data collection or reporting services; professional appraisal organizations; any department, agency, or instrumentality of the United States; and any state, the District of Columbia, or other jurisdictions; without having to obtain the appraiser's or supervisory appraiser's (if applicable) consent. Such consent must be obtained before this appraisal report may be disclosed or distributed to any other party (including, but not limited to, the public through advertising, public relations, news, sales, or other media).

22. I am aware that any disclosure or distribution of this appraisal report by me or the lender/client may be subject to certain laws and regulations. Further, I am also subject to the provisions of the Uniform Standards of Professional Appraisal Practice that pertain to disclosure or distribution by me.

23. The borrower, another lender at the request of the borrower, the mortgagee or its successors and assigns, mortgage insurers, government sponsored enterprises, and other secondary market participants may rely on this appraisal report as part of any mortgage finance transaction that involves any one or more of these parties.

24. If this appraisal report was transmitted as an "electronic record" containing my "electronic signature," as those terms are defined in applicable federal and/or state laws (excluding audio and video recordings), or a facsimile transmission of this appraisal report containing a copy or representation of my signature, the appraisal report shall be as effective, enforceable and valid as if a paper version of this appraisal report were delivered containing my original hand written signature.

25. Any intentional or negligent misrepresentation(s) contained in this appraisal report may result in civil liability and/or criminal penalties including, but not limited to, fine or imprisonment or both under the provisions of Title 18, United States Code, Section 1001, et seq., or similar state laws.

SUPERVISORY APPRAISER'S CERTIFICATION: The Supervisory Appraiser certifies and agrees that:

1. I directly supervised the appraiser for this appraisal assignment, have read the appraisal report, and agree with the appraiser's analysis, opinions, statements, conclusions, and the appraiser's certification.

2. I accept full responsibility for the contents of this appraisal report including, but not limited to, the appraiser's analysis, opinions, statements, conclusions, and the appraiser's certification.

3. The appraiser identified in this appraisal report is either a sub-contractor or an employee of the supervisory appraiser (or the appraisal firm), is qualified to perform this appraisal, and is acceptable to perform this appraisal under the applicable state law.

4. This appraisal report complies with the Uniform Standards of Professional Appraisal Practice that were adopted and promulgated by the Appraisal Standards Board of The Appraisal Foundation and that were in place at the time this appraisal report was prepared.

5. If this appraisal report was transmitted as an "electronic record" containing my "electronic signature," as those terms are defined in applicable federal and/or state laws (excluding audio and video recordings), or a facsimile transmission of this appraisal report containing a copy or representation of my signature, the appraisal report shall be as effective, enforceable and valid as if a paper version of this appraisal report were delivered containing my original hand written signature.

APPRAISER

Signature
Name Gordon Giordano
Company Name The Appraisal Office
Company Address PO Box 1329
Fort Bragg, CA 95437
Telephone Number (707) 964-5800
Email Address gordy@theappraisaloffice.biz
Date of Signature and Report 12/26/2015
Effective Date of Appraisal
State Certification # AR018253
or State License #
or Other (describe) State #
State CA
Expiration Date of Certification or License 10/06/2016

ADDRESS OF PROPERTY APPRAISED

Cazadero, CA 95421
APPRAISED VALUE OF SUBJECT PROPERTY $

LENDER/CLIENT
Name
Company Name W.J. Bradley Mortgage Capital, LLC
Company Address 100 West Towne Ridge Parkway, Suite 300,
Sandy, UT 84070
Email Address

SUPERVISORY APPRAISER (ONLY IF REQUIRED)

Signature
Name
Company Name
Company Address
Telephone Number
Email Address
Date of Signature
State Certification #
or State License #
State
Expiration Date of Certification or License

SUBJECT PROPERTY

☐ Did not inspect subject property
☐ Did inspect exterior of subject property from street
Date of Inspection
☐ Did inspect interior and exterior of subject property
Date of Inspection

COMPARABLE SALES

☐ Did not inspect exterior of comparable sales from street
☐ Did inspect exterior of comparable sales from street
Date of Inspection

Freddie Mac Form 70 March 2005 UAD Version 9/2011 Page 6 of 6 Fannie Mae Form 1004 March 2005

Form 1004UAD — "WinTOTAL" appraisal software by a la mode, inc. — 1-800-ALAMODE

Figure 29: Uniform Residential Appraisal Report Page 6 of 14

Main File No. 15-0365gl Page #1

UNIFORM APPRAISAL DATASET (UAD) DEFINITIONS ADDENDUM

(Source: Fannie Mae UAD Appendix D: UAD Field-Specific Standardization Requirements)

Abbreviations Used in Data Standardization Text

Abbreviation	Full Name	Fields Where This Abbreviation May Appear
ac	Acres	Area, Site
AdjPrk	Adjacent to Park	Location
AdjPwr	Adjacent to Power Lines	Location
A	Adverse	Location & View
ArmLth	Arms Length Sale	Sale or Financing Concessions
ba	Bathroom(s)	Basement & Finished Rooms Below Grade
br	Bedroom	Basement & Finished Rooms Below Grade
B	Beneficial	Location & View
Cash	Cash	Sale or Financing Concessions
CtySky	City View Skyline View	View
CtyStr	City Street View	View
Comm	Commercial Influence	Location
c	Contracted Date	Date of Sale/Time
Conv	Conventional	Sale or Financing Concessions
CrtOrd	Court Ordered Sale	Sale or Financing Concessions
DOM	Days On Market	Data Sources
e	Expiration Date	Date of Sale/Time
Estate	Estate Sale	Sale or Financing Concessions
FHA	Federal Housing Authority	Sale or Financing Concessions
GlfCse	Golf Course	Location
Glfvw	Golf Course View	View
Ind	Industrial	Location & View
in	Interior Only Stairs	Basement & Finished Rooms Below Grade
Lndfl	Landfill	Location
LtdSght	Limited Sight	View
Listing	Listing	Sale or Financing Concessions
Mtn	Mountain View	View
N	Neutral	Location & View
NonArm	Non-Arms Length Sale	Sale or Financing Concessions
BsyRd	Busy Road	Location
o	Other	Basement & Finished Rooms Below Grade
Prk	Park View	View
Pstrl	Pastoral View	View
PwrLn	Power Lines	View
PubTrn	Public Transportation	Location
rr	Recreational (Rec) Room	Basement & Finished Rooms Below Grade
Relo	Relocation Sale	Sale or Financing Concessions
REO	REO Sale	Sale or Financing Concessions
Res	Residential	Location & View
RH	USDA - Rural Housing	Sale or Financing Concessions
s	Settlement Date	Date of Sale/Time
Short	Short Sale	Sale or Financing Concessions
sf	Square Feet	Area, Site, Basement
sqm	Square Meters	Area, Site
Unk	Unknown	Date of Sale/Time
VA	Veterans Administration	Sale or Financing Concessions
w	Withdrawn Date	Date of Sale/Time
wo	Walk Out Basement	Basement & Finished Rooms Below Grade
wu	Walk Up Basement	Basement & Finished Rooms Below Grade
WtrFr	Water Frontage	Location
Wtr	Water View	View
Woods	Woods View	View

Other Appraiser-Defined Abbreviations

Abbreviation	Full Name	Fields Where This Abbreviation May Appear

UAD Version 9/2011 (Updated 4/2012)

Form UADDEFINE1 — "WinTOTAL" appraisal software by a la mode, inc. — 1-800-ALAMODE

Figure 29: Uniform Residential Appraisal Report Page 7 of 14

Main File No. 15-0365g Page #7

Uniform Residential Appraisal Report

20
File # 15-0365g

FEATURE	SUBJECT	COMPARABLE SALE # 4		COMPARABLE SALE # 5		COMPARABLE SALE # 6	
Address Cazadero, CA 95421		1050 Cazadero Hwy Cazadero, CA 95421		21925 Russian River Ave Villa Grande, CA 95462		835 Cazadero Hwy Cazadero, CA 95421	
Proximity to Subject		0.29 miles NE		1.77 miles E		0.32 miles E	
Sale Price	$		$ 415,000		$ 535,000		$ 459,000
Sale Price/Gross Liv. Area	$ sq.ft.	$ 381.43 sq.ft.		$ 412.81 sq.ft.		$ 297.09 sq.ft.	
Data Source(s)		BareisMLS#21522689;DOM 22		BareisMLS#21528245;DOM 21		BareisMLS#21520606;DOM 124	
Verification Source(s)		DOC#89143		Active Listing		Active Listing	
VALUE ADJUSTMENTS	DESCRIPTION	DESCRIPTION	+(-) $ Adjustment	DESCRIPTION	+(-) $ Adjustment	DESCRIPTION	+(-) $ Adjustment
Sales or Financing Concessions		ArmLth Conv;0		Listing Listing;0		Listing Listing;0	
Date of Sale/Time		s10/15;c09/15		Active	-5,350	Active	-4,590
Location	N;Rural;	N;Rural;		N;Rural;		N;Rural;	
Leasehold/Fee Simple	Fee Simple	Fee Simple		Fee Simple		Fee Simple	
Site	1.15 ac	7,802 sf	0	6,098 sf	+1,010	1.79 ac	0
View	N;Mtn;	N;Woods;	0	N;Woods;	0	N;Woods;	0
Design (Style)	DT2;Modern	DT2;A-Frame	0	DT1;Cottage	0	DT2;Contemp	0
Quality of Construction	Q4	Q4	+20,750	Q4		Q4	
Actual Age	40	41	0	14	0	38	0
Condition	C4	C4	+20,750	C4		C4	
Above Grade	Total / Bdrms. / Baths	Total / Bdrms. / Baths		Total / Bdrms. / Baths		Total / Bdrms. / Baths	
Room Count	6 / 2 / 2.0	5 / 2 / 1.0	+10,000	5 / 2 / 2.0	0	5 / 2 / 2.0	0
Gross Living Area	1,806 sq.ft.	1,088 sq.ft.	+23,335	1,296 sq.ft.	+16,575	1,545 sq.ft.	+8,482
Basement & Finished Rooms Below Grade	288sf0sfwo	0sf	0	0sf	0	0sf	0
Functional Utility	Good	Good		Good		Good	
Heating/Cooling	FAU/None	GWH/None	0	FAU/None		Stove/None	0
Energy Efficient Items	Code	Code		Code		Code	
Garage/Carport	2dw	None	0	None	0	1ga5dw	-1,000
Porch/Patio/Deck	Patio/Deck	Patio/Deck		Deck	0	Patio/Deck	
Amenities	None	None		Gazebo	-2,500	Greenhouse	-2,500
Amenities	None	Storage	-2,500	Shed	-2,500	Storage	-2,500
Assessor's Parcel #	097-250-019	097-060-015	0	095-043-004	0	097-230-005	0
Net Adjustment (Total)		☒ + ☐ -	$ 72,335	☒ + ☐ -	$ 7,235	☐ + ☒ -	$ -2,108
Adjusted Sale Price of Comparables		Net Adj. 17.4 % Gross Adj. 18.6 %	$ 487,335	Net Adj. 1.4 % Gross Adj. 5.2 %	$ 542,235	Net Adj. 0.5 % Gross Adj. 4.2 %	$ 456,892

Report the results of the research and analysis of the prior sale or transfer history of the subject property and comparable sales (report additional prior sales on page 3).

ITEM	SUBJECT	COMPARABLE SALE # 4	COMPARABLE SALE # 5	COMPARABLE SALE # 6
Date of Prior Sale/Transfer				
Price of Prior Sale/Transfer				
Data Source(s)	REALIST	REALIST	REALIST	REALIST
Effective Date of Data Source(s)	12/01/2015	12/01/2015	12/01/2015	12/01/2015

Analysis of prior sale or transfer history of the subject property and comparable sales

Analysis/Comments

Freddie Mac Form 70 March 2005 UAD Version 9/2011 Fannie Mae Form 1004 March 2005

Form 1004UAD.(AC) — "WinTOTAL" appraisal software by a la mode, inc. — 1-800-ALAMODE

Figure 29: Uniform Residential Appraisal Report Page 8 of 14

Main File No. 15-0365g Page #8

Loan # 20
File # 15-0365g

USPAP Compliance Addendum

Borrower					
Property Address					
City	Cazadero	County		State CA	Zip Code 95421
Lender/Client	W.J. Bradley Mortgage Capital, LLC				

APPRAISAL AND REPORT IDENTIFICATION

This Appraisal Report is one of the following types:

☒ Appraisal Report — This report was prepared in accordance with the requirements of the Appraisal Report option of USPAP Standards Rule 2-2(a).

☐ Restricted Appraisal Report — This report was prepared in accordance with the requirements of the Restricted Appraisal Report option of USPAP Standards Rule 2-2(b). The intended user of this report is limited to the identified client. This is a Restricted Appraisal Report and the rationale for how the appraiser arrived at the opinions and conclusions set forth in the report may not be understood properly without the additional information in the appraiser's workfile.

ADDITIONAL CERTIFICATIONS

I certify that, to the best of my knowledge and belief:

- The statements of fact contained in this report are true and correct.
- The report analyses, opinions, and conclusions are limited only by the reported assumptions and are my personal, impartial, and unbiased professional analyses, opinions, and conclusions.
- I have no (or the specified) present or prospective interest in the property that is the subject of this report and no (or specified) personal interest with respect to the parties involved.
- I have no bias with respect to the property that is the subject of this report or the parties involved with this assignment.
- My engagement in this assignment was not contingent upon developing or reporting predetermined results.
- My compensation for completing this assignment is not contingent upon the development or reporting of a predetermined value or direction in value that favors the cause of the client, the amount of the value opinion, the attainment of a stipulated result, or the occurrence of a subsequent event directly related to the intended use of this appraisal.
- My analyses, opinions, and conclusions were developed and this report has been prepared, in conformity with the Uniform Standards of Professional Appraisal Practice.
- This appraisal report was prepared in accordance with the requirements of Title XI of FIRREA and any implementing regulations.

PRIOR SERVICES

☐ I have NOT performed services, as an appraiser or in any other capacity, regarding the property that is the subject of this report within the three-year period immediately preceding acceptance of this assignment.

☒ I HAVE performed services, as an appraiser or in another capacity, regarding the property that is the subject of this report within the three-year period immediately preceding acceptance of this assignment. Those services are described in the comments below.

PROPERTY INSPECTION

☐ I have NOT made a personal inspection of the property that is the subject of this report.

☒ I HAVE made a personal inspection of the property that is the subject of this report.

APPRAISAL ASSISTANCE

Unless otherwise noted, no one provided significant real property appraisal assistance to the person signing this certification. If anyone did provide significant assistance, they are hereby identified along with a summary of the extent of the assistance provided in the report.

Patricia Rangel (License # AT043432) materially participated in the research and preparation of this appraisal report in compliance of the requirements of Category 1 experience as set forth in the State of California Bureau of Real Estate Appraiser Licensing handbook.

ADDITIONAL COMMENTS

Additional USPAP related issues requiring disclosure and/or any state mandated requirements: Prior services include an interior appraisal on 7/9/2015.

MARKETING TIME AND EXPOSURE TIME FOR THE SUBJECT PROPERTY

☐ A reasonable marketing time for the subject property is 60-180 day(s) utilizing market conditions pertinent to the appraisal assignment.

☐ A reasonable exposure time for the subject property is 60-180 day(s).

APPRAISER	SUPERVISORY APPRAISER (ONLY IF REQUIRED)
Signature	Signature
Name Gordon Giordano	Name
Date of Signature 12/26/2015	Date of Signature
State Certification # AR018253	State Certification #
or State License #	or State License #
State CA	State
Expiration Date of Certification or License 10/06/2016	Expiration Date of Certification or License
	Supervisory Appraiser Inspection of Subject Property
Effective Date of Appraisal 12/23/2015	☐ Did Not ☐ Exterior-only from Street ☐ Interior and Exterior

USPAP Compliance Addendum 2014 — Page 1 of 1

Form ID14EC — "WinTOTAL" appraisal software by a la mode, inc. — 1-800-ALAMODE

Figure 29: Uniform Residential Appraisal Report Page 9 of 14

Main File No. 15-0365g Page #9

Supplemental Addendum

File No. 15-0365g

Borrower					
Property Address					
City	Cazadero	County		State CA	Zip Code 95421
Lender/Client	W.J. Bradley Mortgage Capital, LLC				

- URAR : Subject - Overall Condition of the Property

The subject is given an effective age of 10 years to reflect good care, maintenance, and additions. The original residence was a 2 bedroom, 1 bath home built in 1975 and was approximately 1,002 sqft. In 1997 a bedroom and a bath were added to the residence (Permit # B-132043) County records only reflects the original living area and does not reflect the addition in the living area. Many homes in the subject's neighborhood have additions and the County does not report these additions in living area. Therefore it is common to have living areas substantially larger than what is reported by the County. The subject reflects minimal wear and tear with quality appointments and finishes that are custom builder grade. The subject meets the definition of C4 and Q4 ratings.

- URAR : Sales Comparison Analysis - Summary of Sales Comparison Approach

The comparables are the most recent and most similar to the subject. Living area is adjusted at $32.50/sqft.derived from the allocated matched pair analysis. Lots have similar utility with a modest adjustment of $1,000/acre when the difference is over 1 acre. Baths are adjusted at $10,000/bath and $5,000/half bath. Age is of little significance to the typical buyer with condition and quality being very Important. Rural properties generally have a limited housing stock with a limited number of listings and closed sales. This often makes it necessary to go back over 9 months for comparables and to go a substantial distance for meaningful comparables. **In the Fannie Mae Handbook for Appraisers it states: "rural areas often have much less real estate activity than more populated locations and the activity that does take place may be on a wide variety of property types. Thus using the sales comparison approach in rural areas: ....you may use older comparable sales (older than 12 months)...comparable sales that are farther away than is typically desired.** In the case of this appraisal report it has been necessary to go back over 9 months for some of the comparables. Basements are not common in the subject's market area and are generally no recognized by the real estate community with no real input into the local MLS which results in a lack of data sufficient to make a market based adjustment for basements. Therefore there are no adjustments made for the subject's basement.

Comp # 1 is adjusted for a seller credit, less living area, a 2 car garage, storage, and a shop.

Comp # 2 is adjusted for larger site size, superior creekside view, more living area, a 2 car garage, and outbuildings.

Comp # 3 is adjusted for a superior creekside view, 1 less bath, less living area, and a 1 car carport.

Comp # 4 is inferior to the subject in quality, condition, with 1 less bath, less living area, and storage.. Comp # 4 has substantially more wear and tear than the subject, and is comprised of standard builder quality and workmanship. Comp # 4 is an "A" frame style and is more of a non-traditional design. The market does not have enough data to develop an adjustment for the "A" frame style as compared to a more traditional style. Therefore, no adjustment is made for the "A" style design. Consequently, Comp # 4 is given least weight.

The difference between the upper and lower range of value ($49,000) indicated by the Sales Comparison Approach (Closed Sales) is approx. 9.6% of the opinion of value stated herein ($512,000). This is considered a narrow range of value is common in rural areas. Most weight is given to Comps #1 & 2 as they are most similar to the subject in primary features. Strong consideration is given to Comp#3. Least weight is given to Comp # 4 due to a non-traditional design. The weighted opinion of value (Comps # 1 & 2 given most weight) is $512,000.

Comp # 5 is adjusted for listing status, less living area, a gazebo, and a shed.

Comp # 6 is adjusted for listing status, less living area, a 1 car garage, greenhouse, and storage.

It is this appraisers opinion that the reasonable exposure time for the subject property would be 60-180 days.

There was a carbon monoxide detector present in the home, and the hot water heater was double strapped at the time of the inspection.

Our office has appraised this property in the past 36 months prior to the effective date of this appraisal.

NEIGHBORHOOD BOUNDARIES DUE TO HWY, FREEWAY, ROAD, TRACKS, OR WATER WAYS

There are major roadway and creeks that separate the subject from some of the comparables. These do not pose any sort of market division between the subject and the comparables and have no impact on value or marketability.

Due to the subject and comparables location, the USPS address tracking system does not recognize the properties, and therefore cannot be converted to USPS standards.

Signature		Signature	
Name	Gordon Giordano	Name	
Date Signed	12/26/2015	Date Signed	
State Certification #	AR018253 State CA	State Certification #	State
Or State License #	State	Or State License #	State

Form TADD2 — "WinTOTAL" appraisal software by a la mode, inc. — 1-800-ALAMODE

Figure 29: Uniform Residential Appraisal Report Page 10 of 14

Main File No. 15-0365g Page #10

Supplemental Addendum File No. 15-0365g

Borrower			
Property Address			
City Cazadero	County	State CA	Zip Code 95421
Lender/Client W.J. Bradley Mortgage Capital, LLC			

12/26/2015

Per the lender, the legal description has been amended to show MAP D6 109-11. A preliminary title report, with the legal description, was not available to the appraiser at the time of preparation of this report.

As stated above "Rural properties generally have a limited housing stock with a limited number of listings and closed sales. This often makes it necessary to go back over 9 months for comparables and to go a substantial distance for meaningful comparables. **In the Fannie Mae Handbook for Appraisers it states: "rural areas often have much less real estate activity than more populated locations and the activity that does take place may be on a wide variety of property types. Thus using the sales comparison approach in rural areas: ....you may use older comparable sales (older than 12 months)...comparable sales that are farther away than is typically desired.** In the case of this appraisal report it has been necessary to go back over 9 months for some of the comparables."

As stated above "The difference between the upper and lower range of value ($49,000) indicated by the Sales Comparison Approach (Closed Sales) is approx. 9.6% of the opinion of value stated herein ($512,000). This is considered a narrow range of value is common in rural areas." Although there is a large difference between the actual age and the effective age, the difference between the actual age and the effective age is not the only criteria to consider.

Again, as stated above "The difference between the upper and lower range of value ($49,000) indicated by the Sales Comparison Approach (Closed Sales) is approx. 9.6% of the opinion of value stated herein ($512,000). This is considered a narrow range of value is common in rural areas. Most weight is given to Comps #1 & 2 as they are most similar to the subject in primary features. Strong consideration is given to Comp#3. Least weight is given to Comp # 4 due to a non-traditional design. The weighted opinion of value (Comps # 1 & 2 given most weight) is $512,000.". The comparables presented are the best indicators of the subjects value and the best avaiable.

The subject has no car storage.

Signature	Signature
Name Gordon Giordano	Name
Date Signed 12/26/2015	Date Signed
State Certification # AR018253 State CA	State Certification # State
Or State License # State	Or State License # State

Form TADD2 — "WinTOTAL" appraisal software by a la mode, inc. — 1-800-ALAMODE

Figure 29: Uniform Residential Appraisal Report Page 11 of 14

Main File No. 15-0365g Page #11

Market Conditions Addendum to the Appraisal Report

File No. 20 15-0365g

The purpose of this addendum is to provide the lender/client with a clear and accurate understanding of the market trends and conditions prevalent in the subject neighborhood. This is a required addendum for all appraisal reports with an effective date on or after April 1, 2009.

Property Address | City Cazadero | State CA | ZIP Code 95421

Borrower

Instructions: The appraiser must use the information required on this form as the basis for his/her conclusions, and must provide support for those conclusions, regarding housing trends and overall market conditions as reported in the Neighborhood section of the appraisal report form. The appraiser must fill in all the information to the extent it is available and reliable and must provide analysis as indicated below. If any required data is unavailable or is considered unreliable, the appraiser must provide an explanation. It is recognized that not all data sources will be able to provide data for the shaded areas below; if it is available, however, the appraiser must include the data in the analysis. If data sources provide the required information as an average instead of the median, the appraiser should report the available figure and identify it as an average. Sales and listings must be properties that compete with the subject property, determined by applying the criteria that would be used by a prospective buyer of the subject property. The appraiser must explain any anomalies in the data, such as seasonal markets, new construction, foreclosures, etc.

MARKET RESEARCH & ANALYSIS

Inventory Analysis	Prior 7–12 Months	Prior 4–6 Months	Current – 3 Months	Overall Trend		
Total # of Comparable Sales (Settled)	3	1	0	[ ] Increasing	[X] Stable	[ ] Declining
Absorption Rate (Total Sales/Months)	0.50	0.33	0.00	[ ] Increasing	[ ] Stable	[X] Declining
Total # of Comparable Active Listings	4	2	2	[ ] Declining	[X] Stable	[ ] Increasing
Months of Housing Supply (Total Listings/Ab.Rate)	8.0	6.1	0.00	[ ] Declining	[X] Stable	[ ] Increasing
Median Sale & List Price, DOM, Sale/List %	Prior 7–12 Months	Prior 4–6 Months	Current – 3 Months	Overall Trend		
Median Comparable Sale Price	535,000	385,000	0	[ ] Increasing	[ ] Stable	[X] Declining
Median Comparable Sales Days on Market	13	88	0	[X] Declining	[ ] Stable	[ ] Increasing
Median Comparable List Price	457,000	348,500	354,000	[ ] Increasing	[ ] Stable	[X] Declining
Median Comparable Listings Days on Market	51	107	79	[ ] Declining	[X] Stable	[ ] Increasing
Median Sale Price as % of List Price	0	86	93	[X] Increasing	[ ] Stable	[ ] Declining
Seller-(developer, builder, etc.)paid financial assistance prevalent?	[ ] Yes	[X] No		[ ] Declining	[X] Stable	[ ] Increasing

Explain in detail the seller concessions trends for the past 12 months (e.g., seller contributions increased from 3% to 5%, increasing use of buydowns, closing costs, condo fees, options, etc.). Seller concessions, although not uncommon, are not prevalent within the subject's market neighborhood. As the market stabilized, Seller concessions became more popular as an incentive to sell properties and to make it easier for Buyers to purchase. More recently, as the market has stabilized and current prices are perceived by the typical buyer to be an excellent value, Seller incentives have decreased.

Are foreclosure sales (REO sales) a factor in the market? [ ] Yes [X] No If yes, explain (including the trends in listings and sales of foreclosed properties).
Along with most of the State of California, there have been a substantial number of foreclosures in the Subject Market Area. Bank owned (ie., foreclosed properties) properties are generally placed on the market, and sell, at market value. Consequently, foreclosures do not appear to have a negative impact the market.

Cite data sources for above information. For the above information we have used BAREIS, the local multiple listing service. Real List, a division of First American Real Estate Information Services, is also a data source used by this appraiser.

Summarize the above information as support for your conclusions in the Neighborhood section of the appraisal report form. If you used any additional information, such as an analysis of pending sales and/or expired and withdrawn listings, to formulate your conclusions, provide both an explanation and support for your conclusions.
The market appears stable with supply and demand in balance and marketing period to be within 3 to 6 months. ***Clearly, The Market Conditions Form, becomes more reliable as there are more listings and sales. In the subject's market area, there has always been few sales due to few listings on the market which do not provide enough data to develop a reliable trend.*** During a listing period many changes can happen. Overpriced properties can be reduced during the listing period and properties can be put into escrow, effectively taken off the market, fall out of escrow and again be offered for sale. In many instances properties will be put on the market substantially over market, "test price" and reduced at a later date. It is not uncommon for a property listed for sale to be in escrow for a substantial amount of the listing period waiting for a potential Buyer to quality for a loan that is eventually declined by the lender with the property put back on the market. Data sources do not take this into account and tend to overstate the days on the market. Subject to the current national economic climate and actions taken by the Federal Reserve, and Congress.

CONDO/CO-OP PROJECTS

If the subject is a unit in a condominium or cooperative project , complete the following: **Project Name:**

Subject Project Data	Prior 7–12 Months	Prior 4–6 Months	Current – 3 Months	Overall Trend		
Total # of Comparable Sales (Settled)				[ ] Increasing	[ ] Stable	[ ] Declining
Absorption Rate (Total Sales/Months)				[ ] Increasing	[ ] Stable	[ ] Declining
Total # of Active Comparable Listings				[ ] Declining	[ ] Stable	[ ] Increasing
Months of Unit Supply (Total Listings/Ab.Rate)				[ ] Declining	[ ] Stable	[ ] Increasing

Are foreclosure sales (REO sales) a factor in the project? [ ] Yes [ ] No If yes, indicate the number of REO listings and explain the trends in listings and sales of foreclosed properties.

Summarize the above trends and address the impact on the subject unit and project.

APPRAISER

Signature		Signature	
Appraiser Name	Gordon Giordano	Supervisory Appraiser Name	
Company Name	The Appraisal Office	Company Name	
Company Address	PO Box 1329, Fort Bragg, CA 95437	Company Address	
State License/Certification #	AR018253 State CA	State License/Certification #	State
Email Address	gordy@theappraisaloffice.biz	Email Address	

Freddie Mac Form 71 March 2009 Page 1 of 1 Fannie Mae Form 1004MC March 2009

Form 1004MC2 — "WinTOTAL" appraisal software by a la mode, inc. — 1-800-ALAMODE

Figure 29: Uniform Residential Appraisal Report Page 12 of 14

Main File No. 15-0365g Page #1

20
File No. 15-0365g

UNIFORM APPRAISAL DATASET (UAD) DEFINITIONS ADDENDUM

(Source: Fannie Mae UAD Appendix D: UAD Field-Specific Standardization Requirements)

Condition Ratings and Definitions

C1

The improvements have been recently constructed and have not been previously occupied. The entire structure and all components are new and the dwelling features no physical depreciation.

Note: Newly constructed improvements that feature recycled or previously used materials and/or components can be considered new dwellings provided that the dwelling is placed on a 100 percent new foundation and the recycled materials and the recycled components have been rehabilitated/remanufactured into like-new condition. Improvements that have not been previously occupied are not considered "new" if they have any significant physical depreciation (that is, newly constructed dwellings that have been vacant for an extended period of time without adequate maintenance or upkeep).

C2

The improvements feature no deferred maintenance, little or no physical depreciation, and require no repairs. Virtually all building components are new or have been recently repaired, refinished, or rehabilitated. All outdated components and finishes have been updated and/or replaced with components that meet current standards. Dwellings in this category are either almost new or have been recently completely renovated and are similar in condition to new construction.

Note: The improvements represent a relatively new property that is well maintained with no deferred maintenance and little or no physical depreciation, or an older property that has been recently completely renovated.

C3

The improvements are well maintained and feature limited physical depreciation due to normal wear and tear. Some components, but not every major building component, may be updated or recently rehabilitated. The structure has been well maintained.

Note: The improvement is in its first-cycle of replacing short-lived building components (appliances, floor coverings, HVAC, etc.) and is being well maintained. Its estimated effective age is less than its actual age. It also may reflect a property in which the majority of short-lived building components have been replaced but not to the level of a complete renovation.

C4

The improvements feature some minor deferred maintenance and physical deterioration due to normal wear and tear. The dwelling has been adequately maintained and requires only minimal repairs to building components/mechanical systems and cosmetic repairs. All major building components have been adequately maintained and are functionally adequate.

Note: The estimated effective age may be close to or equal to its actual age. It reflects a property in which some of the short-lived building components have been replaced, and some short-lived building components are at or near the end of their physical life expectancy; however, they still function adequately. Most minor repairs have been addressed on an ongoing basis resulting in an adequately maintained property.

C5

The improvements feature obvious deferred maintenance and are in need of some significant repairs. Some building components need repairs, rehabilitation, or updating. The functional utility and overall livability is somewhat diminished due to condition, but the dwelling remains useable and functional as a residence.

Note: Some significant repairs are needed to the improvements due to the lack of adequate maintenance. It reflects a property in which many of its short-lived building components are at the end of or have exceeded their physical life expectancy but remain functional.

C6

The improvements have substantial damage or deferred maintenance with deficiencies or defects that are severe enough to affect the safety, soundness, or structural integrity of the improvements. The improvements are in need of substantial repairs and rehabilitation, including many or most major components.

Note: Substantial repairs are needed to the improvements due to the lack of adequate maintenance or property damage. It reflects a property with conditions severe enough to affect the safety, soundness, or structural integrity of the improvements.

Quality Ratings and Definitions

Q1

Dwellings with this quality rating are usually unique structures that are individually designed by an architect for a specified user. Such residences typically are constructed from detailed architectural plans and specifications and feature an exceptionally high level of workmanship and exceptionally high-grade materials throughout the interior and exterior of the structure. The design features exceptionally high-quality exterior refinements and ornamentation, and exceptionally high-quality interior refinements. The workmanship, materials, and finishes throughout the dwelling are of exceptionally high quality.

Q2

Dwellings with this quality rating are often custom designed for construction on an individual property owner's site. However, dwellings in this quality grade are also found in high-quality tract developments featuring residence constructed from individual plans or from highly modified or upgraded plans. The design features detailed, high quality exterior ornamentation, high-quality interior refinements, and detail. The workmanship, materials, and finishes throughout the dwelling are generally of high or very high quality.

UAD Version 9/2011 (Updated 4/2012)

Form UADDEFINE1 — "WinTOTAL" appraisal software by a la mode, inc. — 1-800-ALAMODE

Figure 29: Uniform Residential Appraisal Report Page 13 of 14

Main File No. 15-0365gl Page #13

UNIFORM APPRAISAL DATASET (UAD) DEFINITIONS ADDENDUM

(Source: Fannie Mae UAD Appendix D: UAD Field-Specific Standardization Requirements)

Quality Ratings and Definitions (continued)

Q3

Dwellings with this quality rating are residences of higher quality built from individual or readily available designer plans in above-standard residential tract developments or on an individual property owner's site. The design includes significant exterior ornamentation and interiors that are well finished. The workmanship exceeds acceptable standards and many materials and finishes throughout the dwelling have been upgraded from "stock" standards.

Q4

Dwellings with this quality rating meet or exceed the requirements of applicable building codes. Standard or modified standard building plans are utilized and the design includes adequate fenestration and some exterior ornamentation and interior refinements. Materials, workmanship, finish, and equipment are of stock or builder grade and may feature some upgrades.

Q5

Dwellings with this quality rating feature economy of construction and basic functionality as main considerations. Such dwellings feature a plain design using readily available or basic floor plans featuring minimal fenestration and basic finishes with minimal exterior ornamentation and limited interior detail. These dwellings meet minimum building codes and are constructed with inexpensive, stock materials with limited refinements and upgrades.

Q6

Dwellings with this quality rating are of basic quality and lower cost; some may not be suitable for year-round occupancy. Such dwellings are often built with simple plans or without plans, often utilizing the lowest quality building materials. Such dwellings are often built or expanded by persons who are professionally unskilled or possess only minimal construction skills. Electrical, plumbing, and other mechanical systems and equipment may be minimal or non-existent. Older dwellings may feature one or more substandard or non-conforming additions to the original structure

Definitions of Not Updated, Updated, and Remodeled

Not Updated

Little or no updating or modernization. This description includes, but is not limited to, new homes.

Residential properties of fifteen years of age or less often reflect an original condition with no updating, if no major components have been replaced or updated. Those over fifteen years of age are also considered not updated if the appliances, fixtures, and finishes are predominantly dated. An area that is 'Not Updated' may still be well maintained and fully functional, and this rating does not necessarily imply deferred maintenance or physical/functional deterioration.

Updated

The area of the home has been modified to meet current market expectations. These modifications are limited in terms of both scope and cost.

An updated area of the home should have an improved look and feel, or functional utility. Changes that constitute updates include refurbishment and/or replacing components to meet existing market expectations. Updates do not include significant alterations to the existing structure.

Remodeled

Significant finish and/or structural changes have been made that increase utility and appeal through complete replacement and/or expansion.

A remodeled area reflects fundamental changes that include multiple alterations. These alterations may include some or all of the following: replacement of a major component (cabinet(s), bathtub, or bathroom tile), relocation of plumbing/gas fixtures/appliances, significant structural alterations (relocating walls, and/or the addition of) square footage). This would include a complete gutting and rebuild.

Explanation of Bathroom Count

Three-quarter baths are counted as a full bath in all cases. Quarter baths (baths that feature only a toilet) are not included in the bathroom count. The number of full and half baths is reported by separating the two values using a period, where the full bath count is represented to the left of the period and the half bath count is represented to the right of the period.

Example:
3.2 indicates three full baths and two half baths.

UAD Version 9/2011 (Updated 4/2012)

Form UADDEFINE1 — "WinTOTAL" appraisal software by a la mode, inc. — 1-800-ALAMODE

Figure 29: Uniform Residential Appraisal Report Page 14 of 14

INCOME CAPITALIZATION

INCOME CAPITALIZATION is used to determine the value of income producing properties. An appraiser will provide the usual sale comps and then also include comps that are rental properties.

CAPITALIZATION OF NET INCOME is a method of determining the value of a property based on the income the property is producing or is capable of producing. This method is also used as a method to determine the **potential income**. The real estate professional must know the formula, whether specializing in commercial properties or assisting the occasional purchaser of residential properties.

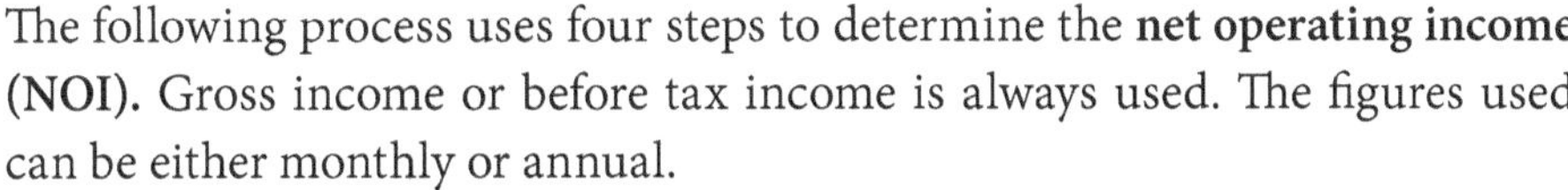

The following process uses four steps to determine the **net operating income (NOI).** Gross income or before tax income is always used. The figures used can be either monthly or annual.

1) Estimate the **adjusted gross income (AGI)** as though the property were fully occupied
2) Deduct **effective gross income (EGI)** by subtracting allowances for uncollected rents and vacancies
3) Deduct **allowable expenses**
4) Equals **net operating income (NOI)** (potential income) Adjusted gross income

   -Vacancy & income loss
   =Effective gross income (EGI)
   -Expenses
   =Net operating income (NOI)

> ***Example:*** *An apartment building with 10 units:*
>
> *$ 15,000 Monthly income (assuming all units are rented) - AGI*
> *$4,500 3 units @ $1,500/mo. vacancy – EGI*
> *$6,000 Maintenance, utilities, mortgage, tax, insurance*
> *= $4,500 NOI*

IRV FORMULA (income, rate & value) is then used to calculate the capitalization from the NOI. **Income, rate, and value** are used in a basic algebraic calculation to determine a rate or a basis to determine the value of a subject property based on a comparable and similar income producing property.

There are three figures in the formula and as long as there are two parts of the formula, the third part can be calculated. There must be at least two parts of the formula that are known.

The required parts of the formula are:

1) NOI or Net Operating Income = I
2) Capitalization Rate (Cap) or Rate =R
3) Value of the property = V

The following algebraic equation is used for calculating:

income (NOI) ÷		
Rate	X	Value

The T formation indicates that the figure on top will be divided by the known figure either to the left or right to calculate the other figure and the figures on either side are multiplied by the other to determine the figure on top or the income.

When working with this formula, it is important to remember that you must have two of the figures to generate or calculate the third figure. In other words, to calculate the value of a property, one must know the cap rate and the income; to calculate income, one must know the value and the rate; to calculate the cap rate, one must know the income and the value.

Another way of showing the equation is:

Income ÷ Rate = Value Income ÷ Value = Rate Rate x Value = Income

Example: *Joe is considering the purchase of a house for rental purposes. He needs to find out what the rent should be to determine the value of the property.*

A house that is rented in the neighborhood recently sold for $200,000. The house is currently rented for $1,500/month. (This can be calculated as monthly or annually, but the cap rate will appear as a considerably different figure if calculated monthly, so it is advisable to use yearly.)

$1,500	*Monthly income*
x 12	*Months per year*
= $18,000	*Annual income*
÷ $200,000	*Value*
= .09 or 9%	*Rate or cap rate*

$18,000 = Income	
9% = Cap Rate	*$200,000 = Value*

This has provided a percentage of the property value that represents income. Now the value of the property being purchased can be calculated or the amount of income that should be charged on the new rental property.

Joe has determined that the subject property can demand a monthly rental income of $1,600 per month. The seller has the property listed for sale at a price of $250,000.

$1,600	*Monthly rental income*
X 12	*Months per year*
= $19,200	*Annual income*
X 9%	*Cap rate*
= $331,776	*Value*

This would be a very good investment. **The cap rate should not exceed 12%.** The higher the cap rate, the higher the risk and: therefore, the lesser the value. The quality of the income is directly related to the quality of the tenant's financial responsibility. A good building that attracts professional tenants in an upscale neighborhood indicates the financial responsibility of the potential tenants, whereas a lesser quality building in a neighborhood of lower income residents will be a higher risk due to a lesser financial stability resulting in lesser financial responsibility. The average cap rate is around 8% to 9% based on annual income.

NOTE

If the cap rate increases, but the income does not change, the property value will decrease.

It does not matter whether the calculations are done on monthly income or annual income, but it is best to be consistent. When the same figures in the previous example are prepared on the monthly income will create the following cap rate:

$1,500	Monthly rental income
÷$200,000	Value
= .007 or .7%	Cap rate

GROSS RENT MULTIPLIER is the same as the capitalization of net income with the exception of not using the net operating income but using the gross income. The gross rent multiplier is the same as the cap rate.

FACTORS TO VALUE

FACTORS TO VALUE include some of the following terms:

- **ASSEMBLAGE** is the combination of two or more properties to create one large lot or parcel of land. The new large parcel may prove to be significant enough to create an assembled value that is greater than the total value of the separate parcels if left as smaller individual parcels.

  Example: *Sam purchased 3 small parcels of vacant land for $30,000 each for a total value of $90,000. The purpose of purchasing all 3 was to assemble them into 1 large lot for building one large structure. Once the individual parcels underwent Assemblage and were recorded with the county recorder's office, the Value of the new large parcel is $120,000.*

- **PLOTTAGE OR PLOTTAGE INCREMENT** is how the increase in the value of the parcels by being assembled into one parcel is referred to.

- **ACTION OF THE SUN** can be an important factor for a retail business in as much as the sun will fade any display items in the store's windows, especially for a retail store that is located on the north side of the street. The sun will also increase the temperature of the building and any pedestrians outside. **The most desirable location for a retail store is the southeast corner** because it has the least exposure to the sun and the morning sun is less harsh then the afternoon sun.

The sun may also be a consideration for residential properties in different climates. Houses in colder climates would prefer to face south and west to get the benefit of the sun's warmth in the winter months. Houses in the southern and warmer climates may prefer to face north and east to receive less sun to the living areas during the summer months.

- **FRONTAGE** is the amount of land that is on the street. This is a lineal measurement from one lot line along the street to the opposite lot line. Building sites have minimum frontage requirements to allow for access to a property. Some areas may require that there is at least enough frontage to allow for a driveway giving access to a property.

- **FRONT FOOT** is related to frontage and refers to the measurement of the property on the street. This is most often used in retail or commercial property evaluations. Retail and commercial structures are valued higher when there is a greater frontage or front feet on the street. A retail business is especially more valuable with a greater amount of space along the sidewalk. It is built-in advertising. Front footage is not used in residential property other than meeting building codes for access to the property.

- **LAND RESIDUAL METHOD** is a way to determine the value of land when there are no comps of vacant land available in the subject property's neighborhood. In order to determine the value of the land, the appraiser must know the value of the entire property with a structure and the value of the structure alone.

  Example: *Appraiser Smith needs to prepare an appraisal for a vacant lot. There are no recent sales of vacant land in the vicinity. Appraiser Smith uses a nearby comp with a recent sales price or value of $225,000. He is able to establish the cost new of the structure at $150,000. By subtracting the value of the structure form the total value of the property, Appraiser Smith can determine the value of the lot:*

$225,000	*Total property value*
-$150,000	*Value of the structure*
= $75,000	*Lot value*

APPRAISAL LICENSING

APPRAISAL LICENSING is required in California. The ***Uniform Standards of Professional Appraisal Practice*** (USPAP) governs the conduct of appraisers. USPAP was established under the Financial Institutions Reform, Recovery, and Enforcement Act (FIRREA) which was established in 1989. FIRREA requires that all appraisals that are prepared for federally related loans must be prepared by appraisers licensed according to the guidelines and requirements of the state in which they are working. Prior to 1989 there were minimal requirements for appraisers. Some states require a real estate broker's license to perform an appraisal. California had none other than an affiliation with the appraisal foundation, which is a professional organization that created an Appraisal Standards Board.

A federally related loan is any real estate transaction that is funded by or involves a federally regulated bank, savings & loan, or lending institutions. This includes almost all mortgage loans on residential property of 1-to 4-units.

California's Office of Real Estate Appraisers (OREA) was established for the regulation of real estate appraisers as part of the Business, Transportation, and Housing Agency and Profession Code on January 1, 1998. Prior regulations had been put into effect on November 1, 1992. The following are education requirements with the current requirements as of January 1, 2017.

THERE ARE FOUR LEVELS OF REAL ESTATE APPRAISER LICENSING:

- AT - Trainee License
- AL - Residential License
- AR - Certified Residential License
- AG - Certified General License

2015 Basic Education Module Requirements

Updated January 1, 2017, a module is a subject matter area and not necessarily the name of the course. A course may consist of one or two complete modules or portions of several different modules.

Degrees and college credit must be from an accredited college or university.

1) TRAINEE LICENSE (AT) 150 Hours of Education
   Qualifying Education hours include instruction in the following modules:
   30 hours - Basic Appraisal Principles
   30 hours - Basic Appraisal Procedures

15 hours - The 15-Hour National USPAP Course
15 hours - Residential Market Analysis and Highest & Best Use
15 hours - Residential Appraiser Site Valuation and Cost Approach
30 hours - Residential Sales Comparison and Income Approaches
15 hours - Residential Report Writing and Case Studies

Trainee applicants must also complete an approved supervisory/trainee appraisers' course prior to obtaining a trainee appraiser license. The supervisory/trainee appraisers' course is not eligible toward the 150 hours of qualifying education.

As of January 1, 2017, all initial applicants must complete an approved state and federal laws course and cultural competency prior to obtaining a license. The laws and regulations course is not eligible toward the 150 hours of qualifying education.

NOTE

Course work for the trainee license taken more than five (5) years prior to the application date is not acceptable.

2) **RESIDENTIAL LICENSE (AL)**

- 150 hours of education and 30 semester hours of college-level education from an accredited college, junior college, community college or university

OR

- An associate's degree or higher (in any field). and
- Work under the supervision of a licensed appraiser for 2,000 hours of acceptable appraisal experience

Licensee may prepare appraisals:
- 1- to 4-unit residential property, value not to exceed $1 million
- Non-residential property with value not to exceed $250,000.

Qualifying Education hours include instruction in the following modules: 30 hours - Basic Appraisal Principles
30 hours - Basic Appraisal Procedures
15 hours - The 15-Hour National USPAP Course
15 hours - Residential Market Analysis and Highest & Best Use
15 hours - Residential Appraiser Site Valuation and Cost Approach
30 hours - Residential Sales Comparison and Income Approaches
5 hours - Residential Report Writing and Case Studies

As of January 1, 2017, all initial applicants must complete an approved state and federal laws course and cultural competency prior to obtaining a license. The Laws and Regulations course is not eligible toward the 150 hours of qualifying education.

3) CERTIFIED RESIDENTIAL LICENSE (AR)

- 200 hours of education and a bachelor's degree or higher from an accredited college or university.
- Associate's degree or 21 college credit hours in related subjects
- 2500 hours appraisal experience
- 2 ½ years acceptable appraisal experience

Licensee may prepare:
- All 1- to 4-unit residential properties
- Non-residential properties up to a value of $250,000

Qualifying Education hours include instruction in the following modules: 30 hours - Basic Appraisal Principles
30 hours - Basic Appraisal Procedures
15 hours - The 15-Hour National USPAP Course
15 hours - Residential Market Analysis and Highest & Best Use
15 hours - Residential Appraiser Site Valuation and Cost Approach
30 hours - Residential Sales Comparison and Income Approaches 15 hours - Residential Report Writing and Case Studies
15 hours - Statistics, Modeling and Finance
15 hours - Advanced Residential Applications and Case Studies
20 hours - Appraisal Subject Matter Electives. May include hours over the minimum requirement in the above modules or in modules not listed above.

As of January 1, 2017, all initial applicants must complete an approved state and federal laws course and cultural competency prior to obtaining a license. The Laws and Regulations course is not eligible toward the 200 hours of qualifying education.

4) CERTIFIED GENERAL LICENSE (AG)

- 300 hours of education and a bachelor's degree or higher from an accredited college or university.
- Bachelor's degree or 30 college credit hours in related subjects
- 3000 hours appraisal experience
- 2 ½ years acceptable appraisal experience
- Minimum of 1,500 hours experience with non-residential properties Licensees may prepare appraisals for all properties.

Qualifying education hours include instruction in the following modules:

30 hours - Basic Appraisal Principles 30 hours - Basic Appraisal Procedures
15 hours - The 15-Hour National USPAP Course
30 hours - General Appraiser Market Analysis and Highest & Best Use 15 hours - Statistics, Modeling and Finance
30 hours - General Appraiser Sales Comparison Approach
30 hours - General Appraiser Site Valuation and Cost Approach
60 hours - General Appraiser Income Approach
30 hours - General Appraiser Report Writing and Case Studies
30 hours - Appraisal Subject Matter Electives. May include hours over the minimum requirement in the above modules or in modules not listed above.

As of January 1, 2017, all initial applicants must complete an approved state and federal laws course and cultural competency prior to obtaining a license. The Laws and Regulations course is not eligible toward the 300 hours of qualifying education.

NOTE

Degrees and college credit must be from an accredited college or university.

TYPES OF APPRAISAL REPORTS that are prepared under USPAP regulations are:

- **Restricted Use Report**: Letter form that appears to be similar to an essay describing the property and its amenities.
- **Summary Report:** Short form report on a prepared form.
- **Self-Contained Report:** Narrative report on a long, prepared form is the most complete and provides the most detail of the three forms. This is the most commonly used report currently and the report required by lenders.

CHAPTER 14
REAL ESTATE AS A BUSINESS

US
Realty School

REAL ESTATE LAW

Real Estate Law and the California Department of Real Estate were formed as a division of the Business, Transportation, and Housing Agency in 1919. ***Real Estate law is found in and is a part of the California Business and Professions Code.***

California was the first state to enact real estate licensing laws recognizing that there was a need to create appropriate laws for the purpose of protecting the public from fraud and unscrupulous acts. The laws have developed over the years and are constantly changing and improving to accommodate the ever-changing influences from society, economy, and business practices.

CALIFORNIA DEPARTMENT OF REAL ESTATE (DRE)

California Department of Real Estate (DRE), which is within the business, Consumer Services, and Housing Agency, is managed by the real estate commissioner appointed by the governor. The DRE is a department under the ***California Business, Consumer Services and Housing Agency (BCSH)***, as well as their own DRE Rules and Regulations, which have the force and effect of law.

The Real Estate Commissioner is responsible for administrative policy of the DRE. The commissioner is responsible for regulating licensees and their activities by:

- **Adopting, amending, and repealing** rules and regulations of the DRE
- **Investigating** written complaints from the public against licensees
- **Conducting hearings** as necessary to the needs of the public and licensees
- **Suspending licenses** or permanently taking away
- **Revoking licenses** or temporarily taking away
- **Restricting licenses** or limiting activities and licensing terms
- **Regulation of new subdivisions** as established by the **Subdivided Lands law.**

The real estate commissioner issues the following **DRE licenses**:

- Real estate broker
- Real estate salesperson license
- Restricted salesperson license
- Prepaid rental listing service (PRLS)

REAL ESTATE ADVISORY COMMISSION is a group of ten members made up of six licensed brokers and four members of the public. The members of the Advisory Commission are appointed by the DRE commissioner. The purpose of the Advisory Commission is to make recommendations and suggestions to the commissioner concerning policy. The Advisory Committee meets four times a year, once in each of the following: Los Angeles, San Diego, San Francisco, and Sacramento.

The ENFORCEMENT OF REAL ESTATE LAWS, AND RULES AND REGULATIONS, other than as they apply to licensing, are the responsibility of the district attorney (DA) in the county where a violation has occurred. Any criminal violations against members of the public by a DRE licensee are prosecuted by the local DA. However, the DRE through its Cite and Fine Program has the authority to fine licensees and collect penalties that have been levied against licensees. The commissioner does not get involved with commission disputes. Commission disputes are generally handled by the local board of realtors or through arbitration.

NOTE

The legal advisor to the commissioner is the California Attorney General.

The REAL ESTATE EDUCATION AND RESEARCH FUND is held by the DRE as a way to provide relief to any members of the public who have obtained a judgment against a real estate licensee.

As license fees are collected by the commissioner, 20% is collected and placed into the fund. A portion of the fund is used for research projects and for education purposes.

If a licensee has had a judgment placed against them and has not paid that judgment, the creditor holding the judgment can request relief from the DRE commissioner. The licensee's license will be suspended until the amount that has been paid out on their behalf has been repaid to the **DRE Consumer Recovery Account**. The Relief Fund will pay out on behalf of a licensee the amount of $50,000 per transaction with a total amount per licensee of $250,000.

REAL ESTATE LICENSE LAW

REAL ESTATE BROKER'S LICENSE allows a natural person or a "legal person," which would be a corporation, to obtain a real estate broker's license for the purpose of performing particular duties for another person for a fee in regard to real property. The duties this license allows the licensee to perform in relation to real property include:

- List
- Sell
- Manage
- Lease
- Exchange
- Negotiate options
- Arrange notes secured by deeds of trust

COMMERCIAL OR BUSINESS TRANSACTIONS may also be performed by a real estate broker licensee as the abovementioned duties pertain to the transaction. Such a situation would include the sale or of a business that includes the sale or rental of a building or other real property.

MOBILE OR MANUFACTURED HOMES TRANSACTIONS that involve homes that are or have previously been licensed under the ***Department of Housing and Community Development (HCD)*** and are now used or occupied and have been placed in a park or otherwise on a private lot may also be conducted by a real estate broker licensee. The sale of new mobile homes must be conducted by a person licensed under the HCD.

REAL ESTATE BROKER LICENSING is required for any of the abovementioned duties to be performed on behalf of a client and any member of the public. There is a distinction between a broker and a salesperson. The real estate broker licensee must successfully complete five additional courses beyond those required for a real estate salesperson licensee and they must successfully pass a DRE exam specific to the broker's licensing requirements.

NOTE

To own and operate a real estate business, one must be a licensed real estate broker. The broker of record is the owner of the business.

Partners in a **PARTNERSHIP** owning a real estate business must all hold a real estate broker's license. A salesperson's license is not acceptable for a business owner of a real estate business.

A **CORPORATION** must have a licensed real estate broker as an officer. A corporation may hold a real estate license as a legal entity, however, there must also be a person that holds an active real estate broker's license as an officer of the corporation. The broker licensee has the final say in regard to any decisions relating to real estate transactions and the consumer.

"RENT-A-BROKER" has been an abusive and fraudulent practice which is the use of another's broker's license even though the broker has nothing to do with the real estate business being operated under their license. The broker is paid for the use of the license.

Rent-a-broker is an illegal practice and is punishable by fines and loss of license for both the party operating the business and renting the license, and the broker that is allowing their license to be used by another. The real estate professional must avoid any actions involving this practice.

REAL ESTATE SALESPERSON'S LICENSEES must work for a licensed real estate broker. It is illegal for a salesperson licensee to collect any payment from anyone other than their broker of record. The broker of record is legally responsible for the actions of all salesperson licensees that have their license hanging under their license. The broker of record must have access to all files and records at all times and is responsible for reviewing documentation during the time that the transaction is in process. *For example, the* DRE *requires that the broker of record review the LE (loan estimate) within three business days of the original or initial MLDS being prepared or signed by the borrower. A broker may assign written authority to another holder of an active real estate broker's license to review files on their behalf.* A person with an active real estate salesperson's license may also be designated to review files for the broker as long as they have two years' experience in the real estate Industry and written authority from the broker of record.

EMPLOYMENT CONTRACTS are used as a means to establish a real estate salesperson licensee as a self-employed person yet legally working under a real estate broker's license. This legal form of employment establishes an association between the broker of record and the salesperson licensee creating the term sales associate when referring to a salesperson licensee in the employ of a real estate broker. The employment contract must clarify that the salesperson licensee is responsible to the broker of record and must obey their laws, and the rules and regulations as they apply to licensing and real estate business. A real estate salesperson licensee is responsible for the broker of record to maintain ethical and legal practices.

UNACCEPTABLE AND/OR ILLEGAL ACTS committed by a salesperson licensee may be subject to fines, loss of license, and even imprisonment. The broker of record will bear the greatest liability for that act by the salesperson. A salesperson licensee has an obligation to act ethically and legally on behalf of the broker of record.

HANGING YOUR LICENSE refers to the legal requirement that all licensed persons working in an office in the business of real estate or requiring a real estate license must have their original license, not a copy, displayed in a conspicuous place on the business premises.

LEAVING THE EMPLOY OF A BROKER or entering into employment by the broker of record requires notification to DRE of that change to DRE. The license change must be reported to DRE within 10 business days of that change. The licensee may report the change, but the brokers of record for **both** the new company and the old company are required to notify DRE.

A SALESPERSON MAY NOT REMOVE FILES FROM THE BROKER'S OFFICE when leaving the employment of that broker. All files belong to the broker, not the salesperson licensee. A salesperson licensee will often expect to take any open files or files in process with them to their new broker's office. They have procured the client and worked on that transaction, and they would like to get paid for their work. As a salesperson is not allowed to perform acts requiring a real estate license without working under the auspices of their broker of record, they may not remove the file. The proper way to ensure payment on a file is to discuss the situation with the current broker to arrange for payment to the new broker who in turn will pay the sales associate or salesperson licensee.

NOTE

A real estate salesperson's licensee may not work independently.

A license can be moved either online or by mail. A variety of acts and information is available to licensees can be done online by contacting DRE online at https://www.dre.ca.gov

Real estate broker's license requirements are as follows:

- GENERAL REQUIREMENTS:
  - **Age**: You must be 18 years of age or older to be issued a license.
  - **Residence**: You do not have to be a California resident.
  - **Honesty**: Applicants must be honest and truthful.

- **EDUCATION:** (360 hours) Eight (8) college level courses of 45 hours each
  - 5 Mandatory classes
    - » Real Estate Principles
    - » Real Estate Practice
    - » Legal Aspects of Real Estate
    - » Real Estate Economics
    - » Real Estate Appraisal
  - 3 Electives
    - » Real Estate Finance
    - » Real Estate Office Administration
    - » Business Law
    - » Property Management
    - » Mortgage Loan Brokering
    - » Real Estate Economics
    - » Credit from previous college classes may be acceptable to DRE

- EXPERIENCE:

  A minimum of two (2) years' full-time licensed salesperson experience within the last five (5) years or the equivalent is required.

- TESTING:

  DRE-prepared 200 multiple-choice questions; time allotted – 4 hours (a score of 75% or more is required to pass the exam)

Real estate salesperson' license requirements are as follows:

GENERAL REQUIREMENTS:

- **Age**: You must be 18 years of age or older to be issued a license.
- **Residence**: You do not have to be a California resident.
- **Honesty**: Applicants must be honest and truthful.

EDUCATION: (135 hours) 45 hours in each of three courses equal to three college level courses
- Real Estate Principles
- Real Estate Practice
- 1 Elective which may be a previous college class if acceptable to DRE: 45 Hours

EXPERIENCE: None

TESTING: California Department of Real Estate (DRE) administered 150 question examination; time allotted - three (3) hours

CONTINUING EDUCATION REQUIREMENTS
Real estate broker's licenses and **salesperson's licenses** are issued for four years. At the end of the four-year license term, the licensee must complete 45 hours of Continuing Education from DRE approved courses.

SALESPERSONS RENEWING FOR THE FIRST TIME
Real estate salespersons renewing an original license for the first time must complete 45 clock hours of DRE-approved continuing education consisting of four (4) separate three-hour courses in:
- *Ethics*
- *Agency*
- *Trust Fund Handling*
- *Risk Management*
  AND
- ***a three-hour course in fair housing*** that must include an ***Interactive Participatory Component*** during which the licensee portrays both a consumer and a real estate professional
- ***a two-hour course in Implicit Bias training***
- ***a minimum of 18 hours of Consumer Protection*** courses, *and*
- ***the remaining clock hours to complete the 45 hours*** of Continuing Education may be related to either Consumer Service or Consumer Protection Courses

NOTE

Effective January 1, 2024, any Real Estate Practice course submitted for purposes of qualifying to take a real estate license exam must include components on implicit bias and fair housing. Also, the fair housing component must include an Interactive Participatory Component where the applicant portrays both the consumer and the real estate professional.

BROKERS RENEWING FOR THE FIRST TIME

Real estate brokers renewing an original license for the first time must complete 45 clock hours of DRE-approved continuing education consisting of five (5) separate three-hour courses in:

- ***Ethics***
- ***Agency***
- ***Trust Fund Handling***
- ***Risk Management***
- ***Management and Supervision***

  AND
- ***A three-hour course in fair housing*** that must include an ***Interactive Participatory Component*** during which the licensee portrays both a consumer and a real estate professional
- ***A two-hour course in Implicit Bias Training***
- ***A minimum of 18 hours of Consumer Protection*** courses, *and*
- ***The remaining clock hours to complete the 45 hours*** of Continuing Education may be related to either Consumer Service or Consumer Protection courses

SALESPERSONS AND BROKERS – SECOND & SUBSEQUENT RENEWALS

For subsequent renewals, all licensees with a license expiration date on or after January 1, 2023, or who are renewing on a late basis after January 1, 2023, must complete 45 hours of DRE-approved continuing education consisting of:

- ***One nine-hour CE survey course that covers the seven mandatory subjects*** (Ethics, Agency, Trust Fund Handling, Risk Management, Management and Supervision, Fair Housing (including Interactive Component), and Implicit Bias training)

  OR
- ***Licensees can choose to take individual courses*** in all of those mandatory subjects
- ***A minimum of 18 hours of CE courses*** in the category of consumer protection, and
- ***The remaining clock hours to complete the 45 hours*** of continuing education may be related to either Consumer Service or Consumer Protection courses

LATE RENWALS

If you fail to renew your license on time (prior to your license expiration date), you may renew your license during the two-year late renewal period immediately following your license expiration date. However, **you cannot perform activities requiring a real estate license** until your license has been renewed.

MISSTATEMENT OF FACTS made on the license application which are fraudulent, deceitful, or misrepresentation of the applicant may result in suspension of the license within 90 days of the application. A hearing will not be required under these circumstances. A real estate licensee is expected to be of good moral character.

NOTE

Conviction of certain felonies or crimes involving moral turpitude may result in the denial of one's application to obtain a real estate license.

CANCELLATION OF LICENSE is temporary and is not the same as revocation. A real estate salesperson's license is canceled under two situations:

- Broker of record dies
- Licensee quits or is terminated

During the time that the license is canceled, the licensee cannot perform any duties that require a real estate license.

SUSPENDED LICENSE is based on stipulations which must be corrected prior to a suspended license being reinstated. A license may be suspended for a variety of reasons to include:

- Non-payment of child support
- Unreimbursed payment to a claimant from the Education and Research Fund
- Lawsuits being investigated by the DA

CHILD SUPPORT IN ARREARS will not be allowed on the part of a DRE licensee.

The DRE will not renew a real estate broker's license or a real estate salesperson's license to a licensee that owes back child support. A temporary or restricted license may be issued for a period of 150 days to allow time to generate the funds to pay the child support that is in arrears. If evidence of payment of that debt is not provided to DRE within the 150-day period, the license will be suspended.

A REVOKED LICENSE occurs under a variety of circumstances, most commonly conviction for a crime involving abuse of the real estate license.

An EXPIRED LICENSE is one that has gone beyond its expiration date without being renewed by completing the required educational requirements.

UNLICENSED PERSONS working in a broker's office may assist with files and transaction, but without a real estate license a person is not allowed to perform any of the following duties:

- Sign contracts
- Discuss price
- Quote interest rates
- Solicit clients
- Discuss terms

NOTE

A real estate salesperson's licensee may not work independently.

An unlicensed person performing the duties requiring a real estate broker's license or representing themselves as a real estate broker are subject to a fine of $10,000 per incident.

EXCEPTIONS to the real estate license requirement allow for persons acting under certain situations to perform real estate related duties without a license.

- **DEALING with ONE'S OWN PROPERTY** does not require a license. A property owner may list, sell, lease, exchange or perform other real estate related duties that would otherwise require a real estate license.

- **BUYING and SELLING LESS THAN 8 REAL ESTATE PAPERS or PROMISSORY NOTES PER YEAR** secured by real property, more commonly referred to as **mortgage loans**. A real estate broker's license is required for any person buying and/or selling **eight or more promissory notes secured by real property within one calendar year**. The involvement to the extent of eight transactions or more during a year classifies one as being "in the business" or actively working in the real estate industry and therefore requires a real estate license.

  Many investors buy and sell real estate paper on a regular basis as an income producing investment. The collection of the monthly principal and interest payments creates a steady income flow.

- **CORPORATIONS** dealing with their own properties in their own offices may conduct duties normally requiring a real estate license. In this capacity, the employees of the corporation are not allowed to be paid special compensation such as commission for these duties.

A corporation is considered an entity, which qualifies the corporation as an individual handling their own property.

- **POWER OF ATTORNEY** allows a person to transact business on behalf of the party giving the power of attorney. This constitutes transacting duties as an individual and, therefore, does not require a real estate license. A real estate transaction generally requires a specific power of attorney for that transaction only.

- **ATTORNEYS** performing an act or duty on behalf of a client or as a part of their duties as an attorney that would otherwise require a real estate license is exempt.

- **COURT APPOINTED PERSONS** acting on behalf of the court in a capacity that would normally require a real estate license is exempt from obtaining a real estate license such as property being sold through probate.

  Example: *Mary's grandmother has passed away and the Will is being handled by the probate court. Mary has been appointed as the executor for her grandmother's estate. As the executor, Mary can sell, lease, exchange, or otherwise dispose of the property without obtaining a real estate license.*

- **BANKS, SAVINGS & LOANS, CREDIT UNIONS,** and their employees are exempt from real estate licensing when transacting on their own behalf. These entities are licensed and governed by the Department of Financial Protection and Innovation (DFPI) at the state level and may also be regulated by federal agencies such as the Office of the Comptroller of the Currency (OCC) or the National Credit Union Administration (NCUA). As a result, they are generally not subject to the Department of Real Estate (DRE) Rules & Regulations, except in cases where specific real estate-related activities may require compliance under other laws.

- **ESCROW COMPANIES** and their employees are exempt from real estate licensing when transacting on their **own** behalf. These entities are corporations licensed and governed by the Department of Financial Protection and Innovation (DFPI) under the California Escrow Law. Escrow companies are limited in the duties they are allowed to perform in a capacity regarding real estate activities to discussing terms, interest rates, and details that would otherwise require a real estate license; however, they would not be allowed to sell, lease, or dispose of property owned by another party.

REAL ESTATE BROKERAGE

REAL ESTATE BROKERAGE can be a business that works in any of a variety of real estate businesses. Brokerage is a term that means that the business does not have items for sale such as a retail business would offer. A brokerage is a type of business that transacts business on behalf of their clients. A real estate brokerage business may sell a parcel of real estate on behalf of the property owner. The business does not own the parcel of land itself but finds a purchaser for the parcel and assists with the sale of the property by bringing the buyer and seller together.

"DOING BUSINESS AS" or DBA is a fictitious name that a business uses instead of using the name of the business owner. A real estate broker may choose to operate their business under their name; however, most businesses will operate under a fictitious name. A fictitious name or a DBA must be recorded with the county recorder's office, and then advertise the recording in a local newspaper under "public notices." The local newspaper personnel know the laws regarding fictitious name filings and will see that the requirements for the filing are met. DRE must be provided with a copy of the fictitious name filing to be placed on the real estate broker's license. A copy of the DBA filing must also be provided to the bank when opening a business bank account and before accepting checks in the business name.

CHANGE TO THE NAME OR ADDRESS of the broker or the business does not require obtaining a new license from DRE. DRE allows for changes to be made manually by the broker as long as the changes have been reported to DRE within 10 business days of the use of the new name.

BUSINESS STRUCTURE OF A REAL ESTATE BUSINESS can be operated under one of several different forms. Whichever way the business is operated, it must be recorded with the county recorder's office and registered with the DRE. Whatever form of ownership, the broker of record will always be responsible for the actions of the business and its employees and is responsible for all decisions regarding the operation of the business.

1. **SOLE PROPRIETOR** is a business owned by one person (or solely). In the real estate industry, a sole proprietor/owner must hold an active real estate broker's license.

2) **PARTNERSHIP** is a business owned and operated by more than one person and can have as many partners as they choose. **All** Partners are required to hold an active real estate broker's license by the DRE. *This was not required*

prior to 2004. DRE recognized the need to have a broker of record on site in real estate businesses as a way to help prevent fraud by unscrupulous business owners.

3) **CORPORATION** is a form of business ownership that is considered to be a legal entity. As a legal entity, the corporation itself can hold a real estate broker's license, but it does require that a person holding an active real estate broker's license be an officer of the corporation and it is recommended that the broker of record be the president.

   A corporation is owned by shareholders or **owners of interest**. Shares may be bought and sold, but the business will be continually operated by a board of directors and its officers. No matter who owns the shares or interest in the business, the business will continue. The result of this type of ongoing business is what allows a corporation to be classified as a legal entity, which is the legal equivalent to an individual.

4) **BRANCH OFFICES** are allowed to be managed under the broker's license by a person holding an active real estate broker's license, or a real estate salesperson's license with a minimum of two years' experience in the real estate Industry.

REAL ESTATE BUSINESS OPPORTUNITIES

Business opportunities that are available to a person holding a real estate license offer a variety of interests.

1. **REAL ESTATE SALES** is the business that is most commonly sought when a person begins the process of becoming a real estate licensee. A real estate sales office performs a variety of duties and can specialize in an area. The duties that are performed in a real estate sales office include:
   - Listing real property for sale
   - Showing homes to potential buyers
   - Negotiating purchase offer contracts
   - Leasing real property on behalf of property owners
   - Showing rental property to potential tenants
   - Preparing leases
   - Managing the property
   - Preparing certain documents such as Notice to Vacate

2. **PROPERTY MANAGEMENT** can be the management of small SFRs, multi-unit residential properties, and all types of commercial properties. This business specialization is usually exercised as a property management business. It is important to remember that residential units of 16 or more require there to be a resident manager. The duties performed in a property management business include:
   - Leasing real property on behalf of property owners
   - Showing property to potential tenants
   - Preparing leases
   - Managing the property
   - Preparing legal documents, such as Notice to Vacate
   - Managing maintenance
   - Bookkeeping

3. **MORTGAGE BROKER** is the business of obtaining mortgages for potential borrowers by locating a lender who matches their needs. The duties performed by a mortgage broker include:
   - Preparing loan applications
   - Working with client's financial needs
   - Providing credit advice
   - Working with lenders
   - Understanding appraisals

4. **PREPAID RENTAL LISTING SERVICE (PRLS)** is a business that provides listings of residential properties that are available for rent for a fee. Unlike other real estate related fees these fees are charged in advance. The PRLS can be operated by a licensed real estate broker or a person holding an active prepaid rental listing service license provided by the California Department of Real Estate.

   The PRLS license is issued for a two-year period and is renewable every two years.

5. **MANUFACTURED/MOBILE HOME TRANSACTIONS** may be performed by a person holding an active real estate license if the manufactured home is "used" (having been located on a lot in a mobile home park and occupied for a period of one year or more). The Department of Housing and Community Development (HCD) provides and enforces licensing for the sale of new mobile homes by issuing a **dealer's license**.

Manufactured/mobile homes in parks are considered chattel, or personal property similar to the ownership of a car and are licensed by the Department of Housing and Community Development (HCD). Until the late 1990s, they were licensed and taxed the same as a car. Some newer models are now assessed through the county tax assessor's office based on local ordinances. They still require registration with the Department of Housing and Community Development (HCD).

Because the property is personal and not real property, mortgage brokers licensed under the California Department of Real Estate (DRE) are not licensed to broker these loans. The required license is a consumer finance lending (CFL) license provided through the Department of Financial Protection and Innovation (DFPI) under the California Financing Law (CFL). DRE mortgage brokers may prepare these loans and submit them to a CFL-licensed broker and collect a fee; however, the CFL broker is the acting broker and will collect their commission and processing fees. The DRE broker may find it cost-prohibitive to perform these loans, as the commissions collected are considerably less than usual, while the CFL broker handles most of the work.

A real estate broker who wishes to also offer mobile home services may obtain a CFL license in addition to the DRE license.

6. **REAL PROPERTY MANUFACTURED HOMES** are manufactured homes on private lots and are considered real property only if the home is permanently fixed on a private lot. Generally, this refers to mobile homes that have been placed on a permanent foundation and the wheels and axles have been removed. Mobile home manufacturers began building the homes with the axles permanently attached in the mid-1990s. If this is the case, it is documentable and can be waived by the Underwriter.

   When a manufactured home has been **permanently affixed to a foundation,** the contractor will provide a state required certificate. A copy of this certificate must be included as part of the transaction documentation required for a loan.

   HUD began establishing guidelines for the construction of manufactured homes in 1976. Any homes built prior to July 1, 1976, are more difficult to finance because they do not meet building standards

   Single-wide mobile homes are not considered acceptable property to residential mortgage lenders even when permanently attached to a private lot.

7. **MINERAL, OIL, AND GAS TRANSACTIONS** may be handled by real estate licensees. *The former licensing designated as a mineral, oil, and gas (MOG) broker license is no longer provided. Those holding an existing MOG broker license may continue to work under that license and must continue to renew the MOG broker license and pay the fees accordingly. There are no longer continuing education requirements for the renewal of this license. New MOG licensing is no longer offered as the real estate broker's license provides for the licensing requirements.*

   » The duties performed by a real estate licensee in a mineral, oil, and gas transaction include:
   - List for sale
   - Solicit prospective buyers and sellers
   - Negotiate and prepare purchase offers
   - Lease
   - Manage lease
   - Exchange
   - Assist with the filing of the application for purchase or lease of related property owned by the federal government
   - Options
   - Offer mining claims
   - Be a principal

Business opportunity brokerage is often handled by a real estate licensee even though the sale may be for personal property only. **Bulk sale of goods** refers to the sale of a business that includes the business and the merchandise that is part of the business. A business sale will involve the sale of the **business name and goodwill:** goodwill is the continuing and ongoing patronage of the clientele.

- **Inventory of business equipment:** Cash register, display selves, machinery or any equipment that is part of running and operating the business.
- **Inventory of business possessions and any product:** A person purchasing a clothing store could expect to purchase the clothing that is currently being offered for sale to the public in the store. Whatever the product the business is providing is a part of the business purchase transaction.
- **Lease of real property:** If the current business is located in a leased space, the transfer of that lease and perhaps new lease terms will be a part of the business purchase transaction.

- **Sale of real property:** If the real property is a part of the business sale transaction, a real property purchase offer will be a part of the overall transaction.
  The negotiations of real property, whether a lease or a purchase offer, is usually handled as a separate simultaneous transaction. **A business sale does not require a real estate license**, however, if the negotiation of real property is a part of the transaction, a real estate broker's license is beneficial. A business sale that does not involve real property negotiations is rare.

- **Review of the records** to include current profit & loss statement, and a minimum of the most recent two years' tax returns, and the seller's books and records are a part of the agent's responsibility when assisting with the sale of a business. The consideration of the business location and the flow of business being generated are also part of the agent's responsibilities. The real estate agent is responsible for assisting the buyer with the review and consideration of all aspects of, not only the purchase of the business, but also the operations of the business being purchased.

- **LOCAL LICENSING LAWS** regarding the operation of a business and those specific to certain businesses is an important part of purchasing a business. The real estate professional specializing in the sale of businesses should be fully prepared to provide advice and assistance with the local requirements.

  - **Franchise Tax Board (FTB)** is responsible for collecting sales tax from businesses that collect sales tax as a part of their business operations such as with retail sales. *The Franchise Tax Board offers seminars for business owners on a regular basis. A real estate professional will learn these intricacies as a part of business when specializing in the sale of businesses.* The owner of a business that is required to collect sales tax must register the business with the Franchise Tax Board. The Franchise Tax Board will provide the forms that will be needed for filing taxes.

NOTE

The licensing provided by the DRE applies to activities involving 1–4-unit residential properties. Although licensing is not required for commercial transactions, the agent that has a DRE license will be recognized as the more capable and knowledgeable agent and therefore the preferred representation.

- » **Uniform Commercial Code (UCC)** is a federal code that has been adopted by California. The purpose of the UCC is to regulate the transfer of goods being held for sale by a business. Most retailers or sellers of goods purchase their stock or items for resale on credit. The normal course of business allows for a retailer to pay for their stock over a period of time, which provides time to generate the money from resale to pay for the merchandise. If the merchandise or stock is part of a business sale, the creditor needs assurance of payment for the merchandise being held as stock in the business being sold. The wholesalers or providers of the product are generally paid through close of escrow.

- » **Bulk sale** is the transfer of a substantial part of the inventory. Inventory will fluctuate as products are sold to customers of the business. An inventory will be conducted; however, business will continue. To protect the creditors, the UCC (Uniform Commercial Code) provides for creditors to be notified of transfer of business ownership:
    - Notice made at least 12 business days prior to transfer
    - Notice recorded with the county recorder's office
    - Transfer published in local newspaper
    - Notice to the county tax collector notified by certified mail
    - Notice posted in a conspicuous place at the place of business

- **Franchises** are businesses that sell to a party or a franchisee the right to operate a business using their name, product, trademark, and any other use to benefit the franchisee in the operation of their business. The franchisee purchases the rights to operate under an already established business name and reputation.

    Example: *McDonalds is perhaps the best-known franchise. The franchisee or the party purchasing a McDonalds franchise purchases the right to use the name, sign, recipes, building design and all else that McDonalds offers. They obtain the right to purchase food from McDonalds' main corporation, which is the franchisor. The franchisee receives the right to advertise and operate as McDonalds.*

The franchisee pays to purchase the franchise and often pays a fee or a percentage of the profits as ongoing payment to operate the franchise. The franchisee is generally required to purchase supplies from the franchisor as part of the agreement. There are a number of large real estate companies that also are franchises.

PROFESSIONAL ASSOCIATIONS

1. "REALTOR" is a registered trademark of the **BOARD OF REALTORS** organization and may not be used by any person who is not a member. A real estate professional must be a member of the Board of Realtors in order to advertise and call themselves "realtor.". Membership in the **California Association of Realtors (CAR)** constitutes membership in the **National Association of Realtors (NAR)**. The organization provides forms created by the CAR Attorneys in an online format for ease in preparing contracts as part of doing business such as a purchase contract. If the broker of record is a member, all associate licensees working for that broker are required to be members per the terms of the organization. See www.car.org and www.realtor.com for information regarding these associations.

2. **MULTIPLE LISTING SERVICE (MLS)** is an organization of real estate sales professionals which provides access to the listings of all member brokers in the organization. It allows a broker to advertise their listings to other member brokers providing information for showings to potential buyers. Members share an agreement to pay commissions to any other member office that procures a party to a real estate transaction. Non-member offices must obtain a contract agreeing to pay commissions for each transaction. If the broker of record is a member, all associate licensees working for that broker are required to be members per the terms of the organization.

3. **REALTIST** is a member of the **NATIONAL ASSOCIATION OF REAL ESTATE BROKERS, INC. (NAREB).** This organization began in Florida in 1947 as an organization of predominantly African American members. It is now a nationwide organization with a number of local groups. *See www.nareb.com for information regarding this association.*

4. CALIFORNIA ASSOCIATION OF MORTGAGE BROKERS (CAMB) is a professional organization for those involved in the mortgage business. Membership in the state association constitutes membership in the National Association of Mortgage Brokers (NAMB). *See www.cambweb.org or www.namb.org for further information regarding these associations.*

Additional Trade Associations may be found on the DRE website https://dre.ca.gov/Licensees/TradeAssociations.html

The following list provides some associations of interest to real estate s:

- Asian American Real Estate Association https://areaa.org
- Californian Association of Realtors www.car.org
- California Association of Real Estate Brokers www.careb.org
- California Association of Mortgage Brokers www.cambweb.org
- California Mortgage Bankers Association www.cmba.com
- California Association of Business Brokers www.cabb.org
- California Association of Community Managers www.cacm.org
- California Building Industry Association www.cbia.org
- National Association of Hispanic Real Estate Professionals www.nahrep.org
- National Association of Realtors https://www.nar.realtor

VIOLATIONS OF THE REAL ESTATE LAWS

REAL ESTATE VIOLATIONS that are the most common offenses and that are prohibited acts are found in the **Business and Professions Code** Section 10176. These acts by a real estate licensee may result in license suspension, revocation, fines, or imprisonment:

- Undisclosed dual agency
- Misrepresentation of material facts
- Comingling of funds
- False promise
- Lack of listing termination date
- Violation of the Transfer Disclosure Civil Code
- Secret profit by licensee
- Dishonest dealing
- Fraud
- Theft
- False advertising
- Criminal activities
- Misuse of trade name
- Negligence
- Negligent supervision of salespersons
- Trust fund violation
- Mishandling of clients' funds
- Inducing panic selling

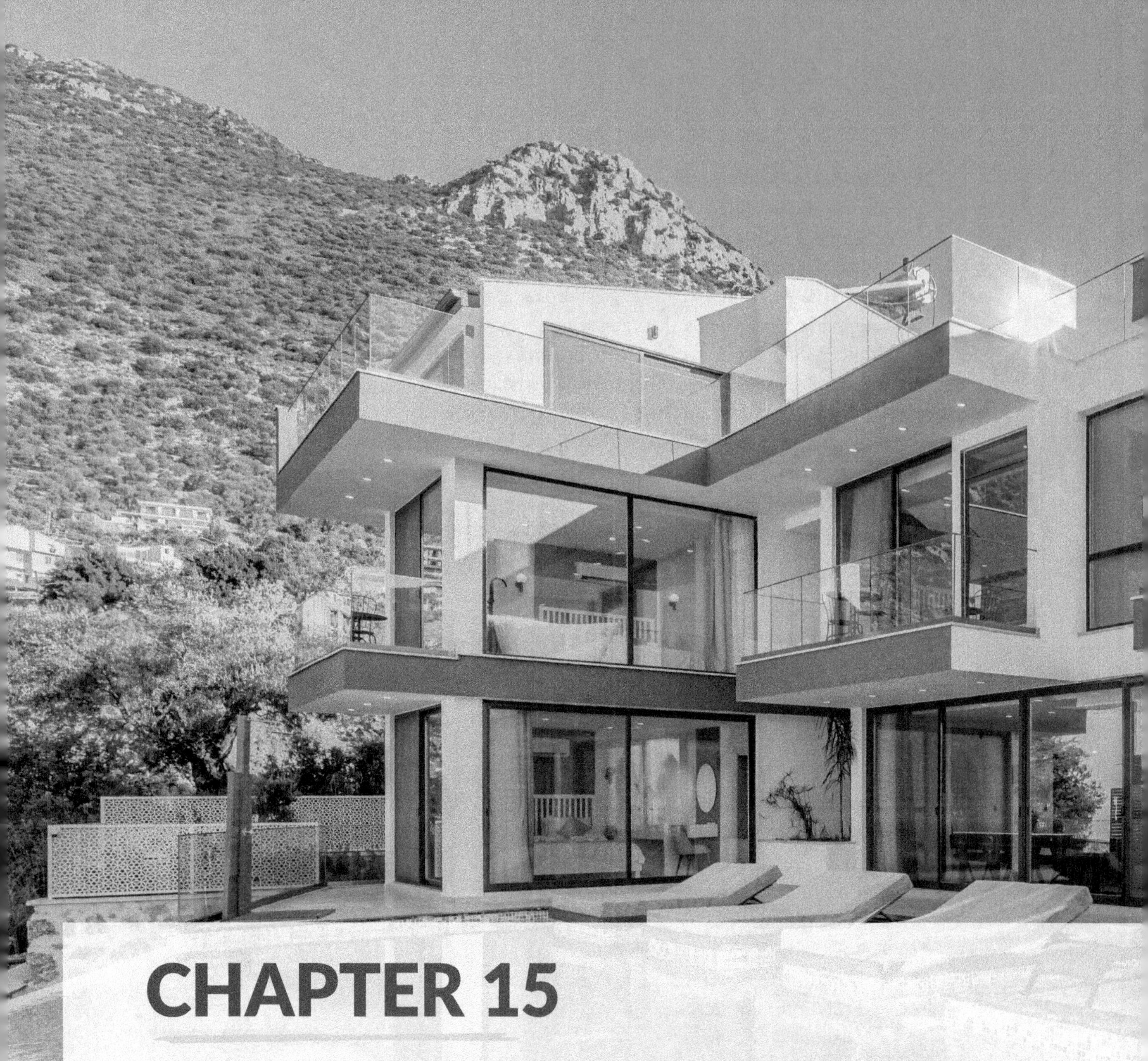

CHAPTER 15

ANTI-DISCRIMINATION LAWS AND DISCLOSURES/SUBDIVISION LAWS OF CALIFORNIA/RESIDENTIAL DESIGN AND CONSTRUCTION

US
Realty School

DISCRIMINATION IN HOUSING

DISCRIMINATION IN HOUSING is illegal and there are various laws protecting the public from various forms and types of discrimination. Owners of real property are prohibited from discrimination in the sale, rental, or leasing of their property. Real estate professionals should not accept a listing or any other type of real property contract from a property owner that is trying to discriminate in any way including making the discriminatory act a condition of the contract. Property owners, real estate professionals, salespeople, lenders, and hotel management are all prohibited from exercising any acts of discrimination in regard to housing accommodations.

FEDERAL LAWS that address discrimination are as follows:

1. ***The Civil Rights Act of 1866*** prohibits racial discrimination and the 13th Amendment abolishes slavery, however, little was done to uphold the Civil Rights Act for nearly one hundred years. Many county records and preliminary title reports still contain CC&Rs from the early 1900s that employ discrimination in the establishment of housing developments and subdivisions. Such CC&Rs are illegal, and the title insurance companies clearly state that, even though they remain a part of the recorded documents with the county recorder's office.

   There are no exemptions to the Civil Rights Act of 1866.

2. ***The Federal Fair Housing Act of 1968*** was created to control discrimination in the housing market. The *Federal Fair Housing Act* applies to all residential property transactions including sale, lease, lending, advertising, and any other acts relating to housing.

   This act became a part of *Title VIII* of the *Civil Rights* Act of 1968. Discrimination in housing is prohibited based on the following:
   - Race
   - Color
   - Religion
   - Sex (including gender identity and sexual orientation)

- National origin
- Ancestry
- Disability
- Familial status

The following are **EXEMPT** from the compliance with this act:

- Families with minor children may prohibit based on familial status.
- Adult communities may discriminate based on age if all residents are 62 or older or 80% of the complex is occupied by residents 55 and older and special services for the elderly are offered.
- Religious organizations, societies, or affiliated non- profit organizations dealing with their privately owned property may limit transactions to their members. Membership may not be restricted based on race, color, or national origin.
- Private clubs limited to members only for lodgings that are not open to the public in a commercial capacity.
- Rental by a property owner of a single-family residence (SFR) if they own three SFR rentals or less.
- Room rental in an owner-occupied dwelling of up to four units.

Exemption from the *Federal Fair Housing Act* does not provide exemption from the *Civil Rights Act of 1866* and does not override any state laws prohibiting discrimination.

Department of Housing and Urban Development (HUD) and the US Attorney General are responsible for hearing complaints of discrimination in housing by the public. A party who has been discriminated against has one year to file a complaint of discrimination with *HUD's Office of Equal Housing Opportunity (OEO)* or two years to file a lawsuit in either state or federal court.

STATE LAWS against discrimination cover more issues than the federal laws and many local areas in California have created stricter laws.

3. **FAIR EMPLOYMENT AND HOUSING ACT (FEHA)** was formerly known as the ***Rumford Act.*** The *Rumford Act* was named for and influenced by Robert Rumford who was a prominent African American businessman and politician. Mr. Rumford was instrumental in establishing rights for minorities in the early 1900s.

The FEHA prohibits discrimination in housing to include sale, lease, or financing in all types of housing accommodations based on:

- Race
- Color
- Religion
- Sex
- Gender identity
- Sexual orientation
- Marital status
- National origin
- Ancestry
- Disability - either physical or mental
- Medical condition
- Familial status
- Source of income

Blockbusting is the discriminatory act of attempting to cause panic selling in a neighborhood. This is done by spreading rumors that people of a different race or another group, such as those of different religious beliefs than the predominant socio-economic occupants of the neighborhood.

This is an illegal act under the *FEHA* and is punishable by loss of real estate license, fines, and/or imprisonment.
Steering is the practice of showing clients properties that are located in similarly ethnic neighborhoods. It is unlawful to restrict or attempt to influence the choices of a person by word or conduct in connection with housing that will perpetuate or affect the make-up of a neighborhood, community, or a housing development through segregation or discriminatory acts.

4. ***The Civil Rights Housing Act of 2006*** became effective January 1, 2007. The act allows for automatic updates as additional areas of discrimination in housing and housing related areas become apparent and a need is proven. This act extends the *FEHA* to prohibit discrimination in housing and housing related areas which include:
   - Real estate licensing
   - Mortgage lending
   - Club membership established by condo associations
   - Housing developments
   - Mobile home parks
   - Community redevelopment

5. ***The Unruh Civil Rights Act*** prohibits discrimination in accommodations and business establishments such as hotels. This act includes all the prohibitions in the *FEHA*. Discrimination is prohibited in all areas of housing accommodations against all categories covered by the *FEHA*.

DISCRIMINATION IN LENDING

DISCRIMINATION IN LENDING is addressed under several laws. Federal banking laws prohibit discrimination in lending by banks, savings & loans, and federal credit unions.

REDLINING became prohibited under anti-discrimination regulation in 1976. Redlining is the practice of denying loans on properties that are located in low income and otherwise unfavorable areas. The state of California prohibits the practice of redlining on all loans secured by 1-to 4-unit residential dwellings. This prohibition applies to conventional loans, insured by FHA, or guaranteed by VA.

Housing Financial Discrimination Act of 1977/ Fair Lending Notice also known as the ***Holden Act,*** which went into effect January 1, 1978, prohibits discrimination by all financial institutions based on the geographic location, neighborhood, or other related characteristics of the property. This prohibition does not apply to negative decisions based on sound business practice such as changing neighborhood, zoning changes, or condition of property. *See Figure 30: Housing Discrimination Act/Fair Lending Notice*

This law applies to all loans on owner-occupied residential properties of 1-to 4-units for purchase, refinance, construction, or remodeling. The law also applies to home improvement loans from a financial institution for owner-occupied and non-owner- occupied properties. All categories covered under the *FEHA* are covered under the *Holden Act.* ***The following categories may not be discriminated against:***

- Race
- Color
- Religion
- Sex
- Sexual orientation
- Marital status
- National origin
- Ancestry
- Disability: either physical or mental

- Medical condition
- Familial status
- Source of income
- Geographic area of subject property
- Condition of the neighborhood
- Characteristics of the neighborhood

COMPLAINTS OF DISCRIMINATION under this act should be filed with the *Secretary for Business, Transportation, and Housing.* The secretary has 30 days from the date of receiving any complaint to act on it by investigating and responding.

When incidences of discrimination are discovered or proven the following remedies are available depending on the extent of the discriminatory act and the damages resulting from the acts:

- Provide the requested loan
- Offer better loan terms
- Monetary damages up to $1,000

Appeals may be presented to the *Office of Administrative Hearings* and the then to a court for a decision to overturn the secretary's decision. Lenders are required to provide borrowers with notification that this law exists and that they have rights under it, and must also provide the necessary information for the borrower to file a complaint.

DISCLOSURES are required to be given to all borrowers of mortgage loans by either state or federal laws. Obtaining a signed copy in the file verifies that the borrower has been given a copy of each. It is imperative that the *Equal Credit Opportunity Act* and *Fair Lending* disclosures are provided to the client.

Equal Credit Opportunity Act (ECOA) is the federal law that prohibits discrimination against credit applicants on the basis of:

- Race
- Color
- Religion
- National origin
- Sex
- Marital status
- Age provided the applicant can legally enter into a contract
- All or part of applicant's income being from public assistance
- Rights under the Consumer Protection Act that were exercised in good faith

THE HOUSING FINANCIAL DISCRIMINATION ACT OF 1977

FAIR LENDING NOTICE

It is illegal to discriminate in the provision of or in the availability of financial assistance because of the consideration of:

1. **Trends, characteristics or conditions in the neighborhood or geographic area surrounding a housing accommodation, unless the financial institution can demonstrate in the particular case that such consideration is required to avoid an unsafe and unsound business practice; or**
2. **Race, color, religion, sex, marital status, domestic partnership, national origin or ancestry.**

It is illegal to consider the racial, ethnic, religious or national origin composition of a neighborhood or geographic area surrounding a housing accommodation or whether or not such composition is undergoing change, or is expected to undergo change, in appraising a housing accommodation or in determining whether or not, or under what terms and conditions, to provide financial assistance.

These provisions govern financial assistance for the purpose of the purchase, construction, rehabilitation or refinancing of one- to four-unit family residences occupied by the owner and for the purpose of the home improvement of any one- to four-unit family residence.

If you have any questions about your rights, or if you wish to file a complaint, contact the management of this financial institution or the Department of Real Estate at one of the following locations:

2550 Mariposa Mall, Suite 3070
Fresno, CA 93721-2273

320 W. 4th Street, Suite 350
Los Angeles, CA 90013-1105

1515 Clay Street, Suite 702
Oakland, CA 94612-1462

651 Bannon Street, STE 505
Sacramento, CA 95811

8620 Spectrum Center Blvd., Suite 301
San Diego, CA 92123

ACKNOWLEDGMENT OF RECEIPT

I (we) received a copy of this notice.

______________________ ______________
Signature of Applicant *Date*

______________________ ______________
Signature of Applicant *Date*

DEPARTMENT OF REAL ESTATE — Mortgage Lending Unit RE 867 (Rev. 6/24)

Figure 30: Housing Discrimination Act/Fair Lending Notice

BORROWERS SIGNATURE AUTHORIZATION gives the real estate professional authorization to acquire a credit report. It is against federal law to run a credit report without written authorization. Authorization is also required to obtain any additional personal information and necessary documentation, such as the verification of employment. The authorization will be required for any real estate related services that requires a credit report and other personal documentation such as for a mortgage loan application or leasing approval. Many related industries such as accountants will often require a copy of the signature authorization prior to talking to the real estate professional. *See Figure 22: Borrower's Signature Authorization.*

RIGHT TO RECEIVE THE APPRAISAL lets the borrower know that they do have a right to receive a copy of the appraisal report on completion of the loan based on the premise that they paid for the appraisal. This disclosure became a requirement in the late 1990s because the buyers/borrowers of real property were required to pay for the appraisal, yet rarely received a copy of the document. The form should provide a space for the buyer/borrower to provide an address for delivery of the appraisal. *See Figure 23: Right to Receive a Copy of the Appraisal in Chapter 12, Real Estate Financing.*

PATRIOT ACT is a requirement of the federal government in conjunction with Homeland Security for a way of tracking any potential terrorist or undesirables mainly through the movement of large amounts of money. The form requires two forms of identification as verification of identity. The driver's license and the Social Security card are the most commonly used forms of ID. One of the forms must include a photo of the person. *See Figure 24: Patriot Act Information Disclosure in Chapter 12, Real Estate Financing.*

MORTGAGE LOAN ORIGINATION AGREEMENT is required by the federal government to explain to the borrower the relationship between the consumer and the mortgage broker/agent and how the mortgage broker gets paid. The disclosure lets the client know that the mortgage broker contracts with a number of different lenders in order to provide options to the client. It also states that the lowest price and terms available on the market cannot be guaranteed. Compensation is paid either entirely by the borrower or it can be received from the lender or a combination of both. The disclosure explains how the lender may provide rebate pricing with a higher interest rate to offset lower fees to the client.

The federal government does not regard the mortgage broker as an agent. According to the federal government's definition, a mortgage broker is an independent contractor. *See Figure 25: Mortgage Loan Origination Agreement in Chapter 12 Real Estate Financing.*

REAL ESTATE AGENCY DISCLOSURE is the similar to the mortgage loan origination agreement; however, is the form required by the State of California's DRE because it states that the mortgage originator is an agent according to California law, whereas the mortgage loan origination agreement states that the mortgage originator is not an agent. The disclosure explains what an agency relationship is and what it means to the borrower.

PMI/ADJUSTABLE-RATE DISCLOSURE is in the form of a HUD pamphlet and was designed by HUD to explain to the consumer the potential problems that may occur as a result of adjustable interest rates.
See Figure 28: Private Mortgage Insurance, Adjustable Rate

ECOA (EQUAL CREDIT OPPORTUNITY ACT) disclosure informs the client that they do not have to disclose any income derived from Alimony or Child Support. The lender does, however, have the right to ask if any of the stated income is from those sources. Verification of income from Alimony or Child Support must be reviewed for a determination of continuance of the income if used for qualifying purposes.
See Figure 31: Equal Credit Opportunity Act (ECOA)

The federal agency that administers compliance with this act is the *Office of the Controller of the Currency.* The *ECOA* requires that all businesses providing lending related services, such as a mortgage broker must give the borrower/client a copy of the ECOA disclosure and provide the address for filing complaints. Complaints should be filed with that Agency at:

Office of the Controller of the Currency Customer Assistance Group
1301 McKinley Street, Suite 3710
Houston, TX 77010

Mortgage brokers and any real estate related businesses that provide lending related services must display the Equal Credit Opportunity symbol/disclosure in a conspicuous place.

CREDIT DISCLOSURE is a relatively new disclosure that is required in all loan packages dated July 1, 2001, or later. In the past, the information on a borrower's credit report was not disclosed. As of July 1, 2001, the information is to be disclosed in a form that explains the way the credit score works, the borrower's credit score, and the information that has directly affected their own credit score. Also included are the addresses of the credit repositories so the borrower may contact them to correct any errors in the report. *See Figure 32, Credit Score Information Disclosure*

SERVICING DISCLOSURE STATEMENT informs the borrower whether the broker or lender retains their loan for servicing or collecting the payments and, if so, how many or if the loan will be sold to other lenders or Investors. In the past, borrowers have found it disconcerting when their loans have been sold on the secondary market without notification and this disclosure helps to explain this to the borrower.

Many borrowers want their loan to stay with the same lender who originally gave them the loan. Unfortunately, selling loans to other lenders and investors is the way the lending business operates. Initially, the borrower gets a "welcome letter" from the lender who is lending the money, but then quite often, a few months after close of escrow, they receive a letter from another lender who has purchased the loan. The servicing disclosure explains what is likely to occur to their loan and it provides a disclosure from the mortgage broker or lender in regard to the number of loans the broker or lender sells or retains. *See Figure 33: Servicing Disclosure Statement.*

PRIVACY POLICY DISCLOSURE is required to notify the borrower that, per *Title V of the Gramm-Leach-Bliley Act*, financial institutions and their affiliates are prohibited from sharing non-public personal information concerning their clients. There are a number of businesses who share or sell their client list to other companies and businesses looking for new client bases. This form gives the client the opportunity to choose to "opt out." Opting out is the choice of the client not to have their information sold or shared for the purpose of soliciting or advertising. *See Figure 34: Privacy Policy Disclosure.*

HUD PAMPHLETS: "Settlement Costs and You," "When Your House Is on the Line," for equity lines of credit and "Adjustable-Rate Mortgages" must also be provided. These pamphlets are provided for both purchase and refinance transactions. They are designed to explain the borrower's rights, costs, and laws in regard to the transaction. Providing the appropriate pamphlet is also a federal law. These pamphlets may be purchased from the companies that sell loan applications and others related forms and documents. *See Figure 35: HUD Pamphlet-Shopping for Your Home Loan.*

EQUAL CREDIT OPPORTUNITY ACT

APPLICATION NO.

PROPERTY ADDRESS:

The Federal Equal Credit Opportunity Act prohibits creditors from discriminating against credit applicants on the basis of race, color, religion, national origin, sex, marital status, age (provided the applicant has the capacity to enter into a binding contract), because all or part of the applicant's income derives from any public assistance program; or because the applicant has in good faith exercised any right under the Consumer Credit Protection Act. The Federal Agency that administers compliance with this law concerning this company is the Office of the Comptroller of the Currency, Customer Assistance Group, 1301 McKinney Street, Suite 3710, Houston, Texas 77010

We are required to disclose to you that you need not disclose income from alimony, child support or separate maintenance payment if you choose not to do so.

Having made this disclosure to you, we are permitted to inquire if any of the income shown on your application is derived from such a source and to consider the likelihood of consistent payment as we do with any income on which you are relying to qualify for the loan for which you are applying.

(Applicant) (Date) (Applicant) (Date)

(Applicant) (Date) (Applicant) (Date)

Figure 31: Equal Credit Opportunity Act (ECOA)

NOTICE TO THE HOME LOAN APPLICANT
CREDIT SCORE INFORMATION DISCLOSURE

APPLICANT(S) NAME AND ADDRESS	LENDER NAME AND ADDRESS (ORIGINATOR): ABC Mortgage 1212 Main St. Oxnard, CA 93030 (P) 805-555-6666, (F) 805-555-0000

In connection with your application for a home loan, the lender must disclose to you the score that a consumer reporting agency distributed to users and the lender used in connection with your home loan, and the key factors affecting your credit scores.

The credit score is a computer-generated summary calculated at the time of the request and based on information a consumer reporting agency or lender has on file. The scores are based on data about your credit history and payment patterns. Credit scores are important because they are used to assist the lender in determining whether you will obtain a loan. They may also be used to determine what interest rate you may be offered on the mortgage. Credit scores can change over time, depending on your conduct, how your credit history and payment patterns change, and how credit-scoring technologies change.

Because the score is based on information in your credit history, it is very important that you review the credit related information that is being furnished to make sure it is accurate. Credit records may vary from one company to another.

If you have questions about your credit score or the credit information that is furnished to you, contact the consumer reporting agency at the address and telephone number provided with this notice, or contact the lender, if the lender developed or generated the credit score. The consumer reporting agency plays no part in the decision to take any action on the loan application and is unable to provide you with specific reasons for the decision on a loan application.

If you have questions concerning the terms of the loan, contact the lender.

The consumer reporting agencies listed below provided a credit score that was used in connection with your home loan application.

Consumer Reporting Agency	Borrower:	Co-Brw:
Experian P.O. Box 2002 Allen, TX 75013 (P)888-397-3742 Model Used: ______ Range of Possible Scores ______ to ______	Score: Created: Factors	Score: Created: Factors

Figure 32: Credit Score Information Disclosure Page 1 of 2

Consumer Reporting Agency	Borrower	Co-Brw:
TransUnion P.O. Box 1000 (P)800-888-4213 Model Used: __________ Range of Possible Scores _____ to _____	Score: Created: Factors	Score: Created: Factors
Equifax P.O. Box 740241 Atlanta, GA 30374 (P)800-685-1111 Model Used: __________ Range of Possible Scores _____ to _____	Score: Created: Factors	Score: Created: Factors

I/We have received a copy of this disclosure.

____________________ __________ ____________________ __________

Applicant Date Applicant Date

Figure 32: Credit Score Information Disclosure Page 2 of 2

SERVICING DISCLOSURE STATEMENT

Lender: **ABC Mortgage**
1212 Main St.
Oxnard, CA 93030

Date:

NOTICE TO FIRST LIEN MORTGAGE LOAN APPLICANTS: THE RIGHT TO COLLECT YOUR MORTGAGE LOAN PAYMENTS MAY BE TRANSFERRED. FEDERAL LAW GIVES YOU CERTAIN RELATED RIGHTS. IF YOUR LOAN IS MADE, SAVE THIS STATEMENT WITH YOUR LOAN DOCUMENTS. SIGN THE ACKNOWLEDGMENT AT THE END OF THIS STATEMENT ONLY IF YOU UNDERSTAND ITS CONTENTS.

Because you are applying for a mortgage loan covered by the Real Estate Settlement Procedures Act (RESPA) (12 U.S.C. Section 2601 et seq.) you have certain rights under that Federal law.

This statement tells you about those rights. It also tells you what the chances are that the servicing for this loan may be transferred to a different loan servicer. "Servicing" refers to collecting your principal, interest and escrow account payments, if any. If your loan servicer changes, there are certain procedures that must be followed. This statement generally explains those procedures.

Transfer practices and requirements

If the servicing of your loan is assigned, sold, or transferred to a new servicer, you must be given written notice of that transfer. The present loan servicer must send you notice in writing of the assignment, sale or transfer of the servicing not less than 15 days before the effective date of the transfer. The new loan servicer must also send you notice within 15 days after the effective date of the transfer. The present servicer and the new servicer may combine this information in one notice, so long as the notice is sent to you 15 days before the effective date of transfer. The 15 day period is not applicable if a notice of prospective transfer is provided to you at settlement. The law allows a delay in the time (not more than 30 days after a transfer) for servicers to notify you, upon the occurrence of certain business emergencies.

Notices must contain certain information. They must contain the effective date of the transfer of the servicing of your loan to the new servicer, and the name, address, and toll-free or collect call telephone number of the new servicer, and toll-free or collect call telephone numbers of a person or department for both your present servicer and your new servicer to answer your questions. During the 60 day period following the effective date of the transfer of the loan servicing, a loan payment received by your old servicer before its due date may not be treated by the new loan servicer as late, and a late fee may not be imposed on you.

Complaint Resolution

Section 6 of RESPA (12 U.S.C. Section 2605) gives you certain consumer rights, whether or not your loan servicing is transferred. If you send a "qualified written request" to your servicer, then your servicer must provide you with a written acknowledgment within 20 Business Days of receipt of your request. A "qualified written request" is a written correspondence, other than notice on a payment coupon or other payment medium supplied by the servicer, which includes your name and account number, and the information regarding your request. Not later than 60 Business Days after receiving your request, your servicer must make any appropriate corrections to your account, or must provide you with a written clarification regarding any dispute. During this 60 Business Day period, your servicer may not provide information to a consumer reporting agency concerning any overdue payment related to such period or qualified written request.

A Business Day is any day in which the offices of the business entity are open to the public for carrying on substantially all of its business functions.

Damages and Costs

Section 6 of RESPA also provides for damages and costs for individuals or classes of individuals in circumstances where servicers are shown to have violated the requirements of that Section.

Page 1 of 2

Figure 33: Servicing Disclosure Statement
Page 1 of 2

Servicing Transfer Estimates

1. The following is the best estimate of what will happen to the servicing of your mortgage loan:

   A. ☐ We may assign, sell or transfer the servicing of your loan while the loan is outstanding.

   We are able to service your loan, and we
   ☐ will service your loan.
   ☐ will not service your loan
   ☐ haven't decided whether to service your loan.

   B. ☐ We do not service mortgage loans ☐ and we have not serviced mortgage loans in the past three years.
   We presently intend to assign, sell or transfer the servicing of your mortgage loan. You will be informed about your servicer.

2. For all mortgage loans that we make in the 12 month period after your mortgage loan is funded, we estimate that the percentage of such loans for which we will transfer servicing is between:

   _____ 0 to 25% _____ 26 to 50% _____ 51 to 75% _____ 76 to 100%

   This estimate ☐ does ☐ does not include assignments, sales or transfers to affiliates or subsidiaries.

   This is only our best estimate and it is not binding. Business conditions or other circumstances may affect our future transferring decisions.

3. A. ☐ We have previously assigned, sold, or transferred the servicing of mortgage loans.

   B. ☐ This is our record of transferring the servicing of mortgage loans we have made in:

Year	Percentage of Loans Transferred
	%
	%
	%

   This information ☐ does ☐ does not include assignments, sales or transfers to affiliates or subsidiaries

Acknowledgment of Mortgage Loan Applicant(s)

I/We have read and understood the disclosure; and understand that the disclosure is a required part of the mortgage application as evidenced by my/our signature(s) below;

Applicant	Date	Applicant	Date
Applicant	Date	Applicant	Date

Page 2 of 2

Figure 33: Servicing Disclosure Statement
Page 2 of 2

PRIVACY POLICY DISCLOSURE

(Protection of the Privacy of Personal Non-Public Information)

Respecting and protecting customer privacy is vital to our business. By explaining our Privacy Policy to you, we trust that you will better understand how we keep our customer information private and secure while using it to serve you better. Keeping customer information secure is a top priority, and we are disclosing our policies to help you understand how we handle the personal information about you that we collect and disclose. This notice explains how you can limit our disclosing of personal information about you. The provisions of this notice will apply to former customers as well as current customers unless we state otherwise.

The Privacy Policy explains the Following:

- Protecting the confidentiality of our customer information.
- Who is covered by the Privacy Policy.
- How we gather information.
- The types of information we share, why, and with whom.
- Opting Out - how to instruct us not to share certain information about you or not to contact you.

Protecting the Confidentiality of Customer Information:

We take our responsibility to protect the privacy and confidentiality of customer information very seriously. We maintain physical, electronic, and procedural safeguards that comply with federal standards to store and secure information about you from unauthorized access, alteration, and destruction. Our control policies, for example, authorize access to customer information only by individuals who need access to do their work.

From time to time, we enter into agreements with other companies to provide services to us or make products and services available to you. Under these agreements, the companies may receive information about you but they must safeguard this information, and they may not use it for any other purposes.

Who is Covered by the Privacy Policy:

We provide our Privacy Policy to customers when they conduct business with our company. If we change our privacy policies to permit us to share additional information we have about you, as described below, or to permit disclosures to additional types of parties, you will be notified in advance. This Privacy Policy applies to consumers who are current customers or former customers.

How We Gather Information:

As part of providing you with financial products or services, we may obtain information about you from the followin sources:

- Applications, forms, and other information that you provide to us, whether in writing, in person, by telephone, electronically, or by any other means. This information may include your name, address, employment information, income, and credit references;
- Your transaction with us, our affiliates, or others. This information may include your account balances, payment history, and account usage;
- Consumer reporting agencies. This information may include account information and information about your credit worthiness;
- Public sources. This information may include real estate records, employment records, telephone numbers, etc

Information We Share:

We may disclose information we have about you as permitted by law. We are required to or we may provide information about you to third-parties without your consent, as permitted by law, such as:

- To regulatory authorities and law enforcement officials.
- To protect against or prevent actual or potential fraud, unauthorized transactions, claims, or other liability.
- To report account activity to credit bureaus.
- To consumer reporting agencies.

Figure 34: Privacy Policy Disclosure
Page 1 of 2

- To respond to a subpoena or court order, judicial process or regulatory authorities.
- In connection with a proposed or actual sale, merger, or transfer of all or a portion of a business or an operating unit, etc.

In addition, we may provide information about you to our service providers to help us process your applications or service your accounts. Our service providers may include billing service providers, mail and telephone service companies, lenders, investors, title and escrow companies, appraisal companies, etc.

We may also provide information about you to our service providers to help us perform marketing services. This information provided to these service providers may include the categories of information described above under "How We Gather Information" limited to only that which we deem appropriate for these service providers to carry out their functions.

We do not provide non-public information about you to any company whose products and services are being marketed unless you authorize us to do so. These companies are not allowed to use this information for purposes beyond your specific authorization.

Opting Out

We also may share information about you within our corporate family of office(s). We may share all of the categories of information we gather about you, including identification information (such as your name and address), credit reports (such as your credit history), application information (such as your income or credit references), your account transactions and experiences with us (such as your payment history), and information from other third parties (such as your employment history).

By sharing this information we can better understand your financial needs. We can then send you notification of new products and special promotional offers that you may not otherwise know about. For example, if you originally obtained a mortgage loan with us, we would know that you are a homeowner and may be interested in hearing how a home equity loan may be a better option than an auto loan to finance the purchase of a new car.

You may prohibit the sharing of application and third-party credit-related information within our company or any third-party company at any time. If you would like to limit disclosures of personal information about you as described in this notice, just check the appropriate box or boxes to indicate your privacy choices.

☐ Please do not share personal information about me with non-affilliated third-parties.

☐ Please do not share personal information about me with any of your affiliates except as necessary to effect, administer, process, service or enforce a transaction requested or authorized by myself.

☐ Please do not contact me with offers of products or services by mail.

☐ Please do not contact me with offers of products or services by telephone.

Note for Joint Accounts: Your Opt Out choices will also apply to other individuals who are joint account holders. If these individuals have separate accounts, your Opt Out will not apply to those separate accounts.

______________________	**ABC Mortgage**
Name	Company Name
______________________	**1212 Main St.**
Address	Address
______________________	**Oxnard CA, 93030**
City, State, Zip	City, State, Zip
______________________	**805-555-6666**
Phone#	Phone #
______________________	
Loan #	
______________________	______________________
Borrower's Signature Date	Co-Borrower's Signature Date

Figure 34: Privacy Policy Disclosure
Page 2 of 2

Procedures Act (RESPA) requires
rs to give you this booklet within
mortgage loan. RESPA is a federal
mers from unfair practices by
during the home-buying and loan

nt financial decision that should be
oklet will help you become familiar
e home-buying process, including
deciding whether you are ready to buy a home, and providing factors to consider in determining how much you can afford to spend. You will learn about the sales agreement, how to use a *Good Faith Estimate* to shop for the best loan for you, required settlement services to close your loan, and the *HUD-1 Settlement Statement* that you will receive at closing.

This booklet will help you become familiar with how interest rates, points, balloon payments, and prepayment penalties can affect your monthly mortgage payments. In addition, there is important information about your loan after settlement, including how to resolve loan servicing problems with your lender, and steps you can take to avoid foreclosure. After you have purchased your home, this booklet will help you indentify issues to consider before getting a home equity loan or refinancing your mortgage. Finally, contact information is provided to answer any questions you may have after reading this booklet. There is also a Glossary of Terms in the booklet"s Appendix.

Using this booklet as your guide will help you avoid the pitfalls and help you achieve the joys of home ownership.

Figure 35: HUD Pamphlet – Shopping for Your Home Loan
Subdivisions Laws of California

SUBDIVISIONS are a common form of residential development. Developers purchase large parcels of land that they will develop by subdividing into five or more smaller parcels and building residential properties for resale to the public. The government controls development through building codes, zoning, and two other laws that were created to protect the consumer:

- Subdivision Land Law
- Subdivision Map Act

SUBDIVISION LAND LAW

SUBDIVISION LAND LAW is found in the ***Business and Professions Code*** and is administered by the *California Department of Real Estate* under the Real Estate Commissioner. The purpose is to protect consumers from misrepresentation, fraud, and deceit in the marketing of properties for sale. The Subdivision Land Law also addresses financing for both construction loans and the buyers of the completed homes.

The Subdivision Land Law addresses ownership and clarifies ownership rights and responsibilities for subdivisions containing 5 parcels or more and containing up to 160 acres of land. The lots do not need to be contiguous or adjacent to each other under this law to be considered a subdivision.

The developer must submit a package or application for development to the DRE providing details of the proposed development. The real estate commissioner then prepares and issues a ***Subdivision Public Report*** which describes the property. As a part of this report, the real estate commissioner reviews and confirms the financial status of the proposed project to ensure that the project is liquid enough to provide for amenities and improvements as advertised to the public and promised to the consumer. Verifying sufficient funds to complete the project also protects the public from losses due to possible bankruptcy by the developer or abandonment of work due to lack of funds.

Material changes cannot be made once the notice of intention has been filed and the public report has been prepared. Items that may be considered material changes may include such items as lot lines or dimensions, or changes to CC&Rs or deed restrictions.

PUBLIC REPORT requirements are stricter on common interest subdivisions than for standard subdivisions. The public report for a **STANDARD SUBDIVISION** includes:

- Project name
- Project location
- Project size
- Developer's name
- Ownership interest to be acquired by potential purchasers
- Payment plan for mortgage, taxes and tax assessments, and insurance
- CC&Rs and/or deed restrictions affecting property use
- Easements and rights-of-way
- Building permits
- Projected expenses for close of escrow
- Projected future expenses
- Environmental factors and hazards

RESERVATIONS may be taken once they have received the **preliminary public report**. The developer is allowed to begin advertising and taking reservations for future purchases from the public on the lots subject to an approved **conditional public report**. A reservation is an agreement to purchase a lot in the future if the reports are acceptable to the buyer. All buyers who make a reservation based on completion of the conditional public report must verify in writing that they have received and read the report prior to moving to the next step of entering into a binding contract.

NOTE

Advertising must not contain any misleading or fraudulent claims, and any deposits made on a reservation are fully refundable to the buyer.

CONDITIONAL PUBLIC REPORT allows the developer to enter into a legal, binding purchase agreement subject to the completion and approval by the buyer of the final public report and the completed improvements or structures.

A FINAL PUBLIC REPORT is issued when the property is completed. Since the properties will be ready for sale or occupancy at different times, a final public report will be prepared for the individual lots to allow the developer to close as they are completed.

Receipt of the final public report must be verified in writing prior to completing the purchase transaction. The written receipt of evidence that the buyer received the report is a DRE form and must be retained by the developer for a minimum of 3 years from the date of signing for the review and audit by the DRE. The receipt and acceptance of the final public report is a contingency of the contract. Deposits are refundable if the contingencies cannot be met, especially an acceptable final public report. A final public report expires five years from issuance. The term can be extended for an additional five years for unsold lots.

RIGHT TO NEGOTIATE is part of the buyer's rights under the *Business and Professions Code*. The buyer has the right to have the property inspected by a party of their choice as part of the purchase contract and prior to the close of escrow.

SUBDIVISION MAP ACT

SUBDIVISION MAP ACT requires that a subdivision of 2 or more contiguous or adjoining parcels meets certain specifications. This act is part of *the California Government Code* and provides for the physical aspects of a subdivision and establishes a uniform filing procedure for the entire state. Local ordinances are allowed as a part of community development and a community's general or master plan. The objectives of the Subdivision Map Act are to:

- Co-ordinate design with the local general or master plan
- Ensure public use areas are developed as a part of each new subdivision

SUBDIVISION MAPS includes the location of streets and parcels. The *Subdivision Map Act* requires three separate stages of the subdivision maps.

TENTATIVE SUBDIVISION MAP is the initial map which does not need to have the final details. Local ordinances may require more details than the Subdivision Map Act requires, and the stricter law or requirement will prevail. A survey prepared by a licensed surveyor or a civil engineer is advisable. Requirements of the Tentative Subdivision Map will generally include:

- Legal description
- Property boundaries
- Individual parcels or lots
- Existing streets including names and widths
- Proposed streets including widths and grade
- Public areas

- Existing utilities, sewers, and drainage
- Proposed utilities, sewers, and drainage
- Water supply
- Property use to include residential, commercial, and public
- Storm overflow
- Watercourses

The developer is usually responsible for the installation of the infrastructure to include utilities, streets, and sewers. The local governments and utility companies usually maintain the infrastructure once installed. The exception would be private streets such as in a PUD or a mutual water company.

Approval of the tentative subdivision map is performed by the local *Building and Planning Department* or any other agency or group that is specified by the local governing entity. Public hearing provides any member of the public to provide input as to the effects the development will have on the surrounding area, natural resources, and drainage. Notice must be given allowing for an appropriate amount of time prior to the hearing to provide sufficient notice to all concerned.

FINAL SUBDIVISION MAP demands that all ordinances, both local and state, must be met prior to preparation and issuance of the final map. The final subdivision map must be/have:

Prepared in black ink on paper that is 18 x 26 inches

- Parcels numbered
- Exact property boundaries
- Blocks numbered or lettered
- Streets named
- Soil reports filed in the public records

NOTIFICATION must be made if any adjoining easements or rights of way are interfered with by the development of the subdivision. Public entities and utility providers must be notified and provided with an opportunity to object to the development or a portion or aspect of the subdivision if they feel necessary. The county surveyor or the city engineer that completed the field survey of the subdivision must certify that the final subdivision map is correct and that it conforms to the details and information that was approved in the tentative subdivision map.

DEDICATIONS are portions of the subdivision that are being given to the local government for public, recreation, and park use. Statutory dedication is a dedication that is required by local ordinance or was part of the agreement when the development was approved by the local government. Clarification of those areas must be clearly made along with a deed granting the property and signed by all necessary parties. A certificate of acceptance for the dedication must be provided by the appropriate agencies.

A PARCEL MAP must:

- Be prepared in black ink on paper that is 18 x 26 inches
- Have individual parcels designated
- Have all boundaries marked
- Be signed by developer and have an acknowledge certificate
- Have accuracy certified by the surveyor or engineer who conducted the field survey

FILING of the final subdivision map must be done prior to the expiration of the tentative subdivision map which is two years from the date of approval.

APPROVAL of the final subdivision map is done by the local Building and Planning Department or any other agency or group that is specified by the local governing entity. Public hearings provide any member of the public with input as to the effects the development will have on the surrounding area, natural resources, and drainage. Notice must be given allowing for an appropriate amount of time prior to the hearing to provide sufficient notice to all concerned.

ENVIRONMENTAL IMPACT REPORT (EIR) must be prepared by a qualified engineer or geologist. The Environmental Impact Report is not required on all proposed subdivisions; these are prepared only if there is an indication that the development will substantially affect any natural or environmental aspects, such as endangered species or watercourse, or any issues such as in the flight pattern to an airport. The *California Environmental Quality Act of 1970 (CEQA)* will either require an EIR or provide a negative declaration stating that there will be no substantial impact on the environment.

California Coastal Act provides for conservation of the coastal areas of California. The coastal zones are defined as land that forms the coastline inland for 1000 yards or more depending on the terrain.

Local government is authorized by the *California Coastal Management Program* to pass ordinances and zoning to control the use of the coastal lands to preserve and maintain the quality of the land.
www.coastal.ca.gov/ccatc.html

The Alquist-Priolo Earthquake Fault Zoning Act regulates the development of land in earthquake fault zones. The construction requirements are stricter in an earthquake fault zone. Full disclosure of the location of a property to a fault zone must be provided to any potential buyers of land within a fault zone. www.conservation.ca.gov
https://www.usgs.gov/programs/earthquake-hazards

The Rangeland, Grazing Land, and Grassland Protection Act provides grants for the acquisition of conservation easements for the purpose of protecting, restoring, or enhancing these areas of California.

TYPES OF SUBDIVISIONS

TYPES OF SUBDIVISIONS are divided into three categories:
1.) Standard subdivision
2.) Common interest subdivision
3.) Undivided interest subdivision

1. **STANDARD SUBDIVISIONS** are developments where the individual purchasers of the lots do not share a common interest in any other portion of the development. They purchase their own lot/property only. A standard subdivision can sell unimproved lots to the public for building purposes or completed buildings ready to move into, but it is required that the utilities be in place prior to the sale of undeveloped, individual lots.
    - **COMMON INTEREST SUBDIVISIONS** offer individual lots for sale plus the common ownership of common areas of the development. A homeowners' association will be created by the developer to manage the common ownership interests. Forms of common interest ownership in California are: **Communally owned common areas**: this may include areas such as swimming pools, tennis courts, and green areas.
    - **Condominium/condo:** own airspace of the individual unit, but communally own building and land

- **Co-operative/co-op**: own stock in a corporation that owns the building and land but have a proprietary right in individual unit.
- **Planned unit developments (PUDs):** individually own the lot and unit but share interest in common grounds.
- **Community apartment:** Communally owned land and building with proprietary right to individual unit.
- **Time share:** Communally owned land and buildings with proprietary right to use for a pre-determined period of time.

2. **UNDIVIDED INTEREST SUBDIVISIONS:** ownership held by all owners as tenants-in-common with a non-exclusive right to use of the entire property by all of the owners. An example of an undivided Interest subdivision is a vacation site with shared amenities and facilities such as a campground.

NOTE

Communally owned properties are generally owned as tenants-in-common while the individual ownership is held as the owner chooses.

RESIDENTIAL DESIGN AND CONSTRUCTION

DESIGN AND FUNCTION of a residential dwelling is determined by many factors and design is a very subjective issue. Every person's taste and idea of design and appeal varies from every other person. The function of a house will also vary from party to party depending on individual personal needs, however, social and economic status will have a major effect on the current style and demands of the consumer.

SITE ORIENTATION is the placement of the structures, especially the house, on the site. It is greatly determined by external influences such as view, traffic flow and noise, and surrounding properties.

- **PROXIMITY TO COMMON AREAS,** such as a swimming pool, or public areas such as a park may be appealing for the access to the amenities; however, properties adjacent to these areas will not have as much privacy as a property away from these areas, especially in properties with communal ownership.

- **TRAFFIC** and the accompanied noise and odor are considerations for site location. A highly traveled street is not as desirable for housing, especially for a family with small children and pets. The location on a quiet street within a subdivision may seem pleasant, unless the back yard is next to a busy street outside of the enclosed neighborhood. The dangers of traffic are not present, but noise and traffic fumes are.
- **THE MOVEMENT OF THE SUN** will also have an influence on the placement of a house on its lot. In warmer climates, the main windows of the house or the main living area inside the house may be facing to the north to help control the heat from the sun on the hot summer days. A south facing house may compensate for this by providing for an extended overhang that will protect the windows from the harsh sunlight of the summer months and allow for the sun's being lower in the sky during the winter months.

  Properties located in northern or colder climates would prefer to have less of an overhang on the south facing side of the house to allow the sun's penetration for warming effects. Homes in a southern or warmer climate would prefer the opposite.

  Other improvements to a property should also take into consideration the sun's angles before beginning to build. A swimming pool on the north side of a house may not be as desirable if it were in the shade for large portions of the day.

CONSTRUCTION STANDARDS

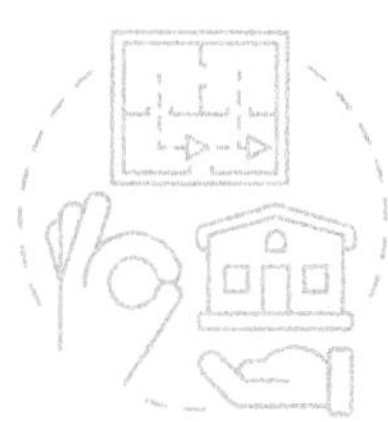

CONSTRUCTION STANDARDS have been established by federal, state, and local government agencies. The standards may vary from one agency to another, and the **strictest rule or law will prevail.** Local building codes are allowed to be more stringent than the state regulations, but they may not be less stringent than the state building standards.

> ***Example:*** *The state requires that a piece of lumber for a particular purpose must be no less than a 2 x 4. The local government requires that the same piece of lumber must be no less than 4 x 6. The builder will use the 4x6 because the requirement of a larger board is the stricter requirement.*

STATE AND LOCAL HEALTH LAWS, as they apply to building and housing, are enforced by the *Local Health Department.*

STATE BUILDING STANDARDS must be adhered to throughout the state. These building standards are enforced by the local agency that oversees buildings.

LOCAL BUILDING CODES set the minimum standards for building within their jurisdiction. Local building codes are instrumental in creating conformity within the area as determined by local ordinances and general or master plans.

Building inspectors are local representatives or agents of the local government and are responsible for enforcing both the state and the local building codes. As each stage of a house is completed during the construction process, the building inspector will inspect the work before the builder can begin the next stage. *For example, the building inspector will inspect electrical and plumbing and approve the completed work before the builder will be allowed to hang dry wall.*

The inspector will initial the building permit for each stage, showing the acceptance of work completed. Any work that is not acceptable to the building inspector will need to be redone until it meets the building codes and is to the satisfaction of the building inspector.

EXCEPTIONS TO THE BUILDING CODES may be requested and it is the building official's decision as to whether the exception is acceptable.

Example: *Local building codes state that a structure must set back a minimum of 15 feet from the street to allow for sufficient off-street parking because of the limited amount of street parking in the area. A homeowner would like to build a balcony on the front of the house from the second floor. This balcony would extend 6 feet out toward the street and would violate the building code because it would mean the front of the house would now be 9 feet from the street.*

The building official approved the project based on the fact that the improvement is on the second floor and will not affect the 15 foot limit on ground level and will not interfere with the ability to park off-street.

A CERTIFICATE OF OCCUPANCY is provided by the inspector when all phases of the construction of the structure have been satisfactorily completed. The certificate of occupancy states that the structure is complete and is acceptable for human occupancy.

PLANS

PLANS are prepared for different stages of development and provide various details.

- **ELEVATIONS** show the designer's conception of the property as it will look when completed. This is in the format of a painting or drawing of the finished structure showing all sides of the structure.

- **FOUNDATION PLAN** is a scale drawing of the dimensions of the foundation and its footings and sub-flooring.

- **PLOT PLAN** shows the lot dimensions and the improvements drawn to scale. It is shown as though it were being looked at from above so that the layout of the plot is shown to include such things as sidewalks and plants and shrubbery.

- **FLOOR PLAN** is the layout of the rooms and living areas within the house. The floor plan provides a scale drawing showing all dimensions and placement of doors, windows, and walls.

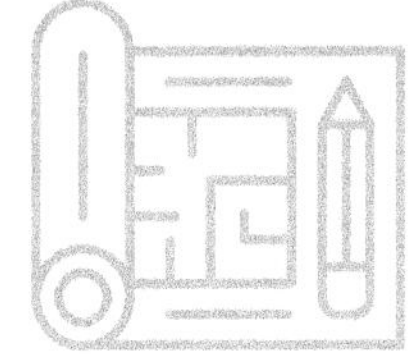

The floor plan of a house needs to provide for a flow of traffic for the occupants of the house. *Acceptable floor plans have varied over the years. Many older homes had a "shotgun" style floor plan with the rooms all in a row leading from one room into the next room. This allowed for little or no privacy and is now considered functionally obsolete.*

The "ranch style" floor plan home has proven the test of time by providing for a living area separated from the bedroom and bathroom area. Current floor plans desired by the public are an expansion of the ranch style floor plan by use of a great room which provides for the family area to be kitchen, dining, and family room in one large area to allow for families to be together in the main area of the house. A private bathroom for the individual bedrooms is also desirable and a half bath for the living area is also a current trend that homebuyers are looking for in new homes. Whether a house is one story or more, the idea of a separate living area is desirable and prevalent.

BASEMENTS are not a common part of homes in most of California. There is little need for the prevention against frost that there is in colder climates. Also, the ground water level is too high in much of California for a basement to be practical. There are areas where a basement or a partial basement is required as a foundation to stabilize the house such as a house that is built on a hillside.

HOME OFFICES are a current trend and often a requirement with more people working at home because of the use of computers. Number of bedrooms, floor plan, square footage, and extra rooms are all individual needs of homebuyers and must be considered when showing homes.

TURNKEY PROJECT is a project that provides a complete newly built home that is in move-in condition. Many projects are sold by choosing the lot and then choosing the desired home from the model homes and having it built to specifications. A turnkey project is completed prior to being offered for sale or the construction of the house was completed before being sold. The term comes from the fact that the buyer can turn the key in the lock and move in.

SQUARE FOOTAGE of a house is very important to potential homebuyers as a matter of comfort and as a socio-economic status. Post-World War II homes tended to be quite small, ranging from around 800 to 1200 square feet in size. During the late 1900s, the housing trends called for larger homes ranging from 1200 to 1800 square feet. Current trends now demand even larger homes, with most new homes being built larger than 2000 square feet.

The sale of a residential property with less than 800 square feet may be difficult. Many lenders will not make a loan for a property that small. The appraiser must verify that it is a typical property for the area.

STANDARD FOR MEASURING SQUARE FOOTAGE of single-family residential property has been established by the ***Board of Standards Review of the American National Standards Institute (ANSI).*** The following must be adhered to when measuring a residential property:

- Exterior of the outside walls to the nearest 1/10 of an inch and final report to the nearest square foot (>50 round up, < 50 round down).
- Only finished areas.
- Garages are considered unfinished areas that are calculated in unfinished area measurements.
- Only spaces with a minimum of 7-foot ceilings except for the presence of exposed beams, eaves or sloping ceilings, and useable area beneath staircases.
- Stairs, but not openings in floors.
- Apartments and other improvements such as guest areas not within the main living area if connected by a hallway or stairway in a finished condition.

CONSTRUCTION

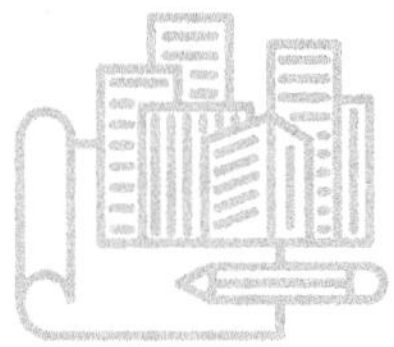

CONSTRUCTION terms, components, and stages are important for the real estate professional to be familiar with, especially for those specializing in new homes and developments. Understanding various aspects of construction will allow the real estate professional to speak intelligently with their clients when looking at houses.

- **A building site** is the land where a house is to be built. The parcel of land must be prepared properly prior to the start of construction of the improvement or house. In order to obtain a building permit to build a house, the contractor will need to obtain several reports for verification that the property is suitable for the construction of a house. There are local, state, and federal requirements and codes that mandate compliance by the builder. Several items and tests that must be obtained are:
- **Soil engineer's report** to confirm that the soil is solid enough to safely support the house and also being clear of any hazardous products. Remediation of a site may be required if the site had previously been used for the production or storage of hazardous materials, such as a gas station. Sites which will require extensive remediation of the soil are classified as "brownfields" by the *Environmental Protection Agency.*

- **Perc test** is a test to determine that the percolation of sub-surface water is adequate to support the potential household and needed water use. A perc test is needed only when a well is used to provide water to the residential dwelling.
- **Environmental impact report** (EIR) to determine if there are potential damage to the environment and hindrance or danger to any species of animal or fish that may be affected by the introduction of a residential dwelling.
- **Seismic or earthquake analysis** to determine the location in respect to earthquake faults. ***Alquist-Priolo Maps*** are available to determine the areas with higher risks.

ORIENTATION is the placement of the structure on the site. As discussed previously, the orientation will take into consideration the exterior influences of traffic, movement of the sun, and surroundings including a view.

INFILL is a process of bringing in fresh or untainted soil to a site as part of the reclamation process. Tests and reports may be required depending on the location and the history of the area and the subject site.

GRADING or leveling of the land will be required. Hillside sites may require extensive grading and retaining walls to stabilize and secure the ground and prevent movement.

DRAINAGE of water must be provided for even when water only occurs seasonally from water flow and flooding. A builder will want to ensure that any water will flow away from the structure and not pool on the site. Mudslides caused by poor drainage are a constant problem for buildings on a hillside or at the foot of a hill.

TEARDOWN PROPERTIES are ones that will be torn down to build a new structure or house. This exists when a building is no longer the highest and best purpose or use and the surrounding property values can support a new home being built on the site. The best candidate for a teardown is an older home that is the lowest valued property in the neighborhood or is under-developed for the neighborhood. The advantages of obtaining a teardown property as a building site is that the utilities are already on the site and will save expense and time of installing, grading generally is minimal, and the site is an established home-site eliminating site preparation issues including zoning and local approvals.

FOUNDATION is the base of the structure being built. Wooden frames are laid into the excavated site and concrete is poured into the framework to create the foundation that the structure is built upon. In California foundations are usually concrete slabs on which the floor rests rather than perimeter footings or basements.

- **FOOTING** is the base of a building that the foundation is placed upon.

- **BACKFILL** is the soil that is packed into the space left by the removed wooden frames after the concrete has set-up.

  Termites *and other insects enter buildings wherever the building touches the ground or soil. The foundation is generally treated to help prevent infestation. Wood that rests on a concrete foundation and does not touch the soil directly may still be subject to termites.*

- **SILL OR MUD SILL** is a wood member secured to the concrete foundation with the use of anchor bolts. The purpose of the sill is to secure the framework of the structure to the foundation to help prevent movement of the structure during an earthquake.

FRAMEWORK is the "bones" of the structure. The framework is built up from the sill creating a skeleton to attach exterior and interior walls

JOISTS OR GIRDERS are beams placed across the foundation as the base of the floor. Plywood sheets are then laid over the joists or girders to create the floor or sub-floor on which the floor covering such as wood, tile or carpeting will be installed.

STUDS are the vertical supports that create the framework for the walls. Building codes require that the studs be no more than 16 to 24 inches apart to create stability in the structure. (16" is the usual standard.)

FIRE STOPS are horizontal pieces of wood that are placed between the studs for stability and to help stop the flow of air that would feed a fire.

BEARING WALLS are the walls that bear the weight of the ceiling, upper floors, and roof. The bearing walls cannot be removed when remodeling without replacing the support in some way such as with beams and posts. *If the bearing walls are removed, the house will collapse.*

PLATFORM FRAME is a form of construction for the purpose of building more than one story to a house. Each story is built separately from the previous floor allowing for the greatest amount of support from the previous floor.

POST AND BEAM method provides for the greatest flexibility and openness to construction. Ceiling boards lay across and rest on the beams within the structure of the house which allows for the studs to be further apart. This provides additional strength which allows for less wall space and more open space inside the structure. The great room design is made possible with the use of this method of framing.

EXTERIOR WALLS begin with a sheathing made of plywood to stabilize and help insulate. The outer siding or stucco can be added to this sheathing. Stucco exterior will consist of a sheet of protective material to help prevent moisture build-up then chicken wire for the stucco plaster to adhere to. Other sidings and shingles can be attached directly to the plywood sheathing.

INSULATION is contained in the exterior walls to keep out both cold and heat. Many older homes, such as those built in the first half of the 1900s or before, may lack insulation. Insulation is usually installed in rolls of fiberglass or other materials when a house is being built by laying the material between the studs of the exterior walls after installation of the exterior sheathing and before installing the drywall.

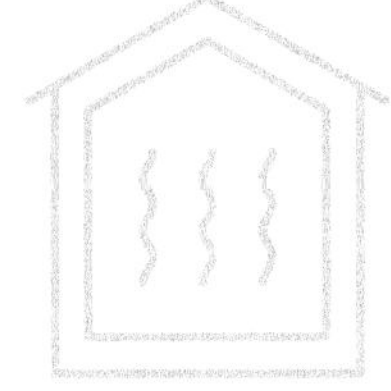

Existing homes without insulation can be insulated using several different types of insulation that can be blown into the walls with special equipment designed for that purpose. There are cellulose products which are a "green product" because it recycles materials such as newspaper and denim. A new foam product is proving to be a very effective insulation that can be installed before or after the installation of drywall. Protective clothing and masks should be worn when installing insulation to protect one's health.

California State Energy Resources Conservation and Development Commission has created a statewide home energy rating program establishing guidelines for builders and homeowners insulating residential properties. The seller or their agent must provide a booklet created by this commission to buyers of 1- to 4-unit residential property.

TERMS that have been established in conjunction with insulation and heating and air conditioning ratings are as follows:

- **R-value/resistance-value** is the measurement used to determine the amount of effectiveness of the insulation. "R" means the amount of resistance the insulation will give to outside temperatures and influences including wind.
- **EER/energy efficiency rating** is used in reference to the efficiency of heating and air conditioning units.
- **HVAC/heating, ventilation, and air conditioning** is used in reference to the efficiency of heating and air conditioning units.
- **BTU/British thermal unit** is used in reference to the efficiency of heating units.
- **SEER/seasonal energy efficiency** is used in reference to the efficiency of air conditioning units.

NOTE

The higher the rating the better the efficiency in all of the measurements.

ASBESTOS had been used in the past as insulation material. This has been determined to be hazardous to human health. When inhaled, asbestos may cause cancer. This material has not been used in new construction since the 1970s, however, it is still present in many homes built before that time. Ceilings were sprayed with asbestos for both esthetic and insulating purposes. Those ceilings are commonly known as "cottage cheese" ceilings. A homeowner removing this product from their ceilings should use protective wear and a mask.

UREA-FORMALDEHYDE is another product that was used in manufactured homes and has been found to emit toxic fumes that are hazardous to health. Both of these products are prohibited from use in residential properties.

There are state and local health laws controlling the use of building products. The local *health department* enforces the controls of the laws.

ELECTRICAL WIRING AND PLUMBING are installed within the framework of the studs prior to installing drywall.

DRYWALL is the covering of interior wall surface. Drywall comes in 4' by 8' sheets of plaster board or sheetrock which are attached to the studs or framework. The seams between the sheets are covered with a plaster product called mud and a paper tape which is sanded for a seamless wall.

WINDOWS AND DOORS come in a wide variety of styles and materials. Older homes were built with wood frame windows and doors, and they are still a popular choice. Aluminum windows and doors have proven to be a cost effective, low maintenance alternative. Doors are now available in various composite materials. For safety reasons, outside doors must be solid but often inside doors are hollow- core for cost effectiveness.

ROOF is the covering of the structure. It keeps the weather out and protects the occupants.

- **RAFTERS** are the skeleton of the roof just as the studs are the skeleton of the walls.
- **RIDGEBOARD** is a board that runs the length of the roof at the peak or highest point of the house. The rafters meet at and are attached to the ridgeboard to act as an anchor for the rafters.
- **PLYWOOD** is attached to the rafters to provide the base for the shingles or the chosen roofing material.
- **SHEATHING** is a covering similar to the sheathing used on the exterior walls to act as a waterproofing and protection for the wood members of the rafters. The chosen roofing materials are attached on top of the sheathing.
- **FLASHING** is metal attached to the roof at joints or changes in the elevation to prevent leakage. An example of this would be at the joint of the chimney and the roof.

ROOF STYLES vary with the architectural design of the house.

A. **GABLE ROOF is the usual roof that has one peak in the center that runs the length of the house with either end straight.**

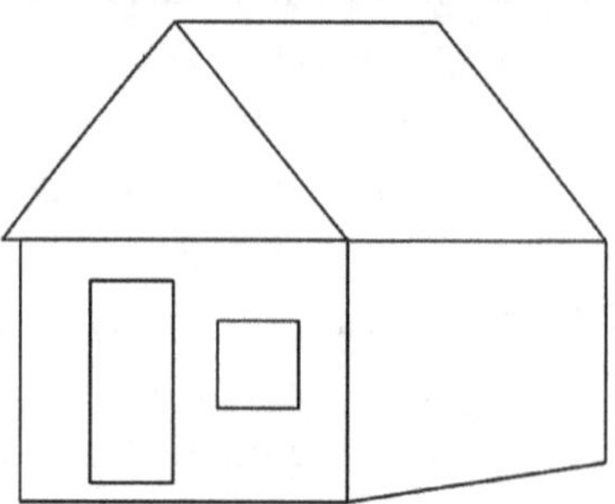

Figure 36: Gable Roof

B. **HIP ROOF is a roof that angles in on all four sides with only two parallel sides meeting at the peak.**

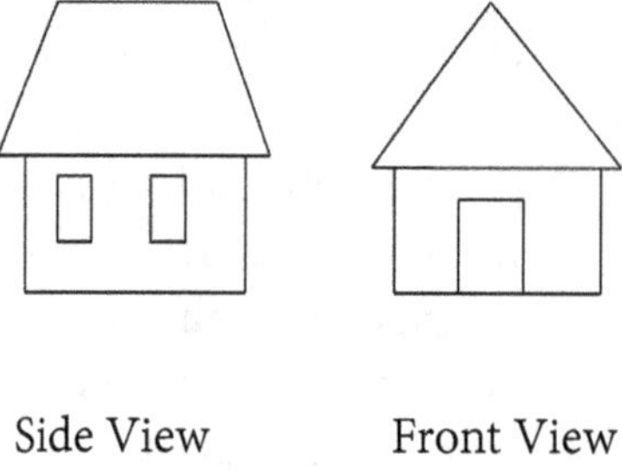

Figure 37: Hip Roof

C. **GAMBREL ROOF is peaked on parallel sides with two angles on each of the parallel sides. This style roof is commonly associated with Dutch Colonial style house or with a barn.**

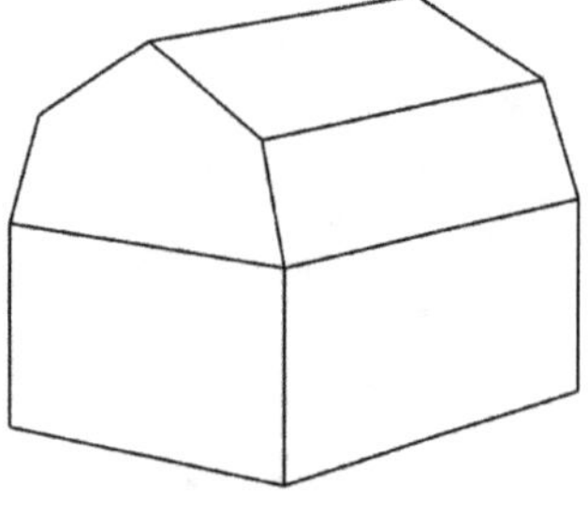

Figure 38: Gambrel Roof

D. **MANSARD ROOF has two angles on all four sides. It is associated with French houses. This is a common style in Eastern Canada.**

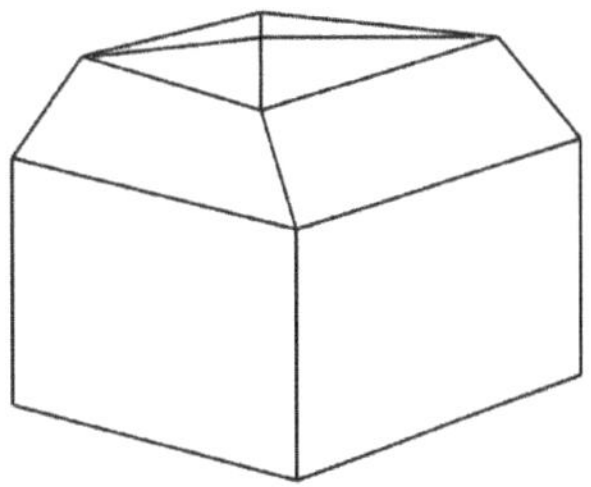

Figure 39: Mansard Roof

ARCHITECTURAL STYLES

ARCHITECTURAL STYLES are as diverse as the people who own the homes. There are certain styles that are more commonly seen than others. The following are several architectural styles that are the most common in today's market.

A. **RANCH has already been discussed as the style that has set the basis for commonly used floor plans. A ranch style house is one story with a floor plan that usually spreads out from the entrance with the living area to one side and the bedroom area to the other. A gable roof is the most commonly used roof style. The ranch style house lends itself to any type of siding, including stone or brick.**

B. **A TOWN HOUSE is also known as a row house. A townhouse is an architectural style that is usually two or more stories. The opposite sides share common walls with the neighboring houses. Commonly found in San Francisco, this also is a common architectural style for condos and PUDs.**

Because this is such a commonly used style for condos, people often confuse "townhouse" as a form of legal ownership by trying to distinguish a property as a "townhouse" instead of a condo.

NOTE

The real estate professional needs to understand that the term "townhouse" is an architectural style not a legal form of ownership, such as a condo.

C. SPANISH STYLE refers to styles that were often built by the early settlers of California from Mexico and Spain. This style also is often referred to as Monterey or Santa Barbara style. The style was developed from the early adobe houses built from mud brick covered with stucco. The homes may be one or two stories with a courtyard and verandas. They often have wrought iron trim.

D. VICTORIAN refers to homes built with elaborate trim often called "gingerbread," and stained-glass windows. Victorian homes are often two-story homes that appear tall and narrow from the front but are quite deep and are usually wood sided. The term Victorian comes from the era of Queen Victoria and this style was very popular late in her reign at the end of the 1800s and the very early years of the 1900s. *Not all houses built during that time are considered Victorian in style.* The most commonly used roof is a steep gable roof.

E. CAPE COD is a style that is very common in the northeastern part of the country or New England - thus the name. A Cape Cod style house can be one or two stories. If two story, the rooms on the second floor have eaves or sloped ceilings and may have dormers or walls extending beyond the sloped walls to accommodate windows. Windows will often be paned or have many small panes making up the one large window. These homes are usually wood sided. The roof is most commonly a hip roof with all four sides peaking in the center.

F. FRENCH PROVINCIAL homes are large, square style, two-story homes often built from brick or stone. French Provincial style homes will usually have a hip roof or a mansard roof.

G. DUTCH COLONIAL homes have a design similar to the classic barn style. They are commonly two-story homes with the eave ceilings on the second floor. This style home has a gambrel roof which is the main distinguishing feature of this architectural style.

H. CRAFTSMAN or CALIFORNIA COTTAGE homes were very popular during the early 1900s. They were originally sold as prefabricated homes sold through the Sears-Roebuck catalogue. They are basically a square structure with a deep front porch extending the width of the house with large front windows on either side of the center front door. A pergola, which is a similar to a garden arbor, is a typical design feature. This style home is usually two-story with eaved ceilings on the second floor that often have dormers. The most commonly used roof is a hip roof.

MANUFACTURED HOMES

Manufactured homes are defined as a "structure transportable in one or more sections, designed and equipped to contain no more than two dwelling units to be used with or without a foundation system." *The definition of a manufactured home does not include recreational vehicles (RVs), camper trailers, or prefabricated homes.*

Although the definition states that it is transportable, that condition is only applicable when it is necessary to move the home. They do have axles and wheels for transportation purposes; however, once set in place, the separate sections are permanently connected, and the home will be left in place for many years and is not mobile. A manufactured home that comes in two sections is called a double-wide and will be about 24' by 60' or have square footage of 1440. *This is the size of many stick-built single-family homes or homes built under standard construction methods.*

If the home is placed on a private lot, it is most often attached to a permanent foundation in which case the wheels and axles are removed. There are companies that specialize in placing manufactured homes on permanent foundations and they will provide a certificate to the homeowner verifying that the home is now a permanent structure. Lenders will require a copy of the certificate as verification of the home's status.

NOTE

A mobile home is not "mobile" once set in place and the sections are connected.

Many manufactured homes are placed in mobile home parks. These parks are similar to subdivisions or PUD complexes that have private lots that are rented by the individual homeowner. The home is placed usually on blocks and/or jacks that support the home on a relatively permanent basis. The home is not placed in a mobile home park with the intention of moving the home. When the homeowner decides to move, they sell the home, leaving it in place. Moving a manufactured home requires several days of preparing the home by separating the sections and preparing the wheels that have been in a state of non-use for a number of years.
Once the home is disassembled and ready to move, a tractor-trailer for each section will be required to move the home. Manufactured homes are still called mobile homes; however, the real estate professional must know that they are not really "mobile."

This type of living accommodation came about in the late 1950s when mobile homes were single-wide. By the late 1960s and early 1970s, double-wide began replacing single-wide and parks were built to accommodate the larger homes by providing larger lots and creating parks that were more of a community, including recreation facilities and swimming pools. Many mobile home parks are designed as retirement communities with facilities designed for senior citizens.

Manufactured homes are stick-built homes that have studs in the walls and follow many of the guidelines established for standard home construction. They are built in factories where the various elements that make up the homes are mass produced for assembly in a controlled environment.

HUD established guidelines for the construction of mobile homes that went into effect July 1, 1978. All Manufactured Homes built since then have met these guidelines making the homes safer and more conducive to family living.

CONSTRUCTION LOANS

Construction loans are used for the purpose of providing funds to build or perform a major renovation to a property. The value of the property is determined by the acquisition cost or purchase price of the land, plus the cost to build a structure. In addition to the usual documentation the following must also be included in the loan package:

- **Closing statement** from the purchase transaction verifying the original cost of the property even if the property has been owned for a long period of time.
- **Receipts or canceled checks** for any expenses already paid by the borrower toward construction.
- **Estimates and contracts** for work to be done.
- Building permits.
- Blueprints and plans.
- **Description of materials** completed by contractor.
- **Line-item cost breakdown**- a form to be provided by the lender which combines all the information gathered in receipts and contracts.
- Contractor's license.
- Contractor's insurance.
- Liability insurance on the property.

Any additional information or documentation that may be helpful to the lender in determining the eligibility of the borrower should be included. The loan amount will be based on the future value of the property, not the present value.

NOTE

The lender will not allow incidental costs, such as meals and phone calls.

Not all lenders will do construction loans. The terms of these loans are usually for a term of 6, 9, or 12 months. During the term, the escrow company holds the funds not already dispersed and will provide payment to the various contractors or service providers on receipt of proof of completion or presentation of a bill. Funds may also be dispersed to the borrower on proof of payment or presentation of a paid receipt.

At the time of locking the loan, the borrower can decide to lock-in the interest rate for the term of the construction loan only or may choose a rollover into a fixed 15- or 30-year loan. The interest rate during the construction term will be higher.

Upon proof of completion of the building, the lender will disperse the remaining funds to the borrower or any remaining service providers and the loan will either roll-over into a conventional mortgage or be refinanced with a new conventional mortgage. The new loan is often called a take-out loan because it is taking-out a short-term construction loan, but it is a regular refinance mortgage.

The following items will be required as part of the refinance take-out loan:

- **Building permits** with all items signed by the building inspector.
- Certificate of completion.
- **Certificate of occupancy** from the local Department of Planning.
- **442 appraisal supplement** which states that the appraiser has re- inspected the property, the work has been completed, and the subject is habitable

Any questions about loan programs should be discussed with the lender. Rate sheets will disclose a great deal of information regarding different loan programs. The lender's representatives or loan agents are the salespeople and are very helpful in determining the ability of their company to do a particular loan scenario. The lender's reps call on mortgage brokers' offices as part of their job and will be glad to look at a loan package if suggestions or guidance is needed.

www.ingramcontent.com/pod-product-compliance
Lightning Source LLC
Chambersburg PA
CBHW081527120626
46550CB00009B/2637

* 9 7 8 1 9 6 7 3 0 0 0 1 3 *